1001 DAYS OUT
WITH YOUR KIDS

p

This is a Parragon Book
First Published in 2006

Parragon
Queen Street House
4 Queen Street
Bath BA1 1HE, UK

All the information given in this book has come directly
from the attractions included and was correct at the time
of going to press. The Publishers will be grateful for any
information that will assist in keeping future editions up
to date. While every care has been taken in the preparation
of this book, neither the Compilers nor the Publishers
can accept any liability for any consequences arising from
the use thereof, or the information contained therein.
The prices, times and facilities given should be used as
a guide only as they will vary with time.

ISBN 1-40546-311-2

Designed by Butler and Tanner
Printed in Indonesia

Front cover
courtesy of © Cadbury World

Frontispiece
Biome, courtesy of ©The Eden Project

Right
The Tower of London, courtesy of ©Britain on View

IMPORTANT NOTE FOR THE READER

We have made every effort to ensure the information in this
guide is accurate and up to date, but things do change very
quickly. Prices and opening times are sometimes altered at
short notice, and sadly some venues close unexpectedly. We
would therefore urge readers to telephone the venue before
setting out on a visit. This will ensure you are aware of any
changes in ticket prices or opening times, and will avoid
unexpected disappointments or problems.

The contents of this book are believed correct at the time of
printing. The Publisher cannot be held responsible for any errors,
omissions or changes in the information in this guide or for the
consequences of any reliance on the information provided.

Contents

Introduction

Welcome to the fourth edition of *1001 Days Out with Your Kids*. Revised, with updated information and a wealth of brand-new entries, this book will give you fresh ideas for places to visit throughout the year and no matter what the weather, as well as giving you up-to-date information on famous attractions.

There is an amazing variety of places in Britain that can capture a child's imagination. They can be educational, inspirational, or just plain fun!

Attractions range from crumbling castles surrounded by magnificent moats to wildlife parks teeming with fabulous creatures; from exciting river journeys and railway trips to fascinating collections of old vehicles; from beautiful country parks with children's nature trails to theme and adventure parks packed with breathtaking rides for even the biggest 'kids'. We have also included a range of museums where you will find displays on everything from children's writers to Viking warriors.

Children's imaginations are captured by the most unexpected things at times so in order to provide ideas and inspiration for even the most difficult to please we have tried to present the widest possible selection of attractions.

Whatever you choose, don't forget to phone the venue and check the details before setting out.

Most of all, enjoy your days out with the kids!

About this guide

This guide covers England, Scotland (including the Northern and Western Islands) and Wales and is arranged in regions, shown on the national map on page viii. The counties within each region, the towns within each county and the attractions within each town are all, where possible, arranged alphabetically (we have taken the occasional licence with the running order to enable us to include the best images). Each attraction also has a reference number and this is used to identify it on the regional map at the beginning of each section.

Understanding the entries

Coloured bands at the top of each page indicate regions; the numbers in the top corners next to the regional name refer to the numbered range of attractions on the page. The nearest major town or village to the attraction is indicated above the name of the attraction.

Quick-reference icons

an all-weather attraction

an attraction for sunny days only

the expected duration of your visit

when the attraction is open

Description

Each entry has a brief description of the attraction and a flavour of what visitors may expect to find. Additional features are also highlighted beneath the description.

Facilities

toilet facilities available

space available for you to eat your own food

restaurant, café or kiosk facilities available

good access for wheelchairs   restricted access

dogs allowed, but they may have to be kept on a lead

Disabled visitors

Visitors with mobility difficulties should look for the wheelchair symbol showing that all or most of the attraction is accessible to wheelchair users. We strongly recommend that visitors telephone in advance of a visit to check exact details, including access to toilets and refreshment facilities. Assistance dogs are usually accepted unless stated otherwise. For the hard of hearing, please check that hearing induction loops are available by contacting the attraction itself.

Location

These are simple directions, usually for motorists (though Underground directions are given for attractions in London) and have been provided by the attraction itself.

Opening times

These times are inclusive, e.g. Apr–Oct indicates that the attraction will be open from the beginning of April to the end of October. Where an attraction has varied opening times, these are indicated; and if it is open seven days a week, this is simply referred to as 'Daily'. Bank Holiday opening is indicated where provided by the attraction.

If you are travelling a long way, please check with the attraction itself to ensure any unexpected circumstances are not going to prevent your entry.

Admission

Wherever possible, the charges quoted are for the 2005–6 season, but please note that prices are subject to change and are correct only at the time of going to print. If no price is quoted, it does not mean that a charge will not be made. Many places that do not charge admission may ask for a voluntary donation. In some instances discounts may be available to families, groups, local residents or members of certain organisations such as English Heritage and the National Trust.

Contact details

We have given details of the administrative address and telephone number for each attraction. While these are usually those of the attraction itself, some properties are administered by an area office, in which case these details are given (several English Heritage properties fall into this category).

Telephone numbers, email and website addresses are also included wherever possible.

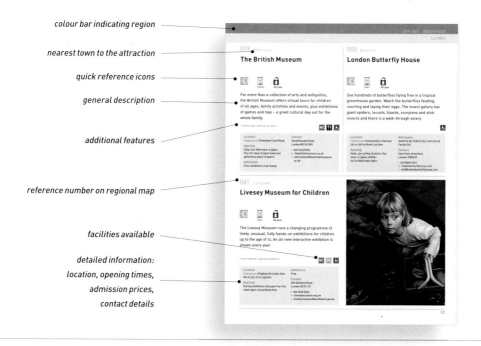

colour bar indicating region

nearest town to the attraction

quick reference icons

general description

additional features

reference number on regional map

facilities available

detailed information:
location, opening times,
admission prices,
contact details

Regional colour key

- South East
- South West
- Eastern
- East Midlands
- West Midlands
- Wales
- Yorkshire
- North West
- North East
- Scotland

HIGHLANDS & ISLANDS

GRAMPIAN

CENTRAL SCOTLAND

SOUTHERN SCOTLAND

NORTHUMBERLAND

TYNE & WEAR

DURHAM

CUMBRIA

NORTH YORKSHIRE

EAST RIDING OF YORKSHIRE

LANCASHIRE

W. YORKSHIRE

MANCHESTER

SOUTH YORKSHIRE

MERSEYSIDE

CHESHIRE

DERBYSHIRE

NOTTINGHAMSHIRE

LINCOLNSHIRE

NORTH WALES

STAFFORDSHIRE

LEICESTERSHIRE

RUTLAND

NORFOLK

SHROPSHIRE

WEST MIDLANDS

NORTHAMPTONSHIRE

CAMBRIDGESHIRE

CENTRAL WALES

WORCESTERSHIRE

WARWICKSHIRE

SUFFOLK

HEREFORDSHIRE

BEDFORDSHIRE

GLOUCESTERSHIRE

BUCKINGHAMSHIRE

HERTFORDSHIRE

ESSEX

SOUTH WALES

OXFORDSHIRE

LONDON

WILTSHIRE

BERKSHIRE

SURREY

KENT

SOMERSET

HAMPSHIRE

WEST SUSSEX

E. SUSSEX

DEVON

DORSET

ISLE OF WIGHT

CORNWALL

Beachy Head, East Sussex

South East

Berkshire Buckinghamshire East Sussex
Hampshire and Isle of Wight Kent London
Oxfordshire Surrey West Sussex

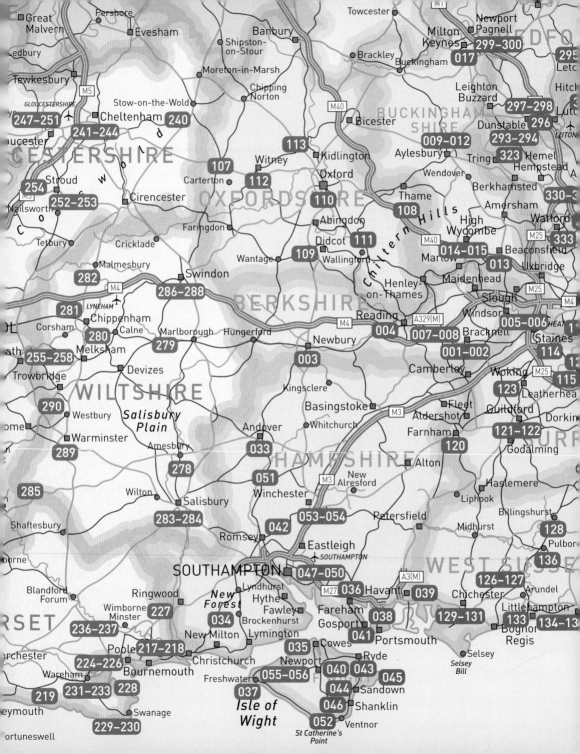

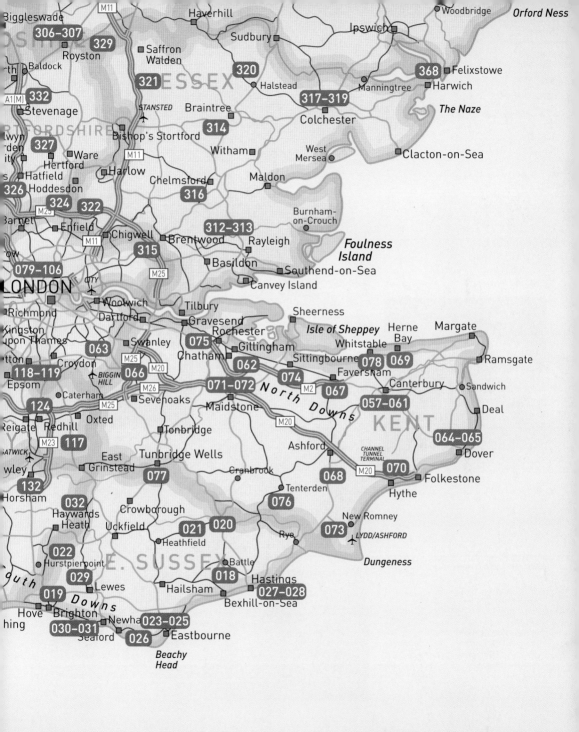

Biggleswade

306–307

329

Royston

Baldock

North

332

Stevenage

A1(M)

Welwyn
Garden
City

327

Ware

Hertford

Hatfield

326

Hoddesdon

324

322

Barnet

Enfield

LONDON

079–106

Richmond

Kingston
upon Thames

Sutton

118–119

Epsom

124

Reigate

Redhill

117

GATWICK

Crawley

132

Horsham

032

Haywards
Heath

022

Hurstpierpoint

029

Lewes

019

Hove

Brighton

030–031

Seaford

Worthing

South

Downs

Haverhill

Woodbridge

Orford Ness

M11

Saffron
Walden

Sudbury

Ipswich

320

321

ESSEX

Halstead

Manningtree

368

Felixstowe

Harwich

317–319

STANSTED

Braintree

Colchester

The Naze

314

Bishop's Stortford

Witham

HERTFORDSHIRE

M11

Harlow

Chelmsford

Maldon

West
Mersea

Clacton-on-Sea

316

Burnham-
on-Crouch

312–313

Brentwood

Rayleigh

Foulness
Island

315

Basildon

M25

Southend-on-Sea

Canvey Island

CITY

Woolwich

Tilbury

Sheerness

Dartford

Gravesend

Rochester

Isle of Sheppey

Herne
Bay

Margate

063

Swanley

Gillingham

Whitstable

078

069

Ramsgate

075

Chatham

Sittingbourne

M25

M20

066

062

Faversham

Canterbury

Sandwich

BIGGIN
HILL

Croydon

Caterham

M26

Sevenoaks

071–072

074

067

057–061

Deal

M25

North Downs

M2

KENT

124

Oxted

Maidstone

064–065

Reigate

Redhill

117

Tonbridge

M20

Dover

East
Grinstead

Tunbridge Wells

Ashford

CHANNEL
TUNNEL
TERMINAL

077

Cranbrook

068

M20

070

Folkestone

Crowborough

076

Tenterden

Hythe

021

020

New Romney

073

LYDD/ASHFORD

Uckfield

Heathfield

Rye

Dungeness

Battle

018

Newhaven

023–025

Hailsham

Hastings

027–028

Bexhill-on-Sea

026

Eastbourne

Beachy
Head

Berkshire

001 Bracknell

Go Ape!

2 hrs+   Mar–Nov

Go Ape! Is a network of rope bridges, trapezes and death slides that stretches for roughly a mile through the tree canopy. A unique experience that consists of an extensive cat's cradle of ropes, netting and platforms, set high above the ground in Bracknell Forest.

* 115 ft aerial walkway for May 2006
* Age limit is 10 & height restriction of 1.4m applies

Location
Follow signs for Look Out Discovery Centre on A322 S of Bracknell

Opening
Mar–Oct 9am 5pm;
Nov Weekends only;
closed Dec–Feb

Admission
Adult £2.80, Child £1.40, Concs £2.10

Contact
The Look Out, Nine Mile Ride
Swinley Forest, Bracknell RG12 7QW

t 0870 444 5562
w goape.co.uk
e info@goape.co.uk

002 Bracknell

The Lookout Discovery Centre

2 hrs+   All year

A hands-on science exhibition with fun for the entire family. 'Pluck' the laser beams of the Light Harp to make a little light music or put all your energy into launching the Hydrogen Rocket. Explore the wonders of the human body or try the amazing puzzles.

* Children's play area
* 2,600 acres of woodlands

Location
Follow signs for Look Out Discovery Centre on A322 S of Bracknell

Opening
Daily: 10am–5pm

Admission
Please phone for details

Contact
Nine Mile Ride, Bracknell RG12 7QW

t 01344 354400
w bracknell-forest.gov.uk/lookout
e thelookout@bracknell-forest.gov.uk

003 Newbury

The Living Rainforest

1 hr+   All year

Experience the sights, sounds and smells of a rainforest under glass at this unique conservation area. There is something for everyone here including special children's activities and art workshops. Visitors can also adopt an animal.

* Endangered Goeldi's monkeys leap among branches
* Birds, butterflies and lizards roam freely as you explore

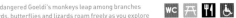

Location
Clearly signed from M4 junction 13

Opening
Daily: 10am–5.15pm (last admission 4.30pm)

Admission
Please phone for details or check the website

Contact
Hampstead Norreys RG18 0TN

t 01635 202444
w livingrainforest.org
e enquiries@livingrainforest.org

004 Reading

Beale Park

4 hrs   All year

Beale Park is dedicated to the conservation of rare birds. It is home to an amazing collection of birds including swans, owls, parrots and pheasants. There is something for everyone, ranging from gentle walks to madcap adventure play areas.

* Meerkat & wallaby enclosures and pets' corner
* Splash pool & miniature golf for children

Location
6 miles from Reading on A329 between Pangbourne & Streatley

Opening
Daily: 1 Oct–13 Apr 10am–5pm;
14 Apr–30 Sep 10am–6pm

Admission
Adult £6.50, Child £4.50, Concs £5.50

Contact
Lower Basildon,
Reading RG8 9NH

t 0870 7777160
w bealepark.co.uk
e administration@bealepark.co.uk

005 Windsor

Legoland Windsor

4 hrs+   Mar–Nov

A land where creativity meets fun, Legoland Windsor has more than 50 rides and attractions based around exhilarating activity areas and surrounded by extensive gardens and parkland.

* Spectactular Lego models
* Daily shows

Location
2 miles from Windsor town centre on B3022 Bracknell–Windsor road

Opening
Please phone or visit the website for details

Admission
Please phone or visit the website

Contact
Winkfield Road
Windsor SL4 4AY

t 0870 504 0404
w legoland.co.uk

006 Windsor

Windsor Castle

2 hrs+   All year

This is an official residence of the Queen and the largest occupied castle in the world. It has been a royal palace and fortress for more than 900 years. The castle and grounds cover 13 acres.

* The magnificent & beautiful St George's Chapel
* Apr–Jun, Changing of the Guard at 11am (not Sun)

Location
Follow brown signs to central Windsor

Opening
Daily; Mar–Oct 9.45am–5.15pm;
Nov–Feb 9.45am–4.15pm

Admission
Please phone for details

Contact
Ticket Sales and Information Office,
The Official Residences of The Queen,
London SW1A 1AA

t 020 7766 7304
w royalcollection.org.uk
e information@royalcollection.org.uk

007 Wokingham

California Country Park

1 hr+   All year

This park offers fishing and walks around a scenic lake. It contains an area of heathland and an ancient bog, which is a Site of Special Scientific Interest (SSSI). A countryside events programme runs all year.

* Conservation Award for management of SSSI 2002
* California Dreamin' café, toy shop & paddling pool

Location
Join Nine Mile Ride from A321, B3016 or A3095

Opening
Daily: Please phone for details

Admission
Free. Car park £1
(weekends & hols)

Contact
Nine Mile Ride, Finchampstead,
Wokingham RG40 4HT

t 0118 934 2016
w wokingham.gov.uk
e countryside@wokingham.gov.uk

Berkshire   Buckinghamshire

008 Wokingham

Dinton Pastures Country Park

2 hrs+   All year

Dinton Pastures Country Park is a 400-acre mosaic
of rivers, lakes, meadows and wooded areas for visitors
to explore. Countryside events are organised throughout
the year, including guided walks, pond dips for children
and activity days.

* Children's nature sessions & wildlife Treasure Hunt
* Join Dinton's weekly conservation volunteer group

Location	Admission
Off A329 Reading–Wokingham road. 15 mins walk from Winnersh station	Free. Car park £1
	Contact
Opening	Davis Street, Hurst RG10 0TH
Daily: summer opening 8am (closing times vary); winter opening 8am (main car park closes 6pm)	t 0118 934 2016
	w wokingham.gov.uk
	e countryside@wokingham.gov.uk

009 Aylesbury

Bucks Goat Centre

3 hrs+   All year

A centre with examples of all the British breeds
of goat as well as donkeys, pets, reptiles, llamas,
wallabies, pigs and poultry. There is also a play
barn with facilities for talks and seminars.

* Petting pen
* Trampoline & play centre

Location	Contact
½ mile S of Stoke Mandeville on A4010	Layby Farm, Old Risborough Road, Stoke Mandeville, Aylesbury HP22 5XJ
Opening	
Daily: summer 10am–5pm; winter 10am–4pm	t 01296 612983
	w bucksgoatcentre.co.uk
Admission	e bucksgoat@ccn.go-free.co.uk
Adult £4.50, Child £3.50, Concs £3.50	

010 Aylesbury

Buckinghamshire Railway Centre

2 hrs+   Apr–Oct

A working steam centre where you can ride behind
full-size steam engines and on the extensive miniature
railway. The museum houses a large collection of
locomotives, carriages and wagons.

* See the Royal Train of 1901
* Santa Steaming the four weekends before Christmas

Location	Contact
Signed from A41 near Waddesdon & A413 at Whitchurch	Quainton Road Station, Quainton Aylesbury HP22 4BY
Opening	
Apr–Oct Wed–Fri 10.30am–4.30pm; weekends 10.30am–5.30pm	t 01296 655720
	w bucksrailcentre.org
Admission	e abaker@bucksrailcentre.btopenworld.com
Adult £6, Child £4, Concs £5	

011 Aylesbury

Roald Dahl Children's Gallery

1 hr   All year

Awaken your senses at this award-winning museum, dedicated to the beloved children's author, with its innovative touchable displays and exciting programme of events. Come along and let your imagination run wild!

Location
In the old part of Aylesbury, near the town centre

Opening
Mon–Sat 10am–5pm, opens 3pm in term time; Sun 2pm–5pm
Please phone for details

Admission
Dahl Gallery Adult £3.25, Child £2.75
Main museum Free

Contact
Church Street,
Aylesbury HP20 2QP

t 01296 331441
w buckscc.gov.uk/museum
e museum@buckscc.gov.uk

012 Aylesbury

Tiggywinkles, The Wildlife Hospital Trust

1½ hrs+   All year

Did you know bread and milk is bad for hedgehogs? Come to the visitor centre to find out why and learn about the hundreds of sick animals the hospital cares for. Visit the gardens and wild areas to see some other permanent disabled residents (birds and badgers).

* Learn how to help wild birds in your garden
* See animals in their natural habitat

Location
Signed off A418 from Aylesbury

Opening
Easter–Sep Mon–Sun 10am–4pm;
Oct–Easter Mon–Fri 10am–4pm

Admission
Adult £3.80, Concs £2.80

Contact
Aston Road, Haddenham,
Aylesbury HP17 8AF

t 01844 292292
w sttiggywinkles.com
e mail@sttiggywinkles.org.uk

©Les Stocker MBE

013 Beaconsfield

Bekonscot Model Village & Railway

2 hrs   Feb–Oct

The oldest model village in the world, Bekonscot is a miniature wonderland depicting rural England in the 1930s. A gauge 1 model railway winds its way through the mini-landscape among castles, thatched cottages and a cricket match on the green.

* Railway available weekends & school holidays
* Children's play area & parties in the new log cabin

Location
Junction 2 off the M40 (near junction 16 of M25). Follow signs to Model Village from A355

Opening
Daily: Feb–Oct 10am–5pm

Admission
Adult £5.80, Child £3.50, Family (2+) £16

Contact
Warwick Road,
Beaconsfield HP9 2PL

t 01494 672919
w bekonscot.com
e info@bekonscot.co.uk

014 High Wycombe

Wycombe Museum

1 hr+   All year

Explore the history of the Wycombe district in the lively modern displays in this museum. There are hands-on activities for children and special events throughout the year.

* Superb collection of Windsor chairs
* Gardens include a Norman 'castle' mound

Location
Off A404 towards Amersham

Opening
Mon–Sat 10am–5pm, Sun 2pm–5pm; closed Bank Hols

Admission
Free, donations appreciated

Contact
Priory Avenue,
High Wycombe HP13 6PX

t 01494 421895
w wycombe.gov.uk/museum
e museum@wycombe.gov.uk

015 High Wycombe

Wycombe Summit Ski & Snowboard Centre

2 hrs   All year

Prepare for the piste at the longest ski slope in England and a world-class ski and snowboard centre for all ages and abilities. It has a 300m main slope, 100m trainer slope and seven nursery areas with three lifts. Training is available for all ability levels.

* Holiday activities
* Special holiday programmes & children's camps

Location
Between junctions 3 & 4 of the M40, just ½ hour from London

Opening
Daily: summer Mon–Fri 10am–10pm, Sat–Sun 10am–6pm; winter 10am–10pm
Please phone for details

Admission
Please phone for details

Contact
Abbey Barn Lane
High Wycombe HP10 9QQ

t 01494 474711/439099
w wycombesummit.com
e info@wycombesummit.com

016 Milton Keynes

Milton Keynes Museum

2 hrs   All year

Housed in a beautiful Victorian farmstead, attractions include room settings depicting Victorian and Edwardian domestic life, plus live demonstrations of cooking and printing from a bygone age.

*Jessie the shirehorse & historical shopping street
* Special events throughout the year

Location
Off McConnell Drive in Wolverton, just off A5 & A422

Opening
Apr–Oct Wed–Sun 11am–4.30pm;
Nov–Mar Sat–Sun 11am–4.30pm;
Christmas opening times vary.
Please phone for details

Admission
Adult £4, Concs £2.50, Family £10

Contact
McConnell Drive, Wolverton,
Milton Keynes MK12 5EL

t 01908 316222
w mkmuseum.org.uk
e enquiries@mkmuseum.org.uk

017 Olney

Emberton Country Park

2 hrs+   All year

A country park with 200 acres of beautiful parkland including five lakes and various children's activities, all bordered by the River Ouse. The park also includes many picnic areas.

* Two children's play areas
* Junior fishing

Location
On A509, 10 miles N of junction 14 off the M1, near Milton Keynes

Opening
Daily 24 hrs *Café* Apr–Oct open weekends 10am–5pm

Admission
Free. Car Park Apr–Oct £3;
Nov–Mar £1.80

Contact
Emberton, nr Olney MK46 5DB

t 01234 711575
w mkweb.co.uk/embertonpark
e embertonpark@milton-keynes.
gov.uk

018 Battle

Battle Abbey & Battlefield

1 hr+   All year

The site of the Battle of Hastings (1066) is now home to the Discovery Centre: a fun, activity-based exhibition open to families at weekends and during school holidays. There's also a children's themed outdoor play area, a battlefield and an audio tour of the abbey.

*Site of the most famous battle in English history
*Free interactive audio tour recreates the battle

Location
In Battle, at S end of high street. Battle is reached by turning off A21 on to A2100 10 mins from Battle station

Opening
Daily: Apr–Sep 10am–6pm;
Oct–Mar 10am–4pm

Admission
Adult £5.30, Child £2.70, Concs £4

Contact
High Street, Battle TN3 30AD

t 01424 773792
w english-heritage.org.uk

019 Bodiam

Bodiam Castle

3 hrs+   All year

Bodiam Castle is one of the most famous and atmospheric castles in the country. Explore the spiral staircases, visit the medieval lavatories and watch out for the enemy from the battlements. You can even try on some medieval armour (please call in advance).

* Bat Pack Discovery fun pack for young children
* Walk the battlements

Location	Contact
Off B2244, 3 miles S of Hawkhurst & 3 miles E of A21 near Hurst Green	Bodiam, nr Robertsbridge, TN32 5UA
Opening	t 01580 830436
1 Nov–6 Feb Sat–Sun 10am–4pm; 7 Feb–31 Oct daily 10am–6pm	w nationaltrust.org.uk
	e bodiamcastle@nationaltrust.org.uk
Admission	
Adult £4.40, Child £2.20, Family £11	

020 Brighton

Brighton Sea Life Centre

2 hrs+   All year

For a fun and educational day out, visit Brighton Sea Life Centre. Walk through the Underwater Tunnel, be amazed by the fantastic Ocean Tank and get close up to sharks, rays, giant sea turtles and tropical fish. Children under 14 must be accompanied.

* One of the longest underwater tunnels in England
* More than 30 modern marine & freshwater habitats

Location	Admission
Take M23/A23 from London or A27 from Portsmouth & Lewes	Adult £9.50, Child £7.50, Concs £8.50
Opening	**Contact**
Daily from 10am; please phone for details of winter opening times	Marine Parade, Brighton BN2 1TB
	t 01273 604234
	w sealifeeurope.com
	e slcbrighton@merlinentertainment. biz

021 Burwash

Bateman's

2 hrs+   Mar–Oct

If you enjoyed *The Jungle Book* or the *Just So Stories*, then take a trip to the home of Rudyard Kipling. See original drawings of Mowgli and Shere Khan, and Kipling's study – just as he left it.

* Children's quiz
* Gardens & watermill

Location
Off A265 or B2096, ½ mile S of Burwash

Opening
House: 19 Mar–30 Oct Sat–Wed 11am–5pm
Wild garden: 5–19 Mar Sat–Sun 11am–4pm; 29 Mar–30 Oct 11am–5pm

Admission
House & Gardens: Adult £5.90, Child £2.95, Family £14.75

Contact
Burwash,
Etchingham TN19 7DF

t 01435 882302
w nationaltrust.org.uk
e batemans@nationaltrust.org.uk

022 Ditchling

Stoneywish Nature Reserve

4 hrs+   All year

Stoneywish Nature Reserve is set in 52 acres of meadows and ponds. A wildlife walk enables visitors to pass through fields to a play and picnic area. There is a farm smallholding area, and freerange animals.

* Pets' corner with pigs & goats
* Shaker-style herb garden

Location
Take A23 from Brighton or London, then B2116. Located ¼mile E of Ditchling

Opening
Daily: summer 9.30am–5pm (last admission 4.30pm); winter 9.30am–4pm (last admission 3.30pm)

Admission
Adult £3.75, Child £2.75, Concs £2.75

Contact
Spatham Lane
Ditchling, Hassocks BN6 8XH

t 01273 843498
w stoneywish.com

023 Eastbourne

Drusillas Park

5 hrs   All year

Drusillas Park has more than 100 animal species in naturalistic environments including meerkats, otters, monkeys, penguins, bats and lemurs. The excellent children's play area includes climbing, sliding and swinging fun with the penguin slide.

* Mokomos Jungle Rock & Jungle Adventure Golf
* Gold panning & Explorer's Lagoon

Location	Admission
Off A27 between Lewes & Eastbourne	Please phone for details
Opening	**Contact**
Daily: summer 10am–6pm; winter 10am–5pm	Alfriston BN26 5QS
	t 01323 874100
	w drusillas.co.uk
	e info@drusillas.co.uk

024 Eastbourne

'How We Lived Then' Museum of Shops

1 hr+   All year

More than 100,000 exhibits of old shops, displays and room sets depicting 100 years of shopping and social history. Stroll through Victorian-styled streets and pay a visit to the grocer, chemist and many more.

* Celebration Inn commemorates 'Admiral Lord Nelson's victory at the Battle of Trafalgar

Location	Admission
Take A22 from London or A27 from Brighton	Adult £4, Child £3.50, Concs £3
Opening	**Contact**
Daily: 10am–5.30pm; winter closing time subject to change	20 Cornfield Terrace
Please phone before visiting	Eastbourne BN21 4NS
	t 01323 737143
	w how-we-lived-then.co.uk
	e howwelivedthen@btconnect.com

025 Eastbourne

Treasure Island

3 hrs   All year

This is a children's adventure playground filled with climbing apparatus and *Treasure Island* characters. There are also trampolines, inflatable slides and remote control boats, cars and bikes.

* Paddling pools & sandpits
* 18-hole golf & indoor play area

Location	Admission
Take A27 from Brighton or A22 from London. Follow signs for seafront E	*Park* Adult £2, Child £4
	Golf £4, £3.50
Opening	**Contact**
Park Easter–Sep daily 10am–6pm	Royal Parade,
Golf Daily 10am– 10pm	Eastbourne BN22 7AA
	t 01323 411077
	w treasure-island.info
	e fun@treasure-island.info

026 Exceat

Seven Sisters Country Park

4 hrs+ All year

A great location for outdoor activities, including family cycle routes, guided bike tours and canoe tuition for all abilities. Sussex Wildlife Trust offers exciting programmes for all age groups. Visit in spring to see newborn lambs on the working farm.

* Bicycle & canoe hire
* Shop selling leaflets, maps & souvenirs

Location
Off A259 between Eastbourne and Seaford or 712, 713 or 714 bus from Eastbourne

Opening
Daily: Easter–Oct;
Nov–Oct weekends only

Admission
Free

Contact
Exceat, Seaford BN25 4AD

t 01323 870280
w sevensisters.org.uk
e sevensisters@southdowns-aonb.gov.uk

027 Hastings

Hastings Castle & 1066 Story

1 hr+ All year

Come to the first Norman castle in Britain. At Hastings you can enjoy a spectacular audio-visual show, The 1066 Story, in a medieval siege tent, and explore the dungeons carved out of solid rock beneath the North Gate.

* Half-price entry to A Smuggler's Adventure when a ticket for the castle is purchased

Location
Leave M25 at junction 5 & follow A21 to Hastings. Take A259 from Eastbourne or Rye

Opening
Daily: Easter–Sep 10am–5pm;
Oct–Easter 11am–3pm

Admission
Adult £3.50, Child £2.30, Concs £2.90, Family £10.50

Contact
Castle Hill Road, West Hill, Hastings

t 01424 781112
w discoverhastings.co.uk
e bookings@discoverhastings.co.uk

028 Hastings

A Smuggler's Adventure

1 hr All year

A hands-on opportunity to learn more about the secrets of smugglers in a series of spooky caverns and passages. Find out what happened when the smugglers got caught and how they were punished!

* Half-price entry to Hastings Castle when a ticket for the A Smuggler's Adventure is purchased

Location
Junction 5 off M25 & follow A21 to Hastings. Take A259 from Eastbourne or Rye

Opening
Daily: Easter–Sep 10am–5.30pm;
Oct–Easter 11am–4.30pm

Admission
Adult £6.20, Child £4.20, Concs £5.20

Contact
West Hill,
Hastings TN34 3HY

t 01424 422964
w discoverhastings.co.uk

East Sussex

029 Lewes

Mohair Centre

2 hrs   All year

A children's farm with Angora goats and other farm animals. Come along and watch the lambing and kidding in the spring. Bookings only.

* Prebooked holiday activity days for children
* Play area

Location
Just off A22 between Eastbourne & East Grinstead. Take B2124 from Lewes

Opening
Sun only 11am–dusk

Admission
Please phone for details

Contact
Lewes Road, Whitesmith, Lewes BN8 6JG

t 01825 872457
e mohaircentre@hotmail.com

030 Newhaven

Newhaven Fort

2 hrs+   Mar–Nov

The massive ramparts, gun emplacements and tunnels fire the imagination with exciting glimpses into England's wartime past.

* Quality Assured Visitor Attraction

Location
M23/A23 from London to Brighton then follow A27 towards Eastbourne. At Lewes follow A26 to Newhaven. Signed from there

Opening
Daily: Mar–early Nov 10.30am–6pm (last admission 5pm); Nov weekends only

Admission
Adult £5. 20, Child £3.50, Concs £4.55 , Family £15.20

Contact
Fort Road, Newhaven BN9 9DL

t 01273 517622
w newhavenfort.org.uk
e info@newhavenfort.org.uk

031 Newhaven

Paradise Park

3–6 hrs   All year

Discover 'Planet Earth' for an unforgettable experience. A unique Museum of Life, Dinosaur Safari, beautiful water-gardens with fish and wildfowl, planthouses, themed gardens, Heritage Trail. Playzone includes crazy golf and adventure play areas.

* Fantasy golf
* Miniature railway

Location
Take A27 Brighton/Lewes bypass, then A26; or take the A259

Opening
Daily: 9am–6pm;

Admission
Please phone for details

Contact
Avis Road, Newhaven BN9 0DH

t 01273 616006 (24-hr info line)
01273 512123
w paradisepark.co.uk
e promotions@paradisepark.co.uk

032 Sheffield Park

Bluebell Railway

1 hr+   All year

The Bluebell Railway operates standard-gauge steam trains through nine miles of scenic Sussex countryside between Sheffield Park, Horsted Keynes and Kingscote.

* Famous Terrier-class engines, Stepney & Fenchurch
* Featured in the film *The Railway Children*

Location
Sheffield Park Station

Opening
Daily: Apr–Oct 11am–4pm;
Oct–Apr Sat–Sun 11am–4pm

Admission
Adult £9.50, Child £4.70, Concs £7

Contact
Sheffield Park Station TN22 3QL

t 01825 720800
w bluebell-railway.co.uk
e info@bluebell-railway.co.uk

033 Andover

The Hawk Conservancy Trust

4 hrs   Feb–Oct

A bird of prey park and hawk conservation centre set in 22 acres of woodland. It has more than 250 birds of prey including hawks, eagles, vultures and owls. There is also the chance to hold and fly a bird of prey. The eagles and vultures flying display is daily at 2pm.

* Flying displays & feeding times
* Duck racing

Location
4 miles W of Andover, off A303

Opening
Daily: 12 Feb–31 Oct 10.30am–5.30pm

Admission
Adult £8, Child & Concs £7.25

Contact
Andover SP11 8DY

t 01264 773850
w hawk-conservancy.org
e info@hawk.conservancy.org

034 Brockenhurst

Beaulieu Abbey & National Motor Museum

3 hrs+   All year

Home of the National Motor Museum, Beaulieu has more than 250 vehicles on display. Visitors can also tour the abbey and Lord Montagu's home, as well as enjoy the many rides and drives.

* Exhibition of James Bond vehicles & props
* Celebrating 800th anniversary of abbey

Location
Going W on M27 take A326. Signed Beaulieu or National Motor Museum

Opening
Daily: May–Sep 10am–6pm; Oct–Apr 10am–5pm; closed 25 Dec

Admission
From Adult £14, Child £7.25, Concs £13

Contact
Brockenhurst SO42 7ZN

t 01590 612345
w beaulieu.co.uk
e info@beaulieu.co.uk

035 East Cowes

Osborne House

3 hrs+   Apr–Sep

Osborne House was bought by Queen Victoria and Prince Albert in 1845 and used as a retreat from the stresses and strains of court life. Today it is one of the most important memorials to Britain's monarchy. Enjoy a horse-and-carriage ride through the grounds.

* Children's play area & interactive displays
* Glorious gardens & Swiss cottage

Location
1 mile SE of East Cowes

Opening
Daily: Apr–Sep 10am–5pm

Admission
Please phone for details

Contact
East Cowes PO32 6JY

t 01983 200022
w english–heritage.org.uk
e customer@english-heritage. org.uk

036 Fareham

The Royal Armouries – Fort Nelson

2 hrs   All year

Fort Nelson is a Victorian fortress overlooking Portsmouth Harbour, home to the Royal Armouries' collection of more than 350 historic big guns. Children can explore the massive fort with its secret underground chambers, tunnels and grass ramparts.

* Big-gun salutes every day & historical performances
* Expert guided tours for the family

Location
Leave M27 at junction 11, taking A27 towards Portchester from Delme Arms roundabout. Left at second traffic lights

Opening
Daily: Apr–Oct 10am–5pm; Nov–Mar 10.30am–4pm; salutes in summer at 12noon & 3pm; in winter at 1pm only

Admission
Free

Contact
Down End Road, Fareham PO17 6AN

t 01329 233734
w armouries.org.uk
e fnenquiries@armouries.org.uk

037 Freshwater

The Needles Park

4 hrs+   All year

Overlooking the famous Needles, the park has attractions and rides for all the family. The chairlift boasts the most famous view on the Isle of Wight of the uniquely coloured sand cliffs.

* Magic in the Skies firework finale (on selected dates)
* Boat trips

Location
Reached via B3322

Opening
Easter–early Nov daily 10am–5pm; 28 Jul–25 Aug late-night opening on Thu; Nov–Mar open partially. Please phone for details

Admission
Free (plus paying attractions/rides)
Car park £3 per vehicle

Contact
Alum Bay,
Isle of Wight PO39 0JD

t 0870 458 0022
w theneedles.co.uk
e info@theneedles.co.uk

038 Gosport

Explosion! The Museum of Naval Firepower

2 hrs+   All year

Everything you've ever wanted to know about naval firepower is here: from gunpowder, cannons, guns, shells and munitions to mines, torpedoes, modern missiles, even an atom bomb. Learn, too, about the 2,500 women who worked here during WWII.

* Gift shop with books & souvenirs
* Café with great views of Portsmouth Harbour

Location
M27 to junction 11. Follow A32 to Gosport & brown tourist signs

Opening
Daily: Apr–Oct 10am–5.30pm;
Nov–Mar Thu, Sat & Sun 10am–4.30pm

Admission
Adult £5.50, Child £3.50, Concs £4.50

Contact
Priddy's Hard, Gosport PO12 4LE

t 02392 505600
w explosion.org.uk
e info@explosion.org.uk

039 Havant

Staunton Country Park

3–4 hrs   All year

Set in 1,000 acres of parkland with huge glasshouses, walled gardens and a folly. This park also has the only remaining ornamental farm in England, with horses, pigs, sheep, llamas, peacocks and waterfowl.

* One-hour walks on Sundays (book at visitor centre)
* Trails, play area & special events

Location
On B2149 between Havant & Horndean, easily accessible by A27 & A3. Follow brown tourist signs

Opening
Daily: 10am–5pm (closes 4pm in winter)

Admission
Adult £4.50, Child £3.30, Concs £4

Contact
Middle Park Way,
Havant PO9 5HB

t 023 9245 3405
w hants.gov.uk/staunton
e staunton.park@hants.gov.uk

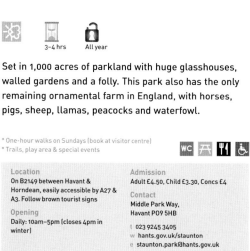

040 Newport

Classic Boat Museum

2 hrs +   Mar–Nov

A great indoor collection of lovingly restored sailing and motorised classic boats, dating from the C19. Highlights include the ultimate sailing classic, a Dragon, WWII airborne lifeboats, and a fragile folding canoe. Also on display are engines, equipment and memorabilia.

* Displays & boats change annually
* Items from *Gypsy Moth IV* on view

Location	Contact
On harbour, free parking	The Quay, Newport Harbour, Newport, Isle of Wight PO30 2EF
Opening	
Daily: Mar–Nov 10am–4.30pm	t 01983 533493
Admission	w netguides.co.uk/wight/boatmus
Adult £3, Child £1, Concs £2	e cbmiow@fsmail.net

041 Portsmouth

Spinnaker Tower

1 hr   All year

A new contemporary national icon on the South coast, providing a unique 'window on the sea'. The Spinnaker Tower is a striking new seamark, soaring 170m above Portsmouth Harbour, offering visitors spectacular views from a great height.

* Lift to upper levels
* Cross Europe's largest glass floor on Level 1

Location	Admission
Come in to Portsmouth on M275 and follow brown signs to Historic Waterfront, and then Spinnaker Tower	Adult £4.95, Child £4, Concs £4.50
	Contact
Opening	Gunwharf Quays, Portsmouth PO1 3TT
Mon–Wed 10am–6pm; Thu–Sat 10am–8pm; Sun 11am–5pm	t 02392 857520
	w spinnakertower.co.uk
	e info@spinnakertower.co.uk

042 Romsey

Paultons Park

5 hrs+   All year

A family leisure park with more than 50 attractions for all ages, including big rides, little rides, play areas, museums and entertainment.

* Voted best family theme park in 2003
* New for 2005 are Kontiki & Magic Carpet rides

Location	Admission
Off M27 at junction 2	Adult £14.50, Child £13.50, Family £52
Opening	Contact
Daily: 13 Mar–31 Oct 10am–6.30pm (last admission 4.30pm); Open weekends Nov–Dec	Ower, Romsey SO51 6AL
	t 02380 81 4442
	w paultonspark.co.uk
	e info@paultons.co.uk

043 Ryde

Isle of Wight Steam Railway

2 hrs+   Apr–Oct

A 5-mile steam railway that uses Victorian and Edwardian locomotives and carriages. New carriages and wagon works, adapted to be wheelchair-friendly.

* Children's playground
* Woodland walks

Location
3 miles SW of Ryde by road

Opening
Apr–Oct selected days;
Jun–mid Sep daily,
Please phone for details

Admission
Adult £8–£11 Child (4–15) £4–£7,
Family £20

Contact
Railway Station, Havenstreet
Ryde PO33 4DS

t 01983 882204
w iwsteamrailway.co.uk
e havenstreet@iwsteamrailway.co.uk

044 Sandown

Isle of Wight Zoo

2 hrs+   Apr–Oct

Situated on Sandown's beautiful seafront, this zoo is renowned for its collection of magnificent tigers and big cats. There are also rare lemurs and the Nightmares of Nature exhibit.

Location
On B3395

Opening
Apr–Oct daily 10am–6pm,
Please phone to confirm

Admission
Adult £5.95, Child £4.95, Concs £4.95,
Family £19.25

Contact
Granite Fort, Yaverland Seafront
Sandown PO36 8QB

t 01983 403883
w isleofwightzoo.com
e enquiries@iow-zoo.freeserve.co.uk

045 Seaview

Seaview Wildlife Encounter

3–4 hrs   Mar–Oct

Set in acres of landscaped gardens overlooking the Solent, this wildlife park has penguins, pelicans, flamingos, parrots, beavers and fish, and a Discovery Zone where visitors can learn all about animal conservation.

* New tropical house
* Events such as feeding the animals are run

Location
Off B3330 between Ryde & Seaview.
Well signposted from Ryde

Opening
Daily; Mar–Oct 10am–5pm (last admission 4pm)

Admission
Adult £6.75, Child £4.75, Concs £5.75

Contact
Springvale
Seaview, Isle of Wight PO34 5AP

t 01983 612153
w flamingoparkiw.com
e flamingo.park@virgin.net

046 Shanklin

Shanklin Chine

1 hr   Easter–Oct

A natural scenic gorge with a 45ft waterfall and stream leading to a beach. Shanklin Chine was once a site for shipwrecks and smuggling. It was later used for training Commandos during WWII.

* The Chine drops 105ft to sea level

Location
Enter via old village, off A3055 or through W end of Shanklin Esplanade, off Chine Hill

Opening
Please phone for details
31 March–25 May 10am–5pm;
26 May–10 Sep 10am–10pm;
11 Sep–29 Oct 10am–5pm

Admission
Adult £3.75, Child £2, Concs £2.75

Contact
12 Ponona Road, Shanklin
Isle of Wight PO37 6PF

t 01983 866432
w shanklinchine.co.uk
e jill@shanklinchine.co.uk

047 Southampton

Calshot Castle

2 hrs   Apr–Oct

Calshot Castle formed part of the chain of coastal forts built by Henry VIII in 1539. Its strategic importance, alongside the deep-water channel between Southampton and Portsmouth, led to it being manned throughout the centuries.

* Best known as a flying boat & RAF base in the C20
* Played a key support role in WWII

Location
From M27 (junction 2) take A326 to Fawley & Calshot

Opening
Daily: Apr–Oct 10am–4pm

Admission
Adult £2.50, Child £1.50, Concs £1.80

Contact
Calshot Spit, Fawley,
Southampton SO45 1BR

t 02380 892023
w calshot.com
e calshot.ac@hants.gov.uk

048 Southampton

Longdown Activity Farm

3 hrs+   Feb–Dec

There is fun for all the family at Longdown Activity Farm, with a variety of hands-on activities every day, including small animal handling and bottle-feeding young animals. Excellent indoor and outdoor play areas, with trampolines and ball pools.

* Bottle-feeding & hand-feeding calves & goat kids
* Great for school visits, playgroups & birthday parties

Location
Just off A35 from Southampton to Lyndhurst

Opening
Daily: Feb–Dec 10am–5pm

Admission
Adult £5.50, Child £4.50, Family £19

Contact
Deerleap Lane, Longdown
Ashurst, Southampton SO40 7EH

t 02380 293326
w longdownfarm.co.uk
e enquiries@longdownfarm.co.uk

049 Southampton

Royal Victoria Country Park

5 hrs+   All year

There are more than 240 acres of parkland, woodland and foreshore to be explored. The park is in the grounds of an old military hospital that now houses a fascinating exhibition depicting its history, with superb views and a shop.

* Miniature railway & activity sheets
* Programme of events, play area & sensory garden

Location	Admission
Take junction 8 off M27 & follow the tourist signs	Adult 70p, Child 35p, Concs 35p
	Contact
Opening	Netley Abbey,
Park Daily: Apr–Oct 8am–9pm;	Southampton SO31 5GA
Nov–Mar 8am–5pm	t 02380 455157
Exhibition, tower & shop Daily: Apr–Sep	w hants.gov.uk/rvcp
12pm–4.30pm	e rvcp@hants.gov.uk

050 Southampton

Southampton Maritime Museum

1½ hrs   All year

The museum is a medieval stone warehouse containing exhibitions on the port of Southampton and the *Titanic*. There are ship models and All Hands on Deck, an interactive exhibition.

* Titanic Voices exhibition
* Exhibitions change reularly

Location	Contact
Corner of Town Key Road and Bugel Street	Wool House, Town Quay, Southampton SO14 2AR
Opening	t 02380 635904
Tue–Fri 10am–5pm,	w southampton.gov.uk/heritage
Sat 10–4pm, Sun 2pm–5pm	e museums@southampton.gov.uk
Admission	
Free	

051 Stockbridge

Museum of Army Flying

2 hrs+   All year

This museum traces the development of army flying, from balloons and kites through both world wars up to the present day. Aircraft include a Sopwith Pup, a Miles Magister and a collection of WWII gliders.

* Children's science & education centre
* Viewing gallery overlooking airfield

 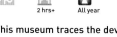

Location	Contact
A343 6 miles from Andover & 12 miles from Salisbury. Accessible from A30, A303 & M3	Middle Wallop, Stockbridge SO20 8DY
	t 01980 674421
Opening	w flying-museum.org.uk
Daily: 10am–4pm	e enquiries@flying-museum.org.uk
Admission	
Adult £5, Child £3.50, Concs £4	

052 Ventnor

Blackgang Chine Fantasy Park

4 hrs   Mar–Oct

This park, originally Victorian gardens, has been developed into a family-friendly theme park, water-gardens and maze. The fun-themed areas include Frontierland, Smugglerland, Fantasyland and Nurseryland.

* New Cliffhanger rollercoaster
* High-speed family watercoaster

Location	Contact
On A3005 Chale–Ventnor road	Chale, Ventnor
	Isle of Wight PO38 2HN
Opening	
End Mar–end Oct daily 10am–5pm;	t 01983 730330
Jul & Aug daily 10am–10pm (floodlit	w blackgangchine.com
until 10pm)	e info@blackgangchine.com
Admission	
Please phone for details	

053 Winchester

INTECH-Hands-on Science & Technology Centre

2 hrs+   All year

This centre houses an interactive technology exhibition set up to bring the worlds of science, technology, engineering and mathematics to life. Here you can bend light, create your own tornado spout and vortex and work out how much energy it takes to power a light bulb.

* Regularly changing exhibitions
* Gift shop with unusual & educational items

Location
Junction 9 off M3, take B3404
towards Alton

Opening
Daily 10am–4pm

Admission
Adult £5.95, Child £3.90, Concs £4.50

Contact
INTECH, Telegraph Way
Morn Hill, Winchester SO21 1HX

t 01962 86379
w intech-uk.com
e htct@intech-uk.com

054 Winchester

Marwell Zoological Park

4 hrs+   All year

A 100-acre park with more than 200 species of animals in large paddocks and thoughtfully designed enclosures. Come face to face with an Amur tiger and hear the jungle call of the gibbons.

*Children's adventure playground

Location
On B2177 Winchester–Bishops
Waltham road. Signed from M27 & M3

Opening
Daily: summer 10am–6pm;
winter 10am–4pm;

Admission
Please phone for details

Contact
Colden Common,
Winchester SO21 1JH

t 01962 777407
w marwell.org.uk
e marwell@marwell.org.uk

055 Yarmouth

Fort Victoria Marine Aquarium

1 hr+   Easter–Oct

See poisonous weever fish, graceful rays, beautiful anemones and amazing cuttlefish that change colour before your eyes. Extraordinary tropical fish and much more can be seen at this aquarium.

Location
W from Yarmouth on A3054

Opening
Daily: Easter–31 Oct 10am–6pm

Admission
Adult £1.90, Child (5–16) 95p,
Family £5, Concs £1.70

Contact
Fort Victoria Country Park
off Westhill Lane, Yarmouth
Isle of Wight PO41 0RR

t 01983 760283
w fortvictoria.co.uk
e pfblake@tiscali.co.uk

056 Yarmouth

Fort Victoria Model Railway

1 hr+   Easter–Sep

This is the largest and most technically advanced model railway in Britain. It is entirely computer-controlled and has more than 450 model buildings, 800 model people and 180 vehicles.

Location
Take Alum Bay/Freshwater road out
of Yarmouth. Take 1st turning right at
brown tourist sign, then follow
Westhill Lane to the end

Opening
Easter–Sep open daily 10am–5pm
Oct weekends & half-term 10am–5pm

Admission
Adult £4, Child £3, Concs £3

Contact
Westhill Lane, Yarmouth
Isle of Wight PO41 0RR

t 01983 761553
w wight-attractions.co.uk

057 Canterbury

The Canterbury Tales

1 hr+   Mar–Jan

This fascinating audio-visual experience, sited in the centre of Canterbury, is one of the town's most popular visitor attractions. Step back in time to experience the sights, sounds and smells of the Middle Ages in this stunning reconstruction of C14 England.

* Uses headsets with earphones
* Recreates the pilgrimages of Chaucerian England

Location
City centre, off high street

Opening
Daily: Mar–Jun 10am–5pm; Jul–Aug 9.30am–5pm; Sep–Oct 10am–5pm; Nov–Jan 10am–4.30pm

Admission
Adult £6.95, Child £5.25, Concs £5.95

Contact
St Margaret's Street,
Canterbury CT1 2TG

t 01227 479227
w canterburytales.org.uk
e info@canterburytales.org.uk

058 Canterbury

Druidstone Park & Art Park

2 hrs+   Mar–Nov

Set in attractive gardens and woodland, Druidstone caters for the imaginations of all ages. Go on a discovery trail through the enchanted woodland, and enjoy hands-on experiences in the farmyard.

* Farm animals
* Play areas for all ages

Location
On A290, between Canterbury & Whitstable

Opening
Daily: Mar–Nov 10am–5.30pm

Admission
Adult £5.10, Child £3.80, Concs £4.30, Family £15

Contact
Honey Hill, Blean,
Canterbury CT2 9JR

t 01227 765168
w druidstone.net

059 Canterbury

Howletts Wild Animal Park

2 hrs   All year

Howletts Wild Animal Park is set in mature parkland and contains John Aspinall's collection of animals. See one of the largest collections of tigers in the world and the largest breeding colony of gorillas in captivity.

* Animals include deer, leopards & elephants
* Jurassic Mine & dinosaur & fossil shop

Location
On A2, 3 miles S of Canterbury

Opening
Daily: 10am–dusk

Admission
Adult £12.95, Child £9.95,
Concs £10.95, Family £38–£44

Contact
Bekesbourne,
Canterbury CT4 5EL

t 01303 264647
w totallywild.net
e info@howletts.net

---

060 Canterbury

Museum of Canterbury with Rupert Bear Museum

1 hr   All year

This museum offers new and exciting interactive displays including a medieval discovery gallery, the Blitz Gallery and the Rupert Bear Museum. They're all set in one of the city's finest medieval buildings.

Location
Follow M2/A2 from London; take A28
from Ashford. Located in city centre,
on Stour Street

Opening
Mon–Sat 10.30am–5pm,
except Jun–Sep 1.30pm–
5pm (last admission 4pm)

Admission
Adult £3.10, Child £2.10, Concs £2.10

Contact
Stour Street,
Canterbury CT1 2NR

t 01227 475202
w canterbury-museum.co.uk

---

061 Canterbury

Roman Museum

1 hr   All year

This underground museum of the Roman town is an exciting mix of excavated real objects, authentic reconstructions, and the remains of a Roman town house with mosaics. Reconstructions also include a Roman market place, with a shoemaker, fruit and vegetable stall.

* Computer reconstruction shows the Roman house
* Touch-screen computer game on Roman technology

Location
Butchery Lane, close to cathedral

Opening
Mon–Sat 10am–5pm (last admission
4pm); Jun–Oct also open Sun
1.30pm–5pm

Admission
Adult £2.90, Child & Concs £1.80

Contact
Longmarket, Butchery Lane,
Canterbury CT1 2JE

t 01227 785575
w canterburymuseums.co.uk
e museums@canterbury.gov.uk

062 Chatham

The Historic Dockyard Chatham

4 hrs+   Feb–Nov

Visitors can enjoy 400 years of exciting naval history and architecture set in an 80-acre site. Explore HMS *Cavalier*, Britain's last WWII destroyer, the submarine *Ocelot* and the Victorian sloop *Gannet*, now fully restored.

* Wooden Walls exhibit with animatronic adventure
* Riverfront museum

Location
Leave M2 at junction 1, 3 or 4 and follow signs

Opening
Daily: 11 Feb–25 Mar 10am–4pm; 26 Mar–29 Oct 10am–6pm (last admission 4pm); Nov weekends only 10am–4pm

Admission
Adult £10, Child £6.50, Concs £7.50

Contact
Chatham ME4 4TZ

t 01634 823800
w thedockyard.co.uk
e info@chdt.org.uk

063 Chislehurst

Chislehurst Caves

1 hr   All year

Grab a lantern and get ready for an amazing adventure! Visit the caves and your whole family can travel back in time as you explore the maze of passageways deep beneath Chislehurst. During a 45-minute guided tour, visit the Caves Church, Druid altar and Haunted Pool.

* Facilities for children's parties
* Private tours of the caves

Location
Take A222 between A20 & A21. At railway bridge turn into Station Road then right again to Caveside Close

Opening
School hols daily 10am–4pm (except Christmas). Rest of the year Wed–Sun 10am–4pm

Admission
Adult £4, Child & Concs £2

Contact
Old Hill, Chislehurst BR7 5NB

t 020 8467 3264
w chislehurstcaves.co.uk
e enquiries@chislehurstcaves.co.uk

064 Dover

Crabble Corn Mill

1 hr+   All year

A restored watermill dating from 1812 and in full working order with devices not seen elsewhere. Demonstrations of flour milling take place and there is a programme of craft and art exhibitions.

Location
M2/A2 from London to Canterbury then A256 to River. From Folkestone follow B2060

Opening
Daily (except Mon); Easter–Sep 11am–5pm; winter weekends only 11am–5pm

Admission
Adult £3, Child £2.50, Concs £2.50, Family 14

Contact
Lower Road, River, Dover CT17 0UY

t 01304 823292
w ccmt.org.uk
e miller@ccmt.org.uk

065 Dover

Dover Castle

4 hrs+   All year

Commanding the shortest Channel sea crossing, this site has been the UK's most important defence against invasion since the Iron Age. It was built in the C12 and reinforced by Henry VIII in the 1530s. Underneath the nearby white cliffs is a series of underground tunnels.

* Reconstruction of Henry VIII's visit in 1539
* Visit the Dunkirk command room

Location
Clearly signed to E of the city, on the white cliffs

Opening
Mar–Sep daily 10am–6pm; Oct daily 10am–5pm; Nov–Jan Thu–Mon 10am–4pm; Feb–Mar daily 10am–4pm

Admission
Please phone for details

Contact
Dover CT16 1HU

t 01304 211067
w english-heritage.org.uk

066 Eynsford

Eagle Heights
Bird of Prey Centre

4 hrs+   All year

Home to birds of prey (eagles, falcons and vultures) and reptiles (pythons, crocodiles and iguanas), the centre offers daily flying displays, indoor demonstrations of owls and reptiles, falconry courses, and Bird of Prey Experience days. It also operates as a sanctuary.

* Facilities for birthday parties
* A range of courses offering hands-on experience

Location
Off M25 at junction 3 on to A20, or M20 at junction 1

Opening
Daily: Mar–Nov 10.30am–5pm; Nov–Feb weekends 11am–4pm; closed Dec

Admission
Adult £6.60, Child £4.60, Concs £5.60

Contact
Lullingstone Lane, Eynsford DA4 0JB

t 01322 866466
w eagleheights.co.uk
e office@eagleheights.co.uk

067 Faversham

Farming World

4 hrs   Mar–Oct

There are more than 100 traditional breeds of farm animals to meet in this safe environment. In the Hawking Centre visitors can see many indigenous birds of prey in spectacular displays. There are also indoor play and crafts.

* Only indoor play, crafts & animal barn open in winter
* 4 times winner of Tourism for All Award

Location
Off A299, ¼ mile E of M2 junction 7

Opening
Daily: Mar–Oct 9.30am–5.30pm

Admission
Adult £6.50, Child £5.50, Concs £6

Contact
Nash Court, Boughton, Faversham ME13 9SW

t 01227 751144
w farming-world.com
e enquiries@farming-world.co.uk

South of England Rare Breeds Centre

3 hrs All year

Here's a chance to meet and pet all your favourite friendly farm animals as you wander around a farm trail. The centre is also home to many endangered and rare British animals. Set in acres of beautiful woodland, there are plenty of places to picnic while the kids play.

* Mysterious Marsh woodland adventure
* Piglet racing in season & trailer rides all year

Location
Leave M20 at junction 10, follow signs to Brenzett and Hamstreet. Situated between Hamstreet & Woodchurch

Opening
Daily: Apr–Sep 10.30am–5.30pm; Oct–Mar Tue–Sun 10.30am–4.30pm

Admission
Adult £6, Child £6, Concs £5

Contact
Woodchurch, Ashford TN26 3RJ

t 01233 861493
w rarebreeds.org.uk
e visit@rarebreeds.org.uk

Wildwood

2 hrs All year

Set in 40 acres of ancient woodland, this unique discovery park is home to more than 300 animals from more than 50 species. See owls and otters, bees and beavers, wild boar and wolves – plus many more.

* Quality Assured Visitor Attraction
* Conservation programmes & woodland play area

Location
Close to Canterbury, just off A291, near Herne Bay

Opening
Daily: 10am–5pm (last admission 4pm)

Admission
Adult £8, Child £6, Concs £6.50, Family £26

Contact
Herne Common, Herne Bay CT6 7LQ

t 01227 712111
w wildwoodtrust.org
e info@wildwoodtrust.org

070 Hythe

Port Lympne Wild Animal Park

4 hrs   All year

A 400-acre wild animal park situated in the gardens of historic Port Lympne Mansion. The collection includes the largest herd of captive-bred black rhino outside Africa, plus elephants, tigers and many more.

Location
Leave M20 at junction 11 & follow signs to Lympne

Opening
Daily: summer 10am–6pm (last admission 4.30pm); winter 10am–dusk (last admission 3pm)

Admission
Adult £12.95, Child £9.95, Concs £10.95, Family £38–£44

Contact
Lympne, Hythe CT21 4PD

t 01303 264647
w totallywild.net
e info@howletts.net

071 Maidstone

Leeds Castle

3 hrs   All year

This medieval castle, situated on two islands in a lake set in 500 acres of parkland is a popular attraction. Once a Norman stronghold, the castle has since been a residence for six of England's medieval queens, a palace for Henry VIII, and a retreat for the powerful.

* Open-air concert programme
* Grand Fireworks spectacular

Location
Leave M20 at junction 8, castle is 7 miles E of Maidstone

Opening
Daily: Apr–Oct 10am–5.30pm; Nov–Mar 10am–3pm

Admission
Adult £13, Child £9, Concs £11
Gardens & attractions £10.50, £6.50, £8.50

Contact
Maidstone ME17 1PL

t 01622 765400
w leeds-castle.com
e enquiries@leeds-castle.co.uk

072 Maidstone

Museum of Kent Life

2 hrs+   Feb–Nov

A unique open-air living museum that celebrates 300 years of Kentish history. Traditional crafts are demonstrated in a working farm. This is one of the only places in England where hops are grown, harvested, dried and packed using time-honoured techniques.

* Calendar of events throughout the year
* Hop-picking festival in September

Location
Off M20 at junction 6. Follow signs

Opening
Daily: Feb–Nov 10am–5pm

Admission
Adult £6.50, Child £4.50, Concs £5

Contact
Cobtree, Lock Lane, Sandling, Maidstone ME14 3AU

t 01622 763936
w museum-kentlife.co.uk
e enquiries@museum-kentlife.co.uk

073 New Romney

Romney, Hythe & Dymchurch Railway

2 hrs   All year

This was the world's smallest public railway when it opened in July 1927. It now runs regular passenger services covering a distance of $13\frac{1}{2}$ miles from the picturesque Cinque Port of Hythe to the fishermen's cottages and lighthouses at Dungeness.

* Thomas the Tank Engine & Santa specials
* Dining-train specials

Location	Admission
The stations at New Romney, Dungeness and Hythe are all on or near A259 trunk road	Adult £5–£11, Child half fare
	Contact New Romney TN28 8PL
Opening Trains run daily Apr–Sep & weekends Oct–Mar; please phone or see the website for timetable	t 01797 362353 w rhdr.org.uk e info@rhdr.org.uk

074 Sittingbourne

Bredgar & Wormshill Light Railway

2 hrs+   May–Oct

One of the best narrow-gauge railways in the UK, this steam-train service runs along the line between Warren Wood and Stony Shaw, through attractive Kent countryside. There are 11 restored steam locomotives, plus steam traction engines.

* Woodland walks
* Vintage cars, a beam engine & a model railway

    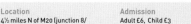

Location	Admission
4½ miles N of M20 (junction 8/ Leeds Castle exit) on B2163. 1 mile S of Bredgar	Adult £6, Child £3
	Contact The Warren, Bredgar, Sittingbourne ME9 8AT
Opening 1 May–2 Oct open 1st Sun of month 11am–5pm	t 01622 884254 w bwlr.co.uk e thewarren@prquis.net

075 Strood

Diggerland

4 hrs+   All year

A unique adventure park based on the world of construction machinery, where children and adults can ride and drive real diggers and dumpers in safety.

* ROSPA Award for saftey
* Suitable for adults & children

Location	Admission
Exit M2 at junction 2 on to the A228; follow signs to Strood; turn right at roundabout & park is on right	Adult £2.50, Child £2.50, Concs £1.25
	Contact Medway Valley Leisure Park, Strood ME2 2NU
Opening Feb–Nov open weekends, Bank Hols & School Hols 10am–5pm; Dec–Jan daily 10am–5pm	t 08700 344437 w diggerland.com e mail@diggerland.com

076 Tenterden

Kent & East Sussex Railway

2 hrs   Mar–Oct

Take a nostalgic trip behind a full-size steam engine on Britain's first light railway. Journey through 10½ miles of unspoilt countryside between Tenterden and the Sussex village of Bodiam and experience the sights and sounds of steam engines.

* Video theatre, children's play area & museum
* Quality Assured Visitor Attraction

Location
Follow A28 from Ashford or Hastings

Opening
Mar–April & Oct weekends;
May–Sep Mon & Fri, daily in Jul

Admission
Adult £10, Child £5, Concs £9

Contact
Tenterden Town Station,
Tenterden TN30 6HE

t 01580 765155
w kesr.org.uk
e enquiries@kesr.org.uk

077 Tunbridge Wells

Groombridge Place Gardens & The Enchanted Forest

4 hrs+   Apr–Nov

In addition to the formal gardens, visit the enchanted forest and enjoy exciting playgrounds, huge swings, strange plants, giant rabbits and shy deer. Don't miss the raised wooden adventure boardwalk, the Dinosaur and Dragon Valley and the Serpent's Lair.

* Home to one of only two zeedonks (zebra-donkeys) in the UK
* Largest centre for birds of prey in the South East

Location
A26 towards Tunbridge Wells, turn right on to B2176 towards Penshurst. 3 miles past Penshurst village, turn left at T junction with A264. Follow signs

Opening
Daily Apr–Nov 9.30am–6pm

Admission
Adult £8.70, Child & Concs £7.20

Contact
The Estate Office, Groombridge Place,
Groombridge,
Royal Tunbridge Wells TN3 9QG

t 01892 863999/861444
w groombridge.co.uk
e office@groombridge.co.uk

078 Whitstable

Snappy's Adventure Play Centre

2 hrs+   All year

Snappy's is a large indoor adventure play centre with an extensive range of approved play equipment all designed to an exciting dinosaur theme. There is a dedicated area for under-fours, a twin wavy-board slide, and a Game Zone for older children.

Location
From Whitstable take A290 up Borstal Hill & turn left on to A2990. At next roundabout turn right then right again

Opening
Daily: 10am–6.30pm

Admission
Adult free, Child £3.95

Contact
45b Joseph Wilson Estate,
Millstrood Road
Whitstable CT5 3PS

t 01227 282100
w snappysadventureplay.co.uk

079 Bloomsbury

The British Museum

2 hrs+   All year

Far more than a collection of arts and antiquities, the British Museum offers virtual tours for children of all ages, family activities and events, plus exhibitions of games and toys – a great cultural day out for the whole family.

* Spectacular covered courtyard

Location
Underground Tottenham Court Road

Opening
Daily: Sat–Wed 10am–5.30pm, Thu–Fri 10am–8.30pm (selected galleries 5.30pm–8.30pm)

Admission
Free, exhibitions may charge

Contact
Great Russell Street,
London WC1B 3DG

t 020 7323 8299
w thebritishmuseum.ac.uk
e information@thebritishmuseum.ac.uk

080 Brentford

London Butterfly House

1 hr+   All year

See hundreds of butterflies flying free in a tropical greenhouse garden. Watch the butterflies feeding, courting and laying their eggs. The insect gallery has giant spiders, locusts, lizards, scorpions and stick insects and there is a walk-through aviary.

Location
Underground Gunnersbury, then 237 or 267 bus to Brent Lea Gate

Opening
Daily: Jan–27 Mar & 25 Oct–Dec 10am–3.30pm; 28 Mar–24 Oct daily 10am–5pm;

Admission
Adult £5.25, Child £3.95, Concs £4.25, Family £16

Contact
Syon Park, Brentford,
London TW8 8JF

t 020 8560 7272
w londonbutterflyhouse.com
e info@londonbutterflyhouse.com

081 Camberwell

Livesey Museum for Children

1 hr+   All year

The Livesey Museum runs a changing programme of lively, unusual, fully hands-on exhibitions for children up to the age of 12. An all-new interactive exhibition is shown every year.

* New Myths & Legends exhibitions

Location
Underground Elephant & Castle, then 21, 53, 172 or 453 bus

Opening
During exhibitions open only Tue–Sat 10am–5pm; closed Bank Hols

Admission
Free

Contact
682 Old Kent Road,
London SE15 1JF

t 020 7639 5604
w liveseymuseum.org.uk
e livesey.museum@southwark.gov.uk

Museum of London

2 hrs   All year

Experience London as you've never seen it before. Meet the Romans, take a walk down a Victorian street, or hear a cockney tale of London life.

* Covers the history of the city since it began
* Regular calendar of exhibitions & special events

Location
Underground Barbican, St Paul's

Opening
Mon–Sat 10am–5.50pm,
Sun 12 noon–5.50pm

Admission
Free

Contact
London Wall,
London EC2Y 5HN

t 0870 444 3852
w museumoflondon.org.uk
e info@museumoflondon.org.uk

London Aquarium

2 hrs   All year

London Aquarium offers more than 350 species from oceans, lakes, rivers and streams around the world. Visitors can stand face to face with spectacular sharks in a two-storey tank, get hands-on with a ray at the touchpool or spot animals in the coral reef.

* Late–night opening times in summer
* Themed activity weeks

Location
Inside County Hall on the south bank
of the Thames by Westminster Bridge
Underground Westminster

Opening
Daily: 10am–6pm (7pm on selected
summer evenings)

Admission
Please phone for details

Contact
County Hall, Westminster Bridge
Road, London SE1 7PB

t 020 7967 8000
w londonaquarium.co.uk
e info@londonaquarium.co.uk

London Eye

½ hr   All year

This is the most popular tourist attraction in London. The 443ft (135m) big wheel provides the most spectacular views of one of the biggest cities in the world. On a clear day you can see 25 miles in every direction from a safe and comfortable capsule.

* More than 15,000 people a day travel on the Eye
* Views are breathtaking in all conditions

Location
On the south bank of the Thames by
County Hall
Underground Waterloo

Opening
Daily: May, Jun & Sep 9.30am–9pm;
Jul & Aug 9.30am–10pm; Jan–Apr &
Oct–Dec 9.30am–8pm

Admission
Adult £12.50, Child £6.50, Concs £10

Contact
BA London Eye, Riverside Building,
County Hall, London SE1 7PB

t 0870 5000 600
w ba–londoneye.com
e customer.services@ba-londoneye.
   com

085   Green Park

Buckingham Palace

1 hr+   Aug–Sep

Do you fancy being Queen for a day? Take a trip around the official residence of the Royal Family with audio tours introduced by HRH Prince Charles. Enjoy a walk in the palace grounds or take part in an activity trail and catch the Changing of the Guard.

* The State Rooms form the heart of the working palace
* Furnished with treasures from the Royal Collection

Location
Mainline Victoria
Underground Victoria, Green Park
& Hyde Park Corner

Opening
23 Jul–27 Sep daily 9.30am–6pm

Admission
Adult £13.50, Child £7, Concs £11.50

Contact
Ticket Sales and Information Office,
The Official Residences of The Queen,
London SW1A 1AA

t 020 7766 7300
w royalcollection.org.uk
e bookinginfo@royalcollection.org.uk

086   Greenwich

The *Cutty Sark*

1 hr   Jan–Sep

It's 1880 and the *Cutty Sark*'s Captain has just jumped overboard, you're 1,000 miles from home and there is a 100ft wave in front of you! Actually, you're in Maritime Greenwich overlooking the River Thames, holding the wheel of the fastest tea clipper ever built.

* Experience life on board one of the world's most famous ships
* Visit now before the £25m conservation programme begins in October 2006

Location
Mainline Docklands Light Railway
Cutty Sark Station
Underground Canary Wharf
By boat from Westminster Pier

Opening
Daily: 10am–5pm (last admission
4.30pm)

Admission
Adult £4.50, Child £3.25, Concs £3.75

Contact
King William Walk, Greenwich,
London SE10 9HT

t 020 8858 3445
w cuttysark.org.uk
e enquiries@cuttysark.org.uk

087 Hendon

Royal Air Force Museum

4 hrs   All year

Soar through the history of aviation for an aerodynamic day of fun. With a brand-new interactive gallery, film shows and more than 80 legendary aircraft on display, this is the place to land for a great family day out.

Location
Easy access from M25. Signed from M1, A41, A5 & A406
Underground Colindale
Mainline Mill Hill Broadway

Opening
Daily: 10am–6pm

Admission
Free, under-16s must be accompanied by an adult

Contact
Grahame Park Way, London NW9 5LL
t 020 8358 4849
w rafmuseum.org
e london@rafmuseum.org

088 Kensington

Natural History Museum

2 hrs+   All year

The Natural History Museum has hundreds of exciting, interactive exhibits. Highlights include Dinosaurs, Creepy-Crawlies, Human Biology, the must-see exhibition about ourselves, and Mammals, with its unforgettable huge blue whale.

* Investigate the wildlife garden

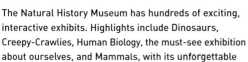

Location
Underground South Kensington

Opening
Mon–Sat, Bank Hols 10am–5.50pm, Sun 11am–5.50pm
(last admission 5.30pm)

Admission
Free

Contact
Cromwell Road, London SW7 5BD
t 020 7942 5000
w nhm.ac.uk
e info@nhm.ac.uk

089 Kensington

Science Museum

3 hrs+   All year

Come and see more than 40 galleries and 2,000 hands-on imaginative exhibits at this amazing museum. You can step into the future in the Wellcome Wing, change your sex, age 30 years in 30 seconds and create your own identity profile – all in a day!

* Interactive exhibits, including new Energy Gallery
* IMAX cinema

Location
Underground South Kensington

Opening
Daily: 10am–6pm

Admission
Free, donations welcomed, exhibitions may charge

Contact
Exhibition Road, South Kensington, London SW7 2DD
t 0870 870 4868
w sciencemuseum.org.uk
e sciencemuseum@nmsi.ac.uk

090 Lambeth

Imperial War Museum

3 hrs+   All year

Come and relive life during WWI and WWII. Walk through the trenches and share the dramatic Blitz experience, complete with the sounds and smells of London during an air raid. Find out about spies in the Secret War exhibition.

* London Family Attraction of the Year 2003

Location
Mainline Waterloo, Elephant and Castle
Underground Lambeth North 5 min walk

Opening
Daily: 10am–6pm

Admission
Free, exhibitions may charge

Contact
Lambeth Road, London SE1 6HZ

t 020 7416 5320
w iwm.org.uk
e mail@iwm.org.uk

---

092 London Bridge

London Dungeon

1 hr+   All year

The London Dungeon is an interactive historic horror attraction that dispenses fear and fun in equal doses. Visitors encounter The Great Fire of London, Jack the Ripper and the Judgement Day boat ride.

* Great Plague exhibition
* The terrible truth about Jack the Ripper

Location
Underground London Bridge

Opening
Daily: 10am–5.30pm

Admission
Adult £15.50, Child £10.95, Concs £12.25

Contact
28–34 Tooley Street,
London SE1 2SZ

t 020 7403 7221
w thedungeons.com
e londondungeon@
   merlinentertainments.biz

---

091 Liverpool Street

Bank of England Museum

1 hr+   All year

This museum housed within the Bank of England traces the history of the bank. Visitors can view gold bars dating from ancient to modern times, as well as coins, a unique collection of bank notes and more.

* Try to lift a real gold bar
* Special events & activities

Location
Underground Bank & Liverpool Street

Opening
Weekdays 10am–5pm; also open on the day of the Lord Mayor's Show; closed Sat, Sun & Bank Hols

Admission
Free

Contact
Threadneedle Street,
London EC2R 8AH

t 020 7601 5491
w bankofengland.co.uk/museum
e museum@bankofengland.co.uk

093   Marylebone

Madame Tussaud's

2 hrs+   All year

Dance like a diva and take to the stage with Beyoncé, Britney and Kylie, see if you can bend it like David Beckham or have a dinner date with George Clooney. Also try out as a Pop Idol, be photographed by the paparazzi, have your DNA checked and explore the galaxy.

* Updated & revamped Chamber of Horrors
* The same building also houses the Planetarium

Location	Contact
Underground Baker Street	Marylebone Road, London NW1 5LR
Opening	t 0870 400 3000
Weekdays 9.30am–5.30pm ;	w madame-tussauds.com
weekends 9am–6pm	e csc@madame-tussauds.com
Admission	
Adult from £19.99, Child from £15.99,	
Concs from £17.99	

094   Marylebone

Sherlock Holmes Museum

1 hr   All year

The museum consists of Holmes's apartment on the first floor, plus the entire second, third and fourth floors, which contain the new exhibition area. It features several life-size wax figures from the best-known Sherlock Holmes adventures – can you identify them?

* New shop selling all kinds of Sherlock Holmes
  novelty goods

Location	Contact
Underground Baker Street	221B Baker Street
	London NW1 6XE
Opening	
Daily: 9.30am–6.30pm	t 020 7935 8866
	w sherlock-holmes.co.uk
Admission	e londonlinks@btconnect.com
Adult £6, Child £4	

095   Regent's Park

London Zoo

4 hrs   All year

Come face to face with some of the hairiest, scariest, tallest and smallest animals on the planet. See our Animals in Action presentation and watch some of our finest flying, leaping and climbing animals showing off their skills. Don't miss a visit to B.U.G.S!

* Regular programme of feeding times & special shows
* New komodo dragon

Location	Admission
At NE corner of Regent's Park on	Adult £14, Child £10.75, Concs £12
Outer Circle	
Underground Camden Town	**Contact**
	Regent's Park, London NW1 4RY
Opening	
Daily: 7 Mar– 23 Oct 10am–5.30pm ; 24	t 020 7722 3333
Oct–31 Oct 10am–4.30pm; Nov–Feb	w zsl.org
10am–4pm	

096 Shepherd's Bush

BBC Television Centre Tours

2 hrs   All year

On this tour you will see behind the scenes of the BBC TV Centre. You may visit areas such as the News Centre, dressing rooms and studios. No two tours are ever the same. All tours must be pre-booked and visitors must be ten years and over.

* Winner of the 2003 Group Travel Awards
* Also new CBBC tours

Location
Underground White City

Opening
Tours run 6 times a day Mon–Sat; booking essential

Admission
Adult £8.95, Child £6.50

Contact
BBC Television Centre,
Wood Lane,
London W12 7RJ

t 0870 603 0304 (bookings)
w bbc.co.uk/tours
e bbctours@bbc.co.uk

097 South Bank

Globe Theatre

1–3 hrs   All year

This museum is an exciting, engaging introduction to the life, works and theatre of Shakespeare's time. Experience a performance in a replica Elizabethan theatre, or enjoy the interactive exhibits about Shakespeare's life.

* Annual programme of Shakespeare's plays
* Permanent exhibition & theatre tours

Location
Mainline London Bridge, Waterloo
Underground Southwark

Opening
Daily: May–Sep *Theatre* 10am–7.30pm
Exhibition 9am–5pm Oct–Apr
Exhibition 10am–5pm (tours available)

Admission
Exhibition Adult £9, Child £6.50,
Concs £7.50

Contact
21 New Globe Walk, London SE1 9DT

t *Enquiries* 020 7902 1400
   Box office 020 7401 9919
w shakespeares-globe.org
e info@shakespearesglobe.com

098 Stepney

Ragged School Museum

1 hr   All year

This museum is dedicated to London's East End. On the old site of Barnardo's ragged school, the museum has a reconstructed Victorian classroom, along with exhibits on housing, education and work in the East End from the 1880s to 1900.

Location
Underground Mile End
Mainline Limehouse

Opening
Wed & Thu 10am–5pm; 1st Sun of month 2pm–5pm

Admission
Free

Contact
46–50 Copperfield Road,
London E3 4RR

t 020 8980 6405
w raggedschoolmuseum.org.uk
e enquiries@raggedschoolmuseum.
   org.uk

099 Stepney

Stepping Stones Farm

2 hrs+   All year

This is an urban working farm with a full range of livestock. Educational sessions and structured demonstrations, such as sheep shearing, can be arranged for groups, according to season.

* Play area & activity room
* Farm trail

Location
Corner of Stepney Way & Stepney High Street,
Underground Stepney Green

Opening
Tue–Sun 9.30am–6pm; closed Mon except Bank Hols; open Easter

Admission
Free; small charges for special events

Contact
Stepney Way, London E1 3DG

t 020 7790 8204
e lynne.rosie@btconnect.com

100 Tower Bridge

Tower Bridge Exhibition

1 hr   All year

Inside the Tower Bridge Exhibition you will learn how the world's most famous bridge works and the history of its construction. Enjoy panoramic views from the walkways situated high above the River Thames and visit the original Victorian engines.

* New interactive computer displays
* Special ticket rate for Tower Bridge & Monument

Location
Underground Tower Hill and London Bridge
Boat from Tower Pier

Opening
Daily: 10am–6.30pm (last admission 5.30pm)

Admission
Adult £5.50, Child £3, Concs £4.25

Contact
Tower Bridge, London SE1 2UP

t 020 7403 3761
w towerbridge.org.uk
e enquiries@towerbridge.org.uk

101 Tower Bridge

Winston Churchill's Britain at War Experience

1 hr+   All year

An educational adventure about the home front of WWII Britain. Special effects and original artefacts recreate everyday life for ordinary people – the Blitz, rationing, blackouts and evacuation.

Location
Underground London Bridge

Opening
Daily: Oct–Mar 10am–4pm; Apr–Sep 10am–5pm

Admission
Adult £8.50, Child £4.50, Concs £5.50

Contact
64–66 Tooley Street, London SE1 2TF

t 020 7403 3171
w britainatwar.co.uk
e info@britainatwar.org.uk

102 Tower Hill

Tower of London

3 hrs   All year

A visit to the Tower of London's 11 towers encompasses 1,000 years of history – some of it bloody. Far more than just a trip to see the Crown Jewels, there are talks, tours, holiday events and family trails, all included in the basic ticket price.

* Ceremony of the Keys (please apply in writing)
* Constant calendar of special events

Location
Underground Tower Hill

Opening
Mar–Oct Tues–Sat 9am–6pm,
Sun & Mon 10am–6pm;
Nov–Feb Tue–Sat 9am–5pm,
Sun & Mon 10am–5pm
(last admission 1 hr before close)

Admission
Adult £14.50, Child £9.50 , Concs £11

Contact
Tower Hill, London EC3N 4AB

t 0870 756 6060
w tower-of-london.org.uk

103 Trafalgar Square

National Gallery

1 hr+   All year

The National Gallery holds one of the finest permanent collections of Western European art. It includes all the greats, and is sure to please even the most reluctant gallery-goer.

* Selection of courses & lectures available
* Weekend & school holiday family events

Location
Trafalgar Square
Underground Leicester Square, Charing Cross

Opening
Daily: 10am–6pm, Wed 10am–9pm

Admission
Free, donations welcome, exhibitions may charge

Contact
Trafalgar Square, London WC2N 5DN
t 020 7747 2885
w nationalgallery.org.uk
e information@ng-london.org.uk

104 Westminster

Houses of Parliament

2 hrs   July–Oct

Take a trip through the history and politics of our country – sit on the backbenches, or become a Lord. This is an invaluable introduction to politics and a great insight into citizenship.

* See & hear debates

Location
Underground Westminster

Opening
Tours available during summer recess end Jul–early Oct
Please phone for details

Admission
Please phone for details

Contact
House of Commons Information Office, Westminster, London SW1A 0AA
t 020 7219 4272
w parliament.uk
e hcinfo@parliament.uk

105 Wimbledon

Polka Theatre

2 hrs   Oct–Aug

Polka is the only theatre building in Britain producing and presenting work just for children. Shows range from classic and contemporary book adaptations to new work for the stage. Children's workshops are also available throughout the year.

* Playground
* Exhibits of costumes & props

Location
Underground Wimbledon, turn left down the Broadway & theatre is on left

Opening
Oct–Aug Tue–Sat 9.30am–4.30pm;
Please phone for performance times

Admission
Please phone for details

Contact
240 The Broadway, London SW19 1SB
t 020 8543 4888
w polkatheatre.com

106 Woolwich

Thames Barrier Learning Centre

1 hr+   All year

The £500 million Thames Barrier spans the river at Woolwich Reach. There is an exhibition with a video and a working model. Please phone or check the website for dates of the monthly test gate closures. There are also riverside walkways and a play area.

Location
On A206. On S side of the Thames between S exit of the Blackwall Tunnel & Woolwich Ferry

Opening
Daily: Apr–Sep 10.30am–4.30pm;
Oct–Mar 11.30am–3.30pm

Admission
Adult £1.50, Child 75p, Concs £1

Contact
1 Unity Way, London SE18 5NJ
t 020 8305 4188
w environment-agency.gov.uk
e learning.centre@environment-agency.gov.uk

107 Burford

Cotswold Wildlife Park & Gardens

3 hrs+   All year

The park, which is set in 160 acres of parkland and gardens around a listed Victorian manor house, has been open to the public since 1970. It's home to a collection of mammals, birds, reptiles and invertebrates, from ants to white rhinos and bats to big cats.

* Insect & reptile houses
* Tikki the 7-year-old, 19¾ft python

Location
On A361, 2 miles S of Burford

Opening
Daily: Mar–Sep 10am–4.30pm;
Oct–Feb 10am–3.30pm

Admission
Adult £8, Child £5.50, Concs £5.50

Contact
Burford OX18 4JW

t 01993 823006
w cotswoldwildlifepark.co.uk

108 Chinnor

Chinnor & Princes Risborough Railway

1 hr   Mar–Dec

Hop aboard a steam or heritage diesel train at Chinnor, then sit back and enjoy the 7-mile round trip as it heads into the country, past a stud farm, the former site of a Roman villa and the local cricket grounds.

* Learn how to drive a train on special training days
* Travel on Thomas the Tank Engine. Phone for details

Location
Station Road just off B4009

Opening
Weekends Mar–Dec 10am–5.30pm
Please phone for timetable details

Admission
Adult £5–£7, Child £2.50–£3.50,
Concs £4–£6

Contact
Chinnor Station, Station Road,
Chinnor OX39 4ER

t 01844 353535/354117
w cprra.co.uk

109 Didcot

Didcot Railway Centre

2 hrs+   All year

A living museum of the Great Western Railway, based around the original depot, and now housing a collection of steam locomotives, carriages and wagons. On steam days the locomotives come to life and visitors can ride in the 1930s trains.

* Recently launched a broad-gauge locomotive engine

Location
Signed from M4 (junction 13) & A34

Opening
Weekends 10am–5pm; May–5 Sep &
School Hols open daily 10am–4pm;
please phone or visit the website

Admission
Adult £4–£9, Child £3–£7.50,
Concs £3.50–£8.50, Family £12–£28

Contact
Great Western Society, Didcot
OX11 7NJ

t 01235 817200
w didcotrailwaycentre.org.uk
e didrlwcf@globalnet.co.uk

110 Oxford

The Oxford Story

1 hr+ · All year

Climb aboard this amazing ride and travel through 900 years of history, complete with sights, sounds and smells of the Middle Ages. Discover the link between *Alice in Wonderland* and the University.

Location
By road via A44. Follow city centre signs. A Park & Ride service is available

Opening
Daily: Jul–Aug 9.30am–5pm;
Jan–Jun & Sep–Dec Mon–Sat
10am–4.30pm, Sun 11am–4.30pm

Admission
Adult £6.95, Child £5.25, Concs £5.95

Contact
6 Broad Street Oxford OX1 3AJ

t 01865 728822
w oxfordstory.co.uk
e info@oxfordstory.co.uk

111 Wallingford

Wellplace Zoo

4 hr+ · All year

A small zoo designed for children, with a museum and garden centre. The zoo houses exotic animals and farmland animals. Residents include rabbits, lemurs, donkeys, meerkats, penguins, otters, tortoises, flamingos, monkeys and many more.

* Children's play area
* Bird feeding

Location
On A4074

Opening
Jan–Mar Sat–Sun 10am–4pm;
Apr–Sep daily 10am–5pm;
Oct–Dec Sat–Sun 10am–4pm;
(last admission 1 hr before close)

Admission
Adult £2.50 , Child £1

Contact
Ipsden, Wallingford OX10 6QZ

t 01491 680473
w wellplacezoo.fsnet.co.uk

112 Witney

Cogges Manor Farm Museum

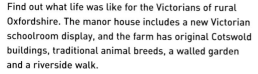

2 hrs · Apr–Oct

Find out what life was like for the Victorians of rural Oxfordshire. The manor house includes a new Victorian schoolroom display, and the farm has original Cotswold buildings, traditional animal breeds, a walled garden and a riverside walk.

* Programme of special events

Location
1/2 mile SE of Witney, off A40

Opening
Apr–Oct Tue–Fri & Bank Hols
10.30am–5.30pm, Sat–Sun
12noon–5.50pm

Admission
2005: Adult £4.40, Child £2.30, Concs
£2.85. Please phone for 2006 prices

Contact
Church Lane, Witney OX28 3LA

t 01993 772602
w westoxon.gov.uk

113 Woodstock

The Oxfordshire Museum

2–3 hrs · All year

This award-winning redevelopment of Fletcher's House provides a home for the new county museum celebrating Oxfordshire. It features local history, art and archaeology, as well as innovative industries.

* Interactive exhibits offer new learning experiences
* Café and large garden

Location
On A44

Opening
Tue–Sat 10am–5pm, Sun & Bank Hols
2pm–5pm (last admission 4.45pm)

Admission
Free

Contact
Fletcher's House, Park Street
Woodstock OX20 1SN

t 01993 811456
w oxfordshire.gov.uk/the_oxfordshire
_museum
e oxon.museum@oxfordshire.gov.uk

114 Chertsey

Thorpe Park

8 hrs   Mar–Nov

A park with thrilling rollercoasters and water rides, including the brand new Rush, the world's biggest air-powered speed swing and Slammer, the ultimate full-throttle free-fall experience. There is also a multitude of rides and experiences for younger children.

* Rumba Rapids, a white-water ride that twists & turns
* Colossus, the world's first 10-looping coaster

Location
Leave M25 at junction 11 or 13 & follow signs via the A320 to Thorpe Park

Opening
Please phone or visit the website

Admission
Adult £30, Child £20, Family £82–£102

Contact
Staines Road, Chertsey KT16 8PN

t 01932 569393
  0870 444 4466 (tickets)
w thorpepark.com

115 Cobham

Painshill Park

2 hrs+   All year

Within its 160 acres created by Charles Hamilton as a series of subtle and surprising vistas, its landscapes include authentic 18th-century plantings, a working vineyard, Gothic Temple, Chinese Bridge, Crystal Grotto, Turkish Tent, newly restored Hermitage and Gothic Tower.

* Historic vineyard now replanted for production
* 14-acre lake fed by a spectacular waterwheel

Location
Off A3 and A245 at Cobham

Opening
Mar–Oct 10.30am–6pm (closed Mon);
Nov–Feb 11am–4pm or dusk
(closed Mon & Tue)

Admission
Adult £6, Child £3.50, Concs £5.25

Contact
Portsmouth Road, Cobham KT11 1JE

t 01932 868 113
w painshill.co.uk
e info@painshill.co.uk

116 East Molesey

Hampton Court Palace

3 hrs+   All year

Embark on a magical journey back through 500 years of royal history. Discover the magnificent State Apartments of Henry VIII and William III, explore 60 acres of immaculate riverside gardens and enjoy the free tours and presentations.

* Tours with costumed guides
* World-famous maze

Location
From M25, junction 10 to A307 or junction 12 to A308

Opening
Daily: 26 Mar–28 Oct 10am–6pm; 29 Oct–25 Mar 10am–4.30pm

Admission
Adult £12, Child £7.80, Concs £9

Contact
East Molesey KT8 9AU

t 0870 752 7777
w hamptoncourtpalace.org.uk
e hamptoncourt@hrp.org.uk

117 Edenbridge

British Wildlife Centre

2 hrs+   Easter–Oct

The British Wildlife Centre is home to one of the finest collections of native mammals, reptiles and birds in the country, with more than 40 species set in 30 acres. Many are rare in the wild but at the centre you have the chance to observe them at close hand.

Location
Leave M25 at junction 6, then follow A22 S to Newchapel

Opening
Easter–Oct Sat, Sun, Bank Hols & daily during School Hols 10am–5pm

Admission
Adult £6, Child £4, Family £18

Contact
Newchapel
Lingfield RH7 6LF

t 01342 834658
w britishwildlifecentre.co.uk
e info@britishwildlifecentre.co.uk

118 Epsom

Chessington World of Adventures

8 hrs   Mar–Oct

An exciting range of themed attractions, games, rides and adventures. There are special Halloween events. Rides and attractions include Beanoland, Trail of the Kings and Toytown & Vampire.

* New Land of the Dragons
* Toadie's Crazy Cars

Location
Just 12 miles from London on the A243, 2 miles from A3 & M25 (junction 9 or 10)

Opening
Mar–Oct; opening times vary. Please phone or visit the website for details

Admission
Please phone or visit the website for details

Contact
Leatherhead Road
Chessington KT9 2NE

t 0870 999 0045
w chessington.com

119 Epsom

Horton Park Children's Farm

4 hrs+   All year

A friendly children's farm set up for the under-nines. There are lots of different farm animals including cows, sheep, pigs, goats, ponies, a donkey, a llama, poultry, rabbits, guinea pigs, gerbils, mice, birds – and even a friendly snake! There is also a play barn.

Location
Leave M25 at junction 9 & follow A243 north

Opening
Daily: summer 10am–6pm; winter 10am–5pm; closed 25, 26 Dec

Admission
Adult £5.30, Child £5.30
1 adult free with each paying child

Contact
Horton Lane
Epsom KT19 8PT

t 01372 743984
w hortonpark.co.uk
e childrensfarm@hortonpark.co.uk

120 Farnham

Rural Life Centre

2 hrs+   All year

The Rural Life Centre is a museum of past village life covering the years from 1750 to 1960. It is set in more than 10 acres of garden and woodland and housed in purpose-built and reconstructed buildings including a chapel, village hall and cricket pavilion.

* Displays show village crafts & trades
* Arboretum with more than 100 species of trees

Location	Contact
Off A287, 3 miles S of Farnham	Old Kiln Museum, Reeds Road Tilford, Farnham GU10 2DL
Opening	t 01252 795571
Mar–Oct Wed–Sun & Bank Hol Mon 10am–5pm; Nov–Feb Wed & Sun 11am–4pm	w rural-life.org.uk e rural.life@lineone.net
Admission	
Adult £6, Child £4, Concs £5	

121 Guildford

Burpham Court Farm Park

2 hrs   All year

A 76-acre conservation centre for endangered breeds of farm livestock including cattle, sheep, pigs, goats and llamas. There is also a nature trail and many opportunities for hands-on contact with the animals including collecting eggs with the farmer.

*Feed the friendly sheep & poultry
*Angling day-tickets available for owner of a rod licence

Location	Admission
From A3 southbound, take Burpham & Merrow exit; signed from A3100, or from A320 at Jacobs Well	Adult £4.75, Child £3.95, Concs £4.35
	Contact
Opening	Clay Lane, Jacobswell Guildford GU4 7NA
Daily: 10am–6pm (or dusk if earlier); feeding time 4pm in summer, 3pm in winter	t 01483 576089 w burphamcourtfarm.com

122 Guildford

River Wey & Godalming Navigations

2 hrs+   Mar–Oct

Discover the story of Surrey's oldest waterway and the people who lived and worked on it. Climb aboard a Wey barge and enjoy the interactive exhibits or take a boat trip.

* Surrey Industrial History Group Conservation Award
* Guildford Borough Council Access Award

Location	Contact
Wharf Road is behind Surrey County Cricket Ground, off Woodbridge Road	Wharf Road, Guildford GU1 4RR
	t 01483 561389
Opening	w nationaltrust.org.uk
End Mar–end Oct Mon & Thu–Sun 11am–5pm	e riverwey@nationaltrust.org.uk
Admission	
Adult £3.50, Child £2	

123 Leatherhead

Bocketts' Farm Park

2 hrs+   All year

This is a working family farm set in beautiful downland countryside with many friendly farm animals who enjoy being fed and handled. The farm boasts tractor and pony rides, a 70ft slide and daily pig races.

* Surrey Farm Diversification Award 2002
* Play barn & trampolines

Location	Contact
Just off A246 Epsom–Guildford road, south of Leatherhead	Young Street, Fetcham Leatherhead KT22 9BF
Opening Daily: 10am–6pm	t 01372 363764 w bockettsfarm.co.uk e jane@bockettsfarm.co.uk
Admission Adult £5.40, Child £4.95, Concs £4.95	

124 Redhill

Godstone Farm

6 hrs+   All year

Set in 40 acres of wooded farmland, Godstone Farm is home to cows, sheep, pigs, horses, ponies, goats, llamas, ducks, chickens, rabbits and more. Children can hold the smaller animals.

* Large indoor soft play area & outdoor play barn
* Toboggan run

Location	Contact
From M25 (junction 6) follow road to Godstone. Signposted from village	Tilburstow Hill Road Godstone RH9 8LX
Opening Daily: 10am–6pm	t 01883 742546 w godstonefarm.co.uk e havefun@godstonefarm.co.uk
Admission Adult & Child £5.50 1 adult free with each paying child	

125 Weybridge

Brooklands Museum

3 hrs+   All year

A family-friendly motorsport and aviation museum with walk-on exhibits, a hands-on discovery centre and regular family activities. There are motorsport events and fly-ins throughout the year. Parts of Concorde are also now ready to assemble for show.

* Extensive programme of motoring events
* Large display of cars, bikes & aircraft

Location	Contact
Off B374, A3 to A245. Follow signs	Brooklands Rd, Weybridge KT13 0QN
Opening Daily: summer 10am–5pm; winter 10am–4pm;	t 01932 857381 w brooklandsmuseum.com e info@brooklandsmuseum.com
Admission Adult £7, Child £5, Concs £6	

126 Arundel

Amberley Working Museum

3 hrs+   Mar–Nov

Amberley is a 36-acre open-air museum set on the South Downs. With its historic buildings, working exhibits and demonstrations, the museum aims to show how science, technology and industry have affected people's lives. The new railway exhibition hall is now open.

* Variety of crafts demonstrated daily
* Trips on vintage bus & narrow-gauge railway

Location
Off B2139 between Arundel
& Storrington

Opening
Mar–Nov Wed–Sun 10am–5.30pm

Admission
Adult £7.80, Child £4.50, Concs £6.80

Contact
Amberley, Arundel,
BN18 9LT

t 01798 831370
w amberleymuseum.co.uk
e office@amberleymuseum.co.uk

127 Arundel

WWT Arundel

2 hrs+   All year

The new visitor centre at Arundel is surrounded by ancient woodland and overlooked by the town's historic castle. The wetlands are home to many rare species of wetland wildlife. Learn more about them in the new Eye-of-the-Wind wildlife art gallery.

* Programme of educational activities & events
* Many rare birds regularly sighted

Location
Close to A27 & A29, follow brown duck
signs on approaching Arundel

Opening
Daily: 9.30am–5.30pm; winter 4.30pm

Admission
Adult £5.95, Child £3.75, Concs £4.75

Contact
Mill Road, Arundel BN18 9PB

t 01903 883355
w wwt.org.uk/visit/arundel
e enquiries@wwt.org.uk

128 Billingshurst

Fishers Farm Park

4 hrs   All year

A mixture of rural farmyard and dynamic adventure playground, Fishers Farm Park has a combine-harvester ride and tractor, pony and horse rides. There are also quad bikes, bumper boats, climbing walls, a mega bouncy slide, a theatre and shows.

* Quality Assured Visitor Attraction

Location
Near village of Wisborough Green.
Follow signs on A272 & B2133

Opening
Daily 10am–5pm

Admission
High season: Adult £9.25, Child £8.75,
Mid-season: £7.25, £6.75,
Low season: £6.25, £5.75

Contact
Newpound Lane,
Wisborough Green RH14 0EG

t 01403 700063
w fishersfarmpark.co.uk
e ffp@aol.com

129 Chichester

Earnley Butterflies & Gardens

3 hrs+   Mar–Nov

At Earnley Gardens visitors can see the ornamental butterfly house and covered theme gardens from around the world. The gardens also house Noah's Ark, a rescue centre for small animals, including reptiles. There is a Shipwreck Museum and exotic bird gardens.

* Rejectamenta - British nostalgia museum from the C20
* 15-hole crazy golf course & animal handling

Location
Follow A286 from Chichester to the
Witterings. After 3 miles turn left &
follow signs

Opening
End Mar–early Nov daily 10am–6pm

Admission
Adult £7, Child £4, Concs £6

Contact
133 Almodington Lane,
Earnley, Chichester PO20 7JR

t 01243 512637
e william.priddle@ntlworld.com

130 Chichester

Military Aviation Museum

4 hrs+   Feb–Nov

Learn about 70 years of military aviation in Sussex, in particular the air war over southern England from 1939 to 1945. Meet the friendly volunteers, many of whom were wartime RAF pilots, navigators and groundcrew. On display are planes, uniforms and other memorabilia.

* Opportunity to 'fly' a fighter simulator
* Direct bus service from Chichester to museum, No. 55

Location
3 miles E of Chichester off A27

Opening
Daily: Feb & Nov 10am–4.30pm;
Mar–Oct 10am–5.30pm

Admission
Adult £5, Child £1.50, Concs £4

Contact
Military Aviation Museum,
Tangmere, Chichester PO20 6ES

t 01243 775223
w tangmere-museum.org.uk
e tangmeretrust@aol.com

131 Chichester

Weald & Downland Open Air Museum

2 hrs+   All year

This museum in 50 acres of beautiful Sussex countryside offers a chance to wander through a collection of nearly 50 historic buildings dating from the C13 to the C19. Many have period gardens and farm animals. There are also woodland walks and a lake.

* The leading museum of historic buildings in England
* See food prepared in the working Tudor kitchen

Location
Situated 7 miles N of Chichester on A286

Opening
Daily: Apr–Oct 10.30am–6pm;
Nov–3 Jan 10.30am–4pm;
4 Jan–12 Feb Wed, Sat–Sun 10.30am–4pm; 13 Feb–31 Mar 10.30am–4pm

Admission
Adult £7.70, Child £4, Concs £6.70,

Contact
Singleton, Chichester PO18 0EU

t 01243 811363/811348
w wealddown.co.uk
e office@wealddown.co.uk

132 Crawley

Tulleys Farm

3 hrs+   All year

A farm with pick-your-own soft fruit and vegetables and a seven-acre maize maze to entertain all the family. At the farm there are also special events, including the Halloween Spooktacular festival. Animals include goats, pigs, chipmunks, rabbits and guinea pigs.

* Play area & pets' corner

Location
Take B2110 from East Grinstead to Turners Hill. Signed from there

Opening
Tearoom 9.30am–4.30pm
Farm shop 9am–6pm; 5pm in winter
Maize Maze Daily: Jul–early Sep 10am–6pm

Admission
Maze: Adult £6, Child £5

Contact
Turners Hill, Crawley RH10 4PE

t 01342 718472
w tulleysfarm.com

133 Ford

The Flying Fortress

2hrs+   All year

The newest Family Entertainment Centre on the South coast boasts an enormous plane-shaped playframe with loads of activities and games to keep all age groups happy from toddlers to teens. The 300+ seater café serves a wide range of freshly prepared foods and drinks.

* Special events programme for holidays

Location
Just off A259 going towards Yapton, look out for blue RAC signs or follow signs to Ford Airfield Industrial Estate

Opening
Daily: Mon,Tue, Thu, Sat & Sun 10am-7pm, Wed & Fri 10am-6pm

Admission
Babies free, under-4s £3.50,
Age 4+ £4.50, Teen club £4.50

Contact
Ford Airfield, Ford BN18 0HY

t 01903 733550
w www.flying-fortress.co.uk
e captain@flying-fortress.co.uk

134 Littlehampton

Harbour Park

3 hrs+   All year

A family amusement park right by the beach, with traditional attractions – dodgems, waltzer, arcade, plus a host of other rides and activities for all ages.

Location
A27, then follow A280 or A284 to Littlehampton

Opening
Arcade, play area & food bar 10am-6pm (later in summer)
Outside attractions Easter-Oct from 12noon; limited opening in winter; please phone for details

Admission
Free, Charges for individual rides

Contact
Sea Front Littlehampton BN17 5LL

t 01903 721200
w harbourpark.com
e fun@harbourpark.com

135 Littlehampton

Look and Sea!

1 hr+   All year

Explore the geology, geography and history of Littlehampton, finishing in the stunning glass-walled viewing tower with fantastic views across the River Arun out to sea and to Arundel. The attractions include an interactive maritime exhibition and a variety of displays.

* Newly opened riverside walks
* Café overlooking the river

Location
By the river, 300 yrds from railway station

Opening
Daily: 9am-5pm

Admission
Adult £2.95, Child & Concs £2.50

Contact
63 Surrey Street
Littlehampton BN17 5AW

t 01903 718984
w lookandsea.co.uk
e info@lookandsea.co.uk

136 Pulborough

Bignor Roman Villa

1 hr+   Mar-Oct

Discovered in 1811, this site, probably dating from the C3, is one of the largest Roman villas in Britain and boasts amazing mosaics of gladiators in combat. It has 65 rooms in the main complex and nine outbuildings, including a bath house and a summer and a winter dining room.

* Spectacular mosaics of Venus & Medusa
* Bathing complex with baths & plunge pool

Location
6 miles N of Arundel, signed from A29 (Bignor–Billingshurst) and A285 (Chichester–Petworth)

Opening
Mar-Apr, Tue–Sun & Bank Hols 10am–5pm;
Daily: May & Oct 10am-5pm;
June-Sep 10am-6pm

Admission
Adult £4.20, Child £1.80, Concs £3

Contact
Bignor Lane,
Pulborough RH20 1PH

t 01798 869259
w pyrrha.demon.co.uk
e bignorromanvilla@care4free.net

Trebarwith Strand, Cornwall

South West

Bristol Cornwall Devon Dorset
Gloucestershire Somerset Wiltshire

Newcastle
Emlyn

Fishguard

St David's

PEMBROKESHIRE   CARMARTHENS

Carmarthen

533

Narberth

Haverfordwest   St Clears   531

536   534
Milford
Haven   Neyland

537   Kidwelly

Pembroke   Tenby   Burry   Llanelli
Dock   Port
Pembroke   Caldey   M4
Island   Swanse

SWANSEA

St Govan's   SWANSEA
Head   Port
Eion   Mumbles
Head

Ilfracombe

176–178

Barns

Hartland
Point   Bideford

180–181

Great
Torrington

DE
148
Bude

Holsworthy

Okehampton

Tintagel   Launceston

156   Dart

147 Bodmin
Wadebridge   Moor

Trevose Head   Tavistock
Padstow   207
Buckfa

NEWQUAY   Bodmin   ORNWAL   PLYMOUTH
172–173   144–146

Newquay   Liskeard   Saltash   PLYMOUTH
157–158
160–163   Plympt
St Austell   199–202
Fowey   Looe   Torpoint
Truro   168–171   159   174
167
175
St Ives Camborne   Redruth
149   Sal
150–151
St Just   Dodman
Penzance   St Mawes   Point
Sennen   164–166   Falmouth
Land's End   153–155   152
Helston

Lizard
Lizard
Point

Isles of Scilly

137 City Centre

@Bristol

3 hrs+   All year

At Explore, you can play virtual volleyball, test your memory and run in a giant hamster wheel. Wildwalk takes you on a journey through life on earth using botanical houses, animals and multimedia. The IMAX® Theatre is the biggest cinema screen in the region.

* Tropical forest with free flying birds & butterflies
* Planetarium – Bristol's very own planetarium

Location
Off Anchor Road in central Bristol

Opening
Daily: 10am–6pm

Admission
Explore
Adult £8, Child £5.50, Concs £6.50
Wildwalk & IMAX® £6.50, £4.50, £5.50

Contact
Harbourside, Bristol BS1 5DB

t 0845 345 1235
w at-bristol.org.uk
e information@at-bristol.org.uk

138 City Centre

Bristol Ice Rink

2 hrs   All year

Bristol Ice Rink offers a variety of family and disco skating sessions every day. Learn-to-ice-skate courses are available throughout the year.

* Birthday parties
* Refreshments available

Location
Bristol city centre

Opening
Daily: 10am–10.30pm

Admission
Adult from £5.50, Child £2.50, please phone for details

Contact
Frogmore Street, Bristol BS1 5NA

t 0117 929 2148
w jnll.co.uk
e jnlbristol@nikegroup.co.uk

139 City Centre

Bristol Zoo Gardens

3 hrs   All year

Bristol Zoo Gardens has more than 400 endangered and exotic species. Visit the Seal & Penguin Coasts, Bug World, Twilight World, the Monkey House, Livingstone's fruit bats, Asiatic lions, the Reptile House and Gorilla Island. Or why not relax in the stunning gardens.

* Voted Zoo of the Year 2004 by the Good Britain Guide

Location
From M5 (junction 17 or 18), follow brown elephant signs

Opening
Daily: 9am–5.30pm in high season, 5.00pm in low season, animal houses close at 4.30pm in winter);

Admission
Adult £9.70, Child £6.20, Concs £8.50, Family £28.50

Contact
Clifton, Bristol BS8 3HA

t 0117 974 7399
w bristolzoo.org.uk
e information@bristolzoo.org.uk

140 City Centre

City Museum & Art Gallery

2 hrs+   All year

The museum and gallery house a wide range of objects, from real Egyptian mummies, fossils and Alfred the gorilla to art, pottery and clothing. Activities include workshops, children's holiday activities, family Sunday Fundays, walks, and arts and crafts sessions.

* World Wildlife Gallery & Eastern art

Location
In Clifton, follow brown signs from town centre

Opening
Daily: 10am–5pm

Admission
Free

Contact
t 0117 922 3571
w bristol-city.gov.uk/museums
e general_museum@bristol-city.gov.uk

141 City Centre

SS *Great Britain*

2 hrs   All year

Visit the world's first great ocean liner, the pinnacle of Victorian engineering and luxury. Take a hard-hat tour and witness the conservation of this historically important iron ship.

* Designed by Isambard Kingdom Brunel
* The largest ship of her day

Location
Follow anchor signs in Bristol Historic Dockyard

Opening
Daily: Apr–Oct 10am–5.30pm
Nov–Mar 10am–4.30pm

Admission
Adult £7.50, Child £4.50, Concs £6.50

Contact
Great Western Dockyard,
Gas Ferry Road, Bristol BS1 6TY

t 0117 926 0680
w ssgreatbritain.org
e admin@ss-great-britain.com

© Alan Russell

142 Whitchurch

Horseworld

3 hrs+   All year

Horseworld Visitor Centre is a great day out for all the family. Support the South West's leading horse welfare charity and meet the rescued horses, ponies and donkeys. There are interactive museums and a nature trail as well as pony rides and pet handling.

* Twice-daily presentations
* Indoor & outdoor play areas

Location
Take A37 from Bristol. Through Whitchurch – Horseworld is on left

Opening
Daily: Mar–Sep 10am–5pm (4pm in winter); Sep–Mar closed Mon

Admission
Please phone for details

Contact
Staunton Manor Farm,
Staunton Lane, Whitchurch,
Bristol BS14 0QJ

t 01275 540173
w horseworld.org.uk
e visitorcentre@horseworld.org.uk

143 Wraxall

Noah's Ark Zoo Farm

3 hrs+   Feb–Oct

This centre has plenty to entertain children – water buffalo, rhinos, yaks, monkeys, reptiles and 80 other species. There are indoor and outdoor adventure play areas and tractor rides; plus the chance to bottle-feed lambs, handle baby chicks and milk a bionic cow!

* Quality Assured Visitor Attraction
* World's longest hedge maze

Location
On B3128 Bristol–Clevedon road

Opening
Feb half-term to Oct, Tue–Sat
10.30am–5pm;
School hols Mon–Sat

Admission Adult £7.50, Child £5.50,
Concs £6.50, Family £23

Contact
Failand Road, Wraxall,
Bristol BS48 1PG

t 01275 852606
w noahsarkzoofarm.co.uk
e info@noahsarkzoofarm.co.uk

144 Bodmin

Bodmin & Wenford Railway

3 hrs   Mar–Oct

A trip on this standard-gauge railway, operating mainly steam engines, covers 6½ miles from Bodmin town to Bodmin Parkway. You'll pass through the beautiful River Fowey valley and stop at Boscarne Junction for the Camel Trail.

* Quizzes available for children

Location
On B3268 in central Bodmin

Opening
Please phone for details

Admission
Adult £10, Child £6, Family £28

Contact
Bodmin General Station,
Lostwithiel Road,
Bodmin PL31 1AQ

t 01208 73666
w bodminandwenfordrailway.co.uk
e enquiries@bodminandwenfordrailway.co.uk

145 Bodmin

Camel Trail

All day   All year

Take a whole day to explore this way-marked path, which runs along 17 miles of the Camel Estuary and Camel Valley from Padstow to Poley's Bridge. The route is suitable for pedestrians, cyclists and horses.

*Local bike hire

Location
Accessible from Wadebridge town, or A389 from Bodmin or main car park in Padstow

Opening
All year: please phone for details

Admission
Free

Contact
3–5 Barn Lane,
Bodmin PL31 1LZ

t 01208 265644
w ncdc.gov.uk

146 Bodmin

Lanhydrock House

3 hrs+   Apr–Oct

One of the finest houses in Cornwall, built in the late C19. It is set in wooded parkland and surrounded by a garden with rare shrubs and trees. 'Below stairs' has a huge kitchen, larder, dairy and bake house.

* Children's guide & quizzes
* Organized activities in school holidays

Location
2 miles E of Bodmin, follow signs off either A30 or A38

Opening
Apr–Oct Tue–Sun & Bank Hol Mon
11am–5.30pm (5pm in Oct)

Admission
Please phone for details

Contact
Lanhydrock, Bodmin PL30 5AD

t 01208 265950
w nationaltrust.org.uk
e lanhydrock@nationaltrust.org.uk

147 Bolventor

Colliford Lake Park

3 hrs+   Easter–Oct

Colliford Lake Park is a farm-based attraction. Spectacularly set on Bodmin Moor, overlooking Colliford Lake, this 40-acre park combines natural beauty with an action-packed day out. There are pedal-karts, challenging agility trails and a target range.

* Extensive indoor and outdoor play areas
* Nature trails around Colliford Lake

Location
500 yards off A30 between Launceston & Bodmin

Opening
Daily: Easter–Oct 11am–6pm

Admission
Adult £5.50, Child £4.50, Concs £4

Contact
Bolventor, Bodmin Moor PL14 6PZ

t 01208 821469
w collifordlakepark.com
e info@collifordlakepark.com

148 Bude

Brocklands Adventure Park

4 hrs+   All year

Younger children will enjoy the sandpit, swings and slides at this activity-packed park. For older kids there is a mini assault course and Aqua Blaster, pony rides, bumper boats, two-seater Supakarts, a new tenpin bowling centre and much more.

* Quality Assured Visitor Attraction
*Evening menus and fully licensed bar

Location
On A39 Atlantic Highway between Bude & Bideford

Opening
Please phone for details

Admission
Standard £7.95, Child £6.95, Concs £5.95

Contact
West Street, Kilkhampton, Bude EX23 9QW

t 01288 321920
w brocklands.com

149 Cambourne

Tehidy Country Park

4 hrs+   All year

Enjoy an active day at this country park in 345 acres of woodland, lakes and ponds, with 9 miles of footpaths to explore. There is also the opportunity to follow horse, cycle and woodland trails.

* Sensory trail for visually impaired visitors
* Redesigned orienteering course

Location
Access on B3301 from Portneath to North Cliffs

Opening
All year: please phone for details

Admission
Free

Contact
Tehidy, Cambourne TR14 0HA

t 01209 714494
w cornwall.gov.uk
e enquiries@cornwall.gov.uk

150 Falmouth

Glendurgan Gardens

2 hrs   Feb–Nov

These delightful subtropical gardens include an extensive laurel maze, the Giant's Stride swing and a reconstructed C19 schoolroom. The gardens run down to the sandy beach of Durgan, with good swimming and rock pools.

Location
4 miles SW of Falmouth, ½ mile SW of Mawnan Smith on road to Helford Passage

Opening
Feb–Nov Tue–Sat 10.30am–5.30pm; (last admission 4.30pm); open Bank Hol Mon

Admission
Adult £4.20, Child £2.10, Concs £3.60

Contact
Mawnan Smith,nr Falmouth TR11 5JZ

t 01326 250906
e glendurgan@nationaltrust.org.uk

151 Falmouth

National Maritime Museum Cornwall

2 hrs   All year

One of only three natural underwater viewing locations in the world. Enjoy hands-on interactives, audio-visual immersive experiences, talks, special exhibitions and the opportunity to get out on to the water and discover the marine life around our coastline.

* Climb to the top of the tower for views over the harbour
* Display of Cornish maritime heritage

Location
SE end of harbourside. Or follow signs from A39 for Park & Float

Opening
Daily: 10am–5pm

Admission
Adult £6.50, Child & Concs £4.30

Contact
Discovery Quay, Falmouth TR11 3QY

t 01326 313388
w nmmc.co.uk
e enquiries@nmmc.co.uk

152 Goonhilly

Goonhilly Satellite Earth Station

2 hrs+   All year

Visit Goonhilly, the largest satellite station on earth, to learn about space and modern communications. There are interactive exhibits, film shows and high-speed touch-screen internet terminals, plus an absorbing multimedia visitor centre.

* 3D virtual head-creation display
* Guided tours

Location
Follow B3293 Helston–St Keverne road

Opening
Daily:from 10am; Closing times vary between 4pm and 6pm. Please phone for details. Closed Mon & Fri

Admission
Adult £6, Child £4, Concs £4.50

Contact
Goonhilly TR12 6LQ

t 0800 679593
w goonhilly.bt.com
e goonhilly.visitorscentre@bt.com

153 Helston

Flambards Theme Park

4 hrs+   Easter–Nov

Set in glorious gardens, this Cornish theme park combines internationally acclaimed exhibitions such as Britain in the Blitz with thrilling playground rides and family shows.

* Firework displays during August

Location
On A3083 Lizard road. Signed from the A394 Truro–Helston road & A394 Penzance–Helston road

Opening
Easter–Nov 10.30am–5pm; peak season open 10am–5.30pm

Admission
Super Family Saver tickets available, please phone for details

Contact
Helston TR13 0QA

t 0845 6018684 (24 hr info line)
w flambards.co.uk
e info@flambards.co.uk

154 Helston

Poldark Mine
& Heritage Complex

3 hrs   All year

Enjoy a guided tour of a genuine C18 Cornish tin mine, with a museum, gardens, children's play areas and craft demonstrations. Pan for real gold, throw a pot or try your hand at woodturning.

* Entry to the site itself is free
* Family attractions in addition to the mine

Location
2 miles from Helston on B3297

Opening
Please phone for details

Admission
Underground tour Adult £6.80, Child £4.40

Contact
Wendron,
Helston TR13 0ES

t 01326 573173
w poldark-mine.co.uk
e info@poldark-mine.co.uk

155 Helston

National Seal Sanctuary

2 hrs   All year

Get to know the seals at this leading marine mammal rescue centre. Watch them at feeding time and learn about their characteristics from informative staff. The centre also has other rescued animals such as ponies and goats.

* Barbecues in summer
* See the otters in Otter Creek

Location	Admission
Follow A3083 from Helston towards the Lizard. Turn left on to B3291 & into Gweek	Adult £10.50, Child £6.95, Concs £7.95, Family £28.95
Opening	**Contact**
Daily from 10am: please phone for last admission	Gweek, Helston TR12 6UG
	t 01326 221361
	w sealsanctuary.co.uk
	e slcgwek@merlinentertainments.biz

156 Launceston

Trethorne Leisure Farm

4–7 hrs   All year

This farm and leisure park offers more than 45,000 square feet of indoor attractions. They include a virtual climbing wall, Jolly Roger Ball Blaster, ball pools, assault course and pony rides. Visitors can also pet and hold the animals.

* Ride on electric cars
* Crazy golf & tenpin bowling

Location	Contact
On A395, 3 miles W of Launceston, just off A30	Kennards House, Launceston PL15 8QE
Opening	t 01566 86324
Daily: *Leisure park* 10am–6pm	w trethorne.co.uk
Tenpin bowling 10am–11pm	e trethorneleisure@eclipse.co.uk
Admission	
Adult £6.50, Child £5.95, Concs £4.50	

157 Liskeard

Porfell Animal Land Wildlife Park

2 hrs+   Apr–Oct

A place where families can enjoy close contact with domestic, exotic and wild animals. Discovery and surprise are all part of the fun as you feed the ducks, chickens, goats and deer. There are also zebras, lemurs, raccoons, wallabies and many more.

* New children's farm opened June 2004
* Small children's play area

Location	Admission
Take A38 from Liskeard to Dobwalls. Turn on to the A390 & at East Taphouse turn left on to B3359. First turning on right	Adult £5 Child (3–13) £4 Concs £4.50
Opening	**Contact**
Daily: 1 Apr–31 Oct 10am–6pm	Trecangate, Nr Lanreath Liskeard PL14 4RE
	t 01503 220211
	w porfellanimalland.co.uk

158 Liskeard

The Yarg Cheese Farm

1 hr+   Mar–Oct

A working farmyard with animals, milking, calf-rearing and cheese making where children can watch and learn about these activities. There is also a farm shop and a picnic orchard.

* Park with nature walk
*Children's willow structure

Location	Admission
From Launceston follow A30 west, then B3257. From Callington follow B3257. From Liskeard follow B3254	Adult £3, Child (5–16) £1.50, Under-5s Free, Concs £2
Opening	**Contact**
Please phone for details	Netherton Farm, Upton Cross Liskeard PL14 5BD
	t 01579 362244
	w cornishyarg.co.uk
	e mhorrell@lynherdairies.co.uk

159 Looe

The Monkey Sanctuary

2 hrs   Easter–Sep

See Amazon woolly monkeys in their own spacious
territory at this environmentally aware centre. Talks
are given throughout the day about the monkeys and
their threatened rainforest habitat. There is also an
opportunity to see a colony of lesser horseshoe bats.

* Wildlife gardens
* Children's activity rooms & play area

Location	Admission
Signed on B387 Looe–Plymouth road at No Man's Land. 4 miles from Looe, 18 miles from Plymouth	Adult £5, Child £3, Concs £4
	Contact
	Looe PL13 1NZ
Opening	
1st Sun before Easter–Sep; plus autumn half-term; Sun–Thu 11am–4.30pm	t 01503 262532
	w monkeysanctuary.org
	e info@monkeysanctuary.org

160 Newquay

Dairyland Farm World

5 hrs   Easter–Oct

One of the UK's leading working farm attractions,
Dairyland has a wealth of animals that children love
to pet. Among the menagerie are kittens, kids, lambs,
rabbits, donkeys, chipmunks and chinchillas. You can
even have a go at milking Clarabelle, the cyber cow.

* Pony rides
* Won Cornish Board Attraction of the Year

Location	Contact
On A3058, 4 miles from Newquay	Tresillian Barton, Summercourt, Newquay TR8 5AA
Opening	
Daily: Easter–Oct 10am–5pm	t 01872 510246
Admission	w dairylandfarmworld.com
Adult £7.25, Child £6.25, Concs £4.95, Family £25	e farmworld@yahoo.com

161 Newquay

Holywell Bay Fun Park

3 hrs   Easter–Oct

Great rides, go-karts, crazy golf and a maze are just
a few of the attractions at this fun park. Others include
bumper boats, children's fun rides, a climbing wall and
a beach near by.

* Quality Assured Visitor Attraction

Location	Admission
Follow A3075 Newquay–Perranporth road, turn right to Cubert. Located on right-hand side, 1 mile past Cubert	'Pay as you play' token system
	Contact
	Holywell Bay, Newquay TR8 5PW
Opening	
Daily: Easter–Oct from 10.30am	t 01637 830531
	w holywellbay.co.uk
	e info@trevornick.co.uk

162 Newquay

Lappa Valley Steam Railway

3-4 hrs   Easter-Oct

Enjoy a 2-mile steam train journey, boating, crazy golf, a maze and woodland walks in scenic countryside. Included in the admission price is entry to the viewing platform of the largest mine-engine house in Cornwall.

Location
Follow A3075 to Newquay. Just past Newquay turn E to St Newlyn East & follow tourist signs to the railway

Opening
Mid Apr-Oct, please phone for details

Admission
Please phone for details

Contact
St Newlyn East,
Newquay TR8 5HZ

t 01872 510317
w lappavalley.co.uk

163 Newquay

Newquay Zoo

2 hrs+   All year

Home to many of the world's endangered species, Newquay Zoo is set in beautiful subtropical gardens. Explore the rainforest and its fascinating wildlife in the Tropical Zone. Events run throughout the year, and group bookings are welcome.

* Quality Assured Visitor Attraction
* Winner of many awards

Location
Off the A3075 Edgcumbe Avenue in Trenance Park, Newquay

Opening
Daily: Apr-Oct, 9.30am-6pm
(last admission 5pm);
Daily: Nov-Mar, 10am-dusk;
closed 25 Dec

Admission
Please phone or check the website for details

Contact
Trenance Park, Newquay TR7 2LZ

t 01637 873342
w newquayzoo.org.uk
e info@newquayzoo.org.uk

164 Penzance

Isles of Scilly Steamship Company

10 hrs   Easter-Nov

Cruise to the Isles of Scilly on a comfortable passenger ferry with a bar, buffet and comfy seating all available. During the journey you can see an interesting exhibition about the islands and enjoy a commentary by the ship's captain.

* Chairlift available between main and 2nd deck
* Family tickets available throughout the year - please phone

Location
On the A30, A394 to Penzance

Opening
Easter-early Nov Mon-Fri 8am-5pm
Sat 8am-4pm

Admission
Day trip Adult £35, Child (2-15) £17.50,
Family £85

Contact
Steamship House, Quay Street
Penzance TR18 4BZ

t 08457 105555
w ios-travel.co.uk
e sales@islesofscilly-travel.co.uk

165 Penzance

Land's End Visitor Centre

2 hrs+   All year

This heritage centre is set amid the breathtaking scenery of Land's End, one of Britain's most famous sites. The centre has exhibitions and shows including the Air Sea Rescue Theatre Experience. There is also a playground.

* Land's End sweet factory
* Stunning scenery

Location	Contact
At end of the A30, 12 miles from Penzance	Land's End, Sennen Penzance TR19 7AA
Opening	t 01736 871501
Daily: *summer* 10am–4pm; *winter* 10am–3pm	w landsend-landmark.co.uk
	e info@landsend.landmark.co.uk
Admission	
Adult £12.95, Child £6.95, Concs £8.95	

166 Penzance

The Pilchard Works

1 hr+   Easter–Oct

A working factory museum that produces salt fish. Learn about Cornwall's fishing heritage over the past 400 years, including the trades of salting, pressing and stencilling. Children can use the pulleys and presses and make their own stencil prints.

Location	Admission
From Penzance follow promenade for 1 mile to Newlyn. From A30 follow signs on Penzance bypass	Adult £3.50, Child £1.95, Concs £3, Family £10.50
Opening	Contact
Easter–Oct Mon–Fri 10am–6pm (last admission 5pm)	Tolcarne, Newlyn, Penzance TR18 5QH
	t 01736 332112
	w pilchardworks.co.uk
	e nick@pilchardworks.co.uk

167 Redruth

Cornish Mines & Engines

2 hrs   Easter–Oct

Learn the story of Cornwall's industrial heritage, and find out what life was like for the miners of tin, copper and china clay. You can also see the enormous working beam engine and find out about the fascinating geology of the area.

* National Trust property

Location	Admission
At Pool, 2 miles W of Redruth on either side of A3047. Midway between Redruth and Camborne.	Adult £5, Child £2.50, Family £12
	Contact
Opening	Pool, Nr Redruth TR15 3NP
31 Mar–30 Jul 11am–5pm (closed Sat) Aug daily 11am–5pm; (Sep–Oct 11am–5pm closed Sat)	t 01209 315027
	w nationaltrust.org.uk

168 St Austell

Charlestown Shipwreck & Heritage Centre

2 hrs   Mar–Oct

Learn about diving, rescues and shipwrecks in this major display of maritime history, the largest shipwreck artefact collection in the British Isles. There is also an exhibition about the *Titanic*.

Location	Contact
Reached via A390	Quay Road, Charlestown, St Austell PL25 3NJ
Opening	
Daily: Mar–Oct 10am–5pm	t 01726 69897
Admission	w shipwreckcharlestown.com
Adult £5.95, Child £2.95, Under-10s free, Concs £3.95	e admin@shipwreckcharlestown.com

169 St Austell

The Eden Project

3 hrs+   All year

Visit the largest greenhouses in the world with plants from many diverse habitats such as the tropical rainforest, Mediterranean fruit groves and the fields of California. There are also free events throughout the year.

* Two million visitors a year
* See coffee plants, palm trees and pineapples

Location	Contact
Follow signs from A390 at St Austell & A30 Bodmin bypass	Bodelva, St Austell PL24 2SG
	t 01726 811900
Opening	w edenproject.com
Daily: summer 9.30am–6pm winter 10am–4.30pm	e info@edenproject.com
Admission	
Adult £12.50, Child £5, Concs £9.50	

170 St Austell

Lost Gardens of Heligan

4 hrs+   All year

These world-renowned gardens comprise 80 acres of pleasure grounds plus a complex of walled gardens. Many spectacular subtropical species thrive in this frost-free Cornish valley. Heligan has undergone one of the largest restoration projects of its kind in Europe.

* Stunning collection of plants from all over the world
* Featured in major Channel Four series

Location	Contact
From St Austell take Mevagissey road (B3273) & follow brown tourist signs	Pentewan, St Austell PL26 6EN
	t 01726 845100
Opening	w heligan.com
Mar–Oct 10am–6pm; Nov–Feb 10am–5pm	e info@heligan.com
Admission	
Adult £7.50, Child £4, Concs £7	

171 St Austell

Polkyth Leisure Centre

2 hrs+   All year

Exercise to your heart's content in this well-equipped sports hall, with badminton courts, squash courts, tennis courts and swimming pools. A Hoist is available for disabled visitors.

* Hydrotherapy pool
* Fitness room

Location	Contact
Accessible via A390 & A391. Follow brown tourist signs	Carlyon Road, St Austell PL25 4DB
	t 01726 223344
Opening	w restormel.gov.uk/polkyth
Daily: Mon–Fri 9am–10pm, Sat & Sun 9am–5pm	e polkythmanagement@restormel.gov.uk
Admission	
Please phone for details	

172 St Columb

Spirit of the West Theme Park

3 hrs+   May–Sep

A theme park dedicated to the Wild West with Native American artefacts and live street-action shows. Set in 100 acres, there are two themed towns. Pan for gold, fish at Retallack and visit the museums. There's also a Western store and a photographic parlour.

* Westworld auto raceway
* Shooting gallery & pony trail rides

Location	Admission
On A39 St Columb–Wadebridge road, just off Winnards Perch roundabout on the B3274	Adult £6, Child, £4, Concs £4, Family £18
	Contact
Opening	Retallack Park, Winnards Perch, nr St Columb TR9 6DE
Theme Park May–Sep Sun–Fri from 10.30am (last admission 4pm)	t 01637 881160
Fishery Open all year	w wildwestthemepark.co.uk
	e sheriffjaybee@aol.com

173 St Columb

Springfields Fun Park & Pony Centre

5 hrs+   Easter–Oct

Have fun along the nature walk, try pond dipping, then sample the indoor and outdoor play zones, free-fall slides, trampolines and more.

* Farm animals & bottle feeding
* Pony cart & train rides

Location
From A30 follow signs for airport for 2 miles. Signed from St Columb roundabout bypass on A39

Opening
Daily: Easter–Sep 10am–6pm (last admission 4pm); Oct weekends & half-term only

Admission
Adult £6.50, Child £5.50, Concs £4.50, Family £21

Contact
Ruthvoes, St Columb TR9 6HU
t 01637 881224
w springfieldsponycentre.co.uk
e info.springfieldsponycentre@btconnect.com

174 Torpoint

Mount Edgcumbe House & Park

2 hrs+   All year

For 400 years this was home to the Earls of Mount Edgcumbe. Its landscaped park overlooking Plymouth Sound has fallow deer, woodland and coastal walks. Mount Edgcumbe offers the opportunity to experience life as a Victorian, including trying on costumes.

*Gowns on display from the film Portrait of a Lady
* Ferry cruise on River Tamar

Location
Take Torpoint ferry or Cremyll foot ferry from Plymouth, then A374 & B3247

Opening
House Apr–Sep, Sun–Thu 11am–4.30pm; Park All year: daily

Admission
House & Earl's Garden Adult £4.50, Child £2.25, Concs £3.50
Combined ticket Adult £7, Child £4.50

Contact
Cremyll, Torpoint PL10 1HZ
t 01752 822236
w mountedgcumbe.gov.uk
e mt.edgcumbe@plymouth.gov.uk

175 Truro

Royal Cornwall Museum

2 hrs   All year

See a myriad of minerals, view our naked mummy, and discover Cornwall's unique culture. Admire the collection of Newlyn School paintings in the decorative arts gallery. The museum presents a range of changing exhibitions from textiles to contemporary art.

* Diverse range of children's activities

Location
Truro town centre

Opening
Mon–Sat 10am–5pm; closed Sun & Bank Hols

Admission
Free

Contact
River Street, Truro TR1 2SJ
t 01872 272205
w royalcornwallmuseum.org.uk
e enquiries@royalcornwallmuseum.org.uk

176 Barnstaple

Arlington Court

3 hrs+   Easter–Oct

The Victorian home of Miss Rosalie Chichester, Arlington Hall is full of fascinating artefacts that she collected. In the basement, from May to September, visitors can follow the activities of Devon's largest colony of lesser horseshoe bats.

* 'Batcam' films bat colony from May to September
* Carriage rides around the grounds

Location	Admission
Follow signs off A39, 8 miles N of Barnstaple	Adult £6.50, Child £3.25
Opening	**Contact**
House Easter–Oct 11am–5.30pm closed Sat	Arlington, Barnstaple EX31 4LP
Gardens Daily: Jul–Aug 10.30am–5.30pm	t 01271 850296
	w nationaltrust.org.uk
	e arlingtoncourt@nationaltrust.org.uk

177 Barnstaple

Barnstaple Heritage Centre

1 hr+   All year

More than 1,000 years of Barnstaple's history is on show here, with hands-on visual and audio displays and life-size models and reconstructions.

* Exhibition has been refurbished and improved

Location	Contact
In centre of Barnstaple, on quayside	Queen Anne's Walk, The Strand, Barnstaple EX31 1EU
Opening	t 01271 373003
Apr–Oct Mon–Sat 10am–5pm; Nov–Mar Mon–Fri 10am–4.30pm, & Sat 10am–3.30pm	w devonmuseums.net/barnstable heritage
Admission	e dteague.barumheritage@ btconnect.com
Adult £2.50, Child £1.50, Concs £2, Family £7.50	

178 Barnstaple

North Devon Farm Park

3 hrs+   Apr–Oct

A visit to this farm park gives children a chance to meet and feed animals in their natural environment, as well as enjoy a choice of beautiful woodland walks.

* Indoor & outdoor play areas
* Pony grooming & ferret racing

Location	Contact
Signed from A361	Marsh Farm, Landkey, Barnstaple EX32 0NN
Opening	t 01271 830255 (Gate)
Apr–Oct Mon–Sat 10am–5pm; closed Wed in term time; Please phone for winter opening details	01271 830111 (Café)
	w farmpark.co.uk
Admission	
£3.99 per person	

179 Beer

Beer Quarry Caves

1 hr+   Easter–Oct

Take an eerie tour of this vast underground quarry with a long and eventful history, from the Romans to the Victorians. Beer Quarry stone was used in 24 cathedrals, plus Hampton Court, Windsor Castle and the Tower of London.

* Used for secret Roman Catholic worship in the past
* A hiding place for contraband

Location	Contact
Take B3174 to Beer, follow brown tourist signs from there	Quarry Lane, Beer, Seaton EX12 3AS
Opening	t 01297 625830
Daily: Mon before Easter–30 Sep 10am–5pm; Oct 11am–4pm	w beerquarrycaves.fsnet.co.uk
Admission	e john@beerquarrycaves.fsnet.co.uk
Adult £5, Child & Concs £3.75, Family £15.50	

180 Bideford

Lundy Island

4 hrs+   All year

Enjoy a day walking on this beautiful island. Three miles long and only 24 miles out in the Bristol Channel, it has a lighthouse and castle and is ideal for bird-watching. It is a great place to take children, not least because there are no roads or cars.

* Lots of wildlife can be seen on the island

Location
Take A361 to Ilfracombe & A386 to Bideford for the MS *Oldenburg* to Lundy Island

Opening
Please phone for details

Admission
Adult £28, Child £14, Concs £25, Family £65 (included in MS *Oldenburg* fare)

Contact
Bideford EX39 2LY

t 01271 863636
w lundyisland.co.uk
e info@lundyisland.co.uk

181 Bideford

The Milky Way Adventure Park

4 hrs   All year

Set in 18 acres of landscaped grounds, this is an all-weather attraction with games and slides for all age groups. The North Devon Bird of Prey Centre is also located here.

* Clone Zone Alien Encounter
* Dodgems

Location
On A39 Bideford–Bude road, 2 miles from Clovelly

Opening
Daily: Apr–Oct 10.30am–6pm; Nov–Mar weekends & school hols 11am–5pm

Admission
Adult £8, Child £7, Concs £5.50, Family £26.50

Contact
Downland Farm, Clovelly, Bideford EX39 5RY

t 01237 431255
w themilkyway.co.uk
e info@themilkyway.co.uk

182 Bovey Tracey

Wonderland & The Cardew Tea Pottery

2 hrs   All year

This venue includes 10 acres of woodland filled with activities, plus the Tea Pottery, where visitors can paint their own pottery to take home. There is also the Cheshire Cat's aerial walkway, duck feeding, an adventure play area and a tour of a working pottery.

Location
On A382 Bovey Tracey to Newton Abbot road, just off A38

Opening
Daily: 10am–5.30pm

Admission
Please phone for details

Contact
Newton Road, Bovey Tracey TQ13 9DX

t 01626 832172
e crafts@cardew.co.uk

183 Buckfastleigh

Buckfast Butterfly Farm & Dartmoor Otter Sanctuary

2 hrs   Easter–Oct

Walk among some of the most beautiful butterflies in the world, flying free in a tropical garden with waterfalls, ponds and bridges. At the otter sanctuary visitors can see the playful otters from above and below the water, and at feeding time.

* Butterfly habitat constructed to maximise viewing
* British, Asian & North American otters on show

Location
Follow signs from A38 at A384 to Buckfastleigh

Opening
Easter–Oct 10am–5.30pm

Admission
Adult £5.95, Child £4.50, Concs £5.50

Contact
Buckfastleigh TQ11 0DZ

t 01364 642916
w ottersandbutterflies.co.uk
e info@ottersandbutterflies.co.uk

184 Buckfastleigh

Pennywell Farm & Wildlife Centre

5 hrs+   Feb–Oct

With a different hands-on activity, show or display every 30 minutes, children won't get bored at this fun farm. From feeding the animals to egg-collecting, this is also a great educational experience. Ride on our miniature railway and quad bikes.

* Visitor Attraction of the Year 2004
* Pony & donkey rides & go-karts

Location
Head for Buckfastleigh on A38 between Plymouth & Exeter

Opening
Daily: Feb half-term–Oct 10am–5pm

Admission
Adult £7.95, Child & Concs £6.95

Contact
Buckfastleigh TQ11 0LT

t 01364 642023
w pennywellfarmcentre.co.uk
e info@pennywellfarmcentre.co.uk

185 Buckfastleigh

South Devon Railway

2 hrs   Apr–Oct

Enjoy a traditional steam-train journey through a beautiful stretch of Devon countryside. There is a free vintage bus service around town in summer.

* Play area
* Small museum

Location
Between Exeter & Plymouth on A38 Expressway

Opening
Daily: Apr–Oct 10am–5pm

Admission
Adult £8.50 return ticket,
Child £5.10 return ticket,
Family £24.50

Contact
The Station, Buckfastleigh TQ11 0DZ

t 0845 345 1420
w southdevonrailway.org
e info@southdevonrailway.org

186 Budleigh Salterton

Bicton Park Botanical Gardens

3 hrs+   All year

Gardeners, young or old, will be interested in this historic garden with its C19 palm house, glasshouses and Italian garden. There are also indoor and outdoor play areas and train rides on offer.

* Indoor play area & guided tours
* Railway, museum & nature trail

Location
Off M5 at junction 30, follow signs via Newton Poppleford

Opening
Daily: *summer* 10am–6pm;
winter 10am–5pm; closed 25, 26 Dec

Admission
Adult £5.95, Child & Concs £4.95

Contact
East Budleigh,
Budleigh Salterton EX9 7BJ

t 01395 568465
w bictongardens.co.uk
e info@bictongardens.co.uk

187 Chulmleigh

Eggesford Country Centre

1 hr   All year

Set within the picturesque Eggesford Gardens, the heritage centre has imaginative displays depicting the local social history of the beautiful Taw Valley. There are bicycles for hire, or you can explore the nearby woodland trails on foot.

* Cycle trails
* Large rural garden centre

Location
Take A377 from Barnstaple or Exeter

Opening
Daily: 9am–5pm

Admission
Free

Contact
Eggesford Gardens,
Chulmleigh EX18 7QU

t 01769 580250

188 Cullompton

Diggerland

3 hrs+   Feb–Nov

Based on the world of construction machinery, this is a unique adventure park where children and adults can experience the thrill of riding and driving real diggers and dumpers in safety.

Location
Exit M5 (junction 27), head E on A38, turn right at the roundabout onto B3181 & the park is 3 miles on the left

Opening
Apr–Nov weekends, Bank Hols & school hols 10am–5pm

Admission
Adult & Child £2.50, Concs £1.25

Contact
Verbeer Manor,
Cullompton EX15 2PE

t 08700 344437
w diggerland.com
e mail@diggerland.com

189 Dartmouth

Blackpool Sands

1hr+   Apr–Oct

Blackpool Sands is an award-winning beach in an unspoilt sheltered bay among evergreens and pines. There is also a watersports centre for kayaking, surfing, snorkelling and more.

* Quality Assured Visitor Attraction
* Dogs allowed Nov–Mar only

Location
On A379, 3 miles from Dartmouth

Opening
Daily: Apr–Oct 10am–4pm

Admission
Please phone for details

Contact
Blackpool,
Dartmouth TQ6 0RG

t 01803 770606
w blackpoolsands.co.uk
e info@blackpoolsands.co.uk

190 Exeter

Crealy Adventure Park

4 hrs+   All year

Visit Crealy for maximum fun in each of its exciting activity realms. Meet Devon's friendliest pets in the Animal Realm, try out the bumper boats and techno race karts in the Action Realm, experience the rides in the Adventure Realm and much more.

* Explore the Natural, Farming and Magical Realms
* Special events throughout the year

Location
Take junction 30 on M5 on to
the A3052. Follow signs to Crealy

Opening
Daily: *summer* 10am–6pm;
winter (dates limited) 10am–5pm;

Admission
Please phone for details

Contact
Clyst St Mary, Sidmouth Road,
Exeter EX5 1DR

t 0870 1163333
w crealy.co.uk
e fun@crealy.co.uk

191 Exeter

Killerton House

2 hrs+   Mar–Oct

Built in the C18, Killerton House offers a display of costumes and has period room sets, laundry, stable yard and chapel. It is set in delightful gardens and parkland, filled with many exotic plants and trees. Children can find the ice house and rustic Bear's Hut.

* Discovery centre
* Family events & extensive woodland walk

Location	Admission
6 miles from Exeter off B3181	*House & Gardens*
	Adult £6.50, Child £3
Opening	**Contact**
15 Mar–29 Oct 11am–5pm,	Broadclyst, Exeter EX5 3LE
closed Tue (&Mon in Oct);	t 01392 881345
Daily: Aug	w nationaltrust.org.uk

192 Exmouth

Exmouth Model Railway

1 hr   Apr–Sep

With more than 7,500 feet of track, this is one of the world's largest scenic 00-gauge model railways. It runs through villages and towns, all exquisitely modelled in great detail. A must for all model railway buffs.

* Model railway accessories for sale

Location	Contact
On Exmouth seafront, via A376	Seafront,
	Exmouth EX8 2AY
Opening	t 01395 278383
Daily: Easter–Sep 10am–5pm	
Admission	
Adult £2.25, Child £1.25, Concs £1.75	

193 Exmouth

Stuart Line Cruises & Boat Trips

1 hr+   All year

Enjoy a pleasureboat cruise along the beautiful River Exe or a sea trip along the South Devon coast (known for the fossils exposed in its rocks and now an official World Heritage Site). There are also day trips to Torquay, Brixham and Sidmouth.

* Guided tours for individuals
* Mackerel & deep-sea fishing trips

Location	Contact
Exmouth Marina on the seafront	Exmouth Marina, Exmouth Docks,
	Exmouth EX8 1DU
Opening	t 01395 279693/222144
Daily: please phone for details	w stuartlinecruises.co.uk
Admission	e info@stuartlinecruises.co.uk
Adult from £4.50, Child from £2.50	
Fares depend on trip	

194 Kingsbridge

Sorley Tunnel Adventure Worlds

4 hrs   All year

A working organic dairy farm with animals, riding stables and pony rides. There's also a children's nature trail that runs through an eerie, reputedly haunted, railway tunnel. Other attractions include trampolines and slides.

* Green Tourism Gold Award
* Four-storey indoor play area

Location	Contact
Off A381 Totnes–Plymouth road	Loddiswell Road, Kingsbridge TQ7 4BP
Opening	t 01548 854078
Daily: Jan–Mar 10am–5pm; Apr–Oct	w sorleytunnel.com
10am–6pm; Nov–Dec 10am–5pm	e info@sorleytunnel.co.uk
Admission	
Adult & Child £5.95, Concs £4.50	

195 Newton Abbot

House of Marbles

1 hr   All year

A working glass-blowing factory that also has a museum of glass artefacts, including toys and marbles. We have probably the largest marble runs in the world! Visitors can watch glass blowing when work is in progress.

Location	Contact
On A382 from Newton Abbot to Bovey Tracey & A38 from Exeter	The Old Pottery, Pottery Road, Bovey Tracey, Newton Abbot TQ13 9DS
Opening	t 01626 835358
Daily: Mon–Sat 9am–5pm,	w houseofmarbles.com
Sun 11am–5pm	e uk@houseofmarbles.com
Admission	
Free	

196 Newton Abbot

Tuckers Maltings

2 hrs+   Easter–Oct

Take a guided tour of England's only working malt house open to the public and watch Victorian machinery producing malt from barley. Visitors of all ages can see, touch, smell and taste, while video and audio guides explain Tuckers Maltings in an educational but fun way.

* Guided tours last one hour
* Video & hands-on discovery centre

Location	Contact
3 min walk from Newton Abbot railway station	Teign Road, Newton Abbott TQ12 4AA
Opening	t 01626 334734
Easter–Oct 10am–5pm, closed Sun;	w tuckersmaltings.com
Please phone for tour times	e info@tuckersmaltings.com
Admission	
Adult £5.45, Child £3.45, Concs £4.95	

197 Paignton

Paignton & Dartmouth Steam Railway

2 hrs+   Apr–Oct

Travel Torbay's spectacular coast and the beautiful River Dart by steam train from Paignton to Kingswear. The trip can be combined with river excursions to picturesque Dartmouth.

* Thomas the Tank Engine weekend
* Santa Specials in December

Location	Admission
Follow brown tourist signs to centre of Paignton. Situated next to mainline trains	Please phone for details
	Contact
Opening	Queens Park Station, Torbay Road, Paignton TQ4 6AF
Daily Jun–Sep; Apr, May & Oct open on selected dates; please phone for details	t 01803 555872
	w paignton-steamrailway.co.uk

198 Paignton

Paignton Zoo Environmental Park

3 hrs+   All year

Home to some of the world's most endangered plants and animals, the zoo has hundreds of different animals and birds, including tigers, rhinoceros and giant tortoises. They are grouped into different climate zones that reflect the world's major habitats.

* 1,500 different plants from around the world
* Starred in the BBC programme *Zoo Keepers*

Location
Situated on the A3022 Totnes Road, 1 mile from Paignton town centre

Opening
summer 10am–6pm;
winter 10am–dusk

Admission
Please phone for details

Contact
Totnes Road, Paignton, TQ4 7EU

t 01803 697500
w paigntonzoo.org.uk
e info@paigntonzoo.org.uk

---

199 Plymouth

Crownhill Fort

2 hrs   Apr–Oct

At the largest of Plymouth's great Victorian forts, visitors can discover the underground tunnels, explore the ramparts, marvel at Victorian architecture and view the guns, including the 'disappearing' Moncrieff.

* Special bookings available for schools and conferences
* Also available for children's parties

Location
Just off A386 Plymouth–Tavistock road

Opening
Daily: Apr–Oct 10am–5pm
Open all year to prebooked groups

Admission
Adult £5, Child £3, Concs £4

Contact
Crownhill Fort Road, Plymouth PL6 5BX

t 01752 793754
w crownhillfort.co.uk
e info@crownhillfort.co.uk

---

200 Plymouth

Dartmoor Wildlife Park

2 hrs+   All year

At this wildlife park visitors can mingle with the friendly animals in a 2-acre walk-in enclosure. There are falconry displays at 12pm and 4pm, a Big Cat talk at 3.30pm and Close Encounters of the Animal Kind at 2pm.

* Adventure playground

Location
6 miles from Plymouth on A38. Follow brown tourist signs

Opening
Daily: 10am–5pm

Admission
Adult £7.95, Child £4.95, Concs £5.95

Contact
Sparkwell, Plymouth PL7 5DG

t 01752 837209
w dartmoorwildlife.co.uk
e ellisdaw@wildlifepark.freeserve.co.uk

201 Plymouth

Plymouth Dome

2 hrs   All year

Learn about the famous explorers who left the shores of Plymouth and travelled the world. These great tales of adventure are accompanied by sight, sound and smell. Walk through an Elizabethan Street, and relive the devastation of the port during WWII.

* Walk the gun deck of a galleon
* See the destructive effects of the Blitz

Location
Follow signs from city centre for Hoe

Opening
Apr–Oct daily 10am–5pm;
Nov–Mar Tue–Sat 10am–4pm

Admission
Adult £4.75, Child £3.25, Concs £3.75

Contact
The Hoe, Plymouth PL1 2NZ

t 01752 603300
w plymouthdome.info
e plymouthdome@plymouth.gov.uk

202 Plymouth

Sound Cruising

1 hr+   Feb–Nov

Sound Cruising offers daily cruises around Plymouth's naval harbour, as well as regular cruises to Calstock on the River Tamar.

Location
Follow signs to Plymouth city centre,
via Plymouth Hoe, then through
Barbican to Phoenix Wharf

Opening
Daily: Feb–Nov 10am–3pm

Admission
Please phone for details

Contact
Phoenix Wharf, Barbican,
Plymouth PL10 1A

t 01752 671166
w soundcruising.com
e pbc@pbc.onyxnet.co.uk

203 Seaton

Pecorama Pleasure Gardens & Exhibition

3 hrs   All year

On a visit to these pleasure gardens, visitors can enjoy a gentle stroll around the Peco Millennium Celebration Garden, which has five linked and themed gardens, and a 1-mile miniature steam locomotive journey on the Beer Heights Light Railway.

* Daily children's entertainment
* Children's activity areas & crazy golf

Location
Follow A3052 W from Lyme Regis or
E from Exeter then B3174 to Beer

Opening
Model exhibition & shop All year daily
Outdoor facilities Easter–Oct Mon–Fri
10am–5.30pm, Sat 10am–1.00pm

Admission
Please phone for details

Contact
Underleys, Beer,
Seaton EX12 3NA

t 01297 21542
w peco-uk.com
e pecorama@btconnect.com

204 Seaton

Seaton Tramway

2 hrs   Feb–Oct

Take a leisurely journey through the glorious Axe Valley in a unique narrow-gauge tramcar. Enjoy panoramic views of the estuary's wading birds and the beautiful countryside from an open-topper. In poorer weather, take shelter in the elegant, enclosed saloon cars.

* Small Visitor Attraction of the Year
* Quality Assured Visitor Attraction

Location
Follow brown tourist signs on A3052 Exeter–Lyme Regis road, or A358 from Taunton, Chard & Axminster

Opening
12–20 Feb & 19 Mar–30 Oct Daily: 26 Feb–13 Mar & 6 Nov–24 Dec Sat & Sun only

Admission
Adult £6, Child £4.90, Concs £3.80, Family £14.10

Contact
Harbour Road, Seaton EX12 2NQ

t 01297 20375
w tram.co.uk
e info@tram.co.uk

205 Sidmouth

The Donkey Sanctuary

2 hrs   All year

This famous donkey sanctuary is home to more than 400 rescued donkeys. Set in beautiful surroundings, it has five walks and a donkey quiz for children.

Location
On A3052 just outside Sidford, towards Lyme Regis. Follow brown tourist signs

Opening
Daily: 9am–dusk

Admission
Free

Contact
Sidmouth EX10 0NU

t 01395 578222
w thedonkeysanctuary.org.uk
e enquiries@thedonkeysanctuary.com

206 Sidmouth

Norman Lockyer Observatory & James Lockyer Planetarium

2 hrs   All year

The solar system, space travel, communications and the weather are all explained and explored in fascinating exhibitions, models and hands-on activities. Visitors can talk to people all over the world in the radio room.

* Exhibition hall with models of the solar system
* Satellite station producing weather pictures

Location
Take A3052 Exeter–Seaton road, turn right after Blue Ball Inn at Sidford & follow signs

Opening
Please phone for details

Admission
Adult £4, Child £2

Contact
Salcombe Hill Road, Sidmouth EX10 0NY

t 01395 579941
w ex.ac.uk/nlo/
e g.e.white@exeter.ac.uk

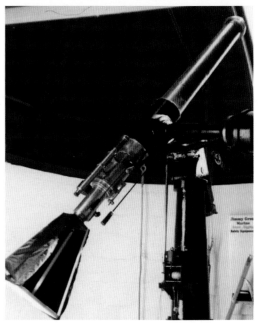

207 Tavistock

Morwellham Quay

4 hrs+   Easter–Oct

Despite being 23 miles from the sea, Morwellham Quay was the Empire's greatest copper port in the time of Queen Victoria. Today the 1860s are recreated with a Tamar ketch moored at the quay, shops, cottages and costumed staff to act as guides.

* Take a tram underground through a copper mine
* Explore the farm, wildlife reserve and parkland

Location
4 miles from Tavistock on River Tamar

Opening
Daily: Easter–Oct 10am–6pm

Admission
Adult £8.90, Child £6, Concs £7.80

Contact
Morwellham, Tavistock PL19 8JL

t 01822 832766
w morwellham-quay.co.uk
e info@morwellham-quay.co.uk

208 Teignmouth

Grand Pier

1 hr+   All year

Enjoy a few hours of simple fun on this traditional pier, with many family amusements and games, including the thrills and spills of a rollercoaster.

* Mini-railway
* Pirate ship

Location
Via A379

Opening
Daily: Easter–Sep 10am–9pm;
Nov–Mar 11am–5pm

Admission
Free. Charges for individual attractions

Contact
The Seafront, Teignmouth TQ14 8BB

t 01626 774367

209 Tiverton

Knightshayes Court

3 hrs   Mar–Oct

This lavish house was built around 1870 by William Burges. Its much-admired garden features a water-lily pond, topiary and a newly restored walled garden.

* National Trust property
* Woodland walks & children's quizzes

Location
2 miles N of Tiverton, turn off A396 (Bampton Road) at Bolham

Opening
House Mar–Oct Sat–Thu 11am–5.30pm (closes 4pm in Oct)
Gardens Mar Sat & Sun 11am–5.30pm; mid-Mar–Oct daily 11am–5.30pm

Admission
Please phone for details

Contact
Bolham, Tiverton EX16 7RQ
t 01884 254665
w nationaltrust.org.uk

210 Tiverton

Tiverton Museum of Mid Devon Life

2 hrs   Feb–Dec

This is a comprehensive regional museum that has a Heathcote lace machine gallery. Also on show are agricultural and domestic implements and a collection of Devon farm wagons.

Location
Via A396, A373 or A361

Opening
Feb–Dec Mon–Fri 10.30am–4.30pm,
Sat 10am–1pm; closed 22 Dec–end Jan

Admission
Adult £3.50, Child £1, Concs £2.50

Contact
Beck's Square, Tiverton EX16 6PJ
t 01884 256295
w tivertonmuseum.org.uk
e curator@tivertonmuseum.org.uk

211 Torquay

Babbacombe Model Village

2 hrs   All year

There are hundreds of 1:12 scale models set in award-winning gardens at this model village. Marvel at villages, farms and rural areas, beautiful lakes and waterfalls, railways and details of everyday life.

* Illuminations & Aquaviva laser show in summer
* Summer evening opening

Location
Take A380 to Torquay, then follow the brown tourist signs

Opening
Daily: from 10am; also open summer evenings, please phone for details

Admission
Adult £6.90, Child £4.20, Cons £5.90, Family £20

Contact
Hampton Avenue, Babbacombe, Torquay TQ1 3LA

t 01803 315315
w babbacombemodelvillage.co.uk
e sw@babbacombemodelvillage.co.uk

212 Torquay

Bygones

2 hrs+   All year

Bygones has a life-size Victorian street with period rooms. Children will enjoy the large Hornby railway layouts, medals and militaria and the illuminated 'fantasyland'.

* Housed in a former cinema
* Christmas winter wonderland in a Victorian setting

Location
Town centre, in the direction of St Mary Church

Opening
Daily: Apr–Jun & Sep 10am–6pm;
Nov–Mar 10am–5pm;
Jul & Aug Sun–Thu 10am–9.30pm,
Fri & Sat 10am–6pm

Admission
Adult £4.95, Child £3.50, Concs £4.50

Contact
Fore Street, St Mary Church
Torquay TQ1 4PR

t 01803 326108
w bygones.co.uk

213 Torquay

Living Coasts

2 hrs+   All year

A unique aquatic visitor attraction, focusing on the conservation of coastal and marine life around the globe. The spacious interior of the meshed aviary allows free flight for the birds and access for visitors, enabling an intimacy unusual in seabird exhibits in this country.

* Adopt an animal & underwater viewing
* Special events throughout the year

Location	Contact
Situated in centre of Torquay, on harbourside	Torquay Harbourside, Beacon Quay Torquay TQ1 2BG
Opening	t 01803 202470
Mar–Sep 10am–6pm; Oct–Feb 10am–5.30pm	w livingcoasts.org.uk e info@livingcoasts.org.uk
Admission	
Adult £5.90, Child £4.10, Concs £4.60	

214 Torquay

The Riviera International Centre & Leisure Pool

2 hrs   All year

There is something for children of all ages at this leisure complex. It has a health and fitness centre, a choice of leisure pool, restaurants and cafés.

* Children's water spray area
* Leisure pool, flume & wave machine

Location	Contact
2 min walk from Torquay seafront	Chestnut Avenue, Torquay TQ2 5LZ
Opening	t 01803 299992
Please phone for details	w rivieracentre.co.uk e enquiries@rivieracentre.co.uk
Admission	
Family swim £10.50; please phone for details	

215 Totnes

Totnes Elizabethan Museum

1 hr   Mar–Oct

This Elizabethan house, built in 1575, features an Elizabethan herb garden, a Tudor bedroom, a kitchen and a Victorian nursery. Displays cover 5,000 years of local history, and there is a special exhibition on Charles Babbage, father of the modern computer.

Location	Contact
On the main street in front of East Gate Arch in Totnes	70 Fore Street, Totnes TQ9 5RU
Opening	t 01803 863821
Mid-Mar–Oct Mon–Fri 10.30–5pm (last admission 4.30pm)	w devonmuseums.net/totnes e totnesmuseum@btconnect.com
Admission	
Adult £1.50, Child 50p, Concs £1	

216 Totnes

Woodlands Leisure Park

3 hrs+   Mar–Oct

You'll be spoilt for choice here by an excellent combination of indoor and outdoor attractions for all ages. Some of the attractions include three watercoasters, a toboggan run, 15 play zones, massive indoor centres and animals.

* UK's biggest indoor venture centre
* Falconry centre with flying displays

Location	Contact
On A3122 between Totnes & Dartmouth	Blackawton, Totnes TQ9 7DQ
Opening	t 01803 712598
Daily: 26 Mar–Oct & school hols	w woodlandspark.com e fun@woodlandspark.com 9
Admission	
Please phone for details	

217 Bournemouth

Dorset Belle Cruises

1 hr+   All year

Take a glorious coastal and harbour cruise on a number of routes linking Bournemouth, Swanage and Poole Quay and the Isle of Wight or explore Brownsea Island. Specialist cruises are also available along this stunning coastline.

* Boats available for charter & evening cruises
* Fireworks & magnificent sunset cruises

Location	Contact
Boats depart from Bournemouth pier, Swanage or Poole	Pier Approach, Bournemouth BH2 5AA
Opening	t 01202 558550
Daily: Apr–Oct 7am–6pm; Nov–Mar 10.30am–6pm	w dorsetbelles.co.uk
	e info@dorsetbelles.co.uk
Admission	
From Adult £5, Child £2.50	

218 Bournemouth

Oceanarium Bournemouth

2 hrs   All year

Explore the secrets of the ocean and some of the world's most amazing waters. Come face to face with a vast array of colourful creatures from stingrays, sharks and exotic fish to piranhas, chameleons, green turtles and tortoises.

* Gift shop
* Great café

Location	Contact
Follow signs to Bournemouth beaches & piers	Pier Approach, Bournemouth BH2 5AA
Opening	t 01202 311993
Please phone for details	w oceanarium.co.uk
	e info@oceanarium.co.uk
Admission	
Adult £6.50, Child £4.50, Concs £5.50	

219 Bovington

Tank Museum

3 hrs+   All year

The Tank Museum houses the world's finest indoor collection of armoured fighting vehicles including a WWII tank visitors can touch. Tanks in Action displays are held throughout the summer.

* Indoor collection of 150 vehicles from 26 countries
* Vehicle rides and live demonstrations

Location	Contact
Off A352, between Dorchester & Wareham, near Wool. Follow signs from Bere Regis	Bovington BH20 6HG
Opening	t 01929 405096
Daily: 10am–5pm	w tankmuseum.co.uk
	e info@tankmuseum.co.uk
Admission	
Adult £8.50, Child £6, Cons £7.50, Family £23	

220 Dorchester
The Dinosaur Museum

1 hr+   All year

The award-winning Dinosaur Museum combines fossils, skeletons and life-size dinosaur reconstructions with video, hands-on and computer displays. This is fascinating fun for all the family.

* Winner of the Dorset Family Attraction Award
* Top 10 Hands-on Museum in Britain

Location	Contact
Centre of Dorchester	Icen Way, Dorchester DT1 1EW
Opening	
Easter–Oct 9.30am–5.30pm; Nov–Mar 10am–4.30pm	t 01305 269880
	w thedinosaurmuseum.com
	e info@thedinosaurmuseum.com
Admission	
Adult £6, Child £4.50, Cons £5.25, Family £18.50	

221 Dorchester
Dorset County Museum

1 hr+   All year

Explore Dorset wildlife, geology and social history in interactive exhibitions and audio-visual displays. Galleries to visit include one devoted to Dorset writers including Thomas Hardy, and the archaeology gallery.

* Interactive audio guide
* Film on Roman invasion of Maiden Castle

Location	Contact
Town centre, follow museum signs	High West Street, Dorchester DT1 1XA
Opening	
Oct–Jun Mon–Sat 10am–5pm; Jul–Sep daily 10am–5pm	t 01305 262735
	w dorsetcountymuseum.org
	e secretary@dor-mus.demon.co.uk
Admission	
Adult £5, Child £1, Concs £4	

222 Dorchester
The Dorset Teddy Bear Museum

1 hr   All year

This is a delightfully unusual museum where the teddy bears are life-size. See the teddy bear family at work, rest and play. A large selection of teddy bears can be bought at the period shop.

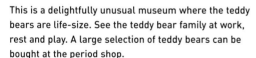

Location	Contact
In town centre	Antelope Walk, Dorchester DT1 1BE
Opening	
Daily: 9.30am–5pm; closed 25, 26 Dec	t 01305 263200
	w teddybearhouse.co.uk
	e info@teddybearhouse.co.uk
Admission	
Adult £3.95, Child £2.50, Family £10.95	

223 Dorchester
Kingston Maurward Gardens

2 hrs+   All year

A formal Edwardian garden with a stunning ornamental lake in front of the C18 mansion house. The animal park has a collection of miniature Shetland ponies, as well as donkeys, rabbits and guinea pigs.

* National Collections of penstemons and salvias
* Edwardian formal & walled demonstration gardens

Location	Contact
1 mile E of Dorchester off A35	Dorchester DT2 8PY
Opening	
Daily: 5 Jan–19 Dec 10am–5.30pm or dusk if earlier	t 01305 215003
	w kmc.ac.uk
	e administration@kmc.ac.uk
Admission	
Adult £5, Child £3	

224 Poole

Brownsea Island National Trust

3 hrs+   Mar–Oct

Just a short boat journey (not National Trust) from Poole or Sandbanks, the island offers spectacular views, a peaceful setting for walks and picnics, a rich variety of habitats for wildlife including the rare red squirrel and a varied and colourful history.

* Family events throughout the year
* Guided walk in nature reserve (summer only)

Location
By boat from Poole, Bournemouth, Swanage or Sandbanks

Opening
24 Mar–29 Oct from 10am; closing time varies

Admission
Adult £4.20, Child £2

Contact
Poole Harbour BH13 7EE

t 01202 707744
w nationaltrust.org.uk/brownsea
e brownseaisland@nationaltrust.org.uk

225 Poole

Farmer Palmer's Farm Park

6 hrs   Feb–Dec

A delightful farm designed for children up to eight years old, where they can enjoy lots of hands-on fun with animals and ride a tractor trailer. There is also an undercover straw mountain, bouncy castles, pedal tractors and a new indoor soft play area.

* Maize maze (in summer)
* Large play area

Location
Off A35 Poole–Dorchester road

Opening
Daily: 12 Feb–30 Oct 10am–5.30pm;
31 Oct–18 Dec Fri 10am–5.30pm,
Sat & Sun 10am–4pm

Admission
Adult £4.95, Child £4.75, Concs £4.50, Family £16

Contact
Organford, Poole BH16 6EU

t 01202 622022
w farmerpalmer.co.uk
e info@farmerpalmers.co.uk

226 Poole

Upton Country Park

2 hrs   All year

Upton House has pretty, formal gardens that lead into woodland, meadow and a saltmarsh teeming with wildlife on the edge of Poole harbour.

* Nature trails
* Cycling allowed on way-marked cycle route

Location
On S side of A35/A3409, 4 miles W of Poole town centre

Opening
Daily: 9am–dusk

Admission
Adult £5, Children £4

Contact
Upton Road, Upton, Poole BH17 7BJ

t 01202 672625

227 St Leonards

Avon Heath Country Park

2 hrs+   All year

Enjoy a day at Dorset's largest country park, walking or cycling in the beautiful heathland and woods. Special events include pond dipping, Easter egg trails, bug hunts, den building, orienteering, animal tracks and signs, and dawn-chorus walks.

* Barbecue hire available
* Birthday parties and school visits

Location
On the A31, 2 miles W of Ringwood

Opening
Park Daily: Apr–Sep 8am–7.30pm;
Oct–Mar 8.30am–5.30pm
Visitor centre Daily 11am–4pm

Admission
Free. Car park charge

Contact
Brocks Pine, St Leonards Ringwood BH24 2DA

t 01425 478470

228 Studland

Studland Beach & Nature Reserve

3 hrs+   All year

There are miles of golden sands at Studland. The shallow waters are perfect for bathing, and the heathland behind the beach is a National Nature Reserve. This haven for birds and wildlife can be enjoyed from several public paths and two nature trails, plus bird hides at Little Sea.

* Guided discovery walks & storytelling (summer)
* Dogs allowed on beach Sep–Jun only

Location
Bournemouth & Swanage motor road ferry or via Corfe Castle on B3351

Opening
Daily: please phone for details

Admission
Parking charges vary through seasons; please phone for details

Contact
Countryside Office, Studland, Swanage BH19 3AX

t 01929 450259
w nationaltrust.org.uk
e studlandbeach@nationaltrust.org.uk

229 Swanage

Durlston Country Park

3 hrs+   All year

A country park with wildflower meadows, downland, cliffs, sea and a wealth of wildlife. There is also a visitor centre for local information.

* Theme trails & ranger-guided walks
* Education service

Location
Take A351 to Swanage & follow brown tourist signs

Opening
Park Daily: dawn–dusk
Visitor centre Apr–Oct daily 10am–5pm;
Nov–Mar weekends & hols
10.30am–4pm

Admission
Free. Car park charge

Contact
Durlston, Swanage BH19 2JL

t 01929 424443
w durlston.co.uk
e info@durlston.co.uk

230 Swanage

Swanage Railway

2 hrs+   All year

Enjoy a nostalgic steam-train journey through magnificent countryside and the village of Corfe Castle, offering good views of the historic ruins. Pass through the eastern gateway to the World Heritage Jurassic Coast.

* Special events programme
* Train-driving lessons

Location
Station is in centre of Swanage, a few mins walk from beach

Opening
Trains daily Apr–Oct. Weekends only rest of the year. Daily: Dec 26–31

Admission
Adult £7.50, Child & Concs £5.50

Contact
Station House, Swanage BH19 1HB

t 01929 425800
w swanagerailway.co.uk
e general@swanrail.freeserve.co.uk

231 Wareham

Corfe Castle

1 hr+   All year

Explore this ruined castle with a long and fascinating history as a fortress, prison and home. The Castle View Visitor Centre has hands-on displays and children are encouraged to touch castle artefacts and try on replica medieval clothing.

* Special events including historical re-enactments
* Guided tours available

Location
On the A352 Wareham–Swanage road

Opening
Daily: closed 25, 26 Dec

Admission
Adult £4.70, Child £2.30

Contact
The National Trust, The Square, Corfe Castle, Wareham BH20 5EZ
t 01929 481294
w nationaltrust.org.uk
e corfecastle@nationaltrust.org.uk

232 Wareham

Lulworth Castle

3 hrs+   All year

There's plenty to entertain children at this historic building. After viewing the house, which has lots of new exhibitions, take a woodland walk and feed the animals at a nearby farm.

* Adventure playground & indoor activity room
* August jousting shows Monday to Friday

Location
3 miles SW of Wareham. Follow signs

Opening
summer 10am–6pm;
winter 10.30am–4pm;
Closed Sat & 24 Dec to early Jan

Admission
Adult £7, Child £4, Concs £6

Contact
East Lulworth, Wareham BH20 5QS
t 01929 400352
w lulworth.com
e estate.office@lulworth.com

233 Wareham

Monkey World

2 hrs+   All year

At this sanctuary for more than 160 primates including chimpanzees, orang-utans and gibbons, learn how they are looked after and live in social groups. Other attractions include a bird pond, a pet's corner with donkeys, and an adventure play area.

* Largest group of chimpanzees outside Africa
* Featured in many TV programmes, including *Animal Hospital*

Location
Between Bere Regis and Wool, 1 mile from Wool station

Opening
Daily 10am–5pm (Jul & Aug 6pm)

Admission
Adult £9, Child & Concs £6.50

Contact
Longthorns, Wareham BH20 6HH
t 01929 462537
w monkeyworld.org
e apes@monkeyworld.org

234 Weymouth

Abbotsbury Swannery

2 hrs   Mar–Oct

Visitors can walk among the only colony of free-flying mute swans in the world that can be visited. During the hatching period (end of May to end June), you can watch the eggs hatch.

* Feeding of up to 1,000 swans daily at 12pm & 4pm
* Children's play area and bail maze

Location	Contact
On B3157 between Bridport and Weymouth	New Barn Road, Abbotsbury Weymouth DT3 4JG
Opening	t 01305 871858
Daily: mid-Mar–Oct 10am–6pm (last admission 5pm)	w abbotsbury-tourism.co.uk
	e info@abbotsbury-tourism.co.uk
Admission	
Adult £6.50, Child £3.80, Concs £5.80 free car park	

235 Weymouth

Brewers Quay

3 hrs+   All year

Visit this redeveloped Victorian brewery in the Old Harbour to enjoy the shops and café, and to see an award-winning exhibition that takes you on a voyage with Miss Paws, the brewery cat, through 19 life-size scenes, recreating 600 years of local history.

Location	Contact
On harbour, 5 mins from town centre	Hope Square, Weymouth DT4 8TR
Opening	t 01305 777622
Daily: 10am–5.30pm	w brewers-quay.co.uk
Admission	e brewersquay@yahoo.co.uk
Free entry to complex	
Timewalk attraction Adult £4.50, Child £3.25, Concs £4, Family £13.50	

236 Wimborne

Stapehill Abbey, Crafts & Gardens

3 hrs   All year

Award-winning gardens and woodland surround this C19 Cistercian Abbey. It has a craft centre, countryside museum, Japanese garden and home farm, where a range of domestic animals can be seen at close quarters.

Location	Admission
8 miles from Ringwood on A31	Adult £7.50, Child £4.50, Concs £7, Family £12
Opening	Please phone for winter rates
Apr–Sep daily 10am–5pm; Oct–Mar Wed–Sun 10am–4pm	Contact
	Wimborne Road West, Stapehill, Wimborne BH21 2EB
	t 01202 861686

237 Wimborne

Wimborne Model Town & Gardens

2 hrs   Mar–Oct

Set in award-winning gardens, the models are exact 1:10 scale replicas of the town of Wimborne Minster as it was in the 1950s. Children will enjoy the play houses in Wendy Street.

Location	Contact
Accessible via A31	16 King Street, Wimborne Minster BH21 1DY
Opening	t 01202 881924
Daily: 26 Mar–3 Oct 10am–5pm	w wimborne-modeltown.com
Admission	e wimbornemodeltown@hotmail.com
Adult £3, Child £2, Concs £3	

238 Berkeley

Berkeley Castle

4 hrs   Apr–Oct

This stunning medieval castle, stately home of the Berkeley family for 900 years, was the scene of Edward II's murder. It is filled with treasures and is set in beautiful Elizabethan terraced gardens. There is a programme of events, with lots of fun activities for children.

Location	Admission
On A38 (M5, exit 13 or 14), W of Dursley	Adult £7, Child £4, Concs £5.50
Opening	Contact
1 Apr–2 Oct Tue–Sat & Bank Hol Mon 11am–4pm, Sun 2pm–5pm; 3–31 Oct Sun only	Berkeley GL13 9BQ
	t 01453 810332
	w berkeley-castle.com
	e info@berkeley-castle.com

239 Berkeley

Cattle Country Adventure Park

3 hrs   Mar–Oct

A farm park with exotic cattle such as American bison. It also has Gloucester Old Spot pigs and a large adventure playground with big slides and an outdoor paddling pool (in summer) and miniature railway.

* Zip wire ride
* Ideal for private parties

Location
On B4066, near Berkeley

Opening
School hols (except Christmas)
Daily: 10am–5pm;
please phone for other opening hours;
Nov–Feb closed

Admission
summer £6 *winter* £5
group discounts available

Contact
Berkeley Heath Farm, Berkeley Heath
Berkeley GL13 9EW

t 01453 810510
w cattlecountry.co.uk
e info@cattlecountry.co.uk

241 Cheltenham

Birdland Park

½ day   All year

Spot the penguins, flamingos, storks, cranes, parrots, ibis, hornbills and many other birds at this centre for all things feathered, set in woodland and gardens.

* Children's play area
* Dogs allowed as long as they are kept on their leads

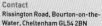

Location
Follow A436 to Bourton-on-the-Water

Opening
Daily: 1 Apr–31 Oct 10am–6pm;
1 Nov–31 Mar open 10am–4pm (last admission 1 hr before closing)

Admission
Adult £4.75, Child (4–14) £3
Concs £4, Family £14.50

Contact
Rissington Road, Bourton-on-the-Water, Cheltenham GL54 2BN

t 01451 820480
w birdland.co.uk
e sb.birdland@virgin.net

240 Bourton-on-the-Water

Cotswold Motor Museum & Toy Collection

½ hr   Feb–Nov

Although the main focus here is on motoring, the museum has a toy collection that includes teddy bears, aeroplanes and rare pedal cars. It's also home to Brum, the little yellow car, from the hit children's BBC TV series, which was filmed here.

* Britain's largest collection of historic motoring signs

Location
Bourton town centre at junction with Sherbourne Street

Opening
Daily: Feb–Nov 10am–6pm

Admission
Adult £2.95, Child £1.95;
Please phone for family details

Contact
The Old Mill, Sherbourne Street, Bourton-on-the-Water, Cheltenham GL54 2BY

t 01451 821255
w cotswold-motor-museum.com
e motormuseum@csma-netlink.co.uk

242 Cheltenham

Chedworth Roman Villa

2 hrs   Mar–Nov

See the remains of one of the largest Romano-British villas in the country. The site comprises more than a mile of walls, several fine mosaics, two bath houses, hypocausts, a water-shrine and a latrine. The museum houses objects from the villa.

* National Trust property
* Audio-visual presentation

Location
3 miles NW of Fossebridge on Cirencester–Northleach road (A429); approach from A429 via Yanworth or from A436 via Withington

Opening
Mar–mid-Nov Tue–Sun 11am–4pm; Bank Hol Mon 10am–5pm

Admission
Adult £5, Child £2.50

Contact
Yanworth, nr Cheltenham GL54 3LJ

t 01242 890256
w nationaltrust.org.uk
e chedworth@nationaltrust.org.uk

243 Cheltenham

Cotswold Farm Park

3 hrs   Mar–Oct

Meet more than 50 flocks and herds of British rare breeds. Enjoy seasonal demonstrations and children's activities, including adventure playgrounds, an indoor tractor school, farm safari rides and a pets' corner.

* Camping site & children's birthday parties
* Lambing, shearing and milking during the year

Location
Follow B4077 from Stow for 5 miles. Signed

Opening
Daily: Mar–Sep 10.30am–5pm; Oct weekends & autumn half-term 10.30am–4pm

Admission
Adult £5.50, Child £4.30, Concs £5

Contact
Guiting Power, Cheltenham GL54 5UG

t 01451 850307
w cotswoldfarmpark.co.uk
e info@cotswoldfarmpark.co.uk

244 Cheltenham

Sandford Parks Lido

2 hrs+   Apr–Oct

Set in beautiful grounds, Sandford Parks Lido tempts the whole family to take the plunge in the 50m heated outdoor pool.

* Playground
* Children's pool

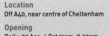

Location
Off A40, near centre of Cheltenham

Opening
Daily: 20 Apr–4 Oct 11am–7.30pm.
Early morning swims, please phone for details

Admission
Adult £3, Child & Concs £1.70

Contact
Keynsham Road, Cheltenham GL53 7PU

t 01242 524430
w sandfordparkslido.org.uk
e swim@sandfordlido.freeserve.co.uk

245 Chipping Sodbury

Dyrham Park

2 hrs   All year

Dyrham Park was built from 1691 to 1702 for William Blathwayt, and its rooms have changed little since they were first furnished. There are restored Victorian domestic rooms, including kitchen, bells passage, bake house, larders, tenants' hall and a Delft-tiled dairy.

* National Trust property
* Peacocks & fallow deer in the park

Location
8 miles N of Bath & 12 miles E of Bristol, off A46

Opening
House Mar–Oct Fri–Tue 12pm–4.45pm (Last admission 4pm)
Gardens Mar–Oct Fri–Tue 11am–5pm
Park All year daily 11am–5.45pm

Admission
Adult £8.80, Child £4.35, Family £21.75
Gardens & park only: £3.40, £1.70, Family £7.75

Contact
Dyrham nr Bath SN14 8ER

t 01179 372501
e dyrhampark@nationaltrust.org.uk

246 Coleford

Puzzle Wood

1 hr+   Feb–Oct

This pre-Roman open-cast iron-ore mine is set in 14 acres of spectacular scenery. Pathways take you through deep ravines and passageways between moss-covered rocks, forming a very unusual maze. There is also an opportunity to meet the farm animals.

* Quality Assured Visitor Attraction
* Indoor wood puzzle with secret doorways

Location
Take B4228 from Coleford to Chepstow. Puzzle Wood is ½ mile from Coleford

Opening
Easter–Sep Tue–Sun 11am–5.30pm (last admission 4.30pm);
Oct & Feb half-term 11am–4pm (last admission 3pm)

Admission
Adult £3.95, Child £2.80

Contact
Lower Perrygrove Farm, Coleford GL16 8RB

t 01594 833187

247 Gloucester

Beatrix Potter's House of The Tailor of Gloucester

½ hr   All year

The attraction and shop are in the very house used by Beatrix Potter to inspire her story of helpful sewing mice, *The Tailor of Gloucester*. Displays and models bring this classic English tale to life.

Location
In city centre, off Westgate Street (pedestrian area). Easily reached from M5 (junction 11, 11A or 12)

Opening
Apr–Oct Mon–Sat 10am–5pm;
Nov–Mar 9.30am–4.30pm;
closed Bank Hols

Admission
Free

Contact
9 College Court
Gloucester GL1 2NJ

t 01452 422856
w heroes-shop.com

248 Gloucester

National Waterways Museum

2 hrs   All year

Take a journey through Britain in this award-winning museum, telling the 200-year story of inland waterways. Investigate interactive displays, historic craft, a traditional blacksmith's and an activities room. You enter through a replica lock complete with running water.

* Learn about Gloucester's role as an important dock
* For boat trips please phone for availability

Location
Follow signs for Historic Docks

Opening
Daily 10am–5pm; closed 25 Dec

Admission
Adult £5, Child £4, Concs £4
Occasionally subject to change, please phone for details

Contact
Llanthony Warehouse,
Gloucester Docks GL1 2EH

t 01452 318200
w nwm.org.uk
e bookingsnwm@thewaterwaystrust.org

249 Gloucester

Prinknash Bird & Deer Park

1 hr   All year

Enjoy a wildlife experience walking in this bird park with fallow deer and pygmy goats, peacocks and cranes. There are bird pavilions and a reputedly haunted fish pond teeming with large trout!

* Tame deer
* Tudor-style wendy house

Location	Contact
Exit M5 at junction 11a then take the A46 towards Stroud	Prinknash Abbey, Cranham Gloucester GL4 8EX
Opening	t 01452 812727
Daily: summer 10am–4pm; winter 10am–4pm	w prinknash-bird-and-deerpark.com
Admission	
Adult £4.50, Child £3, Concs £3.50	

250 Gloucester

Robinswood Hill Country Park

1 hr+   All year

Explore 250 acres of open countryside with way-marked nature trails and a visitor centre. Pay a free visit to the new rare breeds farm and see traditional breeds of farm animals.

Location	Contact
Take Gloucester outer ring road, S of the city road	Reservoir Road Gloucester GL4 6SX
Opening	t 01452 303206
Daily: dawn–dusk	
Admission	
Free	

251 Gloucester

Soldiers of Gloucestershire Museum

1 hr+   All year

The story of Gloucestershire's soldiers and their families in peacetime and war over the past 300 years is told in this award-winning museum.

* Archive film & computer animations
* Life-size displays & sound effects

Location	Contact
Follow signs to Historic Docks	Gloucester Docks GL1 2HE
Opening	t 01452 522682
Daily: 10am–5pm; closed winter Mons & Christmas (last admission 4.30pm)	w glosters.org.uk
	e regimental-secretary@rgbw.army.mod.uk
Admission	
Adult £4.25, Child £2.25, Concs £3.25	

252 Nympsfield

Woodchester Park & Mansion

2 hrs+   Easter –Oct

Known as 'The Secret Valley', this park was formerly an C18 park with five lakes and it is now virtually covered with trees. It contains an unfinished Victorian Gothic mansion. There are way-marked walks and trails through the woods.

* Dogs in park only

Location	Contact
1 mile NW of Nailsworth; 4 miles SW of Stroud	Nympsfield Stonehouse GL10 3TS
Opening	t 01453 861541
Mansion Easter–Oct weekends 11am–4pm; Park Daily	w woodchestermansion.org.uk
	e visitor@woodchestermansion.org.uk
Admission	
Mansion Adult £5, Child Free, Concs £4	
Park Free	

253 Nympsfield

WWT Slimbridge Wildfowl & Wetlands Centre

3 hrs+   All year

Visit a large collection of exotic, rare and endangered ducks, geese and swans in this reserve. The Discovery Centre has hands-on displays.

* Face-painting & badge-making
* Special activities during school holidays

Location
Between Bristol & Gloucester, just off A38, signed from the M5 (junction 13 or 14)

Opening
Daily: 9.30am–5pm; Nov–Mar 4pm; closed 25 Dec

Admission
Adult £6.75, Child £4, Concs £5.50, Family £17.50

Contact
Slimbridge GL2 7BT
t 01453 891900
w wwt.org.uk/visit/slimbridge
e info.slimbridge@wwt.org.uk

254 Stroud

Museum in the Park

1 hr+   All year

An innovative museum set in a park, it has imaginative displays including dinosaur bones, a Roman temple and the world's first lawnmower. There are also family activity packs, special events and exhibitions.

* Quiz trails

Location
From junction 13 of M5 take A419 Ebley bypass towards Stroud

Opening
Please phone or visit the website for details

Admission
Free

Contact
Stratford Park, Stratford Road, Stroud GL5 4AF
t 01453 763394
w stroud.gov.uk
e museum@stroud.gov.uk

255 Bath

Bath Balloon Flights

1 hr   Apr–Oct

Ever wanted to fly over rooftops? You can in a hot-air balloon! You'll ascend as high as 3,000 feet and travel up to 10 miles during the one-hour flight, depending on the weather conditions. Good stout shoes are recommended in case the balloon lands in a field.

* Fantastic views of the city
* No two trips are the same

Location	Contact
Royal Victoria Park is 5 min walk from city centre	8 Lambridge, London Road, Bath BA1 6BJ
Opening	t 01225 466888
Apr–Oct (office open all year)	w balnet.co.uk
Admission	e bath@balnet.co.uk
Please phone for details	

256 Bath

The Jane Austen Centre

1 hr   All year

Jane Austen lived in this street from 1801 to 1806. This exciting and informative centre tells the story of her time in Bath and of the influence the city had on her novels *Northanger Abbey* and *Persuasion*.

Location	Contact
City centre N of Queen Square	40 Gay Street, Bath BA1 2NT
Opening	
Daily: Mon–Sun 10am–5.30pm	t 01225 443000
	w janeausten.co.uk
Admission	e info@janeausten.co.uk
Adult £5.95, Child £2.95, Concs £4.50	

257 Bath

Prior Park Landscape Garden

1 hr+ All year

Enjoy an exhilarating walk through this stunning garden set in a sweeping valley with magnificent views of the city of Bath. This unique C18 garden is in the final stages of restoration and includes the Gothic Temple, Serpentine Lake, Cascades and Palladian Bridge.

* National Trust property
* Access to skyline walk

Location
There is no parking (except prebooked disabled) at the gardens. Please phone for details of public transport connections

Opening
Feb–Nov Wed–Mon 11am–4.30pm;
Dec–Jan Fri–Sun 11am–dusk,
closed Tue

Admission
Adult £4, Child £2, NT free

Contact
Ralph Allen Drive,
Bath BA2 5AH

t 01225 833422
w nationaltrust.org.uk
e priorpark@nationaltrust.org.uk

258 Bath

Roman Baths & Pump Rooms

2 hrs All year

The Roman Baths are one of the best-preserved Roman sites north of the Alps. Below the streets of Bath are the Sacred Spring, a Roman temple and the Roman bath house, while the Georgian pump house stands at street level.

* Taste the water in the C18 Pump Rooms above the Temple
* Displays include sculpture, coins & jewellery

Location
City centre near the abbey

Opening
Jan–Feb & Nov–Dec 9.30am–4.30pm
Mar–June & Sep–Oct 9am–5pm
July–Aug 9am–9pm (Last exit 1 hr
after close)

Admission
Adult £9.50, Child £5.30, Concs £8.50

Contact
Abbey Church Yard, Bath BA1 1LZ

t 01225 477785
w romanbaths.co.uk
e romanbath_bookings@bathsnes.
gov.uk

259 Barrington

Barrington Court

2 hrs+ Mar–Oct

An enchanting garden laid out in a sequence of walled rooms, with a working kitchen garden. The Tudor manor house is an antique furniture showroom.

* Children's activities
* Nature trail

Location
5 miles NE of Ilminster on A358

Opening
Mar & Oct Thu–Sun 11am–4.30pm
Apr–Sep daily (closed Wed)
11am–5.30pm

Admission
Please phone for details

Contact
Barrington TA19 0NQ

t 01460 241938
w nationaltrust.org.uk
e barringtoncourt@nationaltrust.
org.uk

260 Berrow

Animal Farm Adventure Park

4 hrs+   All year

Children can pet and feed many of the friendly animals at this farm. There is a play barn with big indoor slides and a large play park to enjoy.

* Phone for details of special events
* Delightful walks

Location	Admission
10 mins from junction 22 on M5. Head for Berrow & follow signs	Adult & Child £5.50, Concs £4.50, Family £21
Opening	**Contact**
Daily: summer 10am–5.30pm; winter 10am–4.30pm	Red Roan, Berrow TA8 2RW
	t 01278 751628
	w animal-farm.co.uk
	e mike@afap.fsnet.co.uk

261 Chard

Ferne Animal Sanctuary

3 hrs   All year

Take your time to stroll around the 51 acres of tranquil surroundings for 300 rescued and retired animals, ranging from horses to chipmunks.

Location	Contact
3 miles W of Chard in Somerset, signed from A30	Chard TA20 3DH
Opening	t 01460 65214
Daily 10am–5pm; closed 25 Dec & 1 Jan	w ferneanimalsanctuary.org
Admission	e info@ferneanimalsanctuary.org
Free, donations welcome	

262 Chard

The Wildlife Park at Cricket St Thomas

1 hr+   All year

This park is home to more than 600 animals, including lemur, monkeys, leopards, oryx, zebra, camels, wallabies, cheetahs and birds. Through its captive breeding programmes, it plays an important part in the conservation of rare and endangered species.

* Licensed for civil marriages
* Safari train, crazy golf & mini-car ride

Location
3 miles from Chard on A30. Signed from M5 junction 25 and A303

Opening
Mon–Sun *summer* 10am–6pm; *winter* 10am–4.30am

Admission
Please phone for details

Contact
Chard, Somerset TA20 4DB

t 01460 30111
w wild.org.uk
e wildlifepark.cst@bourne-leisure.co.uk

263 Cheddar

Cheddar Gorge & Caves

3 hrs+   All year

The fascinating caves at Cheddar Gorge have long been popular attractions. Wonder at the mysterious stalagmites and stalactites in Gough's Cave and enjoy the Crystal Quest Challenge in the underground fantasy adventure game. There are explorer audio-guide tours.

* New Cheddar Man & the Cannibals attraction
* Open-top bus tour runs through gorge Apr–Sept

Location
Follow signs from junction 22 on M5 & A38 or take B3135 from A37 and the E

Opening
Jul–Aug 10am–5pm;
Sep–Jun 10.30am–4.30pm

Admission
Explorer ticket for all attractions
Adult £10.90, Child £7.90

Contact
Cheddar BS27 3QF

t 01934 742343
w cheddarcaves.co.uk
e info@cheddarcaves.co.uk

264 Dunster

Dunster Castle

2 hrs   Mar–Nov

The fortified home of the Luttrels for 600 years, this castle is set in beautiful parkland and has a terraced garden of rare shrubs. Attic and basement tours with a below-stairs exhibition are popular; a children's guide, trail and activity sheets are available.

* Guided tours available for groups
* Dogs allowed in park only

Location
Off A39, 3 miles SE of Minehead

Opening
Castle Daily: 18 Mar–5 Nov 11am–5pm;
closed Thu & Fri
Gardens & Park Daily: 10am–5pm

Admission
Castle Adult £7.20, Child £3.60
Gardens & Park £3.90, £1.70

Contact
Dunster, nr Minehead TA24 6SL
t 01643 821314
w nationaltrust.org.uk
e dunstercastle@nationaltrust.org.uk

---

265 Farleigh Hungerford

Farleigh Hungerford Castle

2 hrs   All year

In 1370 Sir Thomas Hungerford began the fortification of the original Farleigh Manor, into what became Farleigh Hungerford Castle. The two south towers still remain, as do parts of the curtain wall, the outer gate house, and the C14 chapel and crypt.

* Important collection of lead coffins in chapel crypt
* Programme of living history throughout the year

Location
8 miles SE of Bath off A36

Opening
Daily: Apr–Jun & Sep 10am–5pm;
Jul–Aug 10am–6pm;
Oct–Mar Sat & Sun 10am–4pm

Admission
Adult £3.30, Child £1.70, Concs £2.50

Contact
Farleigh Hungerford,
nr Trowbridge BA2 7RS
t 01225 754026
w english-heritage.org.uk/farleigh
  hungerford
e customers@english-heritage.org.uk

266 Glastonbury

Glastonbury Abbey

2 hrs   All year

Steeped in history and legend, this ancient abbey, though now ruined, is still a Christian sanctuary and an oasis of peace and quiet set in parkland with ponds and wildlife areas. The whole family can relax in its tranquil surroundings.

* Visitor centre with award-winning museum
* Period-dressed guides in summer months

Location	Admission
Take A39 from junction 23 of M5, follow signs once in Glastonbury	Adult £4, Child £1.50, Concs £3.50
	Contact
Opening	Abbey Gatehouse, Magdalene Street, Glastonbury BA6 9EL
Daily: Jun–Aug 9am–6pm (or dusk if earlier); Mar–May & Sep–Nov 9.30am–6pm; Dec–Feb 10am–dusk	t 01458 832267
	w glastonburyabbey.com
	e info@glastonburyabbey.com

267 Highbridge

Alstone Wildlife Park

1 hr+   Easter–Nov

A small, non commercial family-run park and licensed zoo with camels, pigs, deer, ponies, emu, owls and llama. Special features include Theodore the friendly camel, tame red deer, and a pets' corner.

* Heaviest Steer in U.K.

Location	Admission
A38 Highbridge–Bridgwater road, signed turning on the right, ½ mile from Highbridge	Adult £4, Child £3, Concs £3.50
	Contact
Opening	Alstone Road, Highbridge, Somerset TA9 3DT
Daily: Easter–mid-Nov 10am–5.30pm	t 01278 782405

268 Minehead

West Somerset Railway

3 hrs   Feb–Dec

This preserved steam railway operates between Minehead and Bishop's Lydeard, near Taunton. It is the longest independent railway in Britain.

* Visitor centres & museums
* Model railway

Location	Contact
Reached via A39 & A358	The Station, Minehead TA24 5BG
Opening	t 01643 700384
Feb–Dec (daily late May–late Sep); please phone for details	w west-somerset-railway.co.uk
	e info@west-somerset-railway.co.uk
Admission	
Adult £11, Child £5, Concs £10	

269 Minehead

West Somerset Rural Life Museum

1 hr+   Easter–Oct

Visit the schools of the past in this museum, housed in an old school building, with a thatched roof and riverside garden. Children can dress up in Victorian clothes, write on slates and play with traditional toys.

Location	Admission
On A39 from Minehead	Adult £1.50, Child 50p
Opening	**Contact**
Easter & 6 May–mid-Oct Mon–Fri 10.30am–1pm & 2pm–4pm; Sun during school summer hols 2pm–4.30pm	The Old School, Allerford, Minehead TA24 8HN
	t 01643 862529
	w allerfordwebsite.ic24.net

270 Radstock

Radstock Museum

1 hr   Feb–Nov

This award-winning museum depicts the social and industrial heritage of the former North Somerset coalfield. It offers a unique insight into life in the region since the C19.

* Interactive & hands-on displays
* Heritage trail

Location	Admission
10 miles S of Bath	Adult £3, Child & Concs £2
Opening	**Contact**
Feb–Nov Tue–Sat 11am–5pm, Sun 2pm–5pm; Bank Hols 2pm–5pm	The Market Hall, Waterloo Road, Radstock BA3 3EP
	t 01761 437722
	w radstockmuseum.co.uk

271 Sparkford

Haynes Motor Museum

3 hrs   All year

Travel through 100 years of motoring history with Britain's most spectacular collection of historic cars from around the world.

* Fabulous collection of American sports cars
* 70-seater video theatre

Location	Admission
½ mile N of Sparkford on A359	Adult £6.95, Child £3.75, Concs £5.50
Opening	**Contact**
Daily: Mar–Oct 9.30am–5.30pm; Nov–Feb 10am–4pm; closed 25, 26 Dec & 1 Jan	Sparkford BA22 7LH
	t 01963 440804
	w haynesmotormuseum.co.uk
	e info@haynesmotormuseum.co.uk

272 Street

Viaduct Fishery

5 hrs   All year

Set in the beautiful Cary Valley, this fishery offers six coarse fishing lakes spread out over a peaceful 25-acre site. Tuition is available for beginners.

* Tackle shop

Location	Contact
On the N outskirts of Somerton	Cary Valley,
	Somerton TA11 6LJ
Opening	
Daily: dawn–dusk	t 01458 274022
Admission	
Adult £6, Child & Concs £4	

273 Taunton

Somerset County Museum

2–3 hrs   All year

An interesting museum housed in Taunton Castle, it has costumes, silver and a C16 almshouse on display. Recent additions include the shipwreck coin hoard – the largest hoard of Roman silver coins found in Britain.

Location	Contact
Reached via A38 & M5	Taunton Castle, Castle Green,
	Taunton TA1 4AA
Opening	
Tue–Sat 10am–5pm;	t 01823 320201
closed 29 Mar, 25, 26 Dec & 1 Jan	w somerset.gov.uk
Admission	e county-museums@somerset.
Free	gov.uk

274 Weston–super–Mare

The Helicopter Museum

2 hrs   All year

More than 80 helicopters dating from 1931 to the present day are displayed here in hangars. There are open-cockpit days and Helicopter Experience or Air Experience flights available. The museum organises special events throughout the year.

* Guided tours for groups of 12 or more
* The world's largest helicopter museum

Location	Admission
On the A371, off M5 (junction 21)	Adult £4.95, Child £2.95
Opening	Contact
Apr–Oct Wed–Sun 10am–5.30pm;	The Heliport, Locking Moor Road,
Nov–Mar 10am–4.30pm;	Weston-super-Mare BS24 8PP
Easter & school summer hols daily	
10am–5.30pm	t 01934 635227
	w helicoptermuseum.co.uk

275 Weston-super-Mare

Seaquarium, Weston-super-Mare

2 hrs   All year

Walk through the underwater tunnel to view hundreds of fascinating fish, including sharks and rays, in 30 naturally themed marine habitats. There are interactive touch screens as well.

* Discovery trail

Location
On the seafront; take junction 21 or 22 off M5. Follow brown tourist signs

Opening
Daily: 10am–5pm, 4pm in winter (last admission 4pm)

Admission
Please phone for details

Contact
Marine Parade,
Weston-super-Mare BS23 1BE

t 01934 641603
w seaquarium.co.uk
e weston@seaquarium.co.uk

276 Wookey Hole

Wookey Hole Caves & Papermill

4 hrs   All year

It is said that the infamous Witch of Wookey lived in these spectacular caves. Guided tours of the caves are amazing. Visitors can also watch demonstrations of traditional papermaking at a 400-year-old papermill. There are numerous activities for children.

* Magical mirror maze & penny arcade
* New Haunted Witches ghost train

Location
Junction 22 of M5 then follow signs A39 from Bath to Wells

Opening
Daily: Apr–Oct 10am–5pm;
Nov–Mar 10am–4pm

Admission
Adult £9.90, Child & Concs £7.50

Contact
Wookey Hole,
nr Wells BA5 1BB

t 01749 672243
w wookey.co.uk
e witch@wookey.co.uk

277 Yeovil

Fleet Air Arm Museum

3 hrs+   All year

The Fleet Air Arm Museum is one of the 'Must see' attractions when in the South West. Among Europe's largest collection of naval aircraft, see Concorde, Harriers, helicopters and the award-winning Aircraft Carrier Experience. There is even a nuclear bomb.

* *Ark Royal* Aircraft Carrier Experience
* Concorde

Location
1 mile off A303/A37 roundabout

Opening
Daily: Apr–Oct 10am–5.30pm;
Nov–Mar Wed–Sun 10am–4.30pm;
open Bank Hols & school hols;
closed 24–26 Dec

Admission
Adult £9, Child £6, Concs £7

Contact
PO Box D6, RNAS, Yeovilton,
Illchester BA22 8HT

t 01935 840565
w fleetairarm.com
e info@fleetairarm.com

278 Amesbury

Stonehenge

1 hr All year

Now a World Heritage Site, Stonehenge is a powerful witness to the Stone and Bronze Ages. These monolithic stones – whether they were part of a sun-worshipping religion or formed a giant astronomical calendar – are a tribute to their architects and builders.

* World Heritage site
* Audio tours in 9 languages

Location
2 miles W of Amesbury on junction of A303 & A360

Opening
Daily: please phone for details

Admission
Adult £5.50, Child £2.80, Concs £4.10

Contact
Stonehenge Information Line

t 0870 333 1181
w english-heritage.org.uk/stonehenge
e customers@english-heritage.org.uk

279 Avebury

Avebury

1 hr All year

This great stone circle, encompassing part of the village of Avebury, is roughly ¼ mile across. It encloses an area of about 28 acres and contains two smaller circles within. It is believed to be an ancient religious and ceremonial centre.

* World Heritage site
* World's biggest megalithic monument

Location
6 miles W of Marlborough, 1 mile N of Bath road (A4) on A4361 and B4003

Opening
Daily: Apr–Oct 10am–6pm;
Nov–Mar 10am–4pm

Admission
Adult £4.20, Child £2.10

Contact
nr Marlborough SN8 1RF

t 01672 539250
w nationaltrust.org.uk
e avebury.estateoffice@nationaltrust.org.uk

280 Calne

Bowood House

3 hrs Mar–Nov

Fun, beauty and history are all on offer at the magnificent family home of the Marquis and Marchioness of Lansdowne. The house is set in beautiful Capability Brown parkland, and there is an adventure playground, plus the Soft Play Palace, to entertain children.

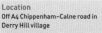

Location
Off A4 Chippenham–Calne road in Derry Hill village

Opening
Daily: 19 Mar–1 Nov 11am–6pm (last admission 5pm)

Admission
Adult £6.60, Child from £3.40–£4.30, Concs £5.50

Contact
Derry Hill, Calne SN11 0LZ

t 01249 812102
w bowood.org
e houseandgardens@bowood.org

281 Chippenham

Lacock Abbey & Fox Talbot Museum

2 hrs+ Mar–Oct

This fine medieval abbey and house, set in gardens and woodland, is home to a museum dedicated to former resident William Henry Fox Talbot, inventor of the positive/negative photographic process.

* Harry Potter movies filmed here
* Beautiful Victorian woodland garden

Location
3 miles S of Chippenham, just E of A350

Opening
Abbey Mar–Oct Wed–Mon 11am–5.30pm
Museum Mar–Oct 11am–5.30pm; *winter* weekends only

Admission
Adult £7.40, Child £3.70

Contact
Chippenham SN15 2LG

t 01249 730141
w nationaltrust.org.uk

282 Malmesbury

Athelstan Museum

½ hr   All year

This museum has local history exhibits such as costumes, an early fire engine, photographs of the town and an educational hands-on activity called the Mini Museum Detective. There is also an activity corner to keep younger children amused.

*No WC facilities on site, but some are situated very
  close to the building

Location	Admission
Off A429, 5 miles from M4 (junction 17)	Free
	Contact
Opening	Town Hall, Cross Hayes,
April–Sep Tue–Sat 10am–2pm;	Malmesbury SN16 9BZ
Oct–Mar Thu 10am–2pm Sat	t 01666 829258
10am–12pm, please phone to confirm	w northwilts.gov.uk
	e athelstanmuseum@northwilts.gov.uk

283 Salisbury

Cholderton Rare Breeds Centre

2 hrs+   All year

This park for rare farm animals has a wealth of things to see and do, and is home to one of Britain's largest collections of rabbit breeds. There is also a replica Iron Age roundhouse farm and nature trail.

* Toddlers' play area & adventure playground
* Pig-racing & tractor rides (in season)

Location	Contact
Reached by A303 from Andover or A338 from Salisbury or Marlborough	Amesbury Road, Cholderton Salisbury SP4 0EW
Opening	t 01980 629438
Daily: 10am–6pm; winter weekends only. Please phone for details	w rabbitworld.co.uk
	e group@rabbitworld.co.uk
Admission	
Adult £5.50, Child (2–16) £3.95, Concs £4.50	

284 Salisbury

Old Sarum

1½ hrs   All year

This great earthwork, with more than 2,000 years of history and its huge banks and ditches was created by Iron Age people around 500 BC, and later occupied by Romans, Saxons and the Normans. See the remains of the prehistoric fortress, the palace, castle and cathedral.

* William the Conqueror paid off his army here in 1070
* Beautiful views to surrounding chalk downs

Location	Contact
2 miles of Salisbury off A345	English Heritage, Castle Road Salisbury SP1 3SD
Opening	
Jul–Aug 9am–6pm;	t 01722 335398
Sep, Oct, Mar 10am–4pm;	w english-heritage.org.uk/oldsarum
Nov–Mar 11am–3pm	e old_sarum.castle@english-heritage. org.uk
Admission	
Adult £2.90, Child £1.50, Concs £2.20	

285 Stourhead

Stourhead Gardens

3 hrs+   Mar–Oct

Stourhead's magnificent landscaped gardens offer space to let off steam and there's plenty to discover and explore. Discover the mini-temples and a spooky grotto and climb Alfred's Tower to enjoy the spectacular views. The house has fine interiors, paintings and furnishings.

* Children's guide & quiz
* Hands-on activities

Location	Contact
Just off A303 at Mere	Stourhead Gardens, nr Warminster BA12 6QD
Opening	
House Mar–Oct; closed Wed & Thu	t 01747 842020
Gardens Daily, please call for details	w nationaltrust.org.uk
	e stourhead@nationaltrust.org.uk
Admission	
House or Gardens Adult £5.80, Child £3.20 Both £9.90, £4.80	

286 Swindon

Link Centre

2 hrs+   All year

This multipurpose sports centre could keep you occupied all day. The Link offers an ice rink, swimming pool, badminton and squash courts, snooker and even a climbing wall. When you need a break, relax in the cafeteria or bar.

Location
In west Swindon, 1½ miles from town centre. Follow brown tourist signs from M4 (junction 16)

Opening
Please phone or visit the website for details

Admission
Please phone or visit the website for details

Contact
Whitehill Way, Westlea, Swindon SN5 7DL

t 01793 445566
w swindon.gov.uk/link

287 Swindon

Oasis Leisure Centre

2 hrs+   All year

This leisure centre has activities for all age groups. The lagoon pool has a new pirate ship for the under-eights, three giant water slides, a wave machine and water cannon. There are also squash courts, a gym and an indoor bowling green.

* Outdoor multiplay pitches

Location
Follow the brown tourist signs on all major roads to Swindon

Opening
Please phone for details

Admission
Please phone for details

Contact
North Star Avenue, Swindon SN2 1EP

t 01793 445401
w swindon.gov.uk/oasis

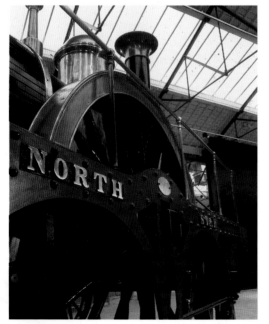

288 Swindon

STEAM – Museum of the Great Western Railway

2 hrs+   All year

STEAM tells the story of workers on the Great Western Railway. Housed in beautiful railway buildings, this award-winning museum has hands-on exhibits and famous locomotives and makes a great day out for all the family.

* Day out with Thomas the Tank Engine
* World-famous GWR locomotives

Location
Follow signs from Swindon town centre

Opening
Daily: 10am–5pm

Admission
Adult £5.95, Child & Concs £3.95

Contact
Kemble Drive, Swindon SN2 2TA

t 01793 466646
w swindon.gov.uk/steam
e steammuseum@swindon.gov.uk

289 Warminster

Longleat

4 hrs+   Feb–Nov

From safari to stately home and from miniature trains to mazes and safari boat rides, there is always something to discover at Longleat. Visitors can enjoy close encounters with some of the world's most exotic animals, King Arthur's mirror maze and a pets' corner.

* Longleat hedge maze
* Featured in the BBC programme *Animal Park*

Location	Contact
Off A36 between Bath & Salisbury (A362 Warminster–Frome road)	The Estate Office, Longleat, Warminster BA12 7NW
Opening	t 01985 844400
Daily: Feb–Nov; times vary please phone for details	w longleat.co.uk
	e enquiries@longleat.co.uk
Admission	
Please phone for details	

290 Westbury

Westbury White Horse & Bratton Camp

3 hrs+   All year

The 300-year-old Westbury white horse is the oldest in Wiltshire. It is in a great location on a very steep slope, which is ideal for kite-flying and hang-gliding, just below the Iron Age hill fort of Bratton camp. There are marvellous views for miles around.

*Neolithic barrow or burial mound

Location	Contact
Between Westbury B3098	Westbury Tourist Information Centre
Opening	t 01373 827158
Daily: please phone for details	w english-heritage.org.uk
Admission	
Free	

Blakeney, Norfolk

Eastern

Bedfordshire Cambridgeshire Essex
Hertfordshire Norfolk Suffolk

Gainsborough

The Wolds

Market Rasen
Louth
410
Mablethorpe

407–408
Lincoln
Horncastle
405–406
Ingoldmells
Skegness

Washingborough

430
Newark-on-Trent
416
417
Coningsby
412–414

404
Grantham
397

Sleaford
Boston

Spalding
415
Holbeach
409
King's Lynn

Bourne

RUTLAND
The Fens
310
Wisbech
351
Swaffham
339

439
Stamford
Peterborough
304–305
March
Downham Market
Watton
Wymondham

437
Uppingham
438
Corby
Oundle
311
Chatteris
Littleport
337
Brandon
362
Thetford
335
Bungay
363–365

420
Kettering
308
Huntingdon
302
Ely
Mildenhall
340
Diss
Eye
373–374
Southwold

426
Rushden
303
Brampton
St Ives
Waterbeach
380
366–367
Saxmundham
381–382
Leiston

Northampton
309
Newmarket
Bury St Edmunds
375–378
Aldeburgh

291
Bedford
372
Cambridge
Stowmarket
SUFFOLK

St Neots
292
Biggleswade
301
Haverhill
379
Woodbridge
369
Orford Ness

Milton Keynes
299–300
306–307
329
Sudbury
Ipswich

017
295
Royston
Saffron Walden
320
368
Felixstowe

Newport Pagnell
Letchworth
328
332
321
Halstead
317–319
Harwich

297–298
296
Hitchin
Baldock
Stevenage
314
Manningtree
The Naze

293–294
323
Luton
Welwyn Garden City
327
Bishop's Stortford
Braintree
Colchester
Clacton-on-Sea

Dunstable
LUTON
STANSTED
Witham
West Mersea

Tring
Hemel Hempstead
St Albans
Hatfield
Hertford
Ware
Harlow
Chelmsford
316
Maldon

Berkhamsted
330–331
326
Hoddesdon
324
322
Burnham-on-Crouch
Foulness Island

Amersham
325
Barnet
Enfield
312–313
Rayleigh

High Wycombe
Watford
333
Chigwell
315
Brentwood
Basildon
Southend-on-Sea

Beaconsfield
013
Uxbridge
Harrow
079–106
Canvey Island

Maidenhead
014–015
LONDON
Woolwich
Tilbury
Gravesend
Sheerness
Isle of Sheppey
Herne Bay
Margate

Slough
Richmond
116
Kingston upon Thames
063
Dartford
Rochester
Gillingham
075
Whitstable
078
069

Windsor
005–006
Staines
Swanley
Chatham
Sittingbourne
Ramsgate

Bracknell
001–002
114
125
Sutton
Croydon

NORFOLK
Norwich
NORWICH
352–357
The Broads
342–345
Great Yarmouth
370–371
Lowestoft
Beccles
Halesworth

Wells-next-the-Sea
336
358
Sheringham
Cromer
346–348
338
359–360
North Walsham
Aylsham
334
350
361
Caister-on-Sea

Hunstanton
349
341
Fakenham
Dereham

CAMBRIDGESHIRE
BEDFORDSHIRE
HERTFORDSHIRE
ESSEX

Sawtry

291 Bedford

Bedford Butterfly Park

2 hrs+   Jan–Dec

Set in a landscape of wildflower hay meadows, this fascinating conservation park features a tropical glasshouse. Visitors walk through a wonderful scene of waterfalls, ponds and lush foliage, with spectacular butterflies flying around.

* Quality Assured Visitor Attraction
* Nature trails & mini-farm

Location
Off A421, near Bedford. From Bedford town centre follow signs for Cambridge. As you leave Bedford turn left for Renhold & Wilden & follow signs for Wilden

Opening
8 Jan–10 Feb Thu–Sun 10am–4pm;
11 Feb–31 Oct daily 10am–5pm;
1 Nov–18 Dec Thu–Sun 10am–4pm;

Admission
Adult £4.50, Child £2.75, Concs £3.50, Family £13

Contact
Renhold Road, Wilden, Bedford MK44 2PX
t 01234 772770
w bedford-butterflies.co.uk
e enquiries@bedford-butterflies.co.uk

292 Biggleswade

The English School of Falconry

3 hrs+   Feb–Oct

Located in woodland, this family-run centre has recreated an environment close to the birds' natural habitat. Here you can see more than 300 birds, including falcons, hawks, eagles, vultures and owls, some of which you can handle or watch fly during the daily displays.

* Three flying displays daily
* Hands-on experience

Location
Old Warden is 2 miles W of A1 where it bypasses Biggleswade

Opening
Daily: Feb–Oct 10am–5pm

Admission
Adult £6.50, Child £4, Concs £5.50

Contact
Old Warden Park, Biggleswade SG18 9EA
t 01767 627527
w shuttleworth.org
e falconry.centre@virgin.net

293 Dunstable

Leighton Buzzard Railway

2 hrs   Mar–Oct

Take a journey into the world of the English light railway – experience sharp curves, steep gradients and level crossings. Passengers can now make a 70-minute round trip from Page's Park to Stonehenge Works.

* Children's play area
* Explore the Guntry terminus

Location
Off A4146 on edge of Leighton Buzzard, close to junction with A505 Dunstable–Aylesbury road

Opening
Early Mar–end Oct Sun & Bank Hols 10.40am–4.30pm; some Sats & Suns in Dec; please phone for details

Admission
Adult £6, Child (2–15) £3, Concs £5

Contact
Billington Road, Leighton Buzzard LU7 4TN
t 01525 373888
w buzzrail.co.uk
e info@buzzrail.co.uk

294 Dunstable

Whipsnade Wild Animal Park

3–5 hrs   All year

Whipsnade Wild Animal Park is home to more than 2,500 rare and exotic animals. Seize the chance to see tigers, elephants, hippos, giraffes, rhino and more in their huge outdoor enclosures. See the 'Lions of the Serengeti' and the park's two baby elephants, Euan and Aneena.

* Children's farm & adventure playground
* Free-flying bird display & penguin feeding

Location	Admission
Follow brown elephant signs from M1 junction 9 or 12. Just 20 mins from M25 junction 21	Adult £14.50, Child (3–15) £11, Concs £12.50, Family £46. Car park £3.50. Book online up to 24 hours in advance and receive a 10% discount
Opening Daily: from 10am Please visit the website for details	**Contact** Dunstable LU6 2LF t 01582 872171 w whipsnade.co.uk

295 Henlow

Stondon Motor Museum

2 hrs   All year

Travel back in time to discover vehicles from the beginning of the century to modern-day classics – 400 vehicles are housed in 5 halls and include Rolls-Royce and Bentley cars. Outside the museum is an exact replica of Captain Cook's ship HM *Endeavour*.

* Large free car park

Location	Contact
At Lower Stondon near Henlow off A600	Station Road, Lower Stondon, Henlow SG16 6JN
Opening Daily: 10am–5pm	t 01462 850339 w transportmuseum.co.uk e info@transportmuseum.co.uk
Admission Adult £6, Child £3, Concs £5	

296 Kensworth

Dunstable Downs Countryside Centre & Whipsnade Estate

2 hrs+   All year

A great place to learn all about flora and fauna, walk, cycle along designated routes, fly kites or watch paragliders. Visit in July to see spectacular displays during the annual kite-flying festival. The centre has exhibitions and a wide range of kites for sale.

* Designated Area of Outstanding Natural Beauty

Location	Contact
4 miles NE of Ashridge between B4540 & B4541	Whipsnade Road, Kensworth, Dunstable LU6 2TA
Opening *Downs* Daily *Centre* Daily: Apr–Oct 10am–5pm; Nov–Apr Sat–Sun 10am–4pm	t 01582 608489 w nationaltrust.org.uk e dunstabledowns@nationaltrust.org.uk
Admission Free	

297 Luton

John Dony Field Centre

1 hr+   All year

The Field Centre is located close to a number of important sites of natural history interest in north-east Luton. There are displays featuring local and natural history, conservation and archaeology.

* Wildlife garden

Location
In Bushmead Estate, near A6, in N Luton. Signed from roundabout at Barnfield College on A6

Opening
Please phone for details

Admission
Free

Contact
Hancock Drive, Bushmead, Luton LU2 7SF

t 01582 486983
w luton.gov.uk
e russells@luton.gov.uk

298 Luton

Stockwood Craft Museum & Gardens

1 hr+   Apr-Oct

This award-winning museum covers nine centuries of garden history and rural life. Its collection of vehicles, on which visitors can ride, illustrates the development of horse-drawn road transport in Britain from Roman times to the 1930s. Events and activities run all year.

* Conservatory tea room set in C18 walled garden
* Largest display of horse-drawn carriages in the UK

Location
2 miles S of town centre, close to junction 10 of M1

Opening
Daily: Apr-Oct 10am-5pm

Admission
Free, donations welcomed

Contact
Farley Hill, Luton LU1 4BH

t 01582 738714
w lutononline.gov.uk
e museum.gallery@luton.gov.uk

299 Milton Keynes

HULA Animal Rescue: South Midlands Animal Sanctuary

1 hr+   All year

HULA Animal Rescue is the headquarters of the charity founded in 1972 and it houses rescued and abandoned animals. Ponies, donkeys, cattle, chickens, ducks, sheep and pigs are residents; and dogs, cats, rabbits, small rodents and birds await adoption into new homes.

* Café & shop open on monthly open days
* Animal houses

Location
From village square in Aspley Guise turn into Church Road, then into Salford Road & entrance to Glebe Farm is on the right

Opening
Fri, Sat-Sun 1pm-3pm
Please phone for details of monthly open days & Bank Hols opening

Admission
Adult £1, Child 50p

Contact
Glebe Farm, Salford Road, Aspley Guise, Milton Keynes MK17 8HZ

t 01908 584000
w hularescue.org
e hularescue@yahoo.co.uk

300 Milton Keynes

Woburn Safari Park

6 hrs   All year

This famous safari drive-through also has an extensive leisure park. You can see rhino, eland, oryx, antelope, giraffe, zebra, elephants, tigers, wolves, bears, monkeys and hippos. It's the only reserve with two species of carnivore, where wolves and bears roam together.

* Animal contact areas, boats & railway train
* Children's indoor & outdoor playgrounds

Location
5 mins off M1 junction 13. Follow signs

Opening
Daily: Mar-Oct 10am-5pm;
Nov-Feb weekends 11am-3pm

Admission
Please phone for details

Contact
Woburn MK17 9QN

t 01525 290407
w discoverwoburn.co.uk
e info@woburnsafari.co.uk

301 Duxford

Imperial War Museum Duxford

3 hrs+   All year

With its air shows, unique history and atmosphere, nowhere else combines the sights, sounds and power of aircraft quite like Duxford. It is home to 200 historic aircaft including biplanes, Spitfires, Concorde and Gulf War jets – many of which still fly regularly.

* D-Day Experience complete with video story
* Flying displays held throughout the summer

Location	Contact
Off junction 10 of M11	Duxford CB2 4QR
Opening	t 01223 835000
Daily: mid-Mar–mid-Oct 10am–6pm;	w iwm.org.uk/duxford
winter 10am–4pm	e duxford@iwm.org.uk
Admission	
Adult £12, Child free, Concs £9	

302 Ely

Oliver Cromwell's House

1 hr+   All year

Home to Ely's most famous former resident, Cromwell's carefully restored house now contains Civil War exhibitions including weapons and armour. It also has illustrations of everyday C17 life and a history of the Fenlands and its transformation from marsh to farmland.

* C15 inglenook fireplace restored to working order
* Kitchen area has display of C17 recipes & ingredients

Location	Contact
Ely town centre next to St Mary's Church	29 St Mary's Street, Ely CB7 4HF
Opening	t 01353 662062
Apr–Oct daily 10am–5.30pm;	w ely.org.uk/tic.htm
Nov–Mar Mon–Fri 11am–4pm;	e tic@ely.org.uk
Sat 10am–5pm, Sun 11.15am–4pm	
Admission	
Adult £3.85, Child £2.60, Concs £3.35	

303 Huntingdon

Houghton Mill

1 hrs   Apr–Oct

Discover how flour is made at this working watermill on an island in the Great Ouse. Have a go at turning the millstone and pull on a rope to lift the bags of flour. There has been a mill on this site since AD 974. The flour is for sale and there are family and children's guides.

* National Trust property
* Hands-on activities & children's quiz & trail

Location
In village of Houghton, signed from A1123 Huntingdon–St Ives road

Opening
Apr & Oct Sat–Sun 1pm–5pm;
May–Sep Sat–Wed 1pm–5pm;
open to groups at other times by arrangement

Admission
Adult £3.20, Child £1.50, Family £7

Contact
Houghton, nr Huntingdon PE17 2AZ

t 01480 301494
w nationaltrust.org.uk
e sally.newton@nationaltrust.org.uk

304 Peterborough

Flag Fen Bronze Age Centre

4 hrs   All year

Travel back in time to the Bronze Age and see how people lived more than 3,000 years ago. The museum displays artefacts including swords, daggers, axes, jewellery and the earliest wheel ever discovered in England.

* Featured on Channel 4's programme *Time Team*
* Set within a 20-acre park

Location
NE of Peterborough, off A1139 or A605

Opening
Daily: 10am–5pm

Admission
Adult £4.25, Child £3.75, Family £11.50

Contact
The Droveway, Northey Road, Peterborough PE6 7QJ

t 01733 313414
w flagfen.com
e office@flagfen.freeserve.co.uk

305 Peterborough

Nene Valley Railway

3 hrs+   All year

Home to a real Thomas the Tank Engine, Nene Valley Railway provides an exciting day out for train enthusiasts both young and old. Travel on a 15-mile round trip through the beautiful Nene Park and enjoy one of Britain's leading collections of engines and carriages, both steam and diesel.

* Train galas in March, June & September
* Talking Timetable 01780 784404

Location
Off southbound A1 at Stibbington between A47 & A605 junctions

Opening
Daily: 9am–4.30pm

Admission
Adult £10, Child £5, Concs £7.50

Contact
Wansford Station, Stibbington, Peterborough PE8 6LR

t 01780 784444
w nvr.org.uk
e nvrorg@aol.com

306 Royston

Shepreth Wildlife Park

2–4 hrs   All year

Shepreth offers a fun and interactive day out for the family. It's home to animals including tigers, meerkats, wolves, deer and farmyard livestock. Children can visit Bug City and Waterworld, where they'll come face to face with scorpions, giant spiders and a dwarf alligator.

* Pirate ship adventure area
* Play area & sandpit for toddlers & children's playroom

Location
Easily reached from A10
Cambridge–Royston road & A1198 Royston–Huntingdon road. Good access by train from London King's Cross to Shepreth station

Opening
Daily: Apr–Sep 10am–6pm;
Oct–Mar 10am–dusk

Admission
Adult £6.50, Child £4.95, Concs £5
Bug City/Waterworld £1.75, £1.10, £1.45

Contact
Willersmill, Station Road, Shepreth, nr Royston SG8 6PZ

t 09066 800031 (info line – 25p/min)
01763 262226 (group bookings)
w sheprethwildlifepark.co.uk

307 Royston

Wimpole Home Farm

2–4 hrs   All year

Built in 1794, Wimpole is a working farm and home to a number of rare farmyard breeds. Children can feed and handle many of the animals, and enjoy the adventure playground with pedal tractors.

* National Trust property

Location
6 miles N of Royston,
8 miles SW of Cambridge

Opening
Sat–Wed 10.30am–5pm (11am–4pm in winter); open Bank hols & extra days in school hols, please phone for details

Admission
Adult £5.40, Child £3.40, Family £26
Discounts for NT members

Contact
Arrington, Royston SG8 0BW
t 01223 206000
e david.watson@nationaltrust.org.uk

308 Sawtry

Hamerton Zoo Park

2 hrs+   All year

Do you know what a curassow, a seriema or a binturong is? Find out by visiting the zoo's fascinating array of beautiful creatures from around the world. There are special enclosures with low windows to give children thrilling views of the most popular animals.

* Spacious indoor-outdoor enclosures for monkeys
* Opportunity to handle many different animals

Location
On A14 turn off to B660 at junction 15 on to A1M. Follow signs

Opening
Daily: 10.30am–6pm (4pm in winter)

Admission
Please phone for details

Contact
Hamerton, nr Sawtry PE28 5RE
t 01832 293362
w hamertonzoopark.com
e office@hamertonzoopark.com

309 Waterbeach

Denny Abbey & The Farmland Museum

1 hr+   Apr–Oct

Learn about local rural life at the Farmland Museum with hands-on displays and interactive exhibits. Visit a traditional farmer's cottage and discover the story of the Benedictine monks, Knights Templar and Franciscan nuns who lived in Denny Abbey.

* Farmland Museum Trust

Location
6 miles N of Cambridge on A10

Opening
Daily: Apr–Oct 12noon–5pm

Admission
Adult £3.80, Child £1.60, Concs £3, Family £9.60

Contact
Ely Road,
Waterbeach CB5 9PQ
t 01223 860489
w dennyfarmlandmuseum.org.uk

310 Wisbech

Fenland & West Norfolk Aviation Museum

1 hr+   Mar–Oct

See a range of aircraft and artefacts, including the cockpit from one of the MiG-29s that collided at RAF Fairford in 1995, a Boeing 747 simulator, uniforms and militaria, and weapons and armour. On a fine day, explore the cockpits of some of the aircraft on display.

* Aircraft park
* Café & souvenir shop

Location
Follow brown tourist signs from A47 Wisbech bypass; or take old B198 to King's Lynn from Wisbech and museum is ½ mile from bypass

Opening
Mar–Oct weekends & Bank Hols 9.30am–5pm (4pm in Mar & Oct)

Admission
Adult £1.50, Child & Concs 75p

Contact
Old Lynn Road, West Walton, Wisbech PE14 7DA

t 01945 461771
w fawnaps.co.uk
e bill@wwelbourne.freeserve.co.uk

---

311 Woodhurst

The Raptor Foundation

2 hrs+   All year

Home to more than 300 birds of prey and more than 43 species, the Raptor Foundation is a unique and exciting place for children and adults alike. Pay a visit to meet and learn about owls, falcons, hawks and buzzards.

* Quality Assured Visitor Centre
* Junior Raptors Club

Location
Off A14 St Ives exit. Turn on to B1040 to Somersham & follow brown tourist signs

Opening
Daily 10am–5pm

Admission
Adult £3.75, Child £2.25, Concs £2.75

Contact
The Heath, St Ives Road, Woodhurst PE28 3BT

t 01487 741140
w raptorfoundation.org.uk
e heleowl@aol.com

---

312 Billericay

Barleylands Craft Village & Farm Centre

2 hrs   All year

A unique attraction with probably the largest collection of working crafts in East Anglia and an impressive farm museum. Children can meet and feed the friendly pigs, cows, goats and sheep in the animal centre. There is also an adventure play area.

* Indoor sand pit & trampolines

Location
Follow brown tourist signs from A127 or A129

Opening
Craft Village All year
Farm Centre Mar–Oct
Tue–Sun 10am–5pm

Admission
Craft Village Free
Farm Centre £3

Contact
Barleylands Road, Billericay CM11 2UD

t 01268 290229
w barleylands.co.uk
e info@barleylands.co.uk

313 Billericay

Hanningfield Reservoir Visitor Centre

2–3 hrs   All year

The visitor centre is the gateway to the 100-acre nature reserve on the shores of Hanningfield Reservoir. Discover a Site of Special Scientific Interest for its breeding of over-wintering birds.

* Events throughout the year
* Children's activities throughout the year

Location	Admission
Turn off B1007 on to Downham Road & turn left on to Hawkswood Road. Centre is just beyond causeway, opposite Crowsheath	Free, donations requested
	Contact
	Hawkswood Road, Downham, Billericay CM11 1WT
Opening	t 01268 711001
Please phone for details	w essexwt.org.uk
	e hanningfield@essexwt.org.uk

314 Braintree

The Original Great Maze

3 hrs+   Jul–Sep

The Great Maze offers more than 5 miles of pathway cut from 10 acres of maize and sunflowers, which reach a height of almost 10 feet. A new maze is designed every year, so enthusiasts can return time and time again to try to beat the latest creation.

* Viewing platform & Lost Souls map available
* Shopping at Blake House Craft Centre

Location	Contact
On B1256 between Great Dunmow & Braintree	Blake House Craft Centre, Blake End Braintree CM77 6RA
Opening	t 01376 553146
Please phone for details	w maze.info
Admission	e davidf@rochesterfm.freeserve.co.uk
Please phone for details	

315 Brentwood

Old MacDonald's Educational Farm Park

3 hrs+   All year

This educational farm park was created to offer a greater understanding of British farm livestock, wildlife and the countryside. There are 17 acres of pasture and woodland, with hard paths to ensure dry feet and wheelchair access and opportunities to get close to the animals.

* Playground
* Otters, red squirrels & owls

Location
Off M25 at junction 28 on to A1023. Left at 1st lights into Wigley Bush Lane, left at junction with Weald Road, 2 miles on Weald Road. Farm is on the left

Opening
Daily: summer 10am–please phone for details of closing times; winter 10am–dusk

Admission
Adult £4.25, Child £3, Concs £3.75

Contact
Weald Road, South Weald, Brentwood CM14 5AY

t 01277 375177/375393
w oldmacdonaldsfarm.org.uk
e info@oldmacdonaldsfarm.org.uk

316 Chelmsford

Chelmsford Museum & Essex Regiment Museum

1 hr+   All year

Chelmsford museum houses three exhibitions showing the story of Chelmsford from the Ice Ages, via the Roman town, to the present day. See the superb Essex Regiment Museum housing many military artefacts as well.

* Bright & colourful Victorian pottery from Hedingham
* Regiment museum houses many military artefacts

Location
In Oaklands Park, off Moulsham Street

Opening
Daily: Mon–Sat 10am–5pm,
Sun 2pm–5pm (winter 1pm–4pm)

Admission
Free, donations welcomed

Contact
Oaklands Park,
Chelmsford CM2 9AQ

t 01245 615100
w chelmsfordmuseums.co.uk
e oaklands@chelmsfordbc.gov.uk

317 Colchester

Colchester Zoo

6 hrs   All year

Colchester Zoo has some of the best cat and primate collections in Europe. See a white tiger eye to eye in White Tiger Valley, or get closer to the zoo's chimpanzees at Chimp World. Other enclosures include Penguin Shores and Lions Rock for African lions.

* Children's jungle safari train
*Kalahari Capers soft play area & rope bridge

Location
Take A1124 exit from A12

Opening
Daily: summer 9.30am–5.30pm;
winter 9.30am–1 hr before dusk

Admission
Please phone for details or visit the website

Contact
Maldon Road, Stanway, Colchester CO3 0SL

t 01206 331292
w colchester-zoo.co.uk
e enquiries@colchester-zoo.co.uk

318 Colchester

High Woods Country Park

2 hrs+   All year

This country park boasts areas of woodland, wetland, grassland and farmland. Numerous footpaths provide an opportunity to see a wide range of wildlife. A visitor centre houses exhibits of local history and natural history.

* Quality Assured Visitor Attraction

Location
Accessible from Mile End Road & Ipswich Road, travelling N from Colchester

Opening
Daily: *Visitor centre* Apr-Sep Mon-Sat 10am-4.30pm, Sun & Bank Hols 11am-5.30pm; Oct-Mar Sat-Sun only 10am-4pm

Admission
Free

Contact
Turner Road
Colchester CO4 5JR

t 01206 853588
w colchester.gov.uk
e yvonne.cook@colchester.gov.uk

319 Colchester

Quasar at Rollerworld

1 hr+   All year

In this futuristic laser game each player is armed with a laser gun and shoots the opposition to win points. Players have unlimited lives and the Game Marshal instructs you on how to play. Under-12s must be accompanied by a playing adult.

* Suitable for ages 8-80
* Supervised by Game Marshal

Location
From A12 take turn off to Harwich & Colchester. Continue straight over roundabouts & follow brown tourist signs

Opening
Please phone for details

Admission
Please phone for details

Contact
Eastgates,
Colchester CO1 2TJ

t 01206 868868
w rollerworld.co.uk

320 Halstead

Hedingham Castle

½ hr+   Apr-Oct

Built in 1140 by the Earls of Oxford, this is one of the best-preserved Norman keeps in England. The castle is set in beautiful parkland and holds special events such as jousts throughout the summer.

* Jousting tournaments

Location
In Castle Hedingham, ½ mile from A1017 between Cambridge & Colchester

Opening
Apr-Oct Thu, Fri & Sun 11am-4pm
Special school hols opening 10am-5pm, please phone for details

Admission
Adult £4.50, Child £3.80, Concs £4, Family £16-£32

Contact
Halstead CO9 3DJ

t 01787 460261
w hedinghamcastle.co.uk
e hedinghamcastle@aspects.net.co.uk

321 Saffron Walden

Mole Hall Wildlife Park

2 hrs   Easter–Oct

The park is in gardens adjoining a fully moated manor (not open to the public) and has otters, chimps, guanaco, lemurs, wallabies, deer and owls. Refreshments are available in the café.

* Butterfly pavilion & pets' corner
* Animal adoption scheme & play areas

Location
Signed from B1383 & junction 8 of M11

Opening
Daily: Easter–Oct 10.30am–6pm

Admission
Adult £5.80, Child £4, Family £18

Contact
Widdington, nr Saffron Walden CB11 3SS

t 01799 540400
w molehall.co.uk
e enquiries@molehall.co.uk

322 Waltham Abbey

Royal Gunpowder Mills

3 hrs+   Apr–Sep

The world of explosives is uncovered with a range of interactive and static displays that follow the trail back to the C17. This unique museum traces the evolution of gunpowder technology and reveals the impact it had on the history of Great Britain.

* Muskets, rifles, pistols & machine guns
* Tours by tractor-trailer train

   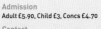

Location
1 mile from junction 26 of M25, take A121 towards Waltham Cross then go straight ahead at traffic lights

Opening
Apr–Sep Sat, Sun & Bank Hols only 11am–5pm (last admission 3.30pm)

Admission
Adult £5.90, Child £3, Concs £4.70

Contact
Beaulieu Drive, Waltham Abbey EN9 1JY

t 01992 707370
w royalgunpowdermills.com
e info@royalgunpowdermills.com

323 Berkhamsted

Ashridge Estate

1 hr+   All year

There's plenty to see and do at Ashridge, no matter what season it is. Enjoy the spring bluebells, a picnic on a sunny day, or a woodland walk in autumn. Make sure you keep your eyes peeled as Ashridge is a wildlife haven – if you are lucky you might spot a badger or a woodpecker.

* Splendid views from Ivinghoe Beacon
* Visitor centre with exhibition room

Location
Between Northchurch & Ringshall just off B4506

Opening
All year Visitor centre Apr–mid-Dec 12noon–5pm

Admission
Estate Free
Monument Adult £1.30, Child 60p

Contact
Ringshall, Berkhamsted HP4 1LT
t 01442 851227
w berkhamsted.info.co.uk
e ashridge@nationaltrust.org.uk

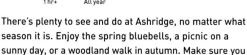

324 Broxbourne

Paradise Wildlife Park

2 hrs+   All year

A friendly, family-run leisure park that offers excitement and enjoyment for all the family. Visitors can touch and feed paddock animals, including zebra and camels, shadow a keeper, and meet wolves and meerkats. There are also play areas and a fun-fair.

* Paradise Lagoon, the brand new paddling pool
* Parrot Olympic training

Location
Junction 25 of M25 on to A10, signed from Broxbourne

Opening
Daily: Mar–Oct 9.30am–6pm; Nov–Feb 10am–5pm

Admission
Adult £10, Child & Concs £7

Contact
White Stubbs Lane, Broxbourne EN10 7QA
t 01992 470490
w pwpark.com
e info@pwpark.com

325 Borehamwood

Aldenham Country Park

7 hrs+   All year

With a 65-acre reservoir, circular footpath and 175 acres of woods and meadowland, Aldenham Country Park has a range of activities and interests for the whole family, from nature trails to Winnie the Pooh features. There are also rare breeds including cattle and sheep.

* Adventure playground
* Angling (day-tickets £4)

Location
Drive via A5, A41, A1(M) or MI (junction 5) & park is just off A5183, N of Elstree on Aldenham road

Opening
Daily: Nov–Feb 9am–4pm; Mar–Apr & Sep–Oct 9am–5pm; May–Aug 9am–6pm

Admission
Free. Car park £4 on exit

Contact
Park Office, Dagger Lane, Elstree, Borehamwood WD6 3AT
t 0208 953 9602
w hertsdirect.org/aldenham

326 Hatfield

Mill Green Museum & Mill

1 hr+   All year

A visit to this fully restored C18 working watermill, which is still producing flour, is interesting and educational. The adjacent miller's house is now the local history museum for the district. There are events throughout the year for all to enjoy.

* Waterwheel in action every day
* Watch milling of organic flour on Tue, Wed & Sun

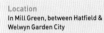

Location
In Mill Green, between Hatfield & Welwyn Garden City

Opening
Tue–Fri 10am–5pm,
Sat, Sun & Bank Hols 2pm–5pm

Admission
Free

Contact
Mill Green, Hatfield AL9 5PD

t 01707 271362
w hertsmuseums.org.uk/millgreen
e museum@welhat.gov.uk

---

327 Hertford

Hertford Museum

1–2 hrs   All year

A local history museum in an old town house with a recreated Jacobean knot garden. There are changing temporary exhibitions to cater for all ages, with related activities for children.

* Special events in school holidays, bookable in advance
* Tea served on Sat

Location
Just off A414 in the centre of Hertford, a short walk from multi-storey car park & within walking distance of train station

Opening
Tue–Sat 10am–5pm
Please phone for details of Bank Hols opening

Admission
Free

Contact
18 Bull Plain, Hertford SG14 1DT

t 01992 582686
w hertfordmuseum.org
e info@hertfordmuseum.org

---

328 Hitchin

Waterhall Farm & Craft Centre

2hrs+   All year

A small open farm featuring rare breeds and offering a hands-on experience for visitors. There is also a play area featuring a straw-bale battlefield, a sandpit, a slide and an old tractor.

* Country walks, garden & tea room
* Dogs permitted only in car park

Location
Off B651 Hitchin–St Albans road, in village of Whitwell

Opening
Weekends & school hols;
summer 10am–5pm;
winter 10am–4pm

Admission
Adult £2.75, Child (2–16) & Concs £1.75

Contact
Whitwell
Hitchin SG4 8BN

t 01438 871256

329 Royston

Maple Street British Museum of Miniatures

2 hrs   All year

The Museum of Miniatures is a doll's house and miniatures museum. Its displays include the largest doll's house in the world, and the on site shop is the largest doll's house shop in Europe.

Location
Take A603 from Cambridge & A1198 to Royston

Opening
Daily: Mon–Sat 9.30am–5pm, Sun 12noon–4pm
Please phone for detail of Bank Hols opening times

Admission
Adult £2.50, Child £1.50

Contact
Maple Street, Wendy, Royston SG8 0AB
t 01223 207025
w maplestreet.co.uk
e info@maplestreet.co.uk

330 St Albans

Verulamium Museum

1–2 hrs   All year

Verulamium Museum is a museum of everyday life in Roman Britain. The award-winning displays include recreated Roman interiors; collections of glass, pottery, jewellery; coins and magnificent mosaics, wall-paintings and reconstructions of Roman rooms.

* Quality Assured Visitor Attraction
* Hands-on discovery areas & playground

Location
Drive via M1 junction 6 or M25 junction 21A. Museum is just off A4147, 1 mile from centre of St Albans

Opening
Daily: Mon–Sat 10am–5.30pm, Sun 2pm–5.30pm

Admission
Adult £3.30, Child & Concs £2

Contact
St Michaels, St Albans AL3 4SW
t 01727 751810
w stalbansmuseums.org.uk
e museum@stalbans.gov.uk

331 St Albans

Willows Farm Village

3 hrs+   Apr–Oct

Children enjoy this farm village where they can get to know the farm animals in a countryside setting. Attractions include a bouncy haystack, Daft Duck trails, a guinea pig village, a children's theatre and a tractor trek.

* Falconry display
* Maze (summer holidays only)

Location
300 metres from junction 22 of M25

Opening
Daily: Apr–Oct 10am–5.30pm

Admission
Please phone for details

Contact
Coursers Road, London Colney,
St Albans AL2 1BB

t 01727 822444
w willowsfarmvillage.com
e info@willowsfarmvillage.com

---

332 Stevenage

Fairlands Valley Park

4 hrs+   All year

This beautiful 120-acre park contains an 11-acre lake used for a range of watersport courses; its waters are kept well stocked for anglers. There is a kids' area with paddling pool and play equipment. The park is also home to a wide selection of wildlife and wildfowl.

* Children's play area
* Paddling pools open during summer

Location
On Six Hills Way, 1 mile E of Stevenage

Opening
Daily: 8am–dusk

Admission
Free

Contact
Six Hills Way, Stevenage SG2 0BL

t 01438 353241
w stevenage-leisure.co.uk/fairlands
e fairlands@stevenage-leisure.co.uk

---

333 Watford

Activity World & Farmyard Fun

3 hrs+   All year

This indoor and outdoor adventure playground has a separate area for toddlers and a baby play pool. Farmyard Fun allows close-up contact with a range of animals, from rabbits and sheep to cows and ponies.

Location
5 mins from M1 junction 5 & 10 mins from M25 junction 19 on Aldenham road

Opening
Daily *Activity World* 10am–6pm
Farmyard Fun 10am–5pm (or dusk if earlier)

Admission
Adult Free, Child (2–5) £3.50,
Child (over 5) £4.50

Contact
Lincolnsfield Centre, Bushey Hall,
Drive, Bushey, Watford WD23 2ES

t 01923 219902
w lincolnsfields.co.uk
e activityworld@lincolnsfield.co.uk

334 Aylsham

Bure Valley Railway

2 hrs+   All year

Bure Valley Railway is one of England's premier narrow gauge railways serving enthusiasts, travellers and tourists. Its steam and diesel trains pass through scenery which is as varied, interesting and beautiful as any to be found on a railway journey in England.

* The two main stations at Aylsham & Wroxham
* Easy to combine with cruise on Norfolk Broads

Location	Admission
Aylsham Station is situated mid-way between Norwich and Cromer on the A140	Please phone for details
Opening	**Contact**
Mar–Sep 10am–5.30pm Plus school holidays Please phone for details for other opening times	Norwich Road, Aylsham Norfolk NR11 6BW
	t 01263 733858
	w bvrw.co.uk
	e info@bvrw.co.uk

335 Banham

Banham Zoo

3–5 hrs   All year

Set in 35 acres of countryside and landscaped gardens, Banham Zoo is home to some of the world's most exotic and endangered animals, ranging from big cats to birds of prey, and siamangs to Shire horses.

* Free safari roadtrain
* All-weather activity centre

Location	Admission
Between Attleborough & Diss; signed from A11 & A140	Vary according to season Please phone for details
Opening	**Contact**
Daily: 10am (seasonal closing times, please phone for details)	The Grove, Banham NR16 2HE
	t 01953 887771
	w banhamzoo.co.uk

336 Blakeney

Blakeney Point

3 hrs   All year

One of Britain's foremost bird sanctuaries, the Point is noted for its colonies of breeding terns and for the rare migrants that pass through in spring and autumn. Common and grey seals can also be seen. Dogs are allowed April–August.

* Information centre at Morston Quay provides further details
* Restricted access during main bird breeding season

Location	Contact
Morston Quay, Blakeney and Cley are all off A149 Cromer to Hunstanton road	The Warden, 35 The Cornfield, Langham, Holt NR25 7DQ
Opening	t 01263 740480 (Apr–Sep)
Daily: all times	01263 740241 (Oct–Mar)
Admission	w nationaltrust.org.uk
Free	e blakeneypoint@nationaltrust.org.uk

337 Brandon

Grimes Graves

1 hr   All year

At Grimes Graves there is a site exhibition with remarkable Neolithic flint mines. The mines are 4,000 years old and were first excavated in the 1870s, with over 433 pits and shafts. One pit is open to the public.

* No children under five allowed down shaft as 30ft drop
* Site of Special Scientific Interest

Location	Contact
Located 7 miles NW of Thetford off A134	Brandon, Lynford IP26 5DE
Opening	t 01842 810656
Please contact for details	w english–heritage.org.uk
Admission	
Adult £2.60, Child £1.30, Concs £2, Family £6.50	

338 Cromer

Norfolk Shire Horse Centre

2 hrs+   Apr–Oct

See magnificent heavy shire horses working on the land just as they did in days gone by. Take time to look around the rural museum and video show, see the small farm animals and the mares with their foals and join in with feeding times.

* Children's farm & riding school
* Special events include blacksmith demonstrations

Location
Off A148 & A149

Opening
Apr–Oct Sun–Fri 10am–5pm;
closed Sat except Bank Hols

Admission
Adult £6, Child £4, Concs £5

Contact
West Runton Stables, West Runton,
nr Cromer NR27 9QH

t 01263 837339
w norfolk-shirehorse-centre.co.uk
e bakewell@norfolkshirehorse.
fsnet.co.uk

339 Dereham

Roots of Norfolk

4 hrs+   Mar–Oct

This is a remarkable museum housed in a former workhouse and in an idyllic rural setting. It has displays on village and rural life plus a farm worked with horses and stocked with rare breeds.

* Riverside trails
* Children's activities

Location
3 miles W of Dereham. Follow signs

Opening
Daily: Mar–Oct 10am–5pm

Admission
Adult £6.60, Child £4.40, Concs £5.50

Contact
Gressenhall, Dereham NR20 4DR

t 01362 860563
w norfolk.gov.uk/museums
e gressenhall.museum@norfolk.
gov.uk

340 Diss

Bressingham Steam Experience & Gardens

4 hrs   Easter–Oct

A working steam experience in a nationally known garden setting with narrow-gauge railway rides, a Victorian steam roundabout, locomotive sheds, stationary engine displays, a royal coach, traction engines and gardens. There are miniature steam-hauled trains.

* Dad's Army National Collection
* Friends of Thomas the Tank Engine

Location
3 miles W of Diss on A1066
Diss–Thetford road

Opening
Daily: Easter–Oct 10.30am– 5.30pm
Please phone for details

Admission
Please phone for details

Contact
Bressingham, Diss IP22 2AB

t 01379 686900
w bressingham.co.uk
e info@bressingham.co.uk

341 Fakenham

South Creake Maize Maze

2 hrs+   Jul–Sep

Looking for excitement and adventure? Then take the challenge of a 7-acre maze in a maize field. Set in 18 acres of unspoilt Norfolk countryside, this is a chance to lose yourself in nature.

* Crazy golf
* Panning for gold

Location
Between Fakenham & Burnham Market on B1355, just off A148 King's Lynn– Fakenham road

Opening
Daily: 9 Jul–14 Sep 10am–6pm (last admission 5pm)

Admission
Adult £4, Child £3, Concs £3

Contact
Compton Hall, South Creake, Fakenham NR21 9JD

t 01328 823224
w amazingmaizemaze.co.uk
e info@amazingmaizemaze.co.uk

342 Great Yarmouth

Great Yarmouth Sealife Centre

3 hrs   All year

Experience the spectacular eye-to-eye views of everything from shrimps and starfish to sharks and stingrays. The City of Atlantis has an underwater tunnel allowing visitors to walk on the seabed and encounter sharks and multi coloured fish. Look for Medusa's head!

* Soft play area
* Lair of the Octopus exhibition

Location
Take A47 from Norwich, A143 from Beccles or A12 from Lowestoft

Opening
Daily: from 10am

Admission
Please phone for details

Contact
Marine Parade, Great Yarmouth NR30 3AH

t 01493 330631
w sealife.co.uk

343 Great Yarmouth

Horsey Mere

2 hrs   Mar–Oct

This area of 1,900 acres on the edge of the Norfolk Broads is ideal for a few hours' walking. It has dunes, farmland and reedbeds and is teeming with wildlife. Nearby is the 90-year-old Horsey Windpump windmill, which still has sails and is open to visitors.

* National Trust property

Location	Contact
Off B1159, 15 miles N of Great Yarmouth, between Martham & Sea Palling	Horsey, Great Yarmouth NR29 4EF
	t 01493 393904
Opening	w nationaltrust.org.uk
Mar Sat–Sun 10am–4.30pm; Apr–Oct Wed–Sun & Bank Hols	e horseywindpump@nationaltrust.org.uk
Admission	
Please phone for details	

344 Great Yarmouth

Pleasure Beach, Great Yarmouth

2 hrs+   Mar–Oct

The Pleasure Beach is situated on the seafront at the southern end of Great Yarmouth's Golden Mile and covers 9 acres. As well as a main ride area with more than 70 rides and the awe-inspiring Ejector Seat, there are two crazy golf courses and gardens.

* 70 rides & attractions
* Firework displays on Sat nights

Location	Contact
Take A12 from Lowestoft or A47 from Norwich	Great Yarmouth NR30 3EH
	t 01493 844585
Opening	w pleasure-beach.co.uk
Please phone for details	e GYPBeach@aol.com
Admission	
Free. Rides paid for at reception or machines	

345 Great Yarmouth

Thrigby Hall Wildlife Gardens

3 hrs+   All year

Meet a wide selection of Asian mammals, birds and reptiles, including tigers, crocodiles and storks. There are superb willow-pattern gardens and a play area. There is also a dramatic swamp house for crocodiles and other tropical swamp dwellers.

* Lime Tree Lookout
* Tiger Tree Walk

Location	Contact
Off A1064 Caister–Acle road	Filby, Great Yarmouth NR29 3DR
Opening	t 01493 369477
Daily: 10am–5pm	w thrigbyhall.co.uk
Admission	
Adult £7.50, Child (4–14) £5.50, Concs £6.50	

346 Holt

Baconsthorpe Castle

1 hr+   All year

Baconsthorpe Castle is a C15 part-moated, semi-fortified house. The remains include the inner and outer gatehouse and curtain wall. The local post office sells guide books and postcards.

* English Heritage property

Location
Off A148 & B1149, ¾ mile N of village of Baconsthorpe, off an unclassified road. 3 miles E of Holt

Opening
Daily: All reasonable times

Admission
Free

Contact
Baconsthorpe, Holt

t 01604 730325
w english-heritage.org.uk

347 Holt

Bishop's Boats Seal Trips

1 hr+   Apr–Oct

Take a boat trip to see the seals and birds on Blakeney Point. There are many species of birds to spot, and both grey and common seals form a colony of approximately 500.

* Optional landing trips
* Warm or waterproof clothing recommended

Location
Trips depart from Blakeney Point reached by A149

Opening
Please phone for details as times vary depending on the tides

Admission
Adult £7, Child £4

Contact
Blakeney Point, Blakeney, Holt

t 0800 0740754/01263 740753
w bishopsboats.co.uk
e bishopsboats@bigfoot.com

348 Holt

Langham Glass

3 hrs+   All year

Langham Glass is based in a large Norfolk barn complex that is pantiled and flint-faced. Teams of glass makers can be seen working with molten glass using blowing irons and hand tools In a way that has been traditional for hundreds of years. There is also a huge 7-acre maze.

* Quality Assured Visitor Attraction
* Museum & video, plus play area

 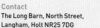

Location
Follow A148 from Holt to Fakenham for 3 miles, turn right on to B1156 & follow brown tourist signs to Langham

Opening
Daily: 10am–5pm

Admission
Glassmaking Adult £3.95, Child & Concs £2.95

Contact
The Long Barn, North Street, Langham, Holt NR25 7DG

t 01328 830511
w langhamglass.co.uk
e enquiries@langhamglass.co.uk

349 Hunstanton

Hunstanton Sea Life Centre

1 hr+   All year

At this sanctuary you will see otters, penguins and more than 30 permanent displays all showcasing the diversity of life under the waves. The centre also provides a safe haven for sick, injured or orphaned seal pups that are cared for at the sanctuary.

* Penguin sanctuary, home to rare Humboldt penguins
* New in 2005 Marine Hospital

Location
Take A140 from King's Lynn to Hunstanton. Follow signs

Opening
Daily: 10am–4pm
Times may vary during winter, please phone for details

Admission
Adult £7.75, Child £4.95, Concs £5.50

Contact
Southern Promenade, Hunstanton PE36 5BH

t 01485 533576
w sealsanctuary.co.uk
e hunstantonsealifecentre
   @merlinentertainments.biz

350 Hoveton

Wroxham Barns

2–3 hrs   All year

Wroxham Barns will keep all the family happy. Watch traditional and contemporary craftworkers at work, indulge in a spot of shopping, feed the friendly animals and have fun at the fair.

* Quality Assured Visitor Attraction
* Traditional farm, junior farm & country food shop

Location
Approximately 10 miles from Norwich.
Follow A1151 towards Wroxham then follow brown tourist signs

Opening
Daily: 10am–5pm

Admission
Admission & car park **Free**
Junior Farm **£2.75**

Contact
Tunstead Road, Hoveton NR12 8QU

t 01603 783762
w wroxham-barns.co.uk
e info@wroxham-barns.co.uk

351 King's Lynn

Caithness Crystal Visitor Centre

2 hrs+   All year

Glassmaking is a magical craft that can transform sand into exquisite glassware using only the heat of a furnace and the skill of hand and eye. Witness it for yourself at the visitor centre in King's Lynn and marvel at a demonstration of the artistry involved.

* Quality Assured Visitor Attraction

Location
Located off A149, A47 & A10.
Follow brown tourist signs

Opening
Daily: Mon–Sat 9am–5pm, Sun 10.15am–4.15pm; closed 31 Mar
Please phone for details of glassmaking demonstration times

Admission
Free

Contact
Paxman Road, Hardwick Industrial Estate, King's Lynn PE30 4NE

t 01553 765111
w caithnessglass.co.uk
e mdennis@caithnessglass.co.uk

352 Norwich

Bank Boats

4 hrs+   All year

Hire all-weather dayboats and take a trip on the beautiful River Ant. Drift lazily past windmills and enjoy a leisurely picnic on the riverbank. Canoes are also available for hire.

* Electric dayboats

Location
On slip road off A149 between Stalham & Wroxham

Opening
Daily: 9am–5pm

Admission
From £25 for 2 hrs

Contact
Staithe Cottage, Wayford Bridge, Stalham, Norwich NR12 9LN

t 01692 582457

353 Norwich

Barton House Railway

2 hrs   Apr–Oct

Barton House has a miniature steam passenger railway and a steam and battery-electric railway. There are full-size Midland and Great Northern accessories, including signals and signal boxes. Guaranteed fun for railway enthusiasts of all ages.

Location
On A1151 from Norwich

Opening
Apr–Oct 3rd Sun each month
2.30pm–5.30pm please phone for details

Admission
Adult £1.50, Child 75p
By boat from Wroxham Bridge:
Adult £2 , Child £1

Contact
Hartwell Road, The Avenue,
Wroxham, Norwich NR12 8TL

t 01603 782470

354 Norwich

Dinosaur Adventure Park

4 hrs+   Apr–Oct

Come face to face with life-size dinosaurs on the ultimate family adventure. The park includes a secret animal garden, adventure play areas, Climb-a-saurus, the Lost World Amazing Adventure and Jurassic Putt.

* New Adventurer's Guide
* Country Capers & Raptor Races

Location
9 miles from Norwich. Follow brown tourist signs from A47 or A1067 to Weston Park

Opening
Please phone or visit the website for details

Admission
Adult £7.25, Child & Concs £6.50

Contact
Weston Park, Lenwade,
Norwich NR9 5JW

t 01603 876310
w dinosaurpark.co.uk
e info@dinosaurpark.co.uk

355 Norwich

Fairhaven Woodland & Water Garden

2–4 hrs   All year

These delightful woodland and water-gardens have a fantastic combination of plants and flowers, together with a wildlife sanctuary for bird-watchers and picturesque waterways spanned by small bridges. There are special events on Sundays in summer.

* 180 acres of woodland
* Private broad

Location
Follow brown tourist signs off A147 at junction with B1140 through South Walsham

Opening
Daily: 10am–5pm; 2 May–31 Aug
Wed–Thu 10am–9pm

Admission
Adult £4, Child £1.50, Concs £3.50,
Dogs 25p Sanctuary £1.50 per person

Contact
School Road, South Walsham,
Norwich NR13 6DZ

t 01603 270449
w norfolkbroads.com/fairhaven
e fairhavengardens@norfolkbroads.com

356 Norwich

Felbrigg Hall, Garden & Park

2 hrs+   Mar–Oct

One of the finest C17 houses in East Anglia, Felbrigg contains original C18 furniture, an outstanding library, and a beautifully restored walled garden with a working dovecote. The house is set in 500 acres of parkland and woodland.

* Many woodland walks
* Changing programme of exhibitions

Location
In Felbrigg, 2 miles SW of Cromer, off B1346. Signed from A140 & A148

Opening
Mar–Oct Sat–Wed
Hall 1pm–5pm
Gardens 11am–5pm

Admission
Please phone for details

Contact
Felbrigg, Norwich NR11 8PR
t 01263 837444
w nationaltrust.org.uk
e felbrigg@nationaltrust.org.uk

357 Norwich

ILPH Hall Farm

1–2 hrs   All year

Visit this centre to learn about the work of the International League for the Protection of Horses. Meet some of the horses and ponies in care, many of whom have been rescued from cruelty and neglect.

* Visitor centre, stabling & indoor riding area

Location
Off A11, signed between Attleborough & Thetford

Opening
Wed, Sat, Sun & Bank Hols 11am–4pm

Admission
Free

Contact
Snetterton,
Norwich NR16 2LR
t 01953 498898
w ilph.org
e info@ilph.org

358 Sheringham

The Muckleburgh Collection

2 hrs Apr–Nov

A collection of more than 120 military vehicles, tanks and guns, plus items from Operation Desert Storm, militaria from the C18 and scale models. Learn how to drive a tank, take a coastal ride on a US Personnel Carrier, or visit by air, landing on the adjoining airstrip.

* Meteor on loan from the Imperial War Museum
* Gama Goat Rides – in a US Personnel Carrier

Location	Contact
Signed from A149 W of Cromer, 3 miles W of Sheringham	Weybourne Military Camp, Holt NR25 7EG
Opening	t 01263 588210
Please phone for details	w muckleburgh.co.uk
Admission	e info@muckleburgh.co.uk
Adult £5.50, Child £3, Concs £4.50	

359 Walsham

Elephant Playbarn

3 hrs All year

A converted Norfolk flint barn filled with bouncy castles, ball pools and toys suitable for the under-eights. There is also a fully enclosed courtyard with an adventure play area and lots of pedal toys.

* Please phone in advance to ensure disabled access

Location	Contact
Off A149, S of Cromer, on B1145, ½ mile from Mundesley	Mundesley Road, Knapton, North Walsham NR28 0RY
Opening	t 01263 721080
Wed–Sun 10am–4pm; daily in school hols	w elephantplaybarn.co.uk
Admission	
Adult Free, Child (1yr & under), £3.50 Child (2-7yrs) £4.50	

360 Walsham

Norfolk Motor Cycle Museum

3 hrs+ All year

Young bike enthusiasts will be fascinated by the displays of more than 100 motor bikes and 100 bicycles covering a wide collection of two-wheelers from 1920–1960.

* Educational visits welcomed

Location	Contact
Near junction of B1150 Norwich road & A149 Great Yarmouth–Cromer road (town bypass)	Railway Yard, North Walsham NR28 0DS
Opening	t 01692 406266
Please phone for details	
Admission	
Adult £3, Child £1.50, Concs £2.50	

361 Wroxham

RAF Air Defence Radar Museum

2 hrs All year

The museum traces the history and development of Air Defence Radar during 1935–1993 including WWII Operations, Surface to Air Missiles, Radar Engineering, Communications and Radar Systems, Air Intelligence Photography and even Space Surveillance and Defence.

* Housed in the original Operations Building
* Battle of Britain 1942 ops Room & Cold War Ops room

Location	Admission
Signed 12 miles NE of Norwich, 2 Miles E of Wroxham	Adult £4, Child £3, Concs £3.50
Opening	Contact
2nd Sat each month & Bank Hols 10am–5pm; Apr–Oct Tue & Thu Visits can be arranged outside these times.	RAF Neatishead, Neatishead, Nr Wroxham NR12 8YB
	t 01692 633309
	w radarmuseum.co.uk
	e curator@radarmuseum.co.uk

362 Brandon

High Lodge Forest Centre

6 hrs+   All year

Thetford Forest is Britain's largest lowland pine forest. High Lodge is located in the heart of the forest with walks, cycle hire, an adventure playground, deer safaris and much more.

* One of the largest mazes in Europe
* Bird walks & family fun walks

Location
Just off A11 on B1107 midway between Thetford & Brandon

Opening
Daily: 9am–dusk,
Please phone for details

Admission
£3.50 per car

Contact
Thetford Forest Park,
Santon Downham,
Brandon IP27 0TJ
t 01842 815434 (High Lodge Centre)
   01842 810271 (Forestry Commission)
w forestry.gov.uk

363 Bungay

Bungay Castle

1 hr   All year

The remains of this large Norman castle contain many interesting features. The massive gatehouse towers still stand, as do the bridge pit and curtain walls. A mine tunnel is exposed, along with the forebuilding with its latrine chamber (garderobe).

* Visitor centre
* Café & shop

Location
Off A143 & A144

Opening
Daily: 5 Jan–23 Dec 10am–4pm

Admission
Adult £1, Child & Concs 50p

Contact
6 Cross Street, Bungay NR35 1AU
t 01986 893002 (tea rooms)
w bungay-suffolk.co.uk

364 Bungay

Norfolk & Suffolk Aviation Museum

2 hrs   All year

This unique museum has 40 aircraft on display, from the early pioneers of flight and Luftwaffe crash planes right up to the machines of the present day. It houses the 446th (H) Bomb Group Museum, the RAF Bomber Command Museum and the Air Sea Rescue Museum.

* 40 aircraft within seven hangars
* Aircraft from before WWI to the present day

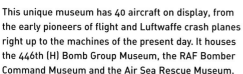

Location
On B1062, off A143, 1 mile W of Bungay

Opening
Apr–Oct Sun–Thu 10am–5pm;
Nov–Mar Tue, Wed & Sun 10am–4pm;
closed 15 Dec–15 Jan

Admission
Free, donations welcomed

Contact
The Street, Flixton NR35 1NZ
t 01986 896644
w aviationmuseum.net
e lcurtis@aviationmuseum.net

365 Bungay

Otter Trust

2 hrs+   Apr–Sep

Children love to watch our beautiful otters and will enjoy a visit to the Trust, which promotes the cause of conserving otters and encourages the public to see, enjoy and learn about them at its centres.

* Three lakes home to otters & wildfowl
* Information centre

Location	Contact
Located off A143, 1 mile W of Bungay	Earsham, Bungay NR35 2AF
Opening	t 01986 893470
Daily: Apr–Sep 10.30am–6pm	w ottertrust.org.uk
Admission	
Adult £5, Child £3	

366 Bury St Edmunds

Bury St Edmunds Abbey

2 hrs   All year

Explore the remains of a Benedictine abbey, church and precinct with Norman tower, set in beautifully kept gardens. The two C14 gateways are the best-preserved buildings. There is also a visitor centre with interactive displays.

* English Heritage property

Location	Contact
Off A14, at E end of Bury St Edmunds	Bury St Edmunds
Opening	t 01284 764667
Daily; all reasonable times please phone for details	w english-heritage.org.uk
Admission	
Free	

367 Bury St Edmunds

Manor House Museum

1 hr+   All year

This magnificent Georgian town house displays some of the finest clocks and watches to be found in the world, costume and textiles from the C17 to the present day, and portrait paintings of national importance.

* Mixes art, science & history
* Three major collections

Location	Contact
Signed within Bury St Edmunds	5 Honey Hill, Bury St Edmunds IP33 1RT
Opening	t 01284 757076/757074
Wed–Sun 11am–4pm	w stedmundsbury.gov.uk/manorhse
Admission	e manor.house@stedsbc.gov.uk
Adult £2.60, Child & Concs £2.10	

368 Felixstowe

Manning's Amusement Park

3 hrs   Apr–Sep

This traditional children's amusement park has numerous rides and slides. There is also an amusement arcade, Sunday market, bowling green, nightclub, a sports bar and indoor Adventure Golf FX.

Location	Admission
Off A14 & A12 on seafront	Rides: Adult Free, Child £3 unlimited rides
Opening	Golf: £1.50–£2
Easter–Sep Sat–Sun & school hols Please phone for further details	Contact
	Sea Road, Felixstowe IP11 2DN
	t 01394 282370

369 Ipswich

Ipswich Transport Museum

1 hr   Mar–Nov

The museum has the largest collection of transport items in Britain devoted to just one town. Everything was either made or used in and around Ipswich. The collection, started in 1965, consists of around 100 major exhibits, and numerous smaller transport-related items.

* Timetables, photographs, maps, tickets & uniforms
* Varied programme of events as advertised

Location
SE of Ipswich near junction 57 of A14

Opening
Mar–Nov Sun & Bank Hols 11am–4pm;
school hols Mon–Fri 1pm–4pm

Admission
Adult £3, Child £2, Concs £2.50

Contact
Old Trolleybus Depot, Cobham Road,
Ipswich IP3 9JD
t 01473 715666
w ipswichtransportmuseum.co.uk
e enquiries@ipswichtransportmuseum.co.uk

370 Lowestoft

Lowestoft Maritime Museum

1 hr+   Easter–Oct

The museum records the history of the Lowestoft fishing fleet, with models of fishing and commercial ships, shipwrights' tools, fishing gear, a lifeboat display, an art gallery and a drifter's cabin with models of fishermen.

* Fine exhibition of evolution of lifeboats
* Collection of shipwright's & cooper's tools

Location
Under Lighthouse on Whaplode Road
in Sparrow's Nest Park

Opening
Daily: May–10 Oct, 23–31 Oct & Easter
hols 10am–5pm

Admission
Adult 75p, Child 25p, Concs 50p

Contact
Whapload Road, Lowestoft
NR32 1XG
t 01502 561963

371 Lowestoft

Pleasurewood Hills Leisure Park

6 hrs+   Easter–Oct

East Anglia's premier leisure park has more than 50 acres of rides, attractions and shows for all the family. Rollercoasters, water rides, go-karts and many more. Fun for both younger members of the family and grandparents.

* Wizzy Dizzy–a spinning pendulum, not for the feinthearted
* Family tickets available

Location
Off A12 N of Lowestoft

Opening
Easter–Oct 10am–5pm
Please phone for details of days &
dates

Admission
Please phone for details

Contact
Leisure Way, Corton,
Lowestoft, Suffolk, NR32 5DZ
t 01502 586000
w pleasurewoodhills.com
e info@pleasurewoodhills.com

372 Newmarket

National Stud

1 hr+   Mar–Sep

Horse-crazy children will enjoy every minute of this stable tour, which takes in the superb stallion unit, along with the stallions in residence, nursery yards, and mares and foals in their paddocks.

* Quality Assured Visitor Attraction

Location
Take A11, A1304 & A1303. Stud
is 2 miles SW of Newmarket on A1304

Opening
Mar–Sep Mon–Sat
Tours 11.15am, 2.30pm & Sun 2.30pm

Admission
Adult £5, Child £3.50, Concs £4

Contact
Newmarket CB8 0XE
t 01638 663464
Tours 01638 666789
w nationalstud.co.uk
e tours@nationalstud.co.uk

373 Southwold

Coastal Voyager

1 hr+ All year

Coastal Voyager a 9m rigid inflatable, offers a variety of sea trips and river cruises. There is a half-hour high-speed blast trip and various tranquil river cruises along the beautiful River Blyth.

* Wrap-round seats, seatbelts and lifejackets
* Smooth, comfortable & safe rides

Location	Contact
Trips depart from Southwold Harbour	6 Strickland Place,
	Southwold IP18 6HN
Opening	
Please phone for details	t 07887 525082
	w coastalvoyager.co.uk
Admission	e thrills@southwold.ws
½-hr High-Speed Blast:	
Adult £16, Child £9	

374 Southwold

Southwold Pier

2–4 hrs Jul–Nov

Visit this seaside pier and amusement centre for good old-fashioned fun. The new pier was completed in 2002 and is the first pier to be built in the UK for over 45 years.

* Pier of the Year 2002
* Educational visits welcomed

Location	Contact
Off A12, follow signs for Southwold	North Parade, Southwold IP18 6BN
Opening	t 01502 722105
Daily: Oct–Nov 10am–5pm; Jul–Sep	w southwoldpier.co.uk
10am–10pm	e admin@southwoldpier.co.uk
Admission	
Free	

375 Stowmarket

Mid-Suffolk Light Railway Museum

2 hrs Apr–Sep

Dedicated to the Mid-Suffolk Light Railway, the museum shows the restoration of the station and trackwork, plus artefacts and memorabilia.

* Check website & press for details of special events

Location	Admission
1 mile from A140 in village of	Adult £1.50, Child 50p
Brockford-cum-Wetheringsett	Rates vary for special events
Opening	**Contact**
Good Fri–end Sep Sun & Bank Hols	Brockford Station, Wetheringsett,
11am–5pm; also Wed in Aug 2pm–5pm	Stowmarket IP14 5PW
	t 01449 766899
	w mslr.org.uk

376 Stowmarket

Playworld Ocean Adventure

1 hr+   All year

An indoor play area for children under 10 years old with ball ponds, scramble nets, slides, an aerial glide and a spooky room. There is also a toddlers' area.

* Large inflatable play area (May-Sep only)

Location	Admission
Easy access from A14 into Stowmarket. Signed to Leisure Centre from town centre	Please phone for details
	Contact
Opening	Mid-Suffolk Leisure Centre, Gainsborough Road, Stowmarket IP14 1LH
Daily: Mon–Fri 9.30am– 7pm, Sat–Sun 9am–6pm	
	t 01449 674980

377 Stowmarket

Redwings Rescue Centre

2 hrs   May–Sep

Redwings Rescue Centre aims to relieve the suffering of horses, ponies and donkeys by providing them with a caring home for the rest of their days. See the animals in their peaceful retirement and learn more about their care and upkeep.

* 20-acre site
* Carriage horses

Location	Contact
Off A1120	Stonham Barns, Stowmarket
Opening	t 0870 040 0033
Daily: May–Sep 10am–4pm	w redwings.co.uk
Admission	
Adult £3.60, Child (3–15) £1.60, Concs £2.60	

378 Stowmarket

Suffolk Owl Sanctuary

2 hrs+   All year

The Suffolk Owl Sanctuary is home to a variety of owls and birds of prey from all over the world, and has spectacular flying displays daily. There is also a woodland walk with a songbird hide and a red squirrel enclosure.

* Kids play area
* Café & shop

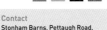

Location	Contact
On A1120, 8 miles from Ipswich & Stowmarket	Stonham Barns, Pettaugh Road, Stonham Aspal, Stowmarket IP14 6AT
Opening	t 01449 711425
Daily: summer 10am–5pm; Oct–Feb 10am–4pm	w suffolk-owl-sanctuary.org.uk
	e info@owl-help.org.uk
Admission	
Free, donations appreciated	

379 Sudbury

Clare Castle Country Park

3 hrs   All year

Spend a few hours exploring a 30-acre site fronting the River Stour. It combines the remains of a Norman motte-and-bailey castle and a Victorian railway station with natural history interest.

* History & nature trail
* Visitor centre

Location	Admission
Signed off A1092 in centre of Clare	Free
Opening	Contact
Park Daily: dawn–dusk	Malting Lane, Clare, Sudbury CO10 8NW
Visitor centre Daily: summer only 10am–5pm	
	t 01787 277491
	w suffolk.gov.uk/e-and-t/countryside
	e john.laws@et.suffolkcc.gov.uk

380 West Stow

West Stow Country Park & Anglo-Saxon Village

1 hr+   All year

West Stow is a reconstructed Anglo-Saxon village, built on the site of an original settlement and set in a 125-acre country park. Finds from the site are displayed in an interpretation centre. This unique village is brought to life when authentic costume groups host special events.

* Nature trail & woodland walks
* River views & lake

Location	Admission
Off A1101, 6 miles NW of Bury St Edmunds	Adult £5, Child & Concs £4. Additional charges during events
Opening	Contact
Daily: summer *Country Park* 8am–8pm *Village* 10am–5pm (last admission 4pm) winter *Country Park* 9am–5pm *Village* 10am–5pm (last admission 3.30pm)	Icklingham Road, West Stow IP28 6HG
	t 01284 728718
	w stedmundsbury.gov.uk/weststow
	e weststow@stedsbc.gov.uk

381 Woodbridge

Deben Cruises

2 hrs+   May–Sep

The MV *Jahan* cruises through 10 miles of lovely countryside, departing from the quay at Waldringfield Boatyard and returning to Waldringfield. The cruises last two to three hours, depending on tides. Visit the picturesque port of Woodbridge or travel to Felixstowe.

* Lunches & afternoon teas
* Group deals by appointment

Location	Admission
From A12 at Orwell Bridge signed to Lowestoft. Take sign at roundabout to Waldringfield & it will take you straight to village	Adult £6 , Child £4
	Contact
	Waldringfield Boatyard Ltd, The Quay, Waldringfield, Woodbridge IP12 4QZ
Opening	
Please phone for details	t 01473 736260

382 Woodbridge

Sutton Hoo

2-3 hrs   All year

Excavations here in 1939 revealed the burial chamber of a 90ft ship, filled with treasures including a warrior's helmet, weapons, armour, ornaments, tableware and a purse with 37 gold coins from c. AD620. The exhibition hall houses a full-size reconstruction of the chamber.

* Most important archaeological find in the UK
* Largest Anglo-Saxon ship ever discovered

Location	Admission
Off B1083 Woodbridge–Bawdsey road, signed from A12	Please phone for details
Opening	Contact
Daily: 11am–5pm school hols Please phone for term-time details	Woodbridge IP12 3DJ
	t 01394 389700
	w nationaltrust.org.uk
	e suttonhoo@nationaltrust.org.uk

Ladybower Reservoir, Derbyshire

East Midlands

Derbyshire Leicestershire Lincolnshire
Northamptonshire Nottinghamshire Rutland

383 Bakewell

Haddon Hall

2 hrs+   Apr–Oct

A perfect example of a Tudor hall set in beautiful gardens. Guided tours are available and are adapted to suit different ages, abilities and interests. A costume room can be booked where the guide will give a talk illustrated with costumes.

* Annual children's weekend
* Film location for *Jane Eyre* & *Elizabeth*

Location
2 miles S of Bakewell on A6

Opening
Apr–Sep daily 10.30am–4.30pm;
Oct Thu–Sun 10.30am–4.30pm

Admission
Adult £7.25, Child £3.75, Concs £6.25

Contact
Bakewell, Derbyshire DE45 1LA

t 01629 812855
w www.haddonhall.co.uk
e info@haddonhall.co.uk

384 Bolsover

Bolsover Castle

1 hr+   All year

An enchanting early C17 castle, set on a hill with restored walled gardens, a magnificent indoor riding house and outstanding craftsmanship everywhere. Visit the Discovery Centre and enjoy the interactive scale model of the castle and the audio tour.

* Regular living history events
* Visitor Attraction of the Year 2001

Location
In Bolsover, on A632, 6 miles E of Chesterfield

Opening
Apr, Sep–Oct Thu–Mon 10am–5pm;
May–Aug daily 10am–6pm;
Nov–Mar Thu–Mon 10am–4pm

Admission
Adult £6.60, Child £3.30, Concs £5

Contact
Castle Street, Bolsover S44 6PR

t 01246 822844
w english-heritage.org.uk
e bolsover.castle@english-heritage.org.uk

385 Castle Donington

Donington Grand Prix Collection

2–4 hrs   All year

Take a spin around the largest collection of Grand Prix cars and journey through motor sport history. Exhibits include a 1999 Ralf Schumacher Williams, a 1997 David Coulthard McLaren and the car in which Ayrton Senna won the 1993 European Grand Prix at Donington Park.

* Ferraris, Lotuses, Tyrells, Maseratis, Alfa Romeos
* Williams F1 cars from 1983 to 1999

Location
M1 junction 23a/24, access from NW via A50

Opening
Daily: 10am–4pm

Admission
Adult £7, Child £2.50, Concs £5

Contact
Donington Park, Castle Donington DE74 2RP

t 01332 811027
w doningtoncollection.com
e enquiries@doningtoncollection.co.uk

386 Castleton

Peak Cavern

1 hr   All year

Set within a 250ft vertical cliff, and once home to a small village, there are various natural caverns within Peak Cavern, including the orchestra gallery, which has amazing acoustic properties, Roger Rain's House with a perpetual waterfall and the devil's cellar.

* Riverside walk past historic miners' cottages
* Guided tours & rope making demonstrations

Location
On A6187, between Hathersage & Whaley Bridge

Opening
Daily: 10am–5pm

Admission
Adult £6, Child £4, Concs £5

Contact
Peak Cavern Road, Castleton, Hope Valley S33 8WS

t 01433 620285
w www.peakcavern.co.uk
e info@peakcavern.co.uk

387 Castleton

Peveril Castle

1 hr+   All year

There are breathtaking views of the Peak District from Peveril Castle, built shortly after the Norman Conquest of 1066 and perched high above the pretty village of Castleton. Come and see the famous Great Square Tower of Henry II.

* Some of the earliest herringbone masonry
* Sir Walter Scott based one of his novels on the castle

Location
On S side of Castleton, on A6187, 15 miles W of Sheffield

Opening
Apr, Sep–Oct daily 10am–5pm;
May–Aug daily 10am–6pm;
Nov–Mar Thur–Sun 10am–4pm

Admission
Adult £3, Child £1.50, Concs £2.30

Contact
Market Place, Castleton S33 8WQ

t 01433 620613
w english-heritage.org.uk

388 Denby

Denby Pottery Visitor Centre

1 hr+   All year

Admire and compare examples of Denby from early salt-glazed bottles and jars to the distinctive tableware of recent years. You can also see how Denby is made and have a go at painting a plate. There are extra activities for children during school holidays.

* Watch free cookery demonstrations
* Tours of the glass studio also available

Location
Next to Denby Pottery on the B6179, off A38, 8 miles N of Derby

Opening
Daily: Mon–Sat 9.30am–5pm;
Sun 10am–5pm

Admission
Factory tour Adult £4.95,
Child & Concs £3.95

Contact
Derby Road, Denby nr Ripley DE5 8NX

t 01773 74099
w denbyvisitorcentre.co.uk
e visitor.centre@denby.co.uk

389 Derby

Derby Museum of Industry & History

1 hr   All year

This museum introduces visitors to the history of Derby's industries. It has a major collection of Rolls-Royce aero engines, railway engineering and research galleries and a Power for Industry Gallery.

* On site of Denby's first silk mill
* History of Midland Railway

Location
Off the A6, near Derby Cathedral

Opening
Daily: Mon 11am–5pm,
Tue–Sat 10am–5pm,
Sun & Bank Hols 1pm–4pm
Please phone to confirm
holiday opening times

Admission
Free

Contact
Silk Mill Lane, off Full Street,
Derby DE1 3AF

t 01332 255308
w derby.gov.uk/museums

390   High Peak

Chestnut Centre Otter Haven & Owl Sanctuary

2 hrs+   All year

Enjoy watching captive-bred otters and owls in their natural surroundings. Extensive nature trails weave through 50 acres of grounds. The sanctuary is a member of the Federation of Zoological Gardens of Great Britain.

* Also see Scottish wild cats & foxes
* Wildlife gift shop

Location	Contact
Off A625. Follow brown tourist signs	Castleton Road, Chapel-en-le-Frith, High Peak, SK23 0QR
Opening	t 01298 814099
Daily: 10.30am–5.30pm; Jan–Feb Sat–Sun only	w ottersandowls.co.uk
Admission	e enquiries@ottersandowls.co.uk
Adult £5.95, Child £3.75	

391   Ilkeston

The American Adventure

7 hrs   Mar–Oct

Visit The American Adventure and discover the epic story of the USA, from the Western Pioneers to the Pioneers of Space. With more than 100 attractions, live shows and rides, The American Adventure is an enjoyable family day out for everyone.

* Events held throughout the year
* Quality Assured Visitor Attraction

Location	Contact
Take junction 26 off M1 & follow signs along A610 to A608 & then A6007	Derbyshire DE7 5SX
Opening	t 0845 330 2929
Daily: Mar–Oct 10am–5pm	w www.americanadventure.co.uk
Admission	e sales@americanadventure.co.uk
Adult (13+) £16.50, Child £13.50	

392   Matlock Bath

Gulliver's Kingdom

6 hrs+   Apr–Sep

The park is designed for Lilliputians, but adults can have as much fun as the children. It is set on a wooded hillside and includes more than 40 attractions ranging from a log flume, rollercoaster and chairlift to the Royal Mine Ride and family shows.

* Outdoor fantasy eating
* Disabled visitors are advised to phone before visiting

Location	Admission
Easily reached from M1 or M6. Off A38 on A6 between Matlock & Cromford	Adult £8.50, Child £8.50, Child under 90cm tall free, Concs £7.50
Opening	Contact
Apr–Sep	Temple Walk, Matlock Bath, Derbyshire DE4 3PG
Please phone for details	t 01925 444888
	w www.gulliversfun.co.uk

393 Ashby-de-la-Zouch

Ashby-de-la-Zouch Castle

1 hr+   All year

Ashby-de-la-Zouch Castle is a late medieval castle with impressive ruins that are dominated by the Hastings Tower. It offers panoramic views of the surrounding countryside and the chance to explore the secret tunnel used in the Siege of Ashby.

* Wonderful views across Leicestershire
* The setting for jousting scenes in the film *Ivanhoe*

Location	Contact
In Ashby-de-la-Zouch, 12 miles S of Derby, on A511	South Street, Ashby-de-la-Zouch LE65 1BR
Opening	t 01530 413343
Please phone for details	w english-heritage.org.uk
	e customers@english-heritage.org.uk
Admission	
Adult £3.20, Child £1.60, Concs £2.40	

394 Ashby-de-La-Zouch

Conkers

4 hrs+   All year

Located at the heart of the national forest, Conkers offers a great mix of hands-on activities, from 4 indoor discovery zones for all ages to 23 outdoor activities, including lakeside walks, sculpture and nature trails, an assault course, train rides, playgrounds and water play.

* Visitor Attraction of the Year finalist
* Adventure playground

Location	Contact
3 miles from Ashby-de-la-Zouch on B5003	Rawden Road, Moira, nr Ashby-de-la-Zouch Leicestershire DE12 6GA
Opening	
Daily: *summer* 10am–6pm	t 01283 216633
winter 10am–dusk	w visitconkers.com
Admission	e info@visitconkers.com
Adult £6.25, Child £4.25, Concs £5.25	

395 Coalville

Snibston Discovery Park

6 hrs   All year

A popular museum, Snibston is situated on the site of a former colliery. It displays a rich collection of historic objects telling the story of transport, mining and quarrying, engineering and the fashion industry. A visit includes a tour of the historic colliery buildings.

* Train ride along the newly restored colliery railway
* Sculpture trail

Location
On A511, on edge of Coalville town centre

Opening
Daily: 10am–5pm; Closed in early Jan, please phone for details

Admission
Adult £5.70, Child £3.60, Concs £3.90

Contact
Ashby Road, Coalville LE67 3LN

t 01530 278444
w leics.gov.uk/museums
e snibston@leics.gov.uk

396 Desford

Tropical Birdland

2 hrs+   All year

Come and see hundreds of beautiful and exotic birds, including macaws, parrots, parakeets, toucans and emus, wander around the walk-through aviary, see where chicks are hatched, or sit with friendly free-to-fly birds in the café. Some might even talk to you!

* Boarding service for pet birds when you go on holiday
* Hundreds of tropical birds from more than 70 species

Location
Just off M1 at junction 22

Opening
Daily: 10am–5pm

Admission
Adult £5, Child & Concs £3.50

Contact
Lindridge Lane, Desford,
Leicester LE9 9N

t 01455 824603
w www.tropicalbirdland.co.uk
e info@tropicalbirdland.co.uk

397 Grantham

Belvoir Castle

3 hrs+   Mar–Oct

Belvoir Castle is still home to the Duke and Duchess of Rutland. This stunning building has a hilltop position, breathtaking views and glorious gardens. Events are staged every weekend throughout the season.

* Hidden spring garden
* Calendar of events

Location
Off A52, 7 miles from Grantham & 9 miles from Melton Mowbray

Opening
Easter–Sep Tue–Thur, Sat–Sun 11am–5pm
Mar & Oct Sun only 11am–5pm

Admission
Adult £8, Child £5, Concs £7

Contact
Grantham,
Leicestershire NG32 1PD
t 01476 871002
w belvoircastle.com
e nwheeler@belvoircastle.com

399 Loughborough

Great Central Railway

2 hrs+   All year

This is one of the few places in the world where you can see scheduled full-size steam trains in operation. Watch a demonstration of a freight or parcel train, jump aboard a classic corridor train or, for the adventurous, learn how to drive a steam or diesel train.

* Steam through the glorious Leicester countryside
* Driver's view of bridges, trains & hidden sidings

Location
SE of town centre

Opening
Trains run at weekends all year & midweek Jun–Aug, please phone for details

Admission
Adult £12, Child & Concs £8

Contact
Great Central Road,
Loughborough LE11 1RW
t 01509 230 726
w gcrailway.co.uk
e booking_office@gcrailway.co.uk

398 Leicester

National Space Centre

4–6 hrs   All year

This centre is dedicated to space science and astronomy. From its futuristic Rocket Tower discover the stories, personalities and technology of the past and present, and explore our current understanding of space and how it affects our future.

* Six themed galleries with hands-on activities
* Space theatre show

Location
Just off A6, 2 miles N of city centre

Opening
Tue–Sun 10am–5pm;
school hols daily 10am–5pm

Admission
Adult £9.95, Child & Concs £7.95

Contact
Exploration Drive, Leicester LE4 5NS
t 0870 607 7223
w spacecentre.co.uk
e info@spacecentre.co.uk

Foxton Canal Museum

3 hrs   All year

A canal museum featuring the story of the local canals and the rare boat lift, set in beautiful countryside with ten locks and all supporting facilities. The museum contains models of the lift, interactive displays, social history and a canal play boat for younger visitors.

* Guided tour & walks
* Calendar of events

Location
Follow brown tourist signs from A6
Market Harborough–Leicester road or
A4304 at Lubenham, or M1 junction 20
to Market Harborough road

Opening
Daily: 10am–5pm; closed Thu–Fri in winter

Admission
Adult £2.50, Child free, Concs £2

Contact
Middle Lock, Gumley Road,
Foxton, Market Harborough
Leicestershire LE16 7RA

t 0116 279 2657
w fipt.org.uk
e info@fipt.co.uk

Rockingham Castle

3 hrs   May–Sep

Built by William the Conqueror more than 900 years ago, the castle stands in beautiful grounds, with superb views across the Welland Valley. As well as a stronghold, it was an important seat of government. It is now home to the Saunders Watson family.

* Winner of numerous education awards
* Regular events including kite & Viking days

   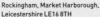

Location
Off A6003, 1 mile N of Corby

Opening
Easter Sun & Mon;
May–Sep Sun, Tue & Bank Hols
12pm–5pm

Admission
Adult £7.50, Child £4.50, Concs £6.50

Contact
Rockingham, Market Harborough,
Leicestershire LE16 8TH

t 01536 770240
w rockinghamcastle.com
e estateoffice@rockinghamcastle.com

Twinlakes Park

7 hrs+   All year

A new family destination with a huge variety of activities for all ages, from climbing Black Knights Castle to shooting foam in the Master Blaster. Other fun attractions include a mini-coaster and water play.

* Rowboats & pedal boats
* Falconry centre

Location
1 mile from Melton Mowbray &
signed from A607 between Melton
Mowbray & Grantham

Opening
Daily: 10am–5.30pm

Admission
Adult £8.50, Child £8.50, Under-3s Free

Contact
Melton Spinney Road,
Melton Mowbray, LE14 4SB

t 01664 567777
w twinlakespark.co.uk
e fun@twinlakes.co.uk

403 Cleethorpes

Cleethorpes Humber Estuary Discovery Centre

1 hr All year

Located on the boating lake surrounded by fantastic views and friendly wildlife. This family-friendly hands-on exhibition explores the Victorian seaside, history and the nature of Cleethorpes. The second-floor observatory has outstanding views of the Humber Estuary.

* On the edge of an important habitat

Location
From A180 & A16 follow signs for the lakeside

Opening
Daily: Jan–Jun, Sep–Oct 10am–5pm;
Jul–Aug 10am–6pm;
Nov–Dec 10am–4pm

Admission
Adult £1.95, Child £1.30

Contact
Lakeside, Kings Road, Cleethorpes
DN35 0AG

t 01472 323232
w cleethorpesdiscoverycentre.co.uk
e lynne.emeny@nelincs.gov.uk

 ©National Trust Photographic Library/Tessa Musgrave

404 Grantham

Woolsthorpe Manor

2 hrs Mar–Oct

This C17 manor house was the birthplace and home of the scientist Sir Isaac Newton. Visitors can see his childhood scribblings on the walls. A gnarled old apple tree in the garden may be a descendant of the famous specimen that inspired Newton in his work.

* Interactive science discovery centre
* Replica of principle of differential calculus

 Location
From A1 take B676 at Colsterworth roundabout, turn right at second crossroads & follow signs

Opening
5 Mar–27 Mar Sat–Sun 1pm–5pm;
1 Apr–30 Sep Wed–Sun 1pm–5pm;
1 Oct–30 Oct Sat–Sun 1pm–5pm

Admission
Adult £4.20, Child £2.10

Contact
23 Newton Way, Woolsthorpe-by-Colsterworth, nr Grantham NG33 5NR

t 01476 860338
w nationaltrust.org.uk
e woolsthorpemanor@national trust.org.uk

405 Ingoldmells

Hardy's Animal Farm

3 hrs   Easter–Oct

Come to Hardy's Animal Farm to see commercial and rare breeds of cattle, sheep and goats. Visit the calf and pig units where you can see how the animals are cared for.

* Large adventure playground
* Horse & cart rides

Location
Take A52 N from Skegness to Ingoldmells. Go through Ingoldmells & take 1st right down Anchor Lane

Opening
Daily: Easter–Oct 10am–5pm

Admission
Please phone for details

Contact
Grays Farm, Anchor Lane, Ingoldmells, Skegness PE25 1LZ

t 01754 872267

406 Ingoldmells

Magical World of Fantasy Island

3–5 hrs   Mar–Oct

This indoor theme park has rides and attractions to suit all ages, as well as live entertainment during the evenings throughout the main season. There are also outdoor rides to try and Europe's largest looping rollercoaster, The Millennium Coaster.

* Movie ride theatre
* Dazzling lightshows in the evenings

Location
Off A52, 4 miles N of Skegness

Opening
Daily: Easter–Oct from 10am; closing times vary, please phone for details

Admission
Free. Tokens available for rides

Contact
Ingoldmells, Skegness PE25 1RH

t 01754 872030
w fantasyisland.co.uk
e info@fantasyisland.co.uk

407 Lincoln

Lincoln Medieval Bishop's Palace

1 hr   All year

Standing in the shadow of Lincoln Cathedral, the palace acted as the administrative centre of the largest diocese in medieval England and now forms an impressive bishop's house. Don't miss the East Hall, with its stunning vaulted undercroft, or the chapel.

* Heritage garden
* Panorama of the Roman, medieval & modern city

Location
S side of Lincoln Cathedral

Opening
Apr–Jun & Sep–Oct 10am–5pm;
Jul–Aug 10am–6pm;
Nov–Mar Thu–Mon 10am–4pm

Admission
Adult £3.60, Child £1.80, Concs £2.70

Contact
Minster Yard, Lincoln LN2 1PU

t 01522 527468
w english-heritage.org.uk

408 Lincoln

Museum of Lincolnshire Life

2 hrs   All year

Experience the domestic, agricultural, industrial and social history of Lincolnshire with agricultural and industrial machinery built in the county. Also on show are Victorian room settings and a WWI tank. Special events are held throughout the year.

* Situated in Royal North Lincoln Military barracks
* Free parking available

Location
Take A15 & the B1398 & follow signs from A46

Opening
May–Sep daily 10am–5pm;
Oct–Apr Mon–Sat 10am–5pm
Last admission 4pm

Admission
Please phone for details

Contact
Burton Road, Lincoln LN1 3LY

t 01522 528448
e lincolnshire.gov.uk/museumof
lincolnshirelife
e lincolnshirelife_museum@
lincolnshire.gov.uk

409 Long Sutton

The Butterfly & Wildlife Park

4 hrs   Mar–Oct

Set in the heart of the Fens, the park has a tropical house, a reptile area with crocodiles and snakes, a creepy-crawlie house, and an ant room. Outdoor attractions include a birds of prey centre that runs twice-daily flying displays, an animal centre and an adventure playground.

* Quality Assured Visitor Attraction
* Lincolnshire Family Attraction of the Year 2003

Location	Contact
Signed off A17 at Long Sutton	Long Sutton, Spalding PE12 9LE
Opening	
Daily: end Mar–end Oct from 10am	t 01406 363833
Please phone for details	w butterflyandwildlifepark.co.uk
	e butterflypark@hotmail.com
Admission	
Please phone for details	

410 Mablethorpe

The Seal Sanctuary

1 hr+   Easter–Sep

The Seal Trust is a registered charity with the twin aims of caring for local wild creatures in distress (especially seals) and encouraging visitors to help wildlife themselves. It acts as a sanctuary for seals, owls and kestrels, as well as lynx, wildcats, snowy owls and harvest mice.

* Specially designed pools
* Educational natural history programmes

Location	Admission
Off A1031 via A1031, A104, A111 or A52	Adult £4.50, Child £2.50, Senior £3.50
Opening	Contact
Daily: Easter–Sept from 10am	North End
Please phone for details of winter	Mablethorpe
opening times	Lincolnshire LN12 1QG
	t 01507 473346

411 Scunthorpe

Normanby Hall Country Park

4 hrs   All year

Set in the heart of tranquil North Lincolnshire, the 300 acres of country park provide the perfect day out for all the family. Learn about Lincolnshire's rich rural heritage in the fascinating Farm Museum or step back in time in the award-winning Victorian walled garden.

* Extensive woodland with a wealth of wildlife
* Adventure playground for younger children

Location	Contact
Four miles N of Scunthorpe on B1430	Normanby, Scunthorpe DN15 9HU
Opening	t 01724 720588
Hall & Museum Easter–Sep 1pm–5pm	w northlincs.gov.uk/normanby
Gardens All year 10.30am–5pm	e normanby.hall@northlincs.gov.uk
Park All year 9am–dusk	
Admission	
Adult £4.20, Child £2.10, Concs £3.80	

Butlins (Skegness)

6 hrs   Apr–Oct

Children can have great fun at Butlins, from Splash, an indoor subtropical waterworld, with its exciting water rides, to Hotshots, a terrific tenpin bowling centre and the amazing Skyline Pavilion. Younger children can meet Bob the Builder in Bob's Yard.

* Quality Assured Visitor Attraction
* Live shows

Location
3 miles N of Skegness, on A52
Ingoldmells, Chapel St Leonards,
Sutton-on-Sea & Mablethorpe roads

Opening
Daily: Apr–Oct 10am–6pm
(last admission 4pm)

Admission
Please phone for details

Contact
Roman Bank, Ingoldmells,
Skegness PE25 1NJ

t 01754 765567 (day-visit hotline)
01754 762311
w butlins.co.uk
butlins.com/dayvisitor

Gibraltar Point Nature Reserve & Visitor Centre

2 hrs+   All year

This area of unspoilt coastline comprises sand dunes, saltmarshes and freshwater habitats for rare plants and animals, including seals, water voles and pygmy shrews. There are five bird-watching hides, a nature trail, an interpretation centre, and various activities and events.

* Area of international scientific interest
* Home to many rare plants, insects & animals

Location
1½ miles S of Skegness, signed from
town centre

Opening
Reserve daily 10.30am–dusk
Visitor centre May–Oct daily
10.30am–4pm;
Nov–Apr Sat–Sun & Bank Hols
10.30am–4pm

Admission
Free

Contact
Gilbraltar Road, Skegness PE24 4SU

t 01507 526667
w lincstrust.org.uk
e info@lincstrust.co.uk

414 Skegness

Skegness Natureland Seal Sanctuary

1 hr+   All year

Skegness Seal Sanctuary is well known for rescuing and rehabilitating orphaned and injured seal pups. It also has crocodiles, penguins, reptiles, insects and tropical birds. There is an aquarium as well and from April to October you can view tropical butterflies.

* Baby seal & penguin pools
* Underwater viewing pool

Location	Contact
Signed from town centre	North Parade, Skegness PE25 1DB
Opening	t 01754 764345
Daily: Jun–Sep 10am–5pm;	w skegnessnatureland.co.uk
Oct–May 10am–4pm	e natureland@fsbdial.co.uk
Admission	
Adult £5.20, Child £3.40, Concs £4.15	

415 Spalding

Baytree Garden Centre & Owl Centre

2 hrs+   All year

Baytree Garden Centre has 72 owls from around the world, and is set in a beautiful landscaped area. There are tame owls to hold or just to enjoy watching in flying displays. It is also home to more than 100 owls and birds of prey, including very rare Mexican striped owls.

* Absorbing interactive experience
* Visit tropical owls in the Hot House

Location	Contact
On main A151 at Weston between	High Road Weston, Spalding,
Spalding & Holbeach	Lincolnshire PE12 6JU
Opening	t Garden Centre 01406 370242
Please phone for details	Owl Centre 01406 372840
Admission	w baytree-gardencentre.com
Please phone for details	e info@baytree-gardencentre.com

416 Spilsby

Lincolnshire Aviation Heritage Centre

4 hrs   All year

The Heritage Centre is part of a wartime bomber airfield under restoration and includes the control tower and displays depicting the history of flying in Lincolnshire. There is also an exhibition by the Royal Air Force Escaping Society.

* Avro Lancaster bomber NX611 Just Jane
* See the barnes Wallis bouncing bomb

Location	Contact
On A155, between Revesey &	East Kirkby Airfield, nr Spilsby
East Kirkby	PE23 4DE
Opening	t 01790 763207
Easter–Oct Mon–Sat 9.30am–5pm;	w lincsaviation.co.uk
Nov–Easter Mon–Sat 10am–4pm	e enquiries@lincsaviation.co.uk
Admission	
Adult £6.50, Child £2, Concs £5.50	

417 Tattershall

Tattershall Castle

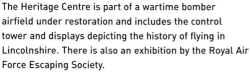

1 hr   Mar–Dec

Tattershall is a vast redbrick tower with a moat, built in medieval times for Ralph Cromwell, Lord Treasurer of England. There are grand tapestries and four great chambers, each with spectacular views across the Fens.

* Tower is more than 100 feet high
* Huge Gothic fireplaces

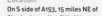

Location	Admission
On S side of A153, 15 miles NE of	Adult £4, Child £2
Sleaford, 10 miles SW of Horncastle	Contact
Opening	Tattershall, Lincoln LN4 4LR
Apr–Oct Mon–Wed & Sat–Sun	t 01526 342543
11am–5pm;	w nationaltrust.org.uk
Mar, Nov–Dec Sat–Sun 12noon–4pm	e tattershallcastle@nationaltrust. org.uk

418 Althorp

Althorp House

4 hrs   Jul–Sep

The home of the Spencer family since 1508. The park came to world attention on 6th September 1997, when Diana, Princess of Wales was laid to rest here. See her final resting place on the island in the Round Oval, surrounded by her family's ancestral heritage.

* Magnificent Palladian stable block for 100 horses
* One of the world's finest collections of portraiture

Location	Contact
7 miles W of Northampton off A428. Clearly signed from Junction 16 of M1	The Stables, Althorp Northampton NN7 4HQ
Opening	t 01604 770107
Jul–Sep 11am–5pm;	w althorp.com
Aug 31 closed	e mail@althorp.com
Admission	
Adult £12, Child £6, Concs £10	

419 Brixworth

Brixworth Country Park

2 hrs+   All year

The park has many facilities including a café, cycle hire, play area, sensory garden and waymarked trails. It is now the main gateway to Pitsford Water and the 10km safe walking/cycling route called the Pitsford Water Trail. The park is also linked with the Brampton Valley Way.

* Take a walk along our sculpture trail
* Watch birds from our bird hide

Location	Contact
Close to Brixworth Village & 7 miles N of Northampton on A508 Northampton –Market Harborough road	Northampton Road Brixworth NN6 9DG
Opening	t 01604 883920
Daily: dawn–dusk	w explorenorthamptonshire.co.uk
	e brixworth@northamptonshire.gov.uk
Admission	
Free	
Car Park £1.20 per hour, £2 all day	

420 Corby

Kirby Hall

1–2 hrs   All year

Featuring decorative carving and ornate gardens fit for a queen, Kirby Hall is one of the great Elizabethan houses, built in the hope of a royal visit. The Great Hall and state rooms have recently been refitted and redecorated to authentic C17 and C18 designs.

* Elizabethan festivals

Location	Admission
On an unclassified road off A43, 4 miles NE of Corby	Adult £4.30, Child £2.20, Concs £3.20
Opening	Contact
24 Mar–30 Jun Thurs–Mon 10am–5pm; 1 Jul–31 Aug daily 10am–6pm; 1 Sep–31 Oct Thurs–Mon 10am–5pm; 1 Nov–31 Mar Thurs–Mon 10am–4pm	Kirby Hall Deene, nr Corby NN17 5EN
	t 01536 203230
	w english-heritage.org.uk

421 Kettering

Rushton Triangular Lodge

1 hr   Apr–Oct

This is probably the strangest building in Britain, built in 1593 by Sir Thomas Tresham. Older children will enjoy this puzzling folly. Wander round the triangular rooms and try to decipher the mysterious quotations and numbers on the walls.

* Colourful house adorned with dates & emblems
* Three windows, three floors, three roof gables

Location	Admission
1 mile W of Rushton, on A6, on unclassified road 3 miles from Desborough	Adult £2.30, Child £1.20, Concs £1.70
Opening	Contact
Apr–Oct Thur–Mon 10am–5pm	Rushton, Kettering NN14 1RP
	t 01536 710761
	w english-heritage.org.uk

422 Kettering

Wicksteed Park

6 hrs+   Mar–Oct

Wicksteed Park has a large playground and an adventure park with more than 30 different amusements including pirate ships, a water chute, the Rockin' Tug and rollercoasters. There are also shows throughout the year in the pavilion.

* UK's oldest theme park
* Regular calendar of events

Location
On A6, 1 mile S of Kettering town centre & 1½ miles from A14 at junction 10. Follow signs

Opening
Grounds All year
Rides Mar–Oct times vary please phone for details

Admission
Please phone for details

Contact
Barton Road, Kettering, Northamptonshire NN15 6NJ

t 01536 512475
w wicksteedpark.co.uk
e information@wicksteedpark.co.uk

423 Northampton

Billing Aquadrome

3 hrs+   Mar–Nov

Billing Aquadrome is a leisure holiday park, set in 235 acres of parkland, woods and lakes. Facilities include an amusement centre, boating, coarse fishing and free children's play areas.

* Calendar of events & rallies

Location
Off A45, 3 miles from Northampton & 7 miles from M1 exit at junction 15

Opening
Daily: Mar–Nov until 8pm;
24-hr access for caravans & tents

Admission
Please phone for details

Contact
Crow Lane, Great Billing, Northampton NN3 9DA

t 01604 408181/784948
w billingaquadrome.com
e brochures@aquadrome.com

424 Northampton

Holdenby House, Gardens & Falconry Centre

 2 hrs   Apr–Sep

Across the fields from Althorp lies Holdenby, a house whose royal connections go back more than 400 years. Its history is complemented by a regal collection of birds of prey, including the only naturally reared male black eagle in captivity anywhere.

* Based on the remaining kitchen wing of the old palace
* Built in 1583 by Sir Christopher Hatton

Location
6 miles NW of Northampton, off A5199 or A428

Opening
Gardens & Falconry Centre
Easter–Sep Sun & Bank Hols
1pm–5pm
House Pre booked tours only

Admission
Gardens & Falconry Centre
Adult £4.50, Child £3, Concs £4

Contact
Holdenby, Northampton NN6 8DJ

t 01604 770074
w holdenby.com
e enquiries@holdenby.com

425   Northampton South

Abington Museum

3 hrs+   All year

The museum includes social and military history. Displays show Northamptonshire life, a Victorian cabinet of curiosities, the history of the building, Northamptonshire military history at home and abroad, and a C19 costume gallery.

* C17 oak-panelled room
* Former home of Shakespeare's granddaughter

Location	Admission
Approximately 1½ miles E of town centre	Free
Opening	**Contact**
March–Oct Sun–Tue 1pm–5pm;	Abington Park, Park Avenue,
Nov–Feb Sun–Tue 1pm–4pm;	South Northampton NN1 5LW
Bank Hol Mon 1pm–5pm	t 01604 838110
	w northampton.gov.uk/
	museums

426   Wellingborough

Irchester Country Park

4–6 hrs   All year

Explore a network of trails running across 83 hectares of mixed woodland and observe the wealth of wildlife, including woodpeckers and sparrowhawks. A Forestry Centre of Excellence, the park balances conservation with timber production and recreation.

* Ironstone railway museum
* Accessible trails & orienteering trail

Location	Contact
2 miles S of Wellingborough, on B570, off A509, in the Nene Valley	Gypsy Lane, Little Irchester, Wellingborough NN29 7DL
Opening	t 01933 276866
Park **Daily:** 24 hrs	w northamptonshire.gov.uk
Car park 24hrs	e irchester@northamptonshire.
Lower car park 9am–6pm	gov.uk
Admission	
Free. Car park £2	

427   Mansfield

Go Ape!

2 hrs+   All year

Discover the thrill of aerial trekking high above the forest floor. Go Ape! offers a high-wire assault course of extreme rope bridges, tarzan swings and zip slides. Full safety instruction is provided.

* Children must be 1m 40cm or over
* All under-18s must be accompanied

Location	Contact
Off B6030 near Old Clipstone	Sherwood Pines Visitor Centre, Nottinghamshire
Opening	t 0870 444 5562
Please phone for details or visit the website	w goape.co.uk
Admission	e info@goape.co.uk
Adult £16, Child (10–17) £12	

428   Mansfield

Making It! Discovery Centre

2 hrs+   All year

Have a fun, engaging, entertaining and educational, interactive, hands-on day out. The galleries celebrate the inventiveness of a variety of industries including shoe manufacture, brewing, soft drinks, textiles, printing, engineering and electronics.

* Nottinghamshire Visitor Attraction of the Year

Location	Contact
Close to town centre & Water Meadows leisure pool. Off A60 & A617	Chadburn House, Weighbridge Road, Littleworth, Mansfield, Nottinghamshire NG18 1AH
Opening	t 01623 473297
Daily: 10am–5pm	w makingit.org.uk
Admission	e info@makingit.org.uk
Adult £6.95, Child £6.25	

429 Mansfield

429 Mansfield

Sherwood Forest Country Park & Visitor Centre

2 hrs   All year

Visit the hiding place of Robin Hood and see the major oak, where he hid with his merry men, discover what life was like in the Middle Ages, learn about ecology in the Forests of the World exhibition or take a walk along one of many waymarked trails.

* Enjoy the trails & discover the forest
* National Nature Reserve

Location
In Edwinstowe village, off B6034

Opening
Visitor centre Daily: summer 10am–5pm, winter 10am–4.30pm
Park dawn–dusk

Admission
Free. Car park £1.50–£3

Contact
Edwinstowe, nr Mansfield NG21 9HN

t 01623 823202
w nottinghamshire.gov.uk/country parks
e sherwood.forest@nottscc.gov.uk

---

430 Newark

Newark Air Museum

2 hrs   All year

An impressive collection of more than 60 aircraft and cockpit sections, including transport, training and reconnaissance aircraft, helicopters, jet fighters and bombers. Learn about the history of RAF Winthorpe, a WWII bomber-training base.

* Post war air-to-air missile display

Location
Easily accessible from A1, A46, A17, A1133 & Newark bypass

Opening
Daily: Mar–Oct 10am–5pm; Nov–Feb 10am–4pm

Admission
Please phone for details

Contact
Winthorpe Showground, Newark NG24 2NY

t 01636 707170
w newarkairmuseum.co.uk
e newarkair@onetel.com

431 Nottingham

City of Caves

1 hr+   All year

Soak up the atmosphere of hundreds of years of local life in this ancient and mysterious labyrinth of sandstone caves buried deep beneath the city. Descend into the depths of these original Anglo-Saxon tunnels, meeting the cave dwellers from its dramatic hidden past.

* Have a go at real archaeology
* Special events throughout the year

Location	Contact
Nottingham city centre. Inside Broadmarsh shopping centre on upper level	Drury Walk, Broadmarsh Centre, Nottingham NG1 7LS
Opening	t 0115 988 1955
Daily: 10.30am–4.30pm	w cityofcaves.org.uk
	e info@cityofcaves.com
Admission	
Adult £4.95, Child & Concs £3.95	

432 Nottingham

Galleries of Justice

2–3 hrs   All year

Journey through 300 years of crime and punishment at this unique and atmospheric site. Actors bring the experience to life as you discover at first hand what prison life was really like. Special family-based events are run throughout the school holidays.

* C18 prison & Edwardian police station
* Series of temporary exhibitions

Location	Contact
In central Nottingham, near Broadmarsh shopping centre	Shire Hall, High Pavement, Lace Market, Nottingham NG1 1HN
Opening	t 0115 952 0555
Tue–Sun & Bank Hols 10am–5pm	w galleriesofjustice.org.uk
	e nnco@galleriesofjustice.org.uk
Admission	
Adult £7.95, Child & Concs £5.95	

433 Nottingham

Nottingham Castle

1–2 hrs   All year

Nottingham Castle is a C17 mansion with a range of historical and contemporary art exhibitions. Interactive displays feature museum collections of silver, ceramics and Nottinghamshire treasures. Children can also explore the hidden passageways under the building.

* Network of caves & passageways beneath the castle
* Robin Hood statue

Location	Contact
In central Nottingham	Lenton Road, Nottingham NG1 6EL
Opening	t 0115 915 3700
Daily: 10am–5pm	w nottinghamcity.gov.uk/museums
Admission	e helens@ncmg.demon.co.uk
Mon–Fri Adult £3, Child &Concs £1.50	
Sat–Sun & Bank Hols £2, £1	

434 Nottingham

Tales of Robin Hood

1–2 hrs   All year

The swashbuckling adventures of Robin Hood have inspired storytellers for more than 700 years. Explore the world of this infamous and endearing outlaw and experience medieval life, legend and adventure by fleeing through the forest to escape the evil Sheriff.

* Regular Robin Hood events
* Medieval banquets are held on Fridays & Saturdays

Location	Contact
In city centre, next to castle, signed from M1	30–38 Maid Marian Way, Nottingham NG1 6GF
Opening	t 0115 948 3284
Daily: 10am–5.30pm	w robinhood.uk.com
Admission	e robinhoodcentre@mail.com
Adult £7.95, Child £5.95, Concs £6.95	

435 Nottingham

Wollaton Hall Museum

3 hrs+   All year

Set in more than 500 acres of deer park, Wollaton Hall is one of the finest Elizabethan houses in England and is now home to Nottingham's natural history collection and industrial museum.

* See George the Gorilla
* Insect exhibition

Location	Admission
3 miles from city centre	Mon–Fri Free, Sat–Sun Each museum Adult £2.50, Child & Concs £1.50
Opening	Contact
Natural History Museum,Industrial Museum & Yard Gallery	Wollaton Park, Nottingham NG8 2AE
Daily: Oct–Mar 11am–4pm; Apr–Sep 11am–5pm	t 0115 915 3900
	w nottinghamcity.gov.uk
	e carolb@ncmg.demon.co.uk

436 Sneiton

Green's Mill & Science Centre

2 hrs   All year

One of the few working inner-city windmills in Britain, with interactive science exhibits, Green's Mill was once home to the C19 miller and mathematician George Green. Tour the mill and discover the fascinating process of turning grain into flour.

* Included in Best 50 Small Museums
* Hands-on experiments exploring magnetism, electricity & light

Location	Contact
1 mile outside city centre	Windmill Lane, Sneinton, Nottingham NG2 4QB
Opening	t 0115 915 6878
Wed–Sun & Bank Hols 10am–4pm	w greensmill.org.uk
Admission	
Free	

© English Heritage Photographic Library

437 Empingham

Rutland Water

  2 hrs+ All year

The whole family can enjoy this award-winning attraction with a 3,100-acre lake set in beautiful countryside and more than 20 miles of off-road cycling or walking. Spend time at the butterfly and aquatic centre, then take in the nature reserve or have a go on the climbing wall.

* Bird-watching, windsurfing & canoeing
* Range of craft available for hire or launch your own

Location
Just off A606, signed from A1

Opening
Daily: 10am–5pm

Admission
Free. Car park charge

Contact
Tourist Information Centre, Sykes Lane, Empingham, Rutland LE 15 8PX
t 01572 653026
w anglianwaterleisure.co.uk
e tic@anglianwaterleisure.co.uk

438 Lyddington

Lyddington Bede House

  1 hr Apr–Oct

Lyddington Bede House was originally a wing of a medieval rural palace belonging to the bishops of Lincoln. In 1600 the building was converted into an alms house and it remained a home for pensioners until the 1930s.

* Great Chamber features a beautiful ceiling cornice
* Bedesmen's rooms with tiny windows & fireplaces

Location
In Lyddington, 6 miles N of Corby, 1 mile E of A6003, next to church

Opening
Please phone for details

Admission
Adult £3.30, Child £1.70, Concs £2.50
Prices for events vary

Contact
Bluecoat Lane, Lyddington LE15 9LZ
t 01572 822438
w english-heritage.org.uk

439 Oakham

Rutland County Museum

  1 hr+ All year

Learn about England's smallest county through the museum's displays of archaeology, architecture, agriculture and domestic life. See the tools and equipment used by tradesmen – the wheelwright, carpenter, blacksmith, farrier and cooper.

* Rare Saunderson tractor
* Tools & equipment of village tradesmen

Location
Off A603, near town centre

Opening
Daily: Mon–Sat 10.30am–5pm, Sun 2pm–4pm

Admission
Free

Contact
Catmose Street, Oakham LE15 6HW
t 01572 758440
e museum@rutland.gov.uk

Lapworth, Warwickshire

West Midlands

Herefordshire Shropshire Staffordshire
Warwickshire West Midlands Worcestershire

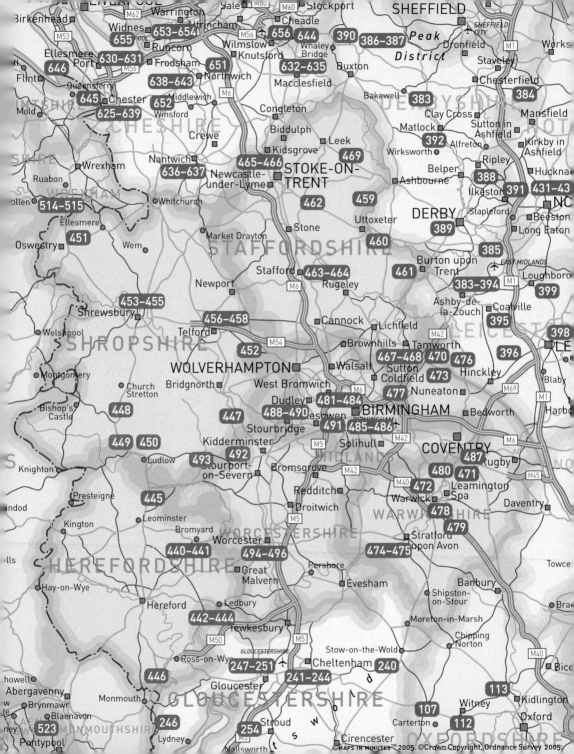

Brockhampton Estate

1 hr   All year

This beautiful park with ancient woodland is a
perfect habitat for wildlife including the dormouse,
raven and buzzard. There are guided walks throughout
the year and a C14 manor house with moat at the
heart of the estate.

* Timber-framed gatehouse & ruined chapel
* Woodland is home to interesting range of wildlife

Location	Admission
2 miles E of Bromyard on A44	Adult £3.60, Child £1.80
Opening	**Contact**
House Mar Sat–Sun 12noon–4pm;	Greenfields, Bringsty WR6 5TB
Apr–Sep Wed–Sun 12noon–5pm;	
Oct Wed–Sun 12noon–4pm	t 01885 488099/482077
Estate All year dawn–dusk	w nationaltrust.org.uk
	e brockhampton@nationaltrust.org.uk

Shortwood Family Farm

4 hrs+   Easter–Oct

Shortwood is an organic farm with a trail to walk and a
pets corner. Guided tours are run between 2pm and
4pm every afternoon. Visitors can collect eggs, feed the
animals, milk a cow and watch a milking machine
in action.

* Play area
* Trailer rides

Location	Admission
Signed from A417 between Burley	Adult £5, Child £3.20
Gate, Bodenham & from Pencombe	
village	**Contact**
	Pencombe,
Opening	Bromyard HR7 4RP
Daily: Easter–Oct from 10am	
	t 01885 400205
	w shortwoodfarm.co.uk

Eastnor Castle

2–3 hrs   Easter–Oct

This fairytale castle in the dramatic setting of the
Malvern Hills is surrounded by a beautiful deer park,
arboretum and lake. Other attractions include the
knight's maze, an assault course and pretty lakeside
and woodland paths.

* Giant redwood grove
* Adventure playground

Location	Admission
2 miles from Ledbury on A438	*Castle & Grounds* Adult £7, Child £4,
Ledbury–Tewkesbury road. 5 miles	Concs £6
from M50 (junction 2) via Ledbury	*Grounds* £5, £3, £4
Opening	**Contact**
Easter–3 Oct Sun & Bank Hol Mon	Eastnor, Ledbury HR8 1RL
11am–5pm; Jul –Aug daily except Sat	
	t 01531 633160
	w eastnorcastle.com

443 Ledbury

Glazydayz Ceramic Café

2 hrs · All year

Paint pottery to your own design and personalise it. When you have created your masterpiece, the staff will glaze and fire the finished article and you can collect it three days later.

* Birthday parties & regular workshops
* Nontoxic & washable paint

Location
In Ledbury; easily reached from Worcester, Gloucestershire & Herefordshire

Opening
Daily: Tue–Fri 11am–6pm, Sat–Sun 11am–5pm (open Mon of school hols)

Admission
Adult £5, Child £3 (+ cost of pottery)

Contact
Homend Trading Estate, Ledbury HR8 1AR
t 01531 636018
w ledburyceramics.net
e ledburyceramics@supanet.com

444 Ledbury

Newbridge Farm Park

2 hrs+ · Easter–Sep

Enjoy a day out on the farm where our visitors are encouraged to touch and feed our many farm animals: chicks, ducklings, geese, peafowl, lambs, kids, goats, rabbits, cows and calves. There are tractor and trailer rides throughout the day and a range of play areas.

* Pony rides (4 & over) for an extra charge
* Indoor & outdoor picnic areas

Location
3 miles W of Ledbury. Take A449 & then A4172

Opening
Easter–Sep Mon–Sat 10am–5pm

Admission
Please phone for details

Contact
Newbridge Farm Park, Little Marcle, nr Ledbury, Herefordshire HR8 2QG
t 01531 670780
w newbridgefarm.co.uk
e gardeners@newbridge-farmpark.freeserve.co.uk

445 Leominster

Berrington Hall

2 hrs · Mar–Oct

Berrington Hall is an C18 mansion with a Georgian dairy, a Victorian laundry, a walled garden and a children's play area. Orienteering courses are available.

* Ugly bug safaris
* Quizzes organised

Location
3 miles N of Leominster

Opening
Times vary, please phone for details

Admission
Adult £5, Child £2.50

Contact
Leominster HR6 0DW
t 01568 615721
w nationaltrust.org.uk
e berrington@nationaltrust.org.uk

446 Symonds Yat West

Amazing Hedge Puzzle

2 hrs · All year

Have fun finding your way to the centre of the maze but try to avoid the 13 deadends. By making your own labyrinths you can follow in the footsteps of the heroes of ancient Greece and India, Roman soldiers, Native Americans, medieval monks and English kings.

* Hands-on displays allow you to build your own maze
* Set in the beautiful countryside of the Wye Valley

Location
Follow signs on B4164, off A40 between Ross-on-Wye & Monmouth

Opening
Daily: Jan–Feb & Nov–Dec 11am–3pm; Apr–Sep and half-terms 11am–5pm; Mar & Oct 11am–4pm

Admission
Please phone for details

Contact
Jubilee Park, Symonds Yat West, Ross-on-Wye HR9 6DA
t 01600 890360
w mazes.co.uk

447 Bridgnorth

Rays Farm Country Matters

2 hrs Mar–Oct

This attraction has unusual animals and birds, including red fallow, Sika and Axis deer, and Bagot, pygmy, angora and other goats. Come and meet the owls, llamas, horses, ponies and donkeys, and follow the Sculpture Trail of Myth and Magic.

* Pull 'Excalibur' from its stone

Location
Signed off B4363 near Billingsley between Bridgnorth & Cleobury Mortimer

Opening
Daily: Mar–Oct 10am–5.30pm

Admission
Adult £5.50, Child £4, Concs £5

Contact
Billingsley, Bridgnorth Shropshire WV16 6PF

t 01299 841255
w raysfarm.com

---

448 Church Stretton

Acton Scott

3 hrs Apr–Oct

Experience daily life on an upland farm at the turn of the C20. The waggoner and his team of heavy horses work the land with vintage farm machines. Every day you can see milking by hand and buttermaking in the dairy. You will also see the farrier and the blacksmith.

* Lambing, shearing & cidermaking in season
* Children's holiday activities

Location
Off A49, 17 miles S of Shrewsbury, 14 miles N of Ludlow

Opening
Apr–Oct Tue–Sun & Bank Hols 10am–5pm

Admission
Adult £4.50, Child £2.25, Concs £4

Contact
nr Church Stretton SY6 6QN

t 01694 781306
w actonscottmuseum.co.uk
e acton.scott.museum@
  shropshire–cc.gov.uk

449 Craven Arms

Secret Hills – Shropshire Hills Discovery Centre

2 hrs+ All year

Learn about ecology, geology, culture and more at this new hands-on discovery centre, set in a grass-roofed building in the Shropshire Hills. Visitors can also take a simulated balloon flight.

* Craft gallery & activities area
* Find out about earthquakes

Location
Off A49, 7 miles N of Ludlow

Opening
Daily: Apr–Oct 10am–4.30pm;
Nov–Mar 10am–3.30pm

Admission
Adult £4.25, Child £2.75

Contact
School Road, Craven Arms SY7 9RS

t 01588 676000/676040
w shropshire-cc.gov.uk/discover.nsf
e secrethills@shropshire-cc.gov.uk

450 Ludlow

Stokesay Castle

1 hr   All year

Stokesay Castle is the finest and best-preserved C13 fortified manor house in England. It includes a medieval Great Hall, a timber-framed Jacobean gatehouse, the parish church and delightful cottage-style gardens.

* Magnificent Great Hall largely untouched

Location	Admission
Off A49, 7 miles NW of Ludlow	Adult £4.60, Child £2.30, Concs £3.50
Opening	**Contact**
Mar–May Thu–Mon 10am–5pm	Craven Arms SY7 9AH
Jun–Aug daily 10am–6pm	
Sep–Oct Thu–Mon 10am–5pm;	t 01588 672544
Nov–Feb Fri–Sun 10am–4pm	w english-heritage.org.uk

451 Oswestry

Park Hall Countryside Experience

5 hrs+   All year

This is an all-weather farm visitor attraction. Popular with young and old alike, Park Hall puts on regular activities at which you can meet and feed the animals. This unique experience combines education, fun and adventure. An impressive 80 per cent of the activities are indoors.

* Children's 4x4 off-road course with replica Land Rovers
* Indoor & outdoor adventure areas

Location	Family £21
In Oswestry, 30 mins from Chester.	**Contact**
Take A495 off Oswestry bypass (A483)	Park Hall,
Opening	Oswestry SY11 4AS
Please phone for details or visit the	
website	t 01691 671123
Admission	w parkhallfarm.co.uk
Adult £5.35, Child & Concs £4.35,	e rachel@parkhallfarm.co.uk

452 Shifnal

The RAF Museum – Cosford

3 hrs+   All year

Follow the story of man's flight – the successes and failures – through one of the largest aviation collections in the UK. More than 70 historic aircraft are displayed in three wartime hangars on an active airfield, which include missiles, motor vehicles and aero-engines.

* Visitor Attraction of the Year 2003
* State-of-the-art flight simulator

Location	Admission
On A41, less than 1 mile from M54	Free. Charges for special events
junction 3	Under-16s must be accompanied
	by an adult
Opening	
Daily: 10am–6pm (last admission 4pm)	**Contact**
	Cosford, Shifnal TF11 8UP
	t 01902 376200
	w rafmuseum.org
	e cosford@rafmuseum.com

453 Shrewsbury

Hawkstone Park

4 hrs   All year

Created in the C18, Hawkstone became one of the greatest historic parklands in Europe. The park is centred around the Red Castle and the awe-inspiring Grotto Hill, and features intricate pathways, ravines, arches and bridges, towering cliffs and follies.

* Woodland full of ancient oaks
* Has won numerous awards

Location	Contact
Off A49, between Shrewsbury & Whitchurch	Weston-under-Redcastle, Shrewsbury SY4 5UY
Opening	t 01939 200611
Jan–Feb Sat–Sun 10am–3pm;	w hawkstone.co.uk
21 Mar–30 Oct daily 10am–4pm	e info@hawkstone.co.uk
Admission	
Adult £5.75, Child £3.75, Concs £4.75	

454 Shrewsbury

Mythstories, Museum of Myth & Fable

1 hr+   Apr–Oct

Enjoy colourful displays of traditional stories from Shropshire and around the world, with illustrations, photographs and artefacts. There are things to touch and play with, puzzles to do and live storytelling in the inglenook fireplace.

* Shropshire Family Attraction of the Year 2001
* Full programme of story walks

Location	Contact
On B5063 just off A49 near Whitchurch	The Morgan Library, Aston Street, Wem, Shrewsbury SY4 5AU
Opening	
Daily: Apr–Oct Sun–Thu 2pm–6pm;	t 01939 235500
prebooked group visits at other times	w mythstories.com
Admission	e info@mythstories.com
Adult £3.50, Child & Concs £2	

455 Shrewsbury

Wroxeter Roman City

1 hr   All year

The largest excavated Roman city in Britain to have escaped development, Wroxeter was once home to 6,000 people. The impressive remains include C2 municipal baths. The site museum offers an insight into the lives of the people who lived here.

* Fourth-largest Roman settlement in Britain

Location	Admission
On B4380, 5 miles E of Shrewsbury	Adult £4, Child £2, Concs £3
Opening	**Contact**
Daily: Apr–Sep 10am–6pm;	Wroxeter, Shrewsbury SY5 6PH
Oct 10am–5pm;	
Nov–Mar 10am–1pm & 2pm–4pm	t 01743 761330
	w english-heritage.org.uk

456 Telford

Enginuity

2 hrs   All year

Based in the Ironbridge World Heritage Site, this museum explains the science and design behind the gadgets we see and use every day. Pull a real locomotive, control the flow of water to generate electricity or even pitch yourself against a robot.

* World Heritage Site
* Be an apprentice engineer for the day

Location
Follow the brown tourist signs from M54 junction 4

Opening
Daily: 10am–5pm

Admission
Adult £5.45, Child & Concs £3.80

Contact
Ironbridge Gorge Museum Trust, Coach Road, Coalbrookdale, Telford TE8 7DQ

t 01952 884391
w ironbridge.org.uk
e tic@ironbridge.org.uk

457 Telford

Ironbridge Gorge Museums

1–6 hrs   All year

There are ten award-winning museums spread along what is often called 'the valley that changed the world'. That valley, beside the River Severn, is still spanned by the world's first iron bridge. See the products that set industry on its way and the machines that made them.

* Various workshops, including ceramic & iron working
* Enginuity – hands-on design & tech experiences

Location
5 miles S of Telford, signed from M54 junction 4

Opening
Daily: 10am–5pm; some areas close in winter

Admission
Passport ticket to all 10 attractions
Adult £13.25, Child £8.75, Concs £11.50

Contact
Ironbridge, Telford TF8 7DQ

t 01952 884391
w ironbridge.org.uk
e tic@ironbridge.org.uk

458 Telford

Wonderland

2 hrs+   All year

Set in a beautiful woodland setting, walks lead you through the world of fairytales where children can find their favourite characters and their houses around every corner. The characters come to life to sing songs and tell stories. Children can also play in the giant indoor softplay area.

* Crazy golf on the *Jolly Roger*
* Extensive hedge maze

Location
Follow signs for Telford Town Park & Wonderland off junctions 4 & 5 of M54

Opening
Easter–Sep 10am–4pm; weekends & school hols; (open until 6pm at peak times)

Admission
Please phone for details

Contact
Telford Town Park
Telford, Shropshire TF3 4AY

t 01952 591633
w wonderlandtelford.com
e info@wonderlandtelford.com

459 Alton

Alton Towers

6 hrs+   Mar–Oct

A famous extensive theme park with a mix of rides and attractions to suit every member of the family. It includes 200 acres of landscaped gardens, rides, live entertainment and the historic Towers building. Come along and enjoy a fun-packed family day out.

* New family spinning rollercoaster
* Two onsite hotels incorporating an indoor water park

Location
Off B5030, near Uttoxeter (A50); take junction 15 or 16 from M6, or junction 23a or 28 from M1. Follow brown tourist signs

Opening
Daily: Mar–end Oct (gates open at 9am) 9.30am–5pm (later in summer) Please phone or visit the website before visiting

Admission
Please phone for details

Contact
Alton, Stoke-on-Trent ST10 4DB

t 08705 204060
w altontowers.com

460 Ashbourne

Sudbury Hall & Museum of Childhood

3 hrs   Mar–Oct

This spectacular late C17 house has sumptuous interiors and a fine collection of portraits. The great staircase is one of the most elaborate of its kind in an English house. The C19 service wing is home to the Museum of Childhood with displays about children from the C18 onwards.

* Featured in the BBC production of *Pride and Prejudice*
* 'Behind the Scenes' tours

Location
6 miles E of Uttoxeter at junction of A50 Derby–Stoke & A515 Ashbourne roads

Opening
Hall & Museum 11 Mar–29 Oct Wed–Sun 1pm–5pm
Grounds 11 Mar–29 Oct Wed–Sun 11am–6pm;
Open Bank Hols

Admission
Hall Adult £5.50, Child £2.50
Museum £5.50, £3.50
Hall & Museum £11, £6

Contact
Sudbury, Ashbourne DE6 5HT

t 01283 585337
w nationaltrust.org.uk
e sudburyhall@nationaltrust.org.uk

461 Burton upon Trent

Coors Visitor Centre

2 hrs+   All year

Beer has been brewed in Burton upon Trent for centuries and the Museum of Brewing charts its heritage. It provides a blend of living heritage, historic galleries and family entertainment. The centre is home to two teams of shire horses and a vintage vehicle collection.

* See a working stationary steam engine
* Visit the micro brewery

Location
A511 in centre of Burton upon Trent (follow signs for Burton North and Stretton)

Opening
Daily: 10am–5pm (last admission 4pm)

Admission
Adult £6, Child £3, Concs £4

Contact
Horninglow Street
Burton upon Trent DE14 1YQ

t 0845 600 0598
w coorsvisitorcentre.com
e enquiries@coorsbrewers.com

© Spinball Whizzer, Alton Towers

462 Longton

Gladstone Working Pottery Museum

2 hrs+   All year

A complete Victorian pottery factory where visitors can get to grips with the history and skills of the potteries. Throw your own pot or try your hand at a range of pottery crafts with the team of friendly expert presentation staff.

* Traditional skills & original workshops
* Cobbled yard & huge bottle kilns

Location	Contact
From M6 follow A500, then take A50 to Longton	Uttoxeter Road, Longton, Stoke-on-Trent ST3 1PQ
Opening	t 01782 319232
Daily: 10am–5pm	w stoke.gov.uk/gladstone
	e gladstone@stoke.gov.uk
Admission	
Adult £4.95, Child £3.50, Concs £3.95	

463 Stafford

British Wildlife Rescue Centre

2 hrs   All year

The whole family will enjoy a visit to this refuge set up for the treatment of sick and injured British wildlife. Also on the farm are a play barn, steam railway, craft shops, a restaurant and a garden centre.

* Guided tours

Location	Contact
On A518 Stafford–Uttoxeter road, 1 mile from Weston	Amerton Working Farm, Stowe-by-Chartley, Stafford ST18 0LA
Opening	t 01889 271308
Daily: 10am–5pm	w thebwrc.co.uk
Admission	
Adult £1.50, Child £1	

464 Stafford

Stafford Castle

3 hrs+   All year

Built by William the Conqueror to subdue rebellious local people, Stafford Castle has dominated the landscape throughout 900 years. Visitors today will find a more peaceful setting – follow the castle trail, explore the castle ruins and take in the panoramic view.

* Try on armour & chainmail
* Host of archaeological finds

Location	Contact
Off A518, 1 mile SW of Stafford	Castle Bank, Newport Road, Stafford ST16 1DJ
Opening	t 01785 257698
Apr–Oct Tue–Sun & Bank Hols 10am–5pm; Nov–Mar Sat–Sun 10am–4pm	w staffordbc.gov.uk
Admission	
Free	

465 Stoke-on-Trent

Etruria Industrial Museum

1 hr   All year

Etruria Industrial Museum is situated on the Calden, Trent and Mersey canals and includes the Etruscan Bone and Flint Mill. It has a family-friendly interactive exhibition, a tea room and a shop. It is also the last steam-powered potter's mill in Britain.

* Family-friendly interactive exhibition & events programme
* Craft activities in school holidays

Location	Contact
Signed from A500. Car park is off Etruria Vale Road	Lower Bedford Street, Etruria Stoke-on-Trent ST4 7AF
Opening	t 01782 233144
Jan–Mar Mon–Wed 12noon–4.30pm Apr–Dec Sat–Wed 12noon–4.30pm	w stoke.gov.uk
	e museums@stoke.gov.uk
Admission	
Adult £2.35, Child £1.20, Family £5.30	

466 Stoke-on-Trent

Waterworld

3–4 hrs　　All year

Children will enjoy this wacky and wild water park. It has 19 exciting rides and attractions including wave machines, flumes, rapids and slides. Very popular attractions include the Spacebowl, aqua assault course, the Python, and Black Hole. Aquadisco parties are also available.

* Best Practice Accolade 2002

Location
Off junction 16 of M6. From M1 follow A50 to Stoke-on-Trent, then follow signs to Festival Park

Opening
Summer Mon–Tue 10am–6pm, Wed–Thu 10am–7pm, Fri 10am–9pm, Sat–Sun 10am–6pm
winter Wed–Thu 2pm–7pm, Fri 2pm–9pm, Sat–Sun 10am–6pm

Admission
Please phone for details

Contact
Etruria, Hanley, Stoke-on-Trent ST1 5PU

t 01782 205747
w waterworld.co.uk

467 Tamworth

Ash End House Children's Farm

4 hrs　　All year

This small family-owned farm has lots of friendly animals to feed and stroke. As well as outdoor activities and a play area, the farm offers many undercover attractions and some fascinating rare breeds. There are activities during weekends and holidays, including Make a Memento.

* Tours for groups
* Birthday parties on the farm

Location
In Middleton, near Tamworth in Staffordshire. Signed off A4091 & on same road as Drayton Manor Park

Opening
Daily: summer 10am–5pm; winter 10am–dusk
Please phone for details

Admission
Adult £3.90, Child £4.90 (includes feed for animals & other activities)

Contact
Middleton Lane, Middleton, nr Tamworth B78 2BL

t 0121 329 3240
w childrensfarm.co.uk
e contact@childrensfarm.co.uk

468 Tamworth

Drayton Manor Family Theme Park

6 hrs+　　Mar–Oct

Everyone's favourite theme park, with more than 100 rides and attractions set in 280 acres of lakes and parkland. It boasts some of the biggest, wettest and scariest rides around – plus family and children's rides, visit the zoo, museums, shops and restaurants.

* Thrills and fun for everyone
* Live entertainment

Location
Near Tamworth on A4091. From M42 take junction 9 or 10

Opening
Daily: mid-Mar–31 Oct
Please phone or visit the website for details

Admission
Please phone or visit the website for details

Contact
Tamworth B78 3TW

t 08708 725252
w draytonmanor.co.uk
e info@draytonmanor.co.uk

469 Winkhill

Blackbrook Zoological Park

2–4 hrs　　All year

Set amid the Staffordshire Moorlands, this zoo contains a large and varied collection of some of the most rare and endangered species to be found in the world, from swans and geese to vultures and flamingos, from meerkats and marmots to piranhas and pythons.

* Pets, aquarium & educational building
* Largest collection of birds from around the world

Location
From Leek, take A523 & 1st right, signed to the park, then 1st right again

Opening
Daily: 10.30am–5.30pm (earlier closing in winter)
Café open in summer only

Admission
Please phone for details

Contact
Winkhill ST13 7QR

t 01538 308293
w blackbrookzoologicalpark.co.uk
e enquiries@blackbrookzoological park.co.uk

470 Atherstone

Twycross Zoo

3–4 hrs   All year

Twycross is the leading primate zoo in the country, but it also hosts hundreds of other animals from around the world including elephants, big cats, birds, reptiles and amphibians.

* Seal & penguin feeding times
* Pets' corner & rare breeds

Location
Just off M42 on A444 in Leicestershire, easily reached from all the Midland counties

Opening
Daily: summer 10am–5.30pm; winter (Nov–Mar) 10am–4pm

Admission
Adult £8, Child £4.50, Concs £5.50

Contact
Burton Road,
Atherstone CV9 3PX

t 01827 880250
w twycrosszoo.com

471 Beandon

Brandon Marsh Nature Centre

1 hr+   All year

A visit to Brandon Marsh Nature Centre starts at the visitor centre, opened by Sir David Attenborough in 1998. This contains displays, hands-on activities and information about the nature reserve, which covers 220 acres and features many lakes and bird hides.

* Warwickshire Wildlife Trust Centre

Location
Off A45

Opening
Daily: Mon–Sat 9am–4.30pm,
Sun 10am–4pm

Admission
Adult £2.50, Child £1, Concs £1.50

Contact
Brandon Lane, Coventry CV3 3GW

t 02476 308999
w wildlifetrust.org.uk
e enquiries@wkwt.org.uk

472 Hatton

Hatton Country World

3 hrs+   All year

Hatton Country World offers acres of fun for everyone, with a fun-packed day of events and activities, such as Farmyard Favourites and Adventure Land. Finish off your day with a relaxing browse round the unique shopping village or a trip to see the animals.

* Daft Duck trials, children's show & Birdobatics
* Soft play centre & Tristan the Runaway Tractor

Location
5 mins from junction 15 off M40. Take A46 towards Coventry, turn on to A4177 & follow brown tourist signs

Opening
Daily: 10am–5pm;

Admission
Please phone or look on website

Contact
Hatton House,
Hatton CV35 7LD

t 01926 843411
w hattonworld.com
e hatton@hattonworld.com

473 Kingsbury

Broomey Croft Children's Farm

2 hrs+   All year

Set in the North Warwickshire countryside, Broomey Croft Children's Farm provides an opportunity for a family day of fun and relaxation. Children can meet and handfeed the farm animals, and see baby goats, sheep shearing, baby chicks and a bee display.

* Free tractor & trailer rides
* Lambing & bottle-feeding lambs

Location
10 mins from junction 9 off M42. Take A4091 towards Drayton Manor & follow brown tourist signs

Opening
Please phone or visit the website for details

Admission
Adult £3.95, Child £3.45

Contact
Bodymoor Heath Lane,
Bodymoor Heath,
Kingsbury B76 OEE

t 01827 873844
w childrens-farm.com
e info@childrens-farm.com

474 Stratford-upon-Avon

Shakespeare's Birthplace

1 hr   All year

The five shakespeare houses open to the public each has its own character and connection to the great man, A visit to the house of his birth will tell you something of the family history and childhood of the world's greatest playwright.

* Exhibitions tell the story of the house
* Exhibits of rare period items including First Folio (1623)

Location
Signed from town centre

Opening
Nov–Mar Mon–Sat 10am–4pm,
Sun 9.30am–5pm;
Apr–May & Sep–Oct Mon–Sat
10am–5pm, Sun 10.30am–5pm;
Jun–Aug Mon–Sat 9am–5pm,
Sun 10.30am–4pm

Admission
Adult £6.70, Child £2.60, Concs £5.50

Contact
Henley Street,
Stratford-upon-Avon CV37 6QW

t 01789 201823
w shakespeare.org.uk
e info@shakespeare.org.uk

475 Stratford-upon-Avon

Stratford Butterfly Farm

1 hr+   All year

Wander through a tropical rainforest with a myriad of multicoloured butterflies, birds and fish. See fascinating animals in Insect City and view deadly spiders in perfect safety in Arachnoland.

* Expert staff
* Wildlife video shows

Location
On River Avon, opposite Royal Shakespeare Theatre. Easily accessible from town centre

Opening
Daily: summer 10am–6pm; winter 10am–dusk

Admission
Please phone for details

Contact
Traway Walk, Swan's Nest Lane, Stratford-upon-Avon CV37 7LS

t 01789 299288
w butterflyfarm.co.uk
e sales@butterflyfarm.co.uk

476 Sutton Cheney

Bosworth Battlefield Visitor Centre & Country Park

2 hrs+   Mar–Dec

This is the site of one of the most famous battles in English history, between Richard III and Henry Tudor. The result gave England a new king and marked the beginning of the Tudor dynasty. Discover what it was like to be a soldier and follow the battle trail.

* Walk down a medieval street
* Annual re-enactment of the battle

Location
2 miles S of Market Bosworth near village of Sutton Cheney

Opening
Visitor centre Mar Sat–Sun 11am–5pm; Apr–Oct daily 11am–5pm
Country Park Jan–Oct daily 7am onwards. Closing times vary

Admission
Adult £3.25, Concs £2.25

Contact
Sutton Cheney, Nuneaton, Warwickshire CV13 0AD

t 01455 290429
w leics.gov.uk
e bosworth@leics.gov.uk

477 Sutton Coldfield

Kingsbury Water Park

2 hrs+   All year

Warwickshire's premier waterside attraction. Kingsbury Water Park has 15 lakes situated in more than 600 acres of country park. Stroll along the surfaced paths, spot birds and wildlife, hire a bike or join an organised event. There is also an adventure playground and a farm.

* Day-ticket fishing
* Miniature railway new for 2006

Location
Exit at junction 9 of M42 & follow A4097 towards Kingsbury

Opening
Please phone for details

Admission
Car park £2.50

Contact
Bodymoor Heath, Sutton Coldfield B76 0DY

t 01827 872660
w warwickshire.gov.uk/countryside
e parks@warwickshire.gov.uk

478 Warwick

Warwick Castle

2 hrs+   All year

Britain's greatest medieval experience – discover 1,000 years of history at Warwick Castle. See the medieval preparation for battle in Kingmaker, join a Victorian Royal Weekend Party and enjoy special events throughout the year.

* Quality Assured Visitor Attraction

Location
2 miles from junction 15 off M40. Warwick Castle is easily accessible by road or rail

Opening
Daily: Apr–Sep 10am–6pm; Oct–Mar 10am–5pm

Admission
Please phone for details

Contact
Warwick CV34 4QU

t 0870 442 2000
w warwick-castle.co.uk
e customer.information@warwick-castle.co.uk

479 Wellesbourne

Wellesbourne Watermill

2 hrs   Easter–Sep

Visitors to this historic watermill can see the mill's machinery being driven by one of the country's largest wooden waterwheels. There are regular demonstrations of how stoneground flour is milled. Coracles are used on the millpond, which is a tranquil haven for wildlife.

* Conservation award from SPAB
* Fishing lake

Location
On B4086, between Kineton & Stratford-upon-Avon

Opening
18 Mar–Sep Wed–Sun & Bank Hols 10am–5pm; 22 Jul–1 Sep Tue–Sun 10am–5pm

Admission
Adult £4.50, Child £3, Concs £3.50

Contact
Kineton Road, Wellesbourne CV35 9HG

t 01789 470237
w wellesbournemill.co.uk
e charhutsby@talk21.com

480 Baginton

Midland Air Museum

2 hrs   All year

See a wide range of aircraft, both international and local. The collection includes WWII aircraft and memorabilia and outside are a number of rare aircraft, plus an anti-aircraft gun. A number of the aircraft have steps up to the cockpit area so you can look inside.

* Giant 1959 Armstrong Whitworth Argosy freighter
* Meteor, Vulcan, Hunter, Starfighter & Phantom

Location
Off A45, between roundabout & Baginton

Opening
Daily: Apr–Oct Mon–Sat 10am–5pm,
Sun 10am–6pm;
Nov–Mar 10am–5pm

Admission
Adult £4.25, Child £2.50, Concs £3.75

Contact
Coventry Airport, Baginton,
Coventry CV8 3AZ

t 02476 301033
w midlandairmuseum.org.uk
e midlandairmuseum@aol.com

481 Birmingham

Lapworth Museum of Geology

1 hr   All year

For an educational few hours, bring the children to visit one of the oldest specialist geological museums in the UK. Dating back to 1880, Lapworth has an extensive and fascinating collection of fossils, minerals and rocks.

* More than 250, 000 specimens
* 420 million-year-old fossils

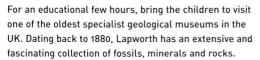

Location
On A38 Bristol road into Birmingham

Opening
Daily: Mon–Fri 9am–5pm; Sat–Sun 2pm–5pm; Please phone for details
Other times by appointment

Admission
Free

Contact
University of Birmingham, Edgbaston
Birmingham B15 2TT

t 0121 414 7294
w lapworth.bham.ac.uk
e lapmus@bham.ac.uk

482 Birmingham

National Sea Life Centre

3 hrs   All year

A unique insight into the lives of a myriad creatures – from shrimps to sharks. The unique, one-million-litre tropical ocean display has a Hawaiian volcanic theme, and the completely transparent 360° submarine tunnel provides a home for two giant green turtles.

* Programme of talks & feeding demonstrations
* Totally tropical centre

Location
Between National Indoor Arena & International Convention Centre

Opening
Summer daily 10am–5pm;
winter Mon–Fri 10am–4pm,
Sat–Sun 10am–5pm

Admission
Adult £11, Child £8.25, Concs £9

Contact
The Waters Edge, Brindleyplace,
Birmingham B1 2HL

t 0121 643 6777/633 4700
w sealifeeurope.com
e slcbirmingham@
merlinentertainments.biz

483 Birmingham

ThinkTank

4 hrs   All year

ThinkTank is Birmingham's science museum. Visitors can explore everything from aircraft and steam engines to intestines and tastebuds! With prestigious exhibitions, events and tours, there really is something here for everyone, plus ThinkTank's new Planetarium.

* Unravel the mysteries of the body
* Medical tour covers techniques & instruments

Location
Follow blue banners, 15 min walk
from New Street

Opening
Daily: 10am–5pm

Admission
Adult £6.95, Child £4.95, Concs £5.50

Contact
Curzon Street, Birmingham B4 7XG
t 0121 202 2222
w thinktank.ac
e findout@thinktank.ac

484 Birmingham

Tolkien's Birmingham

2 hrs   Apr–Sep

Visit many of J R R Tolkien's childhood haunts and see the places that inspired him to write *The Hobbit* and *Lord of the Rings*. This is a fascinating guided tour, and a chance to encounter the young imagination of a literary genius.

* Indepth knowledge from specialist tour guide for groups only
* Please wear appropriate footwear

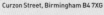

Location
Various areas of Birmingham

Opening
Apr–Sep by appointment
Please phone for details of guided tours

Admission
Adult £5, Child £2.50

Contact
50 Springfield Road,
Kings Heath,
Birmingham B14 7DU
t 0121 444 4046
w birminghamheritage.org.uk
e balti1@compuserve.com

485 Bournville

Cadbury World

3 hrs   Feb–Dec

There is fun for all ages with the magical Cadabra journey and the Cadbury Fantasy Factory. Children can learn all about chocolate – where it came from and who first consumed this mysterious substance – and then visit the largest Cadbury shop in the world!

* Learn how chocolate is used to make famous brands
* Chocolate Coronation Street!

Location
Signed from M42

Opening
Feb–Dec; times vary, please phone for details

Admission
Adult £10.50, Child £7.90, Concs £8.30
Prebooking recommended

Contact
Linden Road, Bournville,
Birmingham B30 2LU

t 0121 451 4159
w cadburyworld.co.uk
e cadbury.world@csplc.com

486 Bournville

Selly Manor

2 hrs   All year

Learn about medieval life, the Tudors, old houses and furniture in this amazing medieval timber-framed house that was moved piece by piece by George Cadbury to the village of Bournville. Portable notes, torches and magnifying glasses are provided.

* In the unique village of Bournville, near Cadbury world

Location
3 miles S of Birmingham city centre on Maple Road next to Bournville village green

Opening
Tue–Fri 10am–5pm;
Apr–Sep, Sat–Sun & Bank Hols only 2pm–5pm

Admission
Adult £3, Child £1, Concs £2

Contact
Bournville, Birmingham B30 1UB

t 0121 472 0199
w bvt.org.uk/sellymanor
e sellymanor@bvt.org.uk

487 Coventry

Ryton Organic Gardens

4 hrs   All year

Ryton Organic Gardens is the UK's national centre for organic gardening, set within 10 acres of glorious gardens. There is a fantastic new interactive visitor centre including The Vegetable Kingdom, an exciting addition especially for children.

* Children's garden
* Computer games

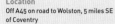

Location
Off A45 on road to Wolston, 5 miles SE of Coventry

Opening
Daily: 9am–5pm

Admission
Adult £4.50, Child £2, Concs £4

Contact
Ryton-on-Dunsmore,
Coventry CV8 3LG

t 02476 303517
w hdra.org.uk
e enquiry@hdra.org.uk

The perfect vegetable?
The perfect vegetable plant would be totally edible.
It might look something like this!

Dudley

Black Country Living Museum

3 hrs+   All year

Discover a fascinating world where an old-fashioned village has been created beside the canal. Wander around original shops and houses, ride on a tramcar or fairground swingboat, go down the mine or just soak up the atmosphere.

* Tramcars & trolleybuses transport visitors
* Costumed demonstrators & working craftsmen

Location	Contact
On A4037, 3 miles from M5 junction 2	Tipton Road, Dudley DY1 4SQ
Opening	t 0121 557 9643
Daily: Mar–Oct 10am–5pm;	w bclm.co.uk
Nov–Feb Wed–Sun 10am–4pm	e info@bclm.co.uk
Admission	
Adult £9.95, Child £5.75, Concs £8.75	

Dudley

Dudley Canal Trust

1 hr   Feb–Nov

Explore Dudley's subterranean world of limestone mines and canal systems. Visitors can see the mining and engineering feats of the men of the C18 and modern tunnelling techniques of today. Computer displays show scenes from the past 200 years of mining.

* See the geological history of the area
* Special events throughout the year

Location	Admission
Follow signs to Dudley past Black Country Living Museum to traffic lights, turn left & the attraction is on the left	Adult £4.15, Child £3.50, Concs £3.80
	Contact
	The Ticket Office, Todds End Towpath, Tipton Road, Dudley
Opening	
Mar–Oct 10am–5pm;	t 01384 236275
Feb & Nov 10am–4pm	w dudleytunneltrips.org
	e dcttrips@btclick.com

Dudley

Dudley Zoological Gardens

3 hrs+   All year

Dudley Zoo is a modern zoo set in the 40-acre wooded grounds of Dudley Castle. Visitors can enjoy a varied day combining zoology, history and geology, as the zoo is built on an important limestone escarpment.

* Breathtaking views over the Black Country
* Audio-visual display & visitor centre

Location	Contact
Just 3 miles from junction 2 of M5	2 The Broadway, Dudley DY1 4QB
Opening	
Daily: Mar–Oct 10am–4pm; Oct–Mar 10am–3pm	t 01384 215313
	w dudleyzoo.org.uk
Admission	
Adult £8.95, Child (4–15) £5.75, Family £31	

491 Edgbaston

Birmingham Botanical Gardens & Glasshouses

2 hrs+   All year

In a series of giant glasshouses, each with different climatic conditions, you can visit a world of environments in just one day. There are four glasshouses (Tropical, Subtropical, Mediterranean and Arid) and a Study Centre running fun workshops aimed at children under 12.

* Designed by J C Loudon, a leading garden planner
* Sculpture trail, waterfowl & exotic birds

Location
Signed from Edgbaston

Opening
Daily: Mon–Sat 9am–5pm
Sun 10am–5pm

Admission
Adult £5.90, Child & Concs £3.50

Contact
Westbourne Road, Edgbaston, Birmingham B15 3TR

t 0121 454 1860
w birminghambotanicalgardens. org.uk
e admin@birminghambotanical gardens. org.uk

492 Bewdley

West Midland Safari & Leisure Park

3 hrs+   Apr–Oct

A 4-mile drive-through safari covers an area of more than 150 acres and is home to a variety of exotic and unusual animals including rare and beautiful white tigers, elephants, rhino, giraffes, lions, wallabies, emus, camels, zebra, bison, wolves and llamas.

* Safari bus tours
* Discovery trail

Location
On A456 between Kidderminster & Bewdley

Opening
Daily: Apr–Oct Mon–Fri 10am–5pm,
Sat–Sun 10am–5.30

Admission
Please phone for details

Contact
Spring Grove,
Bewdley DY12 1LF

t 01299 402114
w wmsp.co.uk
e info@wmsp.co.uk

493 Kidderminster

Mamble Craft Centre

3 hrs   All year

Mamble Craft Centre is housed in C17 barns on an ancient medieval site, with stunning views of the Clee Hills. It offers an insight into past and present crafts through its four craft workshops where you can see items being made.

* Award-winning tea rooms
* Enticing gift shop

Location	Admission
Off A456 in village of Mamble, midway between Bewdley & Tenbury Wells	Free
Opening	**Contact**
Tue–Sun & Bank Hols 10.30am–5pm; Oct–Dec Mon 10.30am–5pm	Mamble, Kidderminster DY14 9JY
	t 01299 832834
	w mamblecraftcentre.co.uk

494 Worcester

The Hop Pocket Craft Centre

4 hrs   All year

The Hop Pocket Craft Centre is located in the beautiful Frome Valley. See work by more than 300 different craftspeople on display, including pottery, glass engraving, jewellery, soft toys, paintings and woodturning – gifts to suit every pocket.

* Demonstrations by appointment
* New 11 shop shopping village

Location	Contact
On B4214 just off A4103 Worcester–Hereford road	New House Farm, Bishops Frome, Worcester WR6 5BT
Opening	t 01531 640323
Open daily except Mon, please phone for details	w thehoppocket.com
Admission	e john@hoppocket.co.uk
Free	

495 Worcester

Upton Heritage Centre

1 hr+   Apr–Sep

This restored bell tower is the oldest surviving building in the town and is a local landmark. It tells the story of the battle of Upton in 1651 during the Civil War. There are also exhibits on local history and the development of Upton-upon-Severn.

* Battle of Upton display
* Sited in old bell tower

Location	Admission
On B4211 from Great Malvern & A38 & A4104 from Worcester	Free
Opening	**Contact**
Daily: Apr–Sep 1.30pm–4.30pm; open some mornings Please phone for details	Church Street, Upton-upon-Severn, Worcester WR8 0HT
	t 01684 592679

496 Worcester

Worcester Cathedral

1 hr   All year

Worcester Cathedral has been a place of prayer and worship since AD680. The present building was begun in 1084. Its many attractions include King John's tomb, Prince Arthur's Chantry, the early C12 Chapter House and St Wulstan's crypt.

* Tower open 10.30am–4.30pm, Sat & summer holidays
* Magnificent Victorian stained-glass windows

Location	Contact
City centre, off College Street	10a College Green, Worcester WR1 2LH
Opening	t 01905 28854
Daily: 7.30am–6pm, services three times daily	w cofe-worcester.org.uk
Admission	e info@worcestercathedral.org.uk
Free, donations welcomed	

Ystradfellte, Powys

Wales

Mid Wales North Wales South Wales

497 Aberystwyth

Animalarium

3 hrs   All year

Meet a wide collection of exotic and domestic animals, birds and reptiles, including monkeys, marmosets, lemurs, and wallabies. Pony rides run twice daily from Easter to September. There is a petting barn, a fruit bat cave and a daily snake-handling demonstration.

* Wales Tourist Board seal of approval

Location
At Borth, between Aberystwyth & Machynlleth

Opening
Daily: summer 10am–6pm; winter 11am–4pm

Admission
Adult £6.50, Child £4.50, Concs £5.50

Contact
Borth, Ceredigion SY25 6RA

t 01970 871224

---

498 Aberystwyth

Vale of Rheidol Railway

1 hr+   Apr–Oct

Take a ride on a steam train for 11 miles from Aberystwyth to Devil's Bridge. During the hour-long journey you'll have spectacular views of the wooded Rheidol Valley. From Devil's Bridge there are walks to Mynach Falls, Devil's Punchbowl and Jacob's Ladder.

* One of the Great Little Trains of Wales
* Last steam railway owned by British Rail

Location
Trains depart from Aberystwyth centre, beside main railway station

Opening
Please phone for details

Admission
Return Adult £12, Child from £3, Concs £10.50

Contact
Park Avenue, Aberystwyth, Cardiganshire SY23 1PG

t 01970 625819
w rheidolrailway.co.uk
e vor@rheidolrailway.co.uk

---

499 Cardigan

Felinwynt Rainforest & Butterfly Centre

1 hr+   Easter–Oct

This tropical rainforest in the heart of Wales is home to exotic and unusual plants, birds, insects and butterflies from all over the world. You'll see the American glass-wing butterfly, the Asian scarlet swallowtail and the giant atlas moth.

* Welsh Tourist Board star attraction
* Video room

Location
Off A487, 6 miles N of Cardigan. Follow brown tourist signs

Opening
Daily: Easter–Oct 10.30am–5pm

Admission
Adult £3.90, Child £1.75, Concs £3.70

Contact
Felinwynt, Cardigan, Ceredigion SA43 1RT

t 01239 810882/810250
w butterflycentre.co.uk

500 Corris

King Arthur's Labyrinth

2 hrs+   Apr–Nov

Take a boat underground through a waterfall and deep into the spectacular caverns under the mountains where tales of King Arthur are told with stunning sound and light effects. Back above ground, join the Bard's Quest to search for legends lost in the Maze of Time.

* Large fully operational craft centre
* Shop sells items on the Arthurian theme

Location
On A487 between Machynlleth & Dolgellau

Opening
Daily: Apr–5 Nov 10am–5pm (last tour 5pm)

Admission
Adult £5.50, Child £3.90, Concs £4.95

Contact
Corris, Machynlleth, Powys SY20 9RF

t 01654 761584
w kingarthurslabyrinth.com
e king.arthurs.labyrinth@corris-wales.co.uk

---

501 Llandrindod Wells

The National Cycle Collection

1 hr+   All year

How big is a penny-farthing's wheel? And just how uncomfortable were those early bikes compared with today's high-tech versions? See more than 250 bicycles from 1819, such as the hobby horse, boneshakers and penny-farthings, up to the most modern cycles of today.

* The Dunlop story
* Displays about past racing stars

Location
Just off Temple Street in town centre. Llandrindod Wells is on A483

Opening
Mar–Oct daily 10am–4pm;
Nov–Feb Tue, Thu & Sun 10am–4pm

Admission
Adult £2.50, Child £1, Concs £2

Contact
The Automobile Palace, Temple Street, Llandrindod Wells, Powys LD1 5DL

t 01597 825531
w cyclemuseum.org.uk
e cycle.museum@care4free.net

---

502 Llangorse

Llangorse Rope & Riding Centre

4 hrs+   All year

The centre offers a range of indoor and outdoor climbing and riding activities, from rock surfaces and rope bridges to trekking and hacking. There are qualified instructors and onsite accommodation is available.

* Largest indoor climbing & riding centre in Wales
* WTB's Best New Business in Wales Award

Location
On B4560, off A40
Brecon–Abergavenny road

Opening
Climb Mon–Sat 9am–10pm,
Sun 9am–6pm
Ride Daily: 9.30am–4.30pm

Admission
Climb From £11.50 per person
Ride From £12.50 per person

Contact
Gilfach Farm, Llangorse, Brecon Beacons, Powys LD3 7UH

t 01874 658272
w activityuk.com
e info@activity.uk.com

515 Chirk

Pony & Quad Treks

1-4 hrs   Easter–Oct

Enjoy the beautiful Ceiriod Valley on horseback. Choose from a variety of treks, from one hour to a full day, on ponies and horses to suit all ages. For the more adventurous over-12s, there's off-road quad biking.

* Full safety equipment provided
* Full protective clothing available

Location
8 miles from Chirk on B4500

Opening
Daily: Easter–Oct 10.30am–4pm

Admission
Pony Trekking Day £45, 2 hrs £25, 1 hr £15.
Quad Trekking 1 hr £25

Contact
Pont-y-Meibion, Pandy,
Glyn Ceiriog, Chirk, Llangollen,
North Wales LL20 7HS

t 01691 718333/718413
w ponytreks.co.uk
e enquiry@ponytreks.co.uk

516 Colwyn Bay

Harlequin Puppet Theatre

2 hrs+   Feb–Sep

The first permanent puppet theatre to be built in Britain opened on July 7th 1958. It was built as the headquarters for The Eric Bramall Marionettes, a touring company that had been founded in 1944. The company presented a repertoire of opera, plays, musical comedies and fantasies.

* Theatre holds 120 people
* Beautiful Italianate interior

Location
From the A55 Expressway, take the exit marked Rhos-on-Sea & follow signs.

Opening
Jul–Sep & half-terms daily show at 3pm; Jul–Aug also show at 8pm on Wed

Admission
Adult £5, Child & Concs £4

Contact
Cayley Promenade, Rhos-on-Sea,
Colwyn Bay LL28 4EP

t 01492 548166
w puppets.inuk.com
e seats@puppets.inuk.com

517 Colwyn Bay

The Welsh Mountain Zoo

4 hrs+   All year

A wildlife collection kept in a natural environment, with many attractions and activities for children, including a Tarzan Trail adventure playground and a virtual zoo tour. Watch falconry displays during the summer and visit Chimpanzee World.

* Children's farm & Jungle Adventureland
* New! Sealions' Rock

Location
3 mins from A55 (Rhos-on-Sea exit).
Follow signs

Opening
Daily: summer 9.30am–6pm;
winter 9.30am–5pm

Admission
Adult £6.95, Child £4.95, Concs £5.95

Contact
Old Highway, Colwyn Bay,
North Wales LL28 5UY

t 01492 532938
w welshmountainzoo.org

518 Gwynedd

Greenwood Forest Park

4 hrs+   Mar–Oct

Enjoy family adventure and fun at Greenwood Forest Park with its exciting Green Dragon family rollercoaster. Ride the Great Green Run, the longest sledge slide in Wales. Have a Jungle Boat Adventure, shoot traditional longbows or build dens.

* Adventure playgrounds & toddlers' village
* Mini-tractors, puzzle barn & big indoor exhibition

Location
Take A4144, leading to B4366

Opening
Daily: mid-Mar–end Aug
10am–5.30pm; school summer hols
10am–6pm; Sep–Oct 10am–5pm

Admission
Please phone for details

Contact
Y Felinheli, Gwynedd,
North Wales LL56 4QN

t 01248 670076
w greenwoodforestpark.co.uk
e info@greenwoodforestpark.co.uk

519 Llanberis

Snowdon Mountain Railway

2½ hrs   Mar–Nov

Travel on the only public rack and pinion railway in Britain to the summit of Snowdon – the tallest mountain in England and Wales (3,560ft), was built and opened in 1896. For those wishing to walk down, a single ticket to the summit station is available.

* 30-minute stay at the top & free audio-visual guide
* Breathtaking views from the train & the summit

Location
Llanberis station on A4086, 7½ miles
from Caernarfon. 15 mins drive from
A55/A5 junction at Bangor. Nearest
railway station is Bangor

Opening
Daily; mid-March–Nov
Please phone for details

Admission
Adult £20, Child £14, Concs £17

Contact
Llanberis, Gwynedd LL55 4TY

t 0870 4580033
w snowdonrailway.co.uk
e info@snowdonrailway.co.uk

520 Llangollen

Llangollen Wharf

1 hr+   Easter–Oct

You can embark on either a horse-drawn canal boat trip up to the spectacular Horseshoe Falls or a motorised cruise that takes you across Thomas Telford's famous aqueduct. There is also a self-steer day-hire boat available for groups of up to 10 people.

* Lunches & cream teas can be preordered

Location
Off A5 Shrewsbury road & near A483 to Chester

Opening
Daily: Easter–Oct 10am–5pm

Admission *Horse-drawn Boats* Adult £4.50, Child £2.50
Aqueduct Cruise £8.50, £6.50

Contact
Welsh Canal Holiday Craft Ltd,
The Wharf, Llangollen LL20 8TA

t 01978 860702

521 Minffordd

Portmeirion

4 hrs+   All year

A private village created by Clough Williams-Ellis on the coast of Snowdonia with woodland, gardens, shops, restaurants and hotels. Built in a fairytale style, it has grottos and cobbled squares. There is a sandy beach and playground for children.

* Used as the location for the cult TV series *The Prisoner*
* Cottages in the village let by Portmeirion Hotel

Location
Signed off A487 at Minffordd between Penrhyndeudraeth & Porthmadog

Opening
Daily: 9.30am–5.30pm

Admission
Adult £6, Child £3, Concs £5

Contact
Gwynedd LL48 6ET

t 01766 770000
w portmeirion-village.com
e info@portmeirion-village.com

522 Porthmadog

The Ffestiniog Railway

4 hrs+   All year

Take a trip on a steam-hauled train with the world's oldest independent railway company. The track runs through 13 miles of spectacular scenery from the sea right up to the mountains. Special events are held throughout the year.

* Refurbished café/bar at Harbour station

Location
Next to harbour in Porthmadog on A487

Opening
Daily: Mar–Nov; limited winter service. Please phone for details

Admission
Adult £16, Child £8, Concs £12.80
(Adult price includes 1 child)

Contact
Harbour Station, Porthmadog,
Gwynedd LL49 9NF

t 01766 516000
w festrail.co.uk
e info@festrail.co.uk

523 Blaenavon

Big Pit National Mining Museum

3 hrs+   Feb–Nov

This was a working coal mine until its closure in 1980. Now you can take an hour-long underground tour, led by ex-miners. Travel down in the pit cage and walk through underground roadways and engine houses. Above ground there's the colliery to explore.

* Enjoy simulated mining
* Winding enginehouse & blacksmith's workshop

Location
Leave M4 at junction 25a/26, follow signs from A465

Opening
Daily: Feb–Nov 9.30am–5pm
Underground tours run 10am–3.30pm

Admission
Free

Contact
Blaenavon, Torfaen NP4 9XP

t 01495 790311
w nmgw.ac.uk
e bigpit@nmgw.ac.uk

524 Caerleon

Roman Legionary Museum

1 hr+   All year

Some 2,000 years ago, Wales was the furthest outpost of the Roman Empire. A fortress was founded at Caerleon that would guard the region for 200 years. Today you can learn what made the Romans such a formidable force and how life would not be the same without them.

* See how the Romans lived & fought
* Most complete amphitheatre in Britain

Location
Caerleon lies N of Newport, just off junction 25 of M4

Opening
Mon–Sat 10am–5pm,
Sun 2pm–5pm

Admission
Free

Contact
High Street, Caerleon,
Gwent NP18 1AE

t 01633 423134
w nmgw.ac.uk
e rlm@nmgw.ac.uk

525 Caerphilly

Caerphilly Castle

1 hr+   All year

One of the largest medieval fortresses in Britain, begun in 1268, the castle is famous for its leaning tower and its ringed stone and water defences. Enjoy the impressive Great Hall, two site exhibitions, an audio-visual display, and replica medieval siege weapons.

* 45-minute audio tours
* Many summer demonstrations & events

Location
Exit M4 at junction 32, then take A470 or A469 for Caerphilly

Opening
Daily: 1 Apr–1 June 9.30am–5pm;
2 Jun–28 Sep 9.30am–6pm;
29 Sep–26 Oct 9.30am–5pm;
27 Oct–31 Mar Mon–Sat 9.30am–4.30pm,
Sun 11am–4pm

Admission
Adult £3, Child & Concs £2.50

Contact
Bridge Street, Caerphilly,
Wales CF83 1JD

t 02920 883143
w cadw.wales.gov.uk
e caerphilly.castle@cadw.co.uk

526 Cardiff

Cardiff Castle

2 hrs+   All year

Discover 2,000 years of history in the heart of the city.
View the Roman wall, climb the Norman keep and take
a guided tour of the fairytale apartments, created in the
C19 for the 3rd Marquess of Bute.

* Guided tours of lavish & opulent interiors
* Set in beautiful grounds

Location
Cardiff city centre

Opening
Daily: Mar–Oct 9.30am–6pm;
Nov–Feb 9.30am–5pm

Admission
Adult £6.50, Child £4, Concs £5

Contact
Castle Street, Cardiff CF10 3RB

t 02920 878100
w cardiffcastle.com
e cardiffcastle@cardiff.gov.uk

---

527 Cardiff

Millennium Stadium Tours

1 hr   All year

Explore the changing rooms, training areas and medical
rooms; imagine the prematch tension; run down the
players' tunnel; climb to the very top row of the highest
tier in the stadium for breathtaking views; sit in the
Royal Box; and have a trophy presented to you.

* World-class venue, home to 5 sporting bodies
* One of the proposed venues for the 2012 Olympics

Location
Cardiff city centre

Opening
Daily: 9.30am–5.30pm

Admission
Adult £5.50, Child £3, Concs £3.50

Contact
Millennium Stadium Shop,
Gate 3, Westgate Street,
Cardiff CF10 1JE

t 02920 822040
w millenniumstadium.co.uk

---

528 Cardiff

Museum of Welsh Life

3 hrs+   All year

Set in 100 acres of beautiful parkland, this is one of
Europe's biggest and most exciting open-air museums.
More than 30 buildings have been transported and rebuilt
here to recreate 500 years of Welsh history. Special events
and craft demonstrations run throughout the year.

* Exhibitions of costume, daily life & farming tools

Location
4 miles W of Cardiff city centre.
Exit M4 at junction 33

Opening
Daily: 10am–5pm

Admission
Free. Car park £2

Contact
St Fagan's, Cardiff CF5 6XB

t 02920 573500
w nmgw.ac.uk
e post@nmgw.ac.uk

529 Cardiff

Techniquest

2 hrs+   All year

Try some of the 160 hands-on exhibits in this amazing
science discovery centre, or experiment in the
laboratory and discovery room. Fire a rocket, launch a
hot-air balloon or play a giant piano. Don't miss the
science theatre. Musiquest was new in Autumn 2005.

* Explore the universe in the planetarium
* Enjoy a fascinating interactive Science Theatre show

Location
Exit M4 at junction 33, then follow
signs on A4232

Opening
Daily: Mon–Fri 9.30am–4.30pm,
Sat, Sun & Bank Hols 10.30am–5pm

Admission
Adult £6.90, Child & Concs £4.80

Contact
Stuart Street, Cardiff CF10 5BW

t 02920 475475
w techniquest.org
e info@techniquest.org

530 Cardigan

Cardigan Heritage Centre

1 hr   Mar–Oct

The heritage centre, in a converted C18 warehouse, tells
the story of Cardigan from just before Norman times to
the present day. A child-friendly place, it has arts
activities for younger children and small quizzes for
older ones.

* Guided tours by appointment
* Static & interactive computer displays

Location
Take A487 to Cardigan. Centre
is on bank of River Teifi, next to
Cardigan Bridge

Opening
Daily: mid-Mar–Oct 10am–5pm

Admission
Adult £2, Child £1, Concs £1.50

Contact
Teifi Wharf, Cardigan

t 01239 614404

531 Carmarthen

National Botanic Garden of Wales

2 hrs+   All year

Learn about the natural world in this 568-acre estate. Attractions include a discovery centre and a 'simply plants' interactive exhibition. Visit the mini-farm, maize maze, children's play area and bee garden. Events include outdoor Shakespeare and helicopter rides.

* Apiary gardens
* Regular calendar of special events

Location	Contact
On A48 E of Carmarthen, signed from M4 & A40	Garden of Wales, Llanarthne, Carmarthenshire SA32 8HG
Opening	t 01558 668768
Daily: Easter–Oct 10am–6pm; Oct–Mar 10am–4.30pm	w gardenofwales.org.uk
	e reception@gardenofwales.org.uk
Admission	
Adult £7, Child £2, Concs £5	

532 Dan-yr-Ogof

National Showcaves Centre for Wales

2 hrs+   Apr–Oct

Descend below ground to explore a wonderland of stalactites, waterfalls and natural cave formations extending over 10 kilometres. The tour of the showcaves is self-guided but commentaries play at selected points so you can enjoy a visit at your own speed.

* Top Wales attraction
* Several other attractions

Location	Admission
On A4067 between Swansea & Brecon. Signed from junction 45 of M4	Adult £9.50, Child £6
Opening	**Contact**
Daily: Apr–Oct 10am–3pm (last admission to caves 3pm)	Dan-yr-Ogof, nr Abercraf, Upper Swansea Valley, Powys SA9 1GJ
	t 01639 730801
	w showcaves.co.uk
	e james@showcaves.co.uk

533 Haverfordwest

Pembrokeshire Motor Museum

2 hrs+   Mar–Sep

More than 40 vehicles give a complete history of the motor car, ranging from a 1906 Rover to a more modern 1969 Jaguar E type series II. In addition to the concourse display, there are a few exhibits in the workshop that are being meticulously restored.

* All cars occasionally used on rallies
* 1924 Buick Open Tourer in restoration

Location
4 miles N of Haverfordwest on A487 to St David's

Opening
Apr–Sep Mon–Fri 10am–5pm
Sun 10am–4pm

Admission
Adult £3, Child £1, Concs £2.50

Contact
Keeston Hill, Keeston, Haverfordwest SA62 6EJ

t 01437 710950
w pembsmotormuseum.co.uk

535 Monmouth

Caldicot Castle & Country Park

2 hrs+   Mar–Oct

A fine medieval castle set in 55 acres of beautiful parkland with plenty on offer for children. Audio tours are available for adults and children. At the activity station children can find out about castles, play giant chess and draughts, and try on historical hats.

* Breathtaking views from the battlements

Location
From M4 take junction 23 & B4245.
From M48 take junction 2, A48 &
B4245. Signed from B4245

Opening
Daily: Mar–Oct 11am–5pm

Admission
Please phone for details

Contact
Church Road,
Monmouthshire NP26 4HU

t 01291 420241
w caldicotcastle.co.uk

534 Kilgetty

Folly Farm

4hrs+   All year

A combination of theme park and animal farm/zoo ensures that Folly Farm has something for everybody. In addition to the farm's traditional animals, the zoo is now home to more than 100 exotic animals including meerkats and zebras. Meet and feed the young animals in the Jolly Barn.

* Vintage fairground attractions
* Indoor play areas for children of all ages

Location
Take A477 Tenby road from A40 towards Kilgetty. Then take A478 road for Narberth. Folly Farm is 1 mile along on left

Opening
Apr–Sep daily 10am–5.30pm;
Oct daily 10am–5pm;
winter Sat–Sun 10am–4pm

Admission
Adult £6.25, Child & Concs £5.25

Contact
Begelly, Kilgetty,
Pembrokeshire SA68 0XA

t 01834 812731
w folly-farm.co.uk
e admin@folly-farm.co.uk

536 Narberth

Oakwood Leisure Park

4 hrs +   Apr–Oct

One of the UK's top ten theme parks and one of Wales's largest tourist attractions. Oakwood has more than 400,000 visitors each year and boasts more than 40 rides and attractions. You can be sure of a great day out, with much to please both older and younger children.

* Carousel, ferris wheel, pirate ship & more
* Megafobia rollercoaster & Hydro (water-coaster)

Location	Contact
Leave M4 at junction 29, take A48 to Carmarthen, then follow signs	Canaston Bridge, Narberth SA67 8DE
Opening	t 08712 206211
Please phone for details	w oakwood-leisure.com
Admission	e park@oakwood-leisure.com
Please phone for details	

537 Tenby

Heatherton Country Sports Park

4hrs   All year

This leisure park has a wide range of activities including clay-pigeon shooting, coarse fishing, archery, pitch and putt, indoor bowls, baseball, go-karting, paintball, adventure golf, horse-riding, bumper boats, a driving range and a maze.

* Play Robot Wars
* Suitable for groups and birthday parties

Location	Admission
2 miles outside Tenby on B4318 Tenby–Pembroke road	Free. Pay-as-you-go activities
Opening	**Contact**
Daily: Jun–Sep 10am–10pm; Oct–May 10am–6pm	St Florence, Tenby, Pembrokeshire SA69 9EE
	t 01646 651025
	w heatherton.co.uk

538 Treharris

Llancaiach Fawr Manor

1 hr+   All year

Llancaiach Fawr Manor offers a unique view of life during the middle of the English Civil War, through the eyes of the many servants. Hear tales of their everyday lives in 1645 and watch them at work. Travel back in time to a long-gone era.

* Listen to the gossip of the day – 300 years ago
* Stroll in the formal gardens

   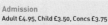

Location	Admission
On B4254 between Nelson & Gelligaer, 2½ miles from A470	Adult £4.95, Child £3.50, Concs £3.75
Opening	**Contact**
Daily: Mon–Fri 10am–5pm, Sat–Sun 10am–6pm; Nov–Feb closed Mon	Nelson, Treharris CF46 6ER
	t 01443 412248
	w caerphilly.gov.uk/visiting

539 Trelewis

Welsh International Climbing & Activity Centre

4 hrs+   All year

In addition to climbing, the centre offers a wealth of indoor and outdoor activities for all abilities, including abseiling, caving, potholing, gorge walking, kayaking, mountain walking and expeditions. It also has a fitness suite and family and bunk-house accommodation.

* One of the biggest indoor climbing walls in Europe
* High-ropes assault course

Location	Contact
From B4255 follow signs to Bedlinog, then ½ mile from Trelewis	Taff Bargoed Centre, Trelewis, Merthyr Tydfil CF46 6RD
Opening	t 01443 710749
Daily: Mon–Fri 9am–10pm, Sat–Sun 9am–7pm	w indoorclimbingwalls.co.uk
Admission	e enquiries@indoorclimbingwalls. co.uk
Prices vary according to activity	

Swaledale, North Yorkshire

Yorkshire

East Riding North Yorkshire
South Yorkshire West Yorkshire

540 Bridlington

Bempton Cliffs Nature Reserve

2 hrs   All year

The best place in England to see seabirds – more than 200,000 nest on the cliffs. Rated one of Britain's most spectacular seabird colonies, it provides superb close-up views of breeding kittiwakes, fulmars, herring gulls, razorbills, guillemots, puffins and gannets.

* Gannets first colonised the cliffs in the 1920s
* Puffins can be seen in spring & summer

Location
On cliff road from Bempton, on B1229 from Flamborough to Filey

Opening
Visitor centre
Daily: Mar–Nov 10am–5pm;
Dec–Feb 9.30am–4pm

Admission
£3.50 car park charge for non members

Contact
11 Cliff Lane, Bempton,
Bridlington YO15 1JD
t 01262 851179
w rspb.org.uk

541 Bridlington

Bondville Model Village

2 hrs   Easter–Sep

Town and countryside in miniature – Bondville is a masterpiece in landscape and gives lasting pleasure to young and old, complemented by hundreds of handmade model figures and buildings.

* One of the best model villages in the UK
* 1-acre site

Location
On A165

Opening
Daily: Apr, May & Sep 11am–4pm;
Jun–Aug 10am–5pm

Admission
Please phone for details

Contact
Sewerby Road, Sewerby,
Bridlington YO15 1EL
t 01262 401736
w bondvillemodelvillage.piczo.com

542 Bridlington

Bridlington Leisure World

4 hrs+   All year

Attractions at this leisure centre include a wave pool with tropical rainstorm and a water-slide. There are main and learner swimming pools, an expanded fitness suite, a refurbished sauna and solarium, a family entertainment centre, plus Kiddies Kingdom.

* 3 quality pools
* One of East Ridings premier attractions

Location
Off A165 (off the M62). Nearest town, is Scarborough

Opening
Please phone for details

Admission
Activities individually priced

Contact
The Promenade,
Bridlington,
Yorkshire YO15 2QQ
t 01262 606715
w bridlington.net/leisureworld

543 Bridlington

Park Rose Owl & Bird of Prey Centre

3 hrs   Mar–Oct

The owl sanctuary is set in 3½ acres of natural woodland. There are 40 aviaries along a woodland walk housing hundreds of owls and birds of prey. There are guided information tours and flying displays daily in the summer season. See our koi carp and aquatic plants.

* School visits & educational talks

Location
On A165/A166, 2 miles S of Bridlington

Opening
Daily: Mar–Oct 10am–5pm

Admission
Adult £2.50, Child £1.50

Contact
Carnaby Covert Lane,
Bridlington YO15 3QF
t 01262 606800

544 Bridlington

Sewerby Hall & Gardens

3 hrs   Apr–Sep

Escape from your parents in the adventure playground, play a game of pitch and putt, hop on a train to the seaside, visit penguins, monkeys and wallabies in the zoo or take a woodland walk where you'll spot small animals, butterflies, birds and unusual plants.

* Display of Amy Johnson's awards & trophies
* Children's zoo includes monkeys & penguins

Location
From Bridlington follow signs for Flamborough & then Sewerby

Opening
Daily: Apr–Sep 10am–5.30pm

Admission
Adult £3.30, Child £1.30, Concs £2.60

Contact
Church Lane, Sewerby, Bridlington YO15 1EA
t 01262 673769
w sewerby-hall.co.uk
e sewerby.hall@eastriding.gov.uk

545 Foston-on-the-Wold

Cruckley Farm

2 hrs+   Easter–Sep

Watch the daily routines of feeding animals and milking cows on a working farm as well as a huge variety of rare breeds. You can also see the collection of vintage farm equipment that is regularly used by film companies. The farm keeps more than 50 varieties of animal.

* Feed hand-reared animals in the paddock
* All seven rare breeds of pig

Location
Just off B1249 between Driffield & Beeford

Opening
Good Fri–Sep 10.30am–5.30pm

Admission
Adult £3.50, Child £2.75, Concs £3.25

Contact
Foston-on-the-Wold, Driffield East YO25 8BS
t 01262 488337
w cruckley.co.uk
e cruckley@aol.com

546 Hull

The Deep

2–3 hrs   All year

Discover the story of the world's oceans in this ship-shaped museum. See seven species of shark, conger eels, rays and hundreds of other stunning sea creatures. Travel in the world's only underwater lift and see sharks swimming overhead.

* 10m-deep tank containing 2.5 million litres of water
* Lots of hands-on and interactive activities

Location
Within walking distance of town centre on banks of Humber

Opening
Daily: 10am–6pm

Admission
Adult £7.50, Child £5.50, Concs £6

Contact
Hull HU1 4DP
t 01482 381000
w thedeep.co.uk
e info@thedeep.co.uk

547 Hull

Ferens Art Gallery

1 hr   All year

This award-winning gallery combines an internationally renowned permanent collection with exciting programmes of exhibitions and live art. The Children's Gallery runs a number of lively events that include educational tours, talks and art workshops.

* Innovative children's gallery
* Masterpieces by Canaletto, Spencer & Hockney

Location
In city centre

Opening
Daily: Mon–Sat 10am–5pm,
Sun 1.30pm–4.30pm

Admission
Free

Contact
Queen Victoria Square,
Kingston upon Hull HU1 3RA

t 01482 613902
w hullcc.gov.uk/museums/ferens
e museums@hull.gov.uk

548 Hull

Fort Paull

2 hrs+   All year

Fort Paull has more than 1,000 years of history that dates back to Viking landings. It has played a part in Britain's sea defences for almost 500 years – from its time as a fortress built by Henry VIII to the anti-aircraft defence visited by Sir Winston Churchill.

* The only remaining Napoleonic fort in Yorkshire
* Explore the underground labyrinths

Location
Village of Paull is S of Hull in the
direction of Hedon

Opening
Apr–Oct 10am–6pm;
Nov–Mar 11am–4pm

Admission
Adults £4.50, Child &Concs £3

Contact
Battery Road, Paull,
Hull HU12 8FP

t 01482 882655
w fortpaull.com
e fortpaull@aol.com

549 Hull

Hands-on History

1 hr+   All year

The museum is a schools curriculum resource centre, created with children in mind. It features Egyptian treasures, Victorian inventions, The Story of the People of Hull exhibition, and much more.

* Ancient Egyptian mummy
* Victorian Britain exhibition

Location
Take A63 to town centre
& A1079 from York

Opening
Daily: Mon–Sat 10am–5pm,
Sun 1.30pm–4.30pm

Admission
Free

Contact
South Church Side,
Hull HU1 1RR

t 01482 613902
e museums@hullcc.gov.uk

550 Hull

Hull Arena

2 hrs+   All year

An Olympic-size ice rink that is home to the Hull Stingrays, who play in the British National Ice Hockey league. The rink is open to the public every day with a variety of family sessions and discos. Times for these vary so it is best to phone in advance.

* One of the North's leading music venues
* See ice hockey played at the highest level

Location
Just off A63 in centre of Kingston upon Hull

Opening
Public skating Mon–Fri 12.15pm–3.30pm;
Sat–Sun 10am–12noon & 2.15pm–4.15pm
Please phone to confirm disco sessions

Admission
All skating £3 + £1 skate hire
Evening disco £3.50

Contact
Kingston Street,
Kingston upon Hull HU1 2DZ
t 01482 325252
w hullcc.gov.uk/leisure
e hullarena@hullcc.gov.uk

551 Hull

Hull & East Riding Museum

1 hr+   All year

Discover the treasures of ancient Britain in a fascinating collection of archaeological finds, including dinosaur bones and treasures from the Bronze and Middle Ages. There is also an Iron Age village and a Roman bath house to explore.

* Bronze Age warriors
* Treasures from the Middle Ages

Location
City centre location, follow signs for the Museum Quarter

Opening
Daily: Mon–Sat 10am–5pm,
Sun 1.30pm–4.30pm

Admission
Free

Contact
36 High Street,
Hull HU1 1PS
t 01482 613902
e museums@hullcc.gov.uk

552 Hull

Streetlife Museum of Transport

2 hrs+   All year

Streetlife has some of the finest period displays in the country on railways, horse-drawn carriages, cycles, cars and trams. Come and meet the animated horses and experience a simulated carriage ride. Costumed figures and smells add to the visual experience.

* Motor car gallery
* Hands-on interactive exhibition area

Location
In high street near Wilberforce House

Opening
Daily: Mon–Sat 10am–5pm,
Sun 1.30pm–4.30pm

Admission
Free

Contact
High Street, Hull HU1 1PS
t 01482 613902
w hullcc.gov.uk/museums/streetlife
e museums@hull.gov.uk

553 Pocklington

Burnby Hall Gardens

4 hrs   Easter–Oct

Home to more water lilies than anywhere else in Europe, Burnby Hall is also famous for its extensive range of ornamental trees, plants, shrubs, flowers and numerous birds and fish, including koi carp, which like to be fed by visitors. Fish food is available to buy.

* Winner of Yorkshire in Bloom 2004
* Two large lakes in 10 acres of beautiful gardens

Location
20 mins E of York off A1079

Opening
Daily: Easter–Oct, 10am–6pm

Admission
Adult £3.25, Child £1.50, Concs £2.60
Gardens free in winter

Contact
The Ball, Pocklington YO42 2QF
t 01759 307125
w burnbyhallgardens.com
e brian@brianpetrie.plus.com

554 Bedale

Big Sheep & Little Cow Farm

2 hrs   All year

This small family-run, family-friendly attraction is home to many farm animals. Under the supervision of a friendly guide, children can bottle feed lambs and piglets, bath a pig, hold small animals, feed the cows and sheep, and talk to the donkey.

* Sand play area & new play barn
* Quad bikes & pony rides

Location
11 miles S of Scotch Corner & 1 mile from A1 on A684 towards Bedale. Follow brown Farm Visitor Centre signs

Opening
Daily: Mar–Sep 10.30am–5pm; Oct–Feb Wed–Sun 10.30am–5pm

Admission
Adult £4.50, Child £3.50, Concs £4

Contact
nr Bedale

t 01677 422125
w farmattraction.co.uk
e enquiries@farmattraction.co.uk

555 Ebberston

The Quad Squad

1 hr+   All year

Enjoy the Quad Squad's trekking facility around the more scenic parts of Pheasant Hill Farm and parts of Dalby Forest. Children will be enthralled by this fun-packed and exhilarating adventure.

* Caters for everyone aged 6 to 65
* On a working farm

Location
On A170 W of Scarborough & E of Pickering

Opening
Daily: *summer* 9.30am–5.30pm; *winter* 9.30am–3pm

Admission
Adult £30 per hour, Child £25 per hour

Contact
Pheasant Hill Farm, Ebberston, Scarborough YO13 9BB

t 0771 575 7706
w quad-squad.biz

556 Harrogate

RHS Garden Harlow Carr

3 hrs   All year

One of Yorkshire's most relaxing yet inspiring locations. Highlights include the spectacular Gardens through Time, a streamside garden and contemporary herbaceous borders; alpines and scented and kitchen gardens; woodland and wildflower meadows.

* Double herbaceous borders
* All year colour & interest

Location
Off B6162, 1½ miles from Harrogate town centre

Opening
Daily: Mar–Oct 9.30am–6pm; Nov–Feb 9.30am–4pm

Admission
Adult £6, Child £1.60, Concs £4
RHS members free

Contact
Crag Lane, Harrogate HG3 1QB

t 01423 565418
w rhs.org.uk/harlowcarr
e admin-harlowcarr@rhs.org.uk

557 Harrogate

Ripley Castle

2 hrs+   All year

Ripley Castle has been the Ingilby family home since 1345. It has fine armour, furniture, chandeliers and panelling, as well as a priest's hiding hole. There are beautiful walled gardens, a deer park guaranteed to thrill children and an extensive tropical plant collection.

* Guided tours leave the front door every hour
* Home to the National Hyacinth Collection

Location
3 miles N of Harrogate on A61

Opening
Daily: Jul–Aug 10.30am–3.30pm;
Sep–Jun Tue, Thu, Sat–Sun & Bank Hols. Please phone for details as they may vary

Admission
Adult £6.50, Child £4, Concs £5.50

Contact
The Ripley Castle Estate,
Harrogate HG3 3AY

t 01423 770152
w ripleycastle.co.uk
e enquiries@ripleycastle.co.uk

558 Hawes

Dales Countryside Museum

1 hr+   All year

This wonderful museum tells the story of the Yorkshire Dales – its people and environment from the Stone Age to Victorian times. Take a walk down a lead mine and see how the industry has changed over the years. There are also regular demonstrations of traditional crafts.

* Tourist Information & National Park Centre
* Guided tours for individuals

Location
Off A684 in Old Station Yard

Opening
Daily: 10am–5pm

Admission
Adult £3, Child free, Concs £2

Contact
Station Yard,
Hawes DL8 3NT

t 01969 666210
w yorkshirevisitor.com
e hawes@ytbtic.co.uk

559 Hutton-le-Hole

Ryedale Folk Museum

1 hr+   All year

Ryedale Folk Museum contains reconstructed local buildings including long houses, an Elizabethan manor house and furnished cottages. See the oldest daylight photographic studio in the country and archaeological displays from prehistory to the C10.

* Sanford Award for Education 2003

Location
Take A170 from Helmsley into Hutton-le-Hole

Opening
Daily: mid-Mar–Oct 10am–5.30pm;
Nov–22 Dec & 22 Jan–mid-Mar
please phone for details
(last admission 4.30pm)

Admission
Please phone for details

Contact
Hutton-le-Hole YO62 6UA

t 01751 417367

560 Ingleton

White Scar Cave

1½ hrs   All year

White Scar is the longest show cave in Britain. You can marvel at underground waterfalls, thousands of stalactites, and the massive 330ft Battlefield Cavern. Take the 80-minute guided tour, which covers over a mile of underground adventure.

* Investigate a hidden world
* 200,000 year-old cavern

Location
In Yorkshire Dales National Park, 17 miles E of M6 (junction 35), 1½ miles from Ingleton on B6255 to Hawes

Opening
Daily: Feb–Oct from 10am (weather permitting)
Nov–Jan weekends only

Admission
Adult £6.95, Child £3.95

Contact
Ingleton LA6 3AW

t 01524 241244
w whitescarcave.co.uk
e info@whitescarcave.co.uk

561 Kirby Misperton

Flamingo Land
Theme Park & Zoo

6 hrs+   Apr–Nov

Flamingo Land offers something for all the family with a dozen white-knuckle thrillers, six great shows, kiddies' attractions and an extensive zoo, which is home to many rare and exotic species including rhino, hippos, giraffes and tigers.

* Lost Kingdom display
* Children's farm

Location
Off A64 Scarborough–York road on A169 Malton–Pickering road

Opening
Daily: Apr–Nov 10am–5pm or 6pm
please phone for details

Admission
Please phone for details

Contact
Kirby Misperton,
Malton YO17 6UX

t 01653 668287
w flamingoland.co.uk
e info@flamingoland.co.uk

562 Knaresborough

Mother Shipton's Cave & Petrifying Well

1 hr+   Mar–Oct

First opened in 1630, Mother Shipton's Cave and Petrifying Well are the oldest tourist attractions in Britain. As well as the cave and well, children will particularly enjoy the playground and 12 acres of riverside grounds.

* Learn about Mother Shipton in the museum
* Free all-day parking

Location
Signed from A1 on A59

Opening
Mar Sat–Sun 10am–5.30pm;
Apr–Oct daily 10am–5.30pm

Admission
Adult £5.50, Child £3.75, Concs £4.50

Contact
Prophecy House,
Knaresborough HG5 8DD

t 01423 864600
w mothershipton.co.uk
e adrian@mothershipton.co.uk

563 Leyburn

Bolton Castle

1 hr+   All year

Bring the family along to this fascinating castle, one of the UK's best preserved, which has dominated its beautiful Yorkshire Dales setting since its completion in 1399. Mary, Queen of Scots, was imprisoned here and it was besieged during the Civil War.

* Location for *Ivanhoe, Elizabeth & Heartbeat*

Location
6 miles W of Leyburn, just off A684.
Signed from Wensley

Opening
Daily: Mar–Nov 10am–5pm;
Dec–Feb 10am–4pm
Please phone for details

Admission
Adults £5, Child & Concs £3.50

Contact
Leyburn North Yorkshire DL8 4ET

t 01969 623981
w boltoncastle.co.uk

578 Scarborough

Sea Life & Marine Sanctuary

2 hrs+   All year

Meet creatures that live in the oceans around the British Isles, ranging from starfish, turtles and crabs to rays, seals and otters. Marvel at the Penguin Sanctuary where seven endangered species including the Humboldt penguin are resident.

* Penguins, sharks & seahorses
* Feeding times

Location
Follow signs to North Bay Leisure Park on Whitby Road, beyond Atlantis & Kinderland; look for white pyramids

Opening
Daily: summer 10am–6pm; winter 10am–5pm

Admission
Adult £8.50, Child (3–14) £6, Concs £6.50

Contact
Scalby Mills,
Scarborough YO12 6RP

t 01723 376125
w sealife.co.uk

579 Scarborough

Staintondale Shire Horse Farm Visitor Centre

2 hrs+   May–Sep

Shire horse and Shetland pony lovers will love Staintondale. Live shows are a regular feature and include the shire horses and Shetland ponies in full Western roping rig. You can even learn how to spin a lariat, whatever the weather!

Location
Signed from A171

Opening
20 May–Sep, Tue–Wed, Fri, Sun & Bank Hols 10.30am–4.30pm

Admission
Adult £4.50, Child (2–15) £3, Concs £4

Contact
Staintondale,
Scarborough YO13 0EY

t 01723 870458
w shirehorsefarm.co.uk

580 Scarborough

Wykeham Lakes

1 hr+   All year

The ideal place to enjoy a range of watersports, including sailing, windsurfing, boating, scuba-diving, and canoeing. Tuition is available. If you prefer fishing there are two trout lakes, three coarse-fishing lakes and pike-fishing all year round.

* Fishing lakes under new management from 2005

Location
6 miles W of Scarborough off the A170 between West Ayton & Wykeham

Opening
Boating & watersports lake Daily: 7am–dusk *Fishing* All year *Bird watching* By arrangement with Wykeham Estate

Admission
Prices vary according to activity/ duration please phone for details

Contact
Charm Park, Wykeham, Scarborough

t fishing 07946 534001
   sailing 0845 4560164
w wykeham.co.uk

581 Skipton

Bolton Abbey Estate

2 hrs+   All year

This estate covers 30,000 acres of beautiful countryside in the Yorkshire Dales. There are medieval buildings, C12 priory ruins to explore, and 80 miles of moorland, woodland and riverside footpaths. A guide book and walks leaflet are available; there is also a gift shop.

* Landscape was inspiration for Wordsworth & Turner
* Grounds include a 6-mile stretch of River Wharfe

Location	Contact
Between Harrogate & Skipton, off A59 on B6160	Skipton BD23 6EX
	t 01756 718009
Opening	w boltonabbey.com
Daily: 9am–dusk	e tourism@boltonabbey.com
Admission	
Vehicle pass £5 (occupants free), £3.50 for disabled badge holders	

582 Skipton

Skipton Castle

1 hr+   All year

For more than 900 years Skipton Castle has stood at the gateway to the Yorkshire Dales through wars and sieges. One of the best-preserved and most complete medieval castles in England, it can be explored in any season. See the dungeon, watch tower, chapel and Conduit Court.

* View the banqueting hall, kitchen & bedchambers
* Comprehensive tour sheets in nine languages

Location	Contact
In town centre	Skipton BD23 1AQ
Opening	t 01756 792442
Mar–Sep Mon–Sat 10am–6pm,	w skiptoncastle.co.uk
Sun 12noon–6pm;	e info@skiptoncastle.co.uk
Oct–Feb 10am–4pm	
Admission	
Adult £5.20, Child £2.70, Concs £4.60	

583 Thirsk

Monk Park Farm Visitor Centre

3 hrs+   Feb–Oct

This open farm in Hambleton Hills has indoor and outdoor viewing and feeding areas, a wildfowl lake and animal attractions. Meet wallabies, rheas, llamas, lambs, piglets, goats and ponies, and birds including ducks, geese, hens, swans and pheasants.

* Farm walks
* Picnic areas

Location	Contact
Bagby, just off A19 S of Thirsk	Monk Park Farm, Bagby, Thirsk YO7 2AG
Opening	
Daily: Feb–Oct 11am–5.30pm	t 01845 597730
Admission	w monkpark.co.uk
Adult £4, Child & Concs £3	

584 Whitby

Captain Cook Memorial Museum

1 hr+   Mar–Oct

This fascinating museum is in the harbourside house, with ship-timbered attic, where the young James Cook lodged as an apprentice. Learn all about his ships, his companions and his amazing explorations.

* Quality Assured Visitor Attraction

Location
Take A171 to Whitby (or A169 from Pickering & York). Museum is in town centre, 100 yards from swing bridge

Opening
Mar weekends only 11am–3pm;
Apr–Oct daily 9.45am–5pm

Admission
Adult £3, Child £2, Concs £2.50

Contact
Grape Lane,
Whitby YO22 4BA

t 01947 601900
w cookmuseumwhitby.co.uk
e captcookmuseumwhitby@ukgateway.net

---

585 York

Castle Howard

2 hrs+   Mar–Oct

Built in 1699, Castle Howard is the private home of the Howard family. Inside are art treasures and sculptures; outside are temples, statues and monuments. There is a whole range of summer activities for children.

* Adventure playground, boat trips & farm shop
* Outdoor guided tours & historical characters

Location
15 miles NE of York

Opening
Daily: Mar–Oct 10am–4pm

Admission
Adult £9.50, Child £6.50, Concs £8.50

Contact
North York YO60 7DA

t 01653 648 333
w castlehoward.co.uk
e house@castlehoward.co.uk

586 York

Jorvik Viking Centre

1 hr   All year

Discover what life was like in AD975 and meet Vikings face to face. See 800 items uncovered here, and journey through reconstructed Viking streets, complete with sounds and smells. Handle replica items, put your own skills to the test, and watch Viking craftsmen at work.

* Jorvik is the name given to York by Vikings in AD 975
* Wheelchair users please phone 01904 543402

Location
Take A64 to York

Opening
Daily: Apr–Oct 10am–5pm;
Nov–Mar 10am–4pm

Admission
Adult £7.45, Child £5.25, Concs £6.30
Prebooking recommended for individual tours

Contact
Jorvik, Coppergate, York YO1 9WT

t 01904 543403/643211
w vikingjorvik.com
e jorvik@yorkarchaeology.co.uk

National Railway Museum

3 hrs+   All year

A collection of more than 103 trains from 1813 to today, including a Japanese bullet train. Learn all about the engines from the Rocket to the Eurostar. Ride on the miniature railway (weekends and school holidays) through the railway-themed children's play area.

* Home of the *Flying Scotsman*
* Literally millions of photographs & artefacts

Location	Contact
200 yrds from train station, signed from town centre	Leeman Road, York YO26 4XJ
Opening	t 01904 621261
Daily: 10am–6pm	w nrm.org.uk
Admission	e nrm@nmsi.ac.uk
Free, except for special events	

Rievaulx Abbey

4 hrs+   All year

Founded by St Bernard of Clairvaux in the C13, this Cistercian abbey was once home to some 150 monks and 500 lay brethren. Although much of what was built by the monks is in ruins, recent digs reveal that the monks ate strawberries and ran a flourishing iron industry.

* Towering medieval architecture
* Exhibition of the works of God

Location	Admission
In Rievaulx, 2¼ miles W of Helmsley on a minor road off B1257	Adult £4, Child £2, Concs £3
	Contact
Opening	Rievaulx, York YO62 5LB
Daily: Apr–Sep 10am–6pm; 14–22 Feb & Oct 10am–5pm; Nov–13 Feb & 23 Feb–Mar 10am–4pm	t 01439 798228
	w english-heritage.co.uk/yorkshire

York Dungeons

1 hr   All year

Deep in the heart of historic York, buried beneath its paving stones, lies the North's most chilling horror attraction. The York Dungeons brings more than 2,000 years of gruesomely authentic history vividly back to life ... and death.

* See how torture was part of everyday life until the C19
* Judgement of sinners new in 2005

Location	Contact
In city centre	The York Dungeons, 12 Clifford Street, York YO1 9RD
Opening	t 01904 632599
Daily: Apr–Sep 10am–5pm; Oct–Mar 10.30am–4.30pm	w thedungeons.com
Admission	e yorkdungeons@merlinentertainments. biz
Adult £9.95, Child (5–14) £7.95, Child (under 5) £7.95 free, Concs £8.95	

590 York

York Minster

1 hr   All year

Built between the C12 and C15, York Minster is the largest Gothic cathedral in England. It is 524 feet long, 249 feet wide and more than 90 feet high. It was constructed on the site of a Norman cathedral, which was itself built on the foundations of a Roman fort.

* Largest Gothic cathedral in Northern Europe
* Visited by 2 million people every year

Location	Admission
In York city centre	Donations appreciated
Opening	**Contact**
Daily: Apr–Oct Mon–Sat	Deangate, York YO1 7HH
9am–4.45pm,	
Sun 12noon–3.45pm;	t 01904 557216
Nov–Mar Mon–Sat 9.30am–4.45pm,	w yorkminster.org
Sun 12noon–3.45pm	e visitors@yorkminster.org
Tower: 30 mins for dusk	

591 York

Yorkshire Air Museum & Allied Air Forces Memorial

3 hrs   All year

This award-winning museum is housed in the largest WWII Bomber Command station now open to the public. Experience fascinating displays, such as the restored control tower, the Air Gunners Museum and the Airborne Forces Display.

* See the only restored Halifax bomber
* Historical aircraft from the earliest days of flight

Location	Contact
Take B1228 off A63/A1079 round-about	Halifax Way, Elvington York YO41 4AU
Opening	t 01904 608595
Daily: *summer* (Apr–Sep) 10am–5pm	w yorkshireairmuseum.co.uk
winter (Oct–Mar) 10am–3.30pm	e museum@yorkshireairmuseum.
Admission	co.uk
Adult £5, Child £3, Concs £4	

592 York

Yorkshire Museum & Gardens

2 hrs   All year

The European award-winning Yorkshire Museum is set in 10 acres of botanical gardens located in the historic centre of York. It displays some of the finest Roman, Anglo-Saxon, Viking and medieval treasures ever discovered in Britain.

* Ruins of St Mary's Abbey in grounds
* 2006 exhibition of Constantine the Great, York's famous emperor

Location	Contact
5–10 min walk from train station	Museum Gardens, York YO1 7FR
Opening	t 01904 687687
Daily: 10am–5pm	w york.yorkshire.museum
Admission	e yorkshire.museum@ymt.org.uk
Adult £4, Child £2.50, Concs £3	

593 Barnsley

Barnsley Metrodome Leisure Complex

3 hrs+   All year

Barnsley Metrodome has a super pool complex offering a total water experience, including the Space Adventure, a fabulous new water-theme park.

* Bowls & karate available
* Holiday activities

Location
Just off M1 junction 37. Follow signs for Metrodome

Opening
Daily: 9am–10pm,
Pool opening times vary please phone for details

Admission
Please phone for details

Contact
Queens Ground, Queens Road,
Barnsley S71 1AN

t 01226 730060
w themetrodome.co.uk

594 Barnsley

Cannon Hall Farm

3 hrs   All year

This working farm is now open to visitors. Come and encounter cattle, pigs and sheep, as well as rabbits, ponies and horses. There are also exotic animals such as chinchillas, wallabies and llamas.

* Best farm attraction in Yorkshire
* Gift shop

Location
Take A635 from Barnsley just after Cawthorne village. Signed on the right

Opening
Mon–Sat 10.30am–4.30pm,
Sun & Bank Hols 10.30am–5pm

Admission
Adult £3.25, Child & Concs £2.75

Contact
Barnsley S75 4AT

t 01226 790427
w cannonhallfarm.co.uk

595 Branton

Brockholes Farm Visitor Centre

3 hrs+   All year

This centre houses farm animals, including a pedigree herd of Limousin cattle, and exotic breeds, such as monkeys, zebra and wallabies. You can also see small animals, including rabbits, guinea pigs and hamsters, and there is a free pony ride for each child.

* Farm is 250 years old
* Woodland walks

Location
Take A638 from Doncaster towards Bawtry & turn on to B1396

Opening
Daily: 10.30am–5.30pm (last admission 4.30pm)

Admission
Adult £4.55, Child & Concs £4

Contact
Brockholes Lane,
Branton DN3 3NH

t 01302 535057
w brockholesfarm.co.uk

596 Conisbrough

Conisbrough Castle

2 hrs+   All year

This spectacular medieval castle was built in the 1180s by the 5th Earl of Surrey, Hamelin Plantagenet, half brother of Henry II. It has been extensively restored with floodlighting and a visitor centre. Educational tours and children's parties are catered for.

* Inspiration for Sir Walter Scott's classic novel Ivanhoe
* Closed for private functions on some Saturdays during summer

 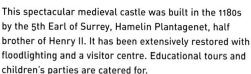

Location
NE of town centre on A630

Opening
Daily: Apr–Sep 10am–5pm;
Oct–Mar 10am–4pm

Admission
Adult £4, Child £2.15, Concs £2.75

Contact
Castle Hill, Conisbrough DN12 3BU

t 01709 863329
w conisbroughcastle.org.uk
e info@conisbroughcastle.org.uk

597 Doncaster

Doncaster Aeroventure

1 hr+   All year

A fascinating day out for any budding plane enthusiast. Come and see this collection of British jets and helicopters. Occupying the last part of the former Doncaster airfield, the site also features other buildings of the WWII period.

* Collection includes a DH Vampire T11, DH Chipmunk T10, DH Dove Westland Scout & Whirlwind HAR 9

Location
Leave M18 at junction 3 & turn on to A6182. Also reached via A638 Doncaster–Bawtry road. Follow brown propeller signs

Opening
Wed–Sun including Bank Hols 10am–5pm (4pm in winter), Tue in school hols

Admission
Adult £3.50, Child £1, Concs £2

Contact
Dakota Way, Airborne Road
Doncaster Leisure Park
Doncaster DN4 7FD

t 01302 761616
w aeroventure.org.uk

598 Doncaster

Thorne Memorial Park Miniature Railway

1 hr+   Varies

Thorne Memorial Park Railway Society operates, builds and maintains this miniature railway, which has recently opened a new second track. Juniors, pensioners and people with disabilities are welcome. There is steam operation at special events and visiting locomotives.

* Operated by volunteers of the Doncaster & District Model Engineering Society Ltd

Location
1 or 2 miles from M18, depending on whether you use junction 5 or 6. Next to Stainforth & Keadby Canal on A614 into town centre

Opening
Please phone for details
Trains Easter–Sep Sun 12noon–4.30pm

Admission
Adult 30p, Child 30p, Under–3s Free

Contact
76 Grange Avenue, Hatfield
Doncaster DN7 6RD

t 01302 842948
w thornerailway.org.uk

599 Doncaster South

Hatfield Water Park

2 hrs+   All year

This all-round watersports centre offers canoeing, kayaking, sailing, windsurfing and power-boating activities. The site also includes a three-star rated caravan and campsite and residential visitor centre.

* Adventure playground

Location
Off A18, just outside Hatfield village on road to Thorne

Opening
Daily: *summer* Mon–Fri 9am–4.30pm & Sat–Sun 9am–5.30pm
winter open Mon–Fri 9am–4.30pm

Admission
Varies depending on activity
Please phone for details

Contact
Old Thorne Road, Doncaster DN7 6EQ

t 01302 841572
w doncaster.gov.uk/leisure
e hatfield.waterpark@doncaster.gov.uk

---

600 Rotherham

Magna Science Adventure Centre

3 hrs+   All year

A high-tech, hands-on centre, organised according to the elements, where you can walk into a wind tunnel, discover how fireworks work, squirt water on hot plates, find out how much water is in your body, make waves, or crawl through an underground tunnel.

* Feel the force of a tornado in the Air Pavilion
* Test your bravery as a virtual fireball races towards you

Location
Just off M1, 1 mile along A6178 from Meadowhall shopping centre

Opening
Daily: 10am–5pm

Admission
Adult £9, Child &Concs £7

Contact
Sheffield Road, Templeborough, Rotherham S60 1DX

t 01709 720002
w visitmagna.co.uk
e info@magnatrust.co.uk

---

601 Sheffield

The Foundry Climbing Centre

2 hrs+   All year

The Foundry Climbing Centre provides indoor climbing experience for visitors of any age and ability – from novices to experts. Instruction is available on request and children's climbing clubs are run regularly. Booking is essential.

* Special events held regularly

Location
Near Sheffield Ski Village, ½ mile from city centre

Opening
Daily: *summer* Mon–Fri 10am–10pm, weekends 10am–6pm
winter Mon–Fri 10am–10pm, weekends 10am–8pm

Admission
Please phone for details

Contact
45 Mowbray Street, Sheffield S3 8EN

t 0114 279 6331
w greatadventures.co.uk
e fma@greatadventures.co.uk

602 Sheffield

Millennium Galleries

2 hrs+   All year

This new museum has four galleries: Special Exhibitions, Metalwork, Craft & Design and the Ruskin Gallery. Many of the exhibitions have hands-on elements that will appeal to children, and exhibitions in other galleries change regularly, keeping the galleries up to date.

* Material regularly borrowed from the Tate & V&A museum
* Metalwork gallery

Location
In city centre near Winter Garden

Opening
Mon–Sat 10am–5pm,
Sun 11am–5pm

Admission
Free, exhibitions may charge

Contact
Arundel Gate, Sheffield S1 2PP

t 0114 278 2600
w sheffieldgalleries.org.uk
e info@sheffieldgalleries.org.uk

603 Sheffield

Renishaw Hall Gardens

4 hrs+   Easter–Sep

Renishaw Hall's gardens, museum and galleries are set in 300 acres of parkland with nature trails, reserves and a sculpture park. Children's events are organised regularly and there is a children's play area.

* Hall open by special arrangement only
* Regular calendar of events

Location
Just 2 miles from junction 30 off M1, between Ecrington & Renishaw on A6135

Opening
Easter–Sep Thu–Sun & Bank Hol Mon 10.30am–4.30pm. Please phone for details of special events

Admission
Please phone for details

Contact
Renishaw Hall, Sheffield

t 01246 432310
w sitwell.co.uk
e info@renishawhall.free-online.co.uk

604 Sheffield

Sheffield Cycle Speedway Club

2 hrs   All year

Sheffield Cycle Speedway Club is a British Cycling
'Go-Ride' club. It provides cycling experience for
children of all ages and abilities.

* Free loan of equipment
* Experienced qualified coach in attendance

Location
Bochum Parkway, Sheffield

Opening
Mar–Oct Mon or Wed 7.30–9.30pm;
Nov–Feb Sun fortnightly 2pm–4pm
Please phone before travelling

Admission
£2 per person

Contact
19 Stockley View, Bolsover,
Chesterfield S44 6HZ

t 01246 824220
w sheffieldstars.net
e martin_gamble@hotmail.com

---

606 Batley

Bagshaw Museum

1 hr+   All year

Bagshaw Museum surrounds you with the sights
and sounds of past times and faraway places. Journey
through the vibrant colours of the Orient and tame the
mythical beasts of four continents.

* Alpine mountain adventure themed play park
* Enchanted Forest

Location
Within easy access of the A652, A62
& M62

Opening
Daily: Mon–Fri 11am–5pm,
Sat–Sun 12noon–5pm,
closed Good Fri

Admission
Free

Contact
Wilton Park,
Batley WF17 0AS

t 01924 326155
w kirkleesmc.gov.uk
e bagshaw.museum@kirkleesmc.
   gov.uk

---

605 Sheffield

Sheffield Ski Village

3½ hrs   All year

If you are looking for a totally unique and exhilarating day
out, the Ski Village at Sheffield is the perfect destination
for all the family. Here at Europe's largest all season ski
resort, you can learn to ski and snowboard, or just chill
out in the authentic Swiss atmosphere!

* More than 1 mile of piste
* Thunder Valley Toboggan Run

Location
5 mins from city centre, off A61
Penistone Road

Opening
Daily: summer Mon–Fri 4pm–10pm,
Sat–Sun 10am–8pm, Bank Hols
10am–10pm; winter Mon–Fri
10am–10pm, Sat–Sun, Bank Hols & 26
Dec–2 Jan 9am–10pm

Admission
Please phone for details

Contact
Vale Road, Sheffield S3 9SJ

t 0114 276 9459
w sheffieldskivillage.co.uk
e info@sheffieldskivillage.co.uk

607 Batley

Oakwell Hall Country Park

2 hrs   All year

History comes alive at Oakwell Hall. This beautiful Elizabethan manor house has delighted visitors for centuries. Stroll around the delightful period garden or check out the inhabitants of the wildlife access garden.

* Setting for Charlotte Brontë's novel *Shirley*
* 100 acres of estate to explore

Location
Take A652 Batley–Bradford road. Park is signed along this road. Take M62 exit at junction 26/27

Opening
Daily: Mon–Fri 11am–5pm, Sat–Sun 12noon–5pm

Admission
Adult £1.40, Child 50p

Contact
Nutter Lane, Birstall, Batley WF17 9LG

t 01924 326240
w kirklees.gov.uk/museums
e oakwell.hall@kirklees.gov.uk

608 Bradford

Bradford Industrial Museum & Horses at Work

2 hrs   All year

The museum has an original C19 spinning mill complex, complete with mill owner's house, back-to-back cottages and job master's stables with working shire horses. There are spinning, weaving and horse demonstrations every day.

* Have a lesson in the Victorian school room
* Experience washday in Gaythorne Row

Location
Take A658 Harrogate road, A6177 ring road

Opening
Tue–Sat 10am–5pm, Sun 12noon–5pm; closed Mon except Bank Hols

Admission
Free

Contact
Moorside Mills, Moorside Road, Bradford BD2 3HP

t 01274 435900
w bradford.gov.uk

609 Bradford

Colour Museum

1 hr   All year

The Colour Museum is unique. Dedicated to the history, development and technology of colour, it is the only museum of its kind in Europe. A truly colourful experience for both kids and adults, it's fun, it's informative and it's well worth a visit.

* Situated in a former wool warehouse
* Workshops educational programme (visit the website)

Location
In city centre, near Metro Interchange

Opening
Tue–Sat 10am–4pm

Admission
Adults £2, Child & Concs £1.50

Contact
PO Box 244, Perkin House, 1 Providence Street, Bradford BD1 2PW

t 01274 390955
w colour-experience.org.uk
e museum@sdc.org.uk

610 Bradford

National Museum of Photography, Film & Television

2 hrs+   All year

Take a voyage of discovery at the National Museum of Photography, Film & Television. Explore the five floors of interactive galleries where you can ride on a magic carpet, read the news or look back at your TV favourites from the past.

* First moving pictures – 1888 film of Leeds Bridge
* IMAX© Cinema

Location	Contact
City centre off Little Horton Lane	Bradford BD1 1NQ
Opening	t 0870 701 0200
Tue–Sun & Bank & Public Hols	w nmpft.org.uk
10am–6pm	e talk.nmpft@nmsi.ac.uk
Admission	
Free, except for cinemas	

611 Halifax

Eureka! The Museum for Children

3 hrs   All year

Eureka! is the UK's first and foremost interactive museum for children aged 12 and under, where they can deliver the post, mix their own music, play 'pinball digestion' and much more. There are fun events at weekends and during holidays – so you'll want to come back again!

* Interactive music gallery

Location	Admission
Next to train station. From M62 junction 24 follow signs to Halifax & then brown tourist signs to Eureka!	Adult £6.50, Child (under 1) free, Child (1–2) £1.95, Child (over 3) £6.50
Opening	Contact
Daily: 10am–5pm	Discovery Road, Halifax HX1 2NE
	t 01422 330069
	w eureka.org.uk

612 Halifax

Shibden Hall

1 hr+   All year

This magnificent C15 hall, home to the Lister family for more than 300 years, is set in 90 acres of parkland with a range of attractions including woodland walks, an orienteering course, children's rides, a miniature railway, pitch and putt, and a boating lake.

* See coopers, a Crispin Inn & an old ale brewery
* Regular events & special children's projects

Location	Admission
Signed from Halifax & M62	Adult £3.50, Child & Concs £2.50
Opening	Contact
Daily: Mar–Nov Mon–Sat 10am–5pm; Sun 12noon–5pm; Dec–Feb Mon–Sat 10am–4pm, Sun 12noon–4pm (doors close 30 mins before closing time)	Lister's Road, Halifax HX3 6XG t 01422 352246 w calderdale.gov.uk/tourism e shibden.hall@calderdale.gov.uk

613 Hebden Bridge

Brontë Boats

1 hr+   Feb–Dec

Enjoy the picturesque Rochdale Canal on our 58ft-long barge equipped with central heating, spacious dining tables and soft furnishing; and pass down locks and through tunnels. Sunday carveries and evening meals are available.

* Boats are also available for private hire
* Daily summer waterbus

Location	Contact
On A646 in middle of Hebden Bridge, 7 miles W of Halifax	The Marina, New Road, Hebden Bridge HX7 8AD
Opening	t 01422 845557
Times vary, please phone for details Advance booking recommended	w bronteboats.co.uk e info@bronteboats.co.uk
Admission	
Please phone for details	

614 Keighley

Cliff Castle Museum

1 hr+   All year

Originally a millionaire's mansion, the castle opened as a museum in 1959. It houses old dolls and toys, the fossilised remains of a 300-million-year-old local giant newt, a working beehive of live honey-bees, and a natural history gallery with an interactive birdsong unit.

* Original 1880s reception rooms

Location	Contact
On A629 N of town centre	Spring Gardens Lane, Keighley BD20 6LH
Opening	t 01535 618231
Tue–Sat & Bank Hols 10am–5pm, Sun 12noon–5pm	w bradford.gov.uk/tourism/museums
Admission	
Free	

615 Keighley

Keighley & Worth Valley Railway

2 hrs+   All year

The fully operational, preserved railway branch line is 5 miles long and runs from Keighley to Oxenhope. Along the line are six award-winning stations.

Location	Admission
Take A650 or A629 to Keighley, or A6033 from Oxenhope	Please phone for details
Opening	Contact
Sat–Sun 9am–6.30pm; Easter & Christmas daily 11.30am–5pm; Jul–Aug Mon–Fri 10am–5.30pm, please phone 01535 647777 for details	Haworth Station, Keighley BD22 8NJ t 01535 645214 w kwvr.co.uk

616 Leeds

Harewood House & Bird Gardens

3–4 hrs   Feb–Nov

This fine Yorkshire home is situated in stunning grounds with lakeside and woodland walks and Capability Brown gardens. The avian collection has more than 100 rare and endangered species of birds.

* Boat trips across the lake and adventure playground
* Below Stairs exhibition

Location	
On A61, 7 miles from Leeds & Harrogate	Grounds Mon–Fri Adult £8.25, Child £5.50, Concs £7.50 Sat–Sun £10.25, £7, £9.50
Opening	Contact
Daily: 4 Feb–Nov 10am–5pm	Harewood Estate, Harewood, Leeds LS17 9LQ
Admission	t 0113 218 1010
All attractions Mon–Fri Adult £11, Child £6.50, Concs £9.50 Sat–Sun £13, £8, £11.50	w harewood.org e info@harewood.org

617 Leeds

Royal Armouries Museum

4 hrs   All year

Learn about arms and armour from around the world in five themed galleries covering war, tournament, self-defence, hunting and the Orient. During the summer months you can watch displays of jousting, falconry and horsemanship. You can even shoot a crossbow.

* See Henry VIII's tournament armour
* Live action events & interactive technology

Location	Contact
S of city centre, near junction 4 of M621	Armouries Drive, Leeds LS10 1LT
Opening	t 08700 344344
Daily: 10am–5pm	w royalarmouries.org.uk e enquiries@armouries.org.uk
Admission	
Free. Car park charge	

618 Leeds

Temple Newsam House & Farm

2 hrs   All year

In the grounds of this beautiful country house is a farm with rare breeds of sheep, pigs, cattle and poultry. On special days visitors can join in with the laundry maids washing at the dolly tub, watch the blacksmith hammer out shoes, and see logs cut at the saw mill.

* Largest rare-breeds centre in the world
* Grounds ideal for picnics

Location	Admission
Temple Newsam Road, off Selby Road, 4 miles from city centre, off A63	House Adult £3.50, Child £2.50 Farm £3.50, £2.50 House & Farm £5.50, £3.50
Opening	Contact
Nov–Mar Tue–Sun 10.30am–4pm; Apr–Oct Tue–Sun 10am–5pm (last admission 30 mins before closing)	Temple Newsam Road, Leeds LS15 0AE t 0113 264 7321 w leeds.gov.uk/templenewsam e tnewsamho.leeds@virgin.net

619 Leeds

Thackray Museum

3 hrs   All year

This award-winning interactive museum offers serious family fun. Explore the slums of Victorian Leeds as one of the city 'characters', discover some of the weird treatments available, and learn how people's lives have improved thanks to medical advances.

* Vast range of surgical instruments from C19 to today
* Unique collection of pharmacy ceramics

Location
Follow signs for St James's Hospital, museum is 100m past main entrance

Opening
Daily: 10am–5pm (last admission 3pm)

Admission
Adult £5.50, Child £4, Concs £4.50
Car park £1

Contact
Beckett Street, Leeds LS9 7LN
t 0113 244 4343
w thackraymuseum.org
e info@thackraymuseum.org

620 Leeds

Tropical World

2 hrs   All year

Walk into a tropical atmosphere among exotic trees, waterfalls and pools containing terrapins and carp. There are also meerkats, lemurs, reptiles, insects and butterflies, as well as a recreated South American rainforest, a desert house and a new tropical beach.

* Largest collection of tropical plants outside Kew
* Nocturnal & Insect zones

Location
Off A58 at Oakwood, 3 miles N of city centre

Opening
Daily: 10am–6pm
(last admission 5.30pm)

Admission
Adult £3, Child (8–15) £2

Contact
Canal Gardens, Roundhay Park,
Leeds LS8 2ER
t 0113 266 1850

621 Shipley

Apollo Canal Cruises

1–3 hrs   All year

Either *Water Prince*, a traditional Leeds and Liverpool wide canal barge, or *Apollo*, a traditional canal narrow boat, will take you on a fantastic cruise through the beautiful Saltaire and Pennine hills.

Location
In town centre, off junction of A657 & A6038

Opening
Daily: as per booking for restaurant boats; waterbus runs during school hols & weekends

Admission
Please phone for details

Contact
Shipley Wharf, Wharf Street,
Shipley BD17 7DW
t 01274 595914
w apollocanalcruises.co.uk
e cruise_apollo@aol.com

622 Shipley

St Leonard's Farm Park

2 hrs   Feb–Oct

Meet Farmer James and his family on their award-winning farm. It has rare and modern breeds of animals (some of which you can feed), play areas, nature footpaths and listed barns and buildings.

* Junior ride-on electric tractors
* Tea room in C16 barn

Location
A6038 from Otley/Ilkley, A6038 from Shipley/Bradford

Opening
Feb–Easter Sat–Sun 10am–4pm;
Easter–Sep Tue–Sun 10am–5pm;
Oct Sat–Sun 10am–5pm

Admission
Adult £3.25, Child & Concs £2.75

Contact
Station Road, Esholt,
Shipley BD17 7RB
t 01274 598795
w stleonardsfarm.com
e farmerjames1@aol.com

623 Wakefield

Sandal Castle

1 hr+   All year

Sandal Castle is an excavated medieval castle that overlooks the site of the Battle of Wakefield in 1460 and was besieged in 1645 during the Civil War. It has beautiful views of the Calder Valley.

* Site of the exploits of 'The Grand Old Duke of York'
* Extensive fortifications

Location
On A61, 2 miles from city centre in the direction of Barnsley

Opening
Castle Daily: dawn–dusk
Visitor centre Daily: Easter–Oct half-term 11am–4.30pm, otherwise weekends only
Please phone for details

Admission
Free

Contact
Manygates Lane, Sandal, Wakefield WF2 7DG

t 01924 249779

---

624 Wakefield

Yorkshire Sculpture Park

2 hrs+   All year

An award-winning centre with changing outdoor sculpture exhibitions sited in 500 acres of landscaped grounds, gardens and parkland. Families are invited to touch and explore the artworks, which include monumental Henry Moore bronzes.

* Four indoor galleries including underground gallery

Location
1 mile from M1 junction 38 on A637

Opening
Daily: *summer* 10am–6pm
winter 10am–5pm

Admission
Free. Car park £3

Contact
West Bretton, Wakefield WF4 4LG

t 01924 832631
w ysp.co.uk
e info@ysp.co.uk

Derwent Water, Cumbria

North West

Cheshire Cumbria Lancashire
Manchester Merseyside

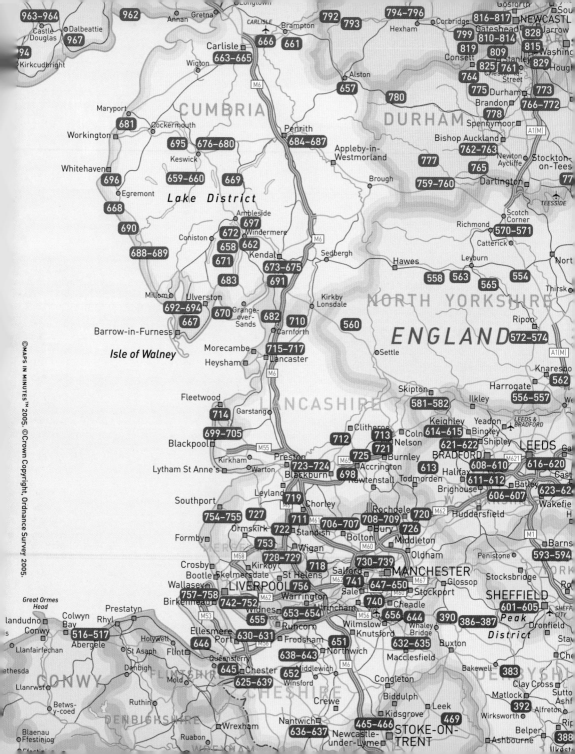

625 Chester

Cheshire Military Museum

1 hr+   All year

Military-minded children will enjoy this museum, which houses an interactive Soldiers of Cheshire exhibition, telling the story of the county's military history.

* Interactive computer displays
* Hands-on exhibits

Location
Close to city centre

Opening
Daily: 10am–5pm (last admission 4pm)

Admission
Adult £2, Child & Concs £1

Contact
The Castle, Chester CH1 2DN

t 01244 403933
w chester.ac.uk/militarymuseum
e museum@chester.ac.uk

626 Chester

Chester Visitor Centre

½ hr+   All year

The ideal starting point for exploring Chester. The Interpretation Centre has a wide variety of features that aim to inform and entertain people of all ages. Activities include guided walks.

* History of Chester displays
* 2 DVD shows & amphi theatre exhibition

Location
Accessible from A483, A56, A51, A41, A55 & M53. Follow signs for city centre

Opening
Daily: Mon–Sat 10am–5pm, Sun 10am–4pm

Admission
Free

Contact
Vicars Lane, Chester CH1 1QX

t 01244 402111
w chestertourism.com
e tis@chestercc.gov.uk

627 Chester

Chester Zoo

5 hrs+   All year

The UK's largest zoological gardens, Chester Zoo has more than 7,000 animals housed in spacious enclosures. The zoo is set in 100 acres of beautiful landscaped gardens and has many attractions specially designed to enthrall children.

* New elephant centre to open in Spring 2006
* Internationally renowned for innovative enclosures

Location
Easily accessible from M53 & M56, follow brown tourist signs

Opening
Daily: from 10am; closing times vary, please phone for details

Admission
Peak season Apr–Sep Adult £13.50, Child £10.50, Concs £12

Off-peak Oct–Mar £9.50, £7.50, £8.50

Contact
Upton-by-Chester, Chester CH2 1LH

t 01244 380280
w chesterzoo.org
e reception@chesterzoo.co.uk

628 Chester

Dewa Roman Experience

    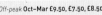
1 hr   All year

Spend a few educational hours discovering what life was like in Roman Britain. Children can step aboard a Roman galley and stroll along reconstructions of Roman streets, experiencing the sights, sounds and smells of Roman Chester.

* Themed Roman games

Location
Accessible from all major road routes. Follow signs for Chester city centre

Opening
Daily: Feb–Nov 9am–5pm; Dec–Jan 10am–4pm

Admission
Adult £4.25, Child £2.50, Concs £3.75

Contact
Pierpoint Lane, Bridge Street, Chester CH1 1NL

t 01244 343407
w dewaromanexperience.co.uk

629 Chester

Mouldsworth Motor Museum

2 hrs   Feb–Nov

Mouldsworth Motor Museum was built in 1937. The Art Deco building is set in its own grounds in the heart of the Cheshire countryside. With more than 60 veteran and classic cars and motorcycles, the museum is also home to a 1920s replica garage, toys and pedal cars.

* Free quiz with prizes for children
* Experience the magic of Harry Potter's car

Location
On B5393 into Ashton & Mouldsworth. 6 miles E of Chester follow brown tourist signs

Opening
3 Feb–Nov Sun & Bank Hol Mon 12noon–5pm; Jul–Aug Wed & Sun 12noon–5pm

Admission
Adult £3, Child £1.50

Contact
Smithy Lane, Mouldsworth Chester, Cheshire CH3 8AR

t 01928 731781
w mouldsworthmotormuseum.com

630 Ellesmere Port

Blue Planet Aquarium

2 hrs   All year

One of Britain's largest aquariums, Blue Planet has two floors of interactive displays and exhibits. Take a voyage through the waters of the world, and see one of the largest collections of sharks in Europe.

* A shark-inhabited Caribbean reef
* Touchpools with anemones & rays & an octopus play park

Location
Nr junction 10 of M53, adjacent to Cheshire Oaks designer outlet village

Opening
Daily: from 10am. Closing times vary, please phone or details

Admission
Adult £9.95, Child & Concs £7.50

Contact
Cheshire Oaks, Ellesmere Port CH65 9LF

t 0151 357 8800
w blueplanetaquarium.com
e info@blueplanetaquarium.com

631 Ellesmere Port

The Boat Museum

2 hrs   All year

This unique award–winning canal museum has more than 5,000 artefacts ranging from large boats to canal company buttons. It covers more than 7 acres of the historic canal port. Dont miss the new interactive exhibition.

* Programme of events throughout the year
* World's largest collection of traditional canal craft

Location
Junction 9 off M53. Follow signs

Opening
Apr–Oct daily 10am–5pm; Nov–Mar Sat–Wed 11am–4pm

Admission
Adult £6.45, Child £4.75, Concs £5.25

Contact
South Pier Road, Ellesmere Port CH65 4FW

t 0151 355 5017
w boatmuseum.org.uk
e bookings@thewaterwaystrust.org

632 Macclesfield

Capesthorne Hall

2–4 hrs   Apr–Oct

Capesthorne Hall is where the Bromley-Davenports and their ancestors have lived since Domesday times. It contains a variety of treasures including fine paintings, furniture, marbles and Greek vases. It lies in gardens and parkland extending over 100 acres.

* Special events including craft fairs
* Car & motorcycle events throughout the year

Location
Off A34 between Manchester & Stoke-on-Trent, 3 miles S of Alderly Edge, junction 6 of M56

Opening
Apr–Oct Sun, Wed & Bank Hols
12noon–5pm

Admission
Adult £6, Child £3, Concs £5

Contact
Siddington, Macclesfield SK11 9JY

t 01625 861221
w capesthorne.com
e info@capesthorne.com

633 Macclesfield

Jodrell Bank Science Centre & Arboretum

2 hrs+   Mar–Oct

Travel aboard the spacecraft *Elysium 7* en route to Mars for an amazing 3D flight over Martian volcanoes and canyons. Special events include meeting astronomers and guided walks of the arboretum for children. There are themed activity trails and hands-on exhibits.

* 35-acre arboretum is a tree-lover's paradise
* Environmental discovery centre

Location
Between Holmes Chapel & Chelford, on A535, 8 miles W of Macclesfield

Opening
Daily: Mar–Oct 10.30am–5.30pm
The centre is under development so please phone for details

Admission
Adult £1.50, Child £1. Car park £3

Contact
Lower Withington, Macclesfield SK11 9DL

t 01477 571339
w jb.man.ac.uk/scicen
e visitorcentre@jb.man.ac.uk

634 Macclesfield

Macclesfield Riverside Park

1 hr+   All year

Bring the whole family to explore and enjoy this pretty country park with woodland, wetland, ponds and a wildflower meadow.

* Visitor centre

Location
Between Macclesfield & Prestbury. Take A538 out of Macclesfield

Opening
Park Daily: Any reasonable times
Visitor centre Daily: 9am–4pm

Admission
Free

Contact
Beechwood Mews, Macclesfield SK10 2SL

t 01625 511086
e bollin@cheshire.gov.uk

635 Macclesfield

Paradise Mill & New Macclesfield Silk Museum

2 hrs+   All year

Set in a restored mill, this venue gives a marvellous idea of working conditions in the 1930s. The Silk Museum is in the restored School of Art and includes six galleries and an audio-visual presentation following the story of local silk manufacturing.

* Includes 26 jacquard hand looms
* Craft club activities & exhibition room

Location
Take A523 & follow signs for Macclesfield town centre. Museum is at foot of high street

Opening
Daily: Mon–Sat 11am–5pm; closed Good Fri, 25, 26 Dec & 1 Jan

Admission
Adult £3.95, Child free, Concs £3.20

Contact
Park Lane, Macclesfield, Cheshire SK11 6UT

t 01625 612045
w macclesfield.silk.museum
e info@macclesfield.silk.museum

636 Nantwich

Hack Green Secret Nuclear Bunker

1 hr+   Jan–Nov

A real government nuclear war headquarters, this place was a secret for more than 50 years. It contains decontamination facilities, a minister of state's office, life-support systems and more. There are two cinemas and many hands-on activities for all age groups.

* Soviet Spy Mouse Trail for children
* WWII radar station

Location	Contact
Off A530 Whitchurch road, outside Nantwich, 30 mins from Chester	PO Box 127, Nantwich CW5 8AQ
Opening	t 01270 623353
Mar–Oct 10.30am–5.30pm;	w hackgreen.co.uk
Nov & Jan–Feb Sat–Sun 11am–4.30pm	e coldwar@hackgreen.co.uk
Admission	
Adult £5.80, Child £4, Concs £5.50	

---

637 Nantwich

Stapeley Water Gardens

3 hrs+   All year

A garden centre specialising in water gardening with display pools, a pet centre and an angling superstore. The Palms Tropical Oasis is a huge glass pavilion housing exotic plants, fish and animals including sharks and toucans.

* Pet centre
* Meet Santa in his grotto at Christmas

 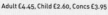

Location	Admission
1 mile S of Nantwich on A51, signed from M6 junction 16	Adult £4.45, Child £2.60, Concs £3.95
Opening	**Contact**
Stapely Water Gardens Daily: Mar–Sep	London Road , Stapeley,
Mon–Sat 9am–6pm (8pm on Wed),	Nantwich CW5 7LH
Sun 10am–4pm; Sep–Mar Mon–Sat	t 01270 623868
9am–5pm, Sun 10am–4pm	w stapeleywg.com
Palms Tropical Oasis Daily: opens 10am	e info@stapeleywg.com

---

638 Northwich

Anderton Boat Lift

1 hr   Mar–Oct

Reopened in 2002 after a £7 million restoration, the Anderton Boat Lift is one of the greatest monuments to Britain's last canal age and is known as the 'Cathedral of the Canals'. Built in 1875, it was the world's first, and is currently England's only boat lift.

* New Operations Centre open
* Quality Assured Visitor Attraction

Location	Admission
Follow A556 & then A559 to Northwich town centre, then follow signs	Adult £6.50, Child £4.50, Concs £5.25
Opening	**Contact**
Daily: Mar–Oct 10am–5pm	Lift Lane, Anderton
Please visit the website or phone for boat & lift times	Northwich CW9 6FW
	t 01606 786777
	w andertonboatlift.co.uk
	e info@andertonboatlift.co.uk

639 Northwich

Lion Salt Works

1 hr   All year

The Lion Salt Works is a unique survival of the traditional inland salt works that once produced this essential commodity. The site illustrates the whole process of salt production and dates from the late C19 and C20. It is the only such surviving site in Cheshire.

* Cheshire once produced 86% of the nation's salt
* Building renovation in progress

Location
Junction 19 from M6 via A556.
Junction 10 from M56 via A559.

Opening
Sun–Thu 1.30pm–4.30pm

Admission
Adult £1, Child 50p

Contact
Ollershaw Lane, Marston
Northwich CW9 6ES

t 01606 41823
w lionsaltworkstrust.co.uk
e afielding@lionsalt.demon.co.uk

640 Northwich

Northwich Community Woodlands

1 hr+   All year

Set in 200 acres of woodland, this park has a large lake and self-guided trails and is great for orienteering. It is also ideal for walkers and picnickers.

* Children's play area
* Lakeside walks

Location
Leave M56 at junction 10, then take A523 & A559

Opening
Daily: Apr–Sep 8am–8pm;
Oct–Mar 8am–5pm

Admission
Free. Car park charge

Contact
Comberbach,
Northwich CW9 6AT

t 01606 77741
w northwichcommunitywoodlands.org.uk
e marbury@cheshire.gov.uk

641 Northwich

Salt Museum

1 hr   All year

The museum tells the fascinating history of mid-Cheshire and the industry that has shaped the landscape and life of the area. Through temporary exhibitions and special activities, find out why salt is vital in so many ways.

* New galleries

Location
Take A533 N to Northwich & follow signs for Salt Museum

Opening
Tue–Fri 10am–5pm,
Sat–Sun 2pm–5pm; Aug Mon 10am–5pm; Bank Hol Mon 10am–5pm

Admission
Adult £2.40, Child £1.20, Concs £2

Contact
162 London Road,
Northwich CW9 8AB

t 01606 41331
w saltmuseum.org.uk
e cheshiremuseums@cheshire.gov.uk

642 Northwich

Stockley Farm

2 hrs+   Mar–Oct

Stockley Farm is a modern working organic dairy farm. It comprises 700 acres on the Arley Estate in the glorious Cheshire countryside. Visitors can watch a herd of 150 British Friesians being milked in one of the most modern computerised milking parlours in the country.

* Birds of prey display
* Tractor & trailer rides

Location
Leave M56 at junction 7, 9 or 10 on M6 at junction 19/20 & follow signs

Opening
End Mar–early Oct Sat–Sun & Bank Hols 11am–5pm; school summer hols, please phone for details

Admission
Adult £4.75, Child & Concs £3.75

Contact
Arley, Northwich CW9 6LZ

t 01565 777323
w stockleyfarm.co.uk
e enquiries@stockleyfarm.co.uk

643 Northwich

Stretton Watermill

1½ hrs   Apr–Sep

Visit this small working watermill set in beautiful Cheshire countryside and discover the traditional skills of flour milling.

* Displays on wildlife

Location
Near Farndon, 10 miles from Chester, signed from A534

Opening
May–Aug Tue–Sun 1pm–5pm; Apr & Sep Sat–Sun 1pm–5pm; open Bank Hols

Admission
Adult £2, Child 75p

Contact
c/o Cheshire Museums, 162 London Road, Northwich CW9 8AB

t 01606 41331
w strettonwatermill.org.uk

644 Poynton

Brookside Miniature Railway

1½ hrs   All year

An extensive miniature railway layout that runs through the grounds of a large garden centre. There are lots of features of interest on the journey such as river bridges, a pond filled with koi carp and a craft centre.

* Steam & diesel locomotives
* Santa specials at Christmas

Location
On A523 midway between Hazel Grove & Poynton. Follow brown tourist signs

Opening
Apr–Sep weekends & Wed 11am–4pm; mid Jul–mid Aug, Bank Hols & school hols daily 11am–4pm. Please phone for details of all other dates

Admission
£1 (10 rides £8)

Contact
Macclesfield Road, Poynton

t 01625 872919
w brookside-miniature-railway.co.uk
e brooksideg.c@tiscali.co.uk

645 Saltney

KK5

1½ hrs   All year

KK5 is a fun-packed children's play centre that helps to develop body and mind through play. Umpteen activities such as ball ponds keep your child amused all day. There is a café and a separate toddler play area, and children under 18 months play free.

* Unlimited play for toddlers until 3pm on weekdays
* Discounts for childminders

Location
From A483, travelling into Chester, take the A5104 into Saltney & turn right into Central Trading Estate

Opening
Daily: 10am–7pm

Admission
Mon–Fri Child (over-4) £3, Child (under-4) £2
Weekends £3.50, £3.50

Contact
Unit 11, Marley Way, Central Trading Estate, Saltney CH5 8SX

646 South Wirral

Rivacre Valley
Local Nature Reserve

1 hr+   All year

A natural area that has been thoughtfully landscaped with an orienteering trail and guided walks. It is a great place for kids to let off steam, and for adults to enjoy the surroundings.

* Guided tours
* Occasional events

Location
Leave M53 at junction 7, follow signs for Overpool, take 1st right at Rivacre Road, then 3rd right

Opening
Daily: 24 hrs

Admission
Free

Contact
Rivacre Road, Ellesmere Port, South Wirral CH64 2UQ

t 0151 357 1991
w cheshire.gov.uk/countryside
e rivacre@cheshire.gov.uk

647 Stockport

Air Raid Shelters

1 hr+   All year

These air raid shelters, now a visitor attraction, were carved into the cliffs in the town centre. Children can experience the sights and sounds of the Blitz and life in general in 1940s Britain.

* Guided tours by arrangement
* Monthly explorer tour

Location
In Stockport town centre. Leave M60 at junction 1. Shelters are in town centre

Opening
Daily: 1pm–5pm

Admission
Adult £3.95, Child £2.50, Concs £2.95

Contact
61 Chestergate, Stockport SK1 1NE

t 0161 474 1940

648 Stockport

Alphabet Zoo

1½ hrs   All year

An indoor adventure playground with the emphasis on purposeful play in a safe environment. Children must be accompanied by an adult.

* Unlimited play for toddlers until 3pm weekdays
* Children's birthday parties

Location
Easily reached from M60 junction 1. On corner of King Street West & Chestergate

Opening
Daily: 10am–7pm

Admission
Mon–Fri Child (over 4) £3, Child (under 4) £2.50
Weekends £3.50, £3.50

Contact
Mentor House, King Street West, Stockport SK3 0DY

t 01614 772225

649 Stockport

Lyme Park

2 hrs+   Mar–Oct

This Tudor house offers beautiful interiors plus extensive gardens and a medieval deer park of moorland, woodland and parkland. Visitors will recognise the place as the setting for Pemberley in the BBC adaptation of *Pride and Prejudice*.

* Children's guide to the house
* Children's quiz & trail

Location
On A6, 6 miles S of city centre. Follow signs

Opening
Daily: late Mar–Oct
House, Park & Gardens please phone for details

Admission
House Adult £5, Child £2.50
Gardens £3.50, £2
House & Gardens £6.50, £3.30

Contact
Disley, Stockport SK12 2NX

t 01663 762023/766492
w nationaltrust.org.uk
e lymepark@nationaltrust.org.uk

650 Stockport

Reddish Vale Country Park

7 hrs   All year

A beautiful country park offering a variety of walks through woodlands, river valleys and meadows. It also features displays on the area's heritage, wildlife and future. Fishing is available on two large mill ponds.

* Cycle trail
* Butterfly park & community organic garden

Location	Admission
Take B6167 Reddish road from Stockport	Free
Opening	Contact
Park Daily	Mill Lane, Reddish,
Visitor centre Please phone for details	Stockport SK5 7HE
	t 01614 775637

651 Tabley

Cuckoo Land

1 hr+   All year

The museum hosts one of the world's largest collections of cuckoo clocks with thousands of assorted exhibits. Most of the clocks are rare or unique, and they combine a number of ingenious methods of time keeping.

* Collection of Black Forest organs
* Display of vintage motorcylces

Location	Contact
Just off Junction 19 of M6	The Old School, Chester Road, Tabley WA16 0HL
Opening	
Daily: 10am–5pm	t 01565 633039
Admission	w cuckoolanduk.net
£5 per person includes guided tour	e mpiekarski@btconnect.com

652 Tarporley

Oulton Park Race Circuit

All day   Apr–Oct

Watch spectacular car and bike racing with British superbikes, Formula 3s and British touring cars. One-to-one instruction with the Racing and Rally Experiences and safe training with the Early Drive Experience are both on offer.

* Full racing programme
* Drive Like a Professional courses

Location	Admission
Take junction 18 off M6 & follow A54 to Chester for 12 miles. Turn left onto A49 to Whitchurch & follow signs	Please phone for details
	Contact
Opening	Motorsport Vision
Apr–Oct open Sat for minor meetings, open Sun & Bank Hols for major meetings	Little Budworth, Tarporley Cheshire CW6 9BW
	t 01829 760301
	w motorsportvision.co.uk

653 Warrington

Gulliver's World

7 hrs   Apr-Nov

A theme park for families set in beautiful woodlands around a lake. It is aimed at children from two to 13 years old and has more than 50 rides, attractions and shows to amuse them. A fun day out for all.

* Lost World Dino area
* Special events

Location
Via M6 junction 21a & M62 junction 8 or 9, then follow the signs

Opening
Apr-5 Nov
Please phone for details

Admission
Please phone for details

Contact
Warrington,
Cheshire WA5 9YZ
t 01925 230088
w gulliversfun.co.uk

654 Warrington

Walton Hall Gardens

2 hrs+   All year

An ideal place for a family day out with attractions including ornamental gardens and woodland trails. Families can try our crazy pitch and putt and bowling, and children can play in our special play area.

* Children's zoo
* Park ranger service & heritage centre

Location
Leave M56 at junction 11 & follow A56. 2 miles from Warrington town centre on A56

Opening
Daily: May-Sep 10.30am-5pm;
Oct-Apr Sat, Sun, Bank Hol Mon & school hols 10.30am-4.30pm;
Park All year 8am-dusk

Admission
Free. Car park charge

Contact
Walton Lea Road, Higher Walton,
Warrington WA4 6SN
t 01925 601617
w warrington.gov.uk/waltongardens
e waltonhall@warrington.gov.uk

655 Widnes

Catalyst Science Discovery Centre

3 hrs   All year

Science and technology come alive through a host of interactive exhibits and hands-on displays. Children and adults can tug, tease and test more than 100 different exhibits in four interactive action-packed galleries.

* Only science centre devoted to chemistry
* Virtual-reality theatre & discovery lab new for Spring 2006

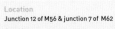

Location
Junction 12 of M56 & junction 7 of M62

Opening
Tue-Fri & Bank Hols 10am-5pm,
Sat & Sun 11am-5pm

Admission
Adult £4.95, Child £3.50, Concs £3.95

Contact
Mersey Road, Widnes WA8 0DF
t 0151 420 1121
w catalyst.org.uk
e info@catalyst.org.uk

656 Wilmslow

Quarry Bank Mill & Styal Estate

2 hrs+   All year

A country park with a Georgian water-powered cotton mill, plus the Apprentice House, where visitors can see where pauper children stayed and the conditions in which they lived. Marvel at the most powerful working waterwheel in Europe.

* Woodland & riverside walks
* Turbine in mill

Location
1½ miles N of Wilmslow off B5166, 2½ miles from M57 junction 5

Opening
Please phone for details

Admission
Please phone for details

Contact
Styal, Wilmslow,
Cheshire SK9 4LA
t 01625 527468
w nationaltrust.org.uk
e quarrybankmill@nationaltrust.org.uk

657 Alston

South Tynedale Railway

2 hrs   Easter–Oct

Visit England's highest narrow-gauge railway and take a trip by diesel or steam from Alston to Kirkhaugh. The 2-mile journey passes through the South Tyne Valley and through an Area of Outstanding Beauty.

* Railway shop & picnic area
* Special events

Location
Alston is on A686, A689, & B6277 16 miles NE of Penrith. Follow signs to railway from village centre

Opening
Easter–Oct, please phone for details

Admission
Please phone for details

Contact
Alston CA9 3JB
t 01434 382828 (timetable)
01434 381696
w strps.org.uk
e mail@strps.org.uk

658 Ambleside

Hawkshead Trout Farm

½ day+   All year

A well-stocked lake where you can fish by boat or from the shore. It is suitable for inexperienced, intermediate and expert anglers. Tuition is available and children can feed and catch their own fish.

* Shop selling tackle, bait & local produce
* Purpose-built children's fishing area

Location
1½ miles S of Hawkshead, on road to Newby Bridge

Opening
Daily: 9am–6pm

Admission
Fishing Adult £21, Child £6, Concs £18

Contact
Ambleside LA22 0QF
t 01539 436541
w hawksheadtrout.com
e trout@hawkshead.demon.co.uk

659 Borrowdale

Honister Slate Mine

1½ hrs   All year

An opportunity to see ancient craftsmanship and to learn the history of bygone years as you take an underground tour of this working mine. Deep inside the mountain you can explore some caverns hacked out by Victorian miners with hand tools by candlelight.

* Quality Assured Visitor Attraction
* All tours are guided

Location
From Keswick take B5289 through Borrowdale & Rosthwaite for 9 miles. From Cockermouth follow B5292 & B5289 for 14 miles

Opening
Daily: 9am–5pm, Sat–Sun 10am–5pm

Admission
Mine tour Adult £9.50, Child £4.50

Contact
Honister Pass, Borrowdale, Keswick CA12 5XN
t 017687 77230
w honister.com
e info@honister-slate-mine.co.uk

660 Borrowdale

Platty+

1 hr+   Mar–Oct

A family-based centre where visitors can enjoy canoeing, kayaking, dinghy sailing, dragonboating, rowing and a Viking longship! Children and adults with special needs are welcomed.

* RYA (Royal Yachting Association) training centre
* British Canoe Union approved

Location
From Keswick take B5289 Borrowdale road for about 3 miles. Park in Lodore Falls Hotel car park & walk down to boat landing

Opening
Daily: Mar–Oct 10am–6pm
Otherwise open by prior arrangment

Admission
Activities priced individually

Contact
Lodore Boat Landings, Derwentwater, Borrowdale, Keswick CA12 5UQ
t 017687 77282
w plattyplus.co.uk
e jplatt@plattyplus.co.uk

Talkin Tarn Country Park

7 hrs   All year

Get active when you visit this park with a 65-acre lake set amid 120 acres of farmland and woodland. A permanent orienteering course is laid out around the park, and there are wooden rowing boats for hire woods to explore.

* Sailing, boating, canoeing & windsurfing
* Coarse fishing available on a day-ticket basis

Location	Admission
On B6413, 9 miles E of Carlisle & 2 miles S of Brampton	Free
	Contact
Opening	Brampton CA8 1HN
Park Daily: Dawn–dusk. Please phone for details of other facilities	t 01697 741050
	Park warden 07976062153
	w visitcumbria.com

662 Bowness-on-Windermere

Blackwell, The Arts & Crafts House

1 hr+   Feb–Dec

Inspired by lakeland wild flowers, trees, berries and birds, Baillie Scott designed every last detail of this house. Outside, from the garden terraces, there are wonderful views of Windermere. Children can have a go at the Blackwell quiz.

* Royal Institute of British Architects' Award for excellence

Location	Admission
Follow A5074 from Bowness (Lyth Valley road). 1 mile from Bowness	Please phone for details
	Contact
Opening	Bowness-on-Windermere LA23 3JT
Daily: Feb–Dec 10.30am–5pm, (4pm in Feb–Mar & Nov–Dec)	t 01539 446139
	w blackwell.org.uk
	e info@blackwell.org.uk

663 Carlisle

Border Regiment & King's Own Royal Border Regiment Museum

½ hr+   All year

This museum has a large collection of uniforms, weapons, medals, trophies, models, silver and pictures. Displays on two floors depict the 300-year history of the Regiment. The museum is in the medieval castle, the regiment's home since 1873.

* Field & antitank guns

Location	Admission
On N side of city centre, accessible from M6 junction 43 or 44	Adult £4, Child £2, Concs £3
	Contact
Opening	Queen Mary's Tower, The Castle, Carlisle CA3 8UR
Daily: Apr–Sep 9.30am–6pm; Oct–Mar 10am–4pm	t 01228 532774
	w armymuseums.org.uk
	e korbrmuseum@aol.com

664 Carlisle

Carlisle Castle

1 hr   All year

A great medieval fortress with a thrilling past. Today visitors can explore fascinating and ancient chambers, stairways and dungeons. The castle is home to the Border Regiment and King's Own Royal Border Regiment Museum.

* Lively exhibitions
* See the legendary 'licking stones'

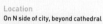

Location
On N side of city, beyond cathedral

Opening
Daily: Apr–Sep 9.30am–6pm;
Oct–Mar 10am–4pm

Admission
Adult £4, Child £2, Concs £3

Contact
Carlisle CA3 8UR

t 01228 591922
w english-heritage.org.uk
e northwest@english-heritage.org.uk

665 Carlisle

Laserquest

1 hr   All year

Unleash a volley of laser fire in the battle zone – the ultimate sci-fi action adventure for children over seven. Each game lasts for 20 minutes.

* Simple or complex games
* Play solo or in a team

Location
In Carlisle city centre

Opening
Daily: Mon–Fri 11am–9pm,
Sat 10am–9pm, Sun 10am–7pm

Admission
£3.50 for 1 game, £6 for 2, £7.50 for 3

Contact
Bush Brow,
Victoria Viaduct CA3 8AN

t 01228 511155
w lquk.com
e info@lquk.com

666 Crosby-on-Eden

The Edward Haughey Solway Aviation Museum

2½ hrs   Apr–Oct

Young people interested in civil and military aviation history will be fascinated by this museum. Among the items on display are aircraft from the 1950s and 1960s and the Blue Streak Rocket Programme. Visitors can sit in the pilot's seat of the Canberra bomber.

* Mock-up control tower
* Vulcan B2, Canberra T4 & Sikorsky S-55a among aircraft

Location
3½ miles E of Carlisle on A689

Opening
Apr–Oct weekends & Bank Hols
10.30am–5pm; also Fri during school hols

Admission
Adult £3.50, Child £1.75, Concs £2.25

Contact
Aviation House, Carlisle Airport,
Crosby-on-Eden CA6 4NW

t 01228 573823
w solway-aviation-museum.co.uk
e info@solway-aviation-museum.co.uk

667 Dalton-in-Furness

South Lakes Wild Animal Park

4 hrs+   All year

One of Europe's leading conservation zoos, this rolling 17-acre park is home to some of the rarest animals on earth. Many, such as lemurs, parrots, kangaroos and wallabies, have complete freedom to wander at will.

* Lake District's only zoological park
* Home of Sumatran Tiger Trust

Location
Follow signs from junction 36 of M6

Opening
summer 10am–5pm;
winter 10am–4.30pm

Admission
Adult £9.50, Child & Concs £6

Contact
South Lakes Wild Animal Park, Dalton-in-Furness LA15 8JR
t 01229 466086
w wildanimalpark.co.uk
e office@wildanimalpark.co.uk

668 Egremont

Florence Mine Heritage Centre

3 hrs   All year

Based at the last deep iron-ore mine in western Europe, this heritage centre offers a mining museum, a geology and mineral room and an authentic reconstruction of an underground mine.

* Guided underground tours

Location
On outskirts of Egremont, just off the A595 on the Haile/Wilton turn off

Opening
Mon–Fri 9.30am–3.30pm; also weekends 10am–4pm in summer
Please phone in the morning to book tours

Admission
Museum Adult £2, Child £1
Underground £6.50, £4.50

Contact
Egremont CA22 2NR
t 01946 825830/820683
w florencemine.co.uk

669 Glenridding

Ullswater 'Steamers'

2 hr+   All year

Cruises between Glenridding, Howtown and Pooley Bridge run daily, weather permitting. There is access to a variety of walks including Howtown to Glenridding and spectacular picnic spots in unspoilt scenery.

* Best Large Visitor Attraction 2004

Location
Accessible from M6 junction 40 or over Kirkstone Pass from Windermere & Ambleside

Opening
Daily: Sailing times vary, please phone or visit the website for details

Admission
Please phone for details

Contact
Pier House, Glenridding LA11 0US
t 017684 82229
w ullswater-steamers.co.uk
e office@ullswater-steamers.co.uk

670 Grange-over-Sands

Lakeland Miniature Village

1 hr   All year

Visit Lakeland in a day at Cumbria's only miniature village. It has more than 100 buildings made from local Coniston slate, including houses, farms, barns and tiny wishing wells. A new Japanese tea house was completed in 2005.

* See Beatrix Potter's house in miniature
* Play area for children

Location
From Grange-over-Sands take B5277 to Flookburgh, follow signs for Ravenstown & turn left after post office

Opening
Daily: 10.30am–dusk

Admission
Adult £3.50, Child £1.50, Concs £3

Contact
Winder Lane, Flookburgh, Grange-over-Sands LA11 7LE
t 015395 58500
w lakelandminiaturevillage.com

671 Grizedale Forest Park

Go Ape!

2½ hrs   Feb–Nov

Discover the thrill of the high wire with an assault course of rope bridges, Tarzan swings and zip slides. Scramble up rope nets and swing through the trees at this award-winning attraction.

* For children over ten & adults only
* Prebooking essential

Location
Off Hawkshead–Satterthwaite road, follow brown tourist signs to Grizedale Forest Park

Opening
Apr–Oct & Feb half-term daily; Mar & Nov open weekends Please phone for details

Admission
Adult £18, Child £12

Contact
Grizedale Forest Visitor Centre' Ambleside LA22 0QJ
t 0870 444 5562
w goape.co.uk
e info@goape.co.uk

672 Hawkshead

Beatrix Potter Gallery

½ hr   Apr–Oct

Housed in what was once Beatrix Potter's husband's office, the gallery has an annually changing exhibition of illustrations from her famous children's books, including *The Tale of Benjamin Bunny*, *The Tale of Jemima Puddle-Duck* and *The Tale of Squirrel Nutkin*.

* Interior remains substantially unaltered
* 2006 exhibit Jeremy Fisher, Miss Moppett and The Story of the Fierce Bad Rabbit

Location
In town centre

Opening
Apr–Oct Sat–Wed 10.30am–4.30pm

Admission
Adult £3.50, Child £1.70

Contact
Main Street, Hawkshead LA22 0NS
t 01539 436355
w nationaltrust.org.uk
e beatrixpottergallery@nationaltrust.org.uk

673 Kendal

Kendal Museum

1 hr+   Feb–Dec

This museum houses displays of the archaeology and natural history of the Lake District, alongside a world wildlife exhibition. There are free quizzes, worksheets and activities for children and events throughout the year.

* Wildlife garden simulates local habitats
* Changing programme of temporary exhibitions

Location
10 mins from junction 36 of M6

Opening
Apr–Oct Mon–Sat 10.30am–5pm;
Feb–Mar & Nov–Dec Mon–Sat
10.30am–4pm

Admission
Adult £2.70, Child free, Concs £2.10

Contact
Station Road, Kendal LA9 6BT

t 01539 721374
w kendalmuseum.org.uk
e info@kendalmuseum.org.uk

674 Kendal

Low Sizergh Barn

2 hrs   All year

Walk on the farm trail and enjoy the beautiful countryside around this organic dairy farm. See the cows and hens, and watch out for wildlife and birds in the fields, pond and woods.

* Watch cows being milked at 3.45pm daily

Location
On A591, 4 miles S of Kendal. From M6 junction 36 take A591 and follow signs

Opening
Daily: 9am–5.30pm;
(5pm closing Jan–Easter)

Admission
Free

Contact
Sizergh, Kendal LA8 8AE

t 01539 560426
w lowsizerghbarn.co.uk
e apark@low-sizergh-barn.co.uk

675 Kendal

Museum of Lakeland Life

1 hr+   All year

The Museum of Lakeland Life shows how the Cumbrian people worked, lived and entertained themselves in the changing social climate of the past 200 years. Exhibits include a street scene, reconstructed workshops and a Victorian bedroom and parlour.

* Captain Flint children's room
* Arthur Ransome's study

Location
Next to Abbots Hall Gallery,
junction 36 of M6

Opening
Apr–Oct Mon–Sat 10.30am–5pm;
20 Jan–Mar & Nov–Dec
Mon–Sat 10.30am–4pm

Admission
Adult £3.75, Child £2.75

Contact
Kendal LA9 5AL

t 01539 722464
w lakelandmuseum.org.uk
e ws@lakelandmuseum.org.uk

Keswick

Cars of the Stars

1½ hrs+   Easter–Nov

Take the opportunity to see some of the most famous cars from film and TV. This incredible collection includes Batmobiles, Bond cars and 'character' cars such as Chitty Chitty Bang Bang, Knightrider and Herbie. New in 2005 was a Starsky and Hutch Ford Torino.

* Exhibition varies, so please phone for details of cars
  currently on show to avoid potential disappointment

Location
Well signed from Keswick town centre

Opening
Easter–Nov: daily 10am–5pm;
Dec–Christmas weekends only
10am–5pm

Admission
Adult £4, Child £3

Contact
Standish Street, Keswick,
Cumbria CA12 5LS

t 017687 73757 (museum)
   017687 72090 (office)
w carsofthestars.com
e cotsmm@aol.com

Keswick

Cumberland Pencil Museum

1 hr   All year

The Cumberland Pencil Museum traces the history of pencilmaking from the discovery of graphite to present-day methods of pencil manufacture. Also on show is the world's largest pencil.

* Brass rubbing
* Children's drawing area

Location
Follow the A66 to Keswick. Located 300 yrds W of town centre

Opening
Daily: 9.30am–4pm

Admission
Adult £3, Child & Concs £1.50

Contact
Southey Works,
Keswick CA12 5NG

t 01768 773626
w pencils.co.uk

678 Keswick

Derwent Water Marina

1 hr+   All year

If you want to go sailing, windsurfing or canoeing, this marina offers lots of RYA watersports courses, with canoe, kayak and dinghy hire available. Other activities include ghyll scrambling, abseiling, climbing and walking. A great experience for families, friends and groups.

Location
From Keswick take A66 & follow signs for Portinscale

Opening
Daily: 9am–5pm; closed 20 Dec–12 Jan

Admission
Activities priced individually

Contact
Portinscale, Keswick,
Cumbria CA12 5RF

t 01768 772912
w derwentwatermarina.co.uk
e info@derwentwatermarina.co.uk

---

679 Keswick

Trotters World of Animals

2–4 hrs   All year

At Trotters you will meet animals from all over the world, as well as many zoo favourites. Handling of the animals is encouraged during audience participation sessions, plus there's a large soft play centre, picnic areas and special events.

* Pony & tractor trailer rides (weekends & holidays)
* Birds of prey centre

Location
Follow brown tourist signs from A591 & A66

Opening
Daily: Feb–Nov 10am–5.30pm
(last admission 5pm)
Christmas hols 11am–4pm
(last admission 3.30pm)

Admission
Adult £5.50, Child £4.25

Contact
Coalbeck Farm, Bassenthwaite,
Keswick CA12 4RD

t 01768 776239
w trottersworld.com
e info@trottersworld.com

---

680 Keswick

Whinlatter Forest Park

2 hrs+   All year

Nestling in England's only mountain forest, this park offers a wide variety of activities, from way-marked walks to orienteering courses, for all abilities and ages.

* Adventure playground
* Live TV pictures of nesting ospreys in season

Location
Follow signs on A66 from Keswick

Opening
Daily: Oct–Easter 10am–4pm;
Easter–summer school hols
10am–5pm;
school hols 10am–5.30pm

Admission
Free. Car park charge

Contact
Braithwaite, Keswick CA12 5TW

t 01768 778469
w forestry.gov.uk/whinlatter
e whinlatter@forestry.gsi.gov.uk

681 Maryport

The Lake District Coast Aquarium

1 hr+   All year

This independently owned aquarium has a comprehensive collection of native marine species. Exciting displays recreate natural habitats, including a 'walk-over' ray pool and 'hands-in' rock pool. There is also a new miniature golf attraction.

Location
Take junction 40 on M6 & A66 to Maryport; or junction 44 & A595 S to connect with A596 coastal route

Opening
Daily: 10am–5pm

Admission
Adult £4.75, Child £3.10, Concs £4

Contact
South Quay, Maryport CA15 8AB

t 01900 817760
w lakedistrict-coastaquarium.co.uk
e info@ld-coastaquarium.co.uk

682 Milnthorpe

Lakeland Wildlife Oasis

1½ hrs+   All year

Enjoy a fascinating journey through the animal kingdom, encountering everything from microbes to monkeys, in this unique, award-winning wildlife exhibition, with live animals and hands-on displays.

* Cumbria Winner, *Good Britain Guide*
* Animal handling sessions

Location
On A6, 2½ miles S of Milnthorpe, near junction 35 on M6

Opening
Daily: 10am–5pm;
(last admission 4pm)

Admission
Adult £6, Child £4, Concs £5

Contact
Milnthorpe LA7 7BW

t 015395 63027
w wildlifeoasis.co.uk

683 Newby Bridge

Aquarium of the Lakes

1 hr   All year

Explore a range of naturally themed Lake District habitats featuring the UK's largest collection of freshwater fish. See otters, British sharks and a variety of British mammals. Discover our underwater tunnel featuring giant carp and diving ducks.

* Midnight at the water's edge new for 2005
* Large number of nocturnal creatures

Location
15 mins from junction 36 of M6, take A590 to Newby Bridge & follow signs

Opening
Daily: Apr–Oct 9am–6pm;
Nov–Mar 9am–5pm
(last admission 1 hr before closing)

Admission
Adult £6.25, Child £3.95, Concs £5.50

Contact
Lakeside, Newby Bridge LA12 8AS

t 01539 530153
w aquariumofthelakes.co.uk
e aquariumofthelakes@reallive.co.uk

684 Penrith

Dalemain Historic House & Garden

2 hrs   Easter–Oct

Dalemain is a beautiful Tudor and Georgian house with fascinating interiors set among fine gardens, parkland with red squirrels and fallow deer and the Lakeland Fells. Children love the nursery, Mrs Mouse House on the back stairs and the hiding hole in the housekeeper's room.

* Children's garden
* Cruises available on nearby Ullswater

Location	Contact
On A592 Penrith–Ullswater road	Penrith CA11 0HB
Opening	t 01768 486450
House 11am–4pm	w dalemain.com
Gardens and tearoom 10.30am–5pm	e admin@dalemain.com
Please phone for details	
Admission	
Adult £6.50, Child free	

685 Penrith

Eden Ostrich World

2 hrs+   All year

Come face to face with African black ostriches, rare breeds of cattle, donkeys, shire horses, pigs, goats, red deer, ducks and geese. There are even zebras, and safari rides (weather permitting).

* New soft play centre & hayloft gallery
* Tractor & trailer rides

Location	Admission
In Eden Valley, 5 miles from M6 (junction 40). Follow A686 towards Alston	Adult £4.50, Child £3.50, Concs £3.75
Opening	Contact
Mar–Oct daily 10am–5pm;	Langwathby Hall Farm, Langwathby,
Nov–Feb Wed–Mon 10am–5pm	Penrith CA10 1LW
	t 01768 881771
	w ostrich-world.com

686 Penrith

Lakeland Bird of Prey Centre

2 hrs+   Apr–Oct

Situated in the walled garden of Lowther Castle and enclosed by parkland, this centre gives visitors the chance to observe fascinating birds of prey at close quarters.

* Daily flying demonstrations at 1pm & 3pm

Location	Admission
From the N take A6,	Adult £6, Child £3, Concs £5
5 miles S of Penrith. From the S leave	Contact
M6 at junction 39 on to A6 through	Old Walled Garden, Lowther,
Shap, about 15 miles N of Kendal	Penrith CA10 2HH
Opening	t 01931 712746
Daily: Apr–Oct 11am–5pm	

687 Penrith

Rheged – The Village in the Hill

2 hrs+   All year

This essential Lake District experience is home to a giant cinema screen showing up to five spectacular films daily, the National Mountaineering Exhibition, a children's indoor play area and a Tourist Information Centre. It is Europe's largest grass-covered building.

* International award-winning attraction
* New bistro, toy shop & two exhibition halls

Location
2 mins from M6 junction 40 at Penrith, on A66 towards Keswick

Opening
Daily: 10am–5.30pm

Admission
Free parking & admission.
Charge per activity or event

Contact
Redhills, Penrith CA11 0DQ

t 01768 868000
w rheged.com
e enquiries@rheged.com

688 Ravenglass

Muncaster Castle

4 hrs+   All year

A historic castle and headquarters of the World Owl Centre, Muncaster has 70 acres of gardens, a meadow vole maze and children's play area. It's also rumoured to be haunted ...

* Cumbria & North West excellence awards
* Darkest Muncaster – a winter evening of magic

Location
On A595, 1 mile S of Ravenglass.
Take junction 40 off M6
S & junction 36 off M6 N

Opening
Castle Sun–Fri 12noon–5pm
Gardens Daily; 10.30am–6pm
Please phone for details of winter opening times

Admission
Castle Adult £2.50, Child £1.50
Gardens £6.50, £4.50

Contact
Ravenglass CA18 1RQ

t 01229 717614
w muncaster.co.uk
e info@muncaster.co.uk

689 Ravenglass

Ravenglass & Eskdale Railway

2 hrs+   All year

Take a gentle steam train ride from the coast at Ravenglass to the foot of England's highest mountain at Eskdale, through the beautiful Lake District landscape. Depending on the weather, visitors can travel in open carriages or cosy covered ones.

* La'al Ratty, water vole stationmaster in summer hols
* New station & visitor centre at Eskdale

Location
On A595 Whitehaven–Barrow road

Opening
Daily: mid-Mar–early Nov 9am–5pm;
winter open weekends, Feb half-term & Christmas–New Year
Please phone for details

Admission
All-day return ticket
Adult £9, Child £4.50

Contact
Ravenglass CA18 1SW

t 01229 717171
w ravenglass-railway.co.uk
e steam@ravenglass-railway.co.uk

690 Seascale

Sellafield Visitor Centre

2 hrs+   All year

With interactive exhibits, exciting science workshops and plenty of hands-on fun, Sellafield Visitor Centre is an educational and entertaining family day out. Join in the great energy debate. Plug in to an attraction that's free, fascinating and fun.

* Recharge your batteries in our bright dairy coffee shop

Location
11 miles S of Whitehaven on A595

Opening
Daily: Apr–Oct 10am–5pm
Nov–Mar 10am–4pm

Admission
Free

Contact
Sellafield, Seascale CA20 1PG

t 019467 27027

691 Sizergh

Sizergh Castle & Garden

2 hrs+   Apr–Oct

This small medieval castle includes a C14 tower and oak-panelled Elizabethan interiors. There are gardens, woodland, pasture and a rock garden with waterfalls and pools to explore.

* Identify butterflies in the ancient woods
* Children's quiz daily in the castle

Location
Follow signs from A590, 3½ miles S of Kendal

Opening
House Apr–Oct Sun–Thu
1.30pm–5.30pm
Gardens Apr–Oct Sun–Thu
12.30pm–5.30pm

Admission
House Adult £5.80, Child £2.90
Gardens £3.50, £1.70

Contact
Sizergh, nr Kendal LA8 8AE

t 01539 560070
w nationaltrust.org.uk
e sizergh@nationaltrust.org.uk

692   Ulverston

Bardsea Country Park

2 hrs+   All year

A beautiful wild location on the north side of Morecambe Bay, its large woodland area reaching down almost to the sea. It is ideal for walking and spotting flora and fauna. Seawood, a Site of Special Scientific Interest, is next to the park and is managed by the Woodland Trust.

* Seashore and woodland walks

Location
S of Ulverston. Take A5087
Ulverston–Barrow coastal road

Opening
Daily: All reasonable times

Admission
Free

Contact
Ulverston Tourist Information Centre,
Coronation Hall, County Square,
Ulverston LA12 7LZ

t 01229 587120
e ulverstontic@southlakeland.gov.uk

693   Ulverston

National Trust Fell Foot Park

4 hrs+   All year

An 18-acre Victorian park, restored to its prior splendour, providing access to the lakeshore of Windermere and its watery activities. Picnic areas and rowing-boat hire, and wonderful spring and summer displays of flowers, are set off by breathtaking views of the Lakeland fells.

* Children's quiz & trail
* Hands-on family activities

Location
At extreme S end of Lake
Windermere, on E shore, entrance
from A592

Opening
Park Daily: 9am–5pm or dusk if earlier
Shop & tea room Daily: Easter–Oct
11am–5pm

Admission
Free, donations welcome.
Car park charge

Contact
Newby Bridge,
Ulverston LA12 8NN

t 01539 531273
w nationaltrust.org.uk
e fellfootpark@ntrust.org.uk

694   Ulverston

Windermere Lake Cruises

1 hr+   All year

Steamers and launches sail daily throughout the year from Ambleside, Bowness and Lakeside with connections for the Lake District Visitor Centre (Brockdale), the World of Beatrix Potter, the Aquarium of the Lakes and the Lakeside & Haverthwaite Railway.

* Cumbria Large Visitor Attraction of the Year 2003
* Rowing boats available for hire

Location
Take junction 36 off M6. Follow brown
tourist signs along A590 to Lakeside
or A591 to Windermere for Bowness &
Ambleside

Opening
Daily: *summer* open during daylight
hours; *winter* 9.45am–4.30pm

Admission
Adult from £5.25, Child from £2.60

Contact
Lakeside, Newby Bridge,
Ulverston LA12 8AS

t 01539 531188
w windermere-lakecruises.co.uk
e mail@windermere-lakecruises.co.uk

Underskiddaw

Mirehouse, Keswick

2½ hrs   Mar–Oct

A comparatively small historic house, given to the
Spedding family in 1802. Standing between mountains
and lake, it is a living home with a tradition of giving a
relaxed welcome. It has an interesting history and links
with many famous writers.

* Best Property for Families in the UK
* NPI Heritage Award 1999

Location
On A591, 4 miles N of Keswick

Opening
House Mar–Oct Sun & Wed; Aug
also open Fri 2pm–5pm
Grounds & tea room Daily:
10am–5.30pm

Admission
Grounds Adult £2.20, Child £1.10
House & Grounds £4.60, £2.30

Contact
Underskiddaw, Keswick CA12 4QE

t 01768 772287
w mirehouse.com
e info@mirehouse.com

---

696 Whitehaven

The Beacon

1½ hrs+   All year

Discover the fascinating history of Whitehaven, West
Cumbria's Georgian port. Situated on the harbourside,
the beacon tells the story of the town's maritime,
social and industrial heritage through audio-visual,
graphic and interactive presentations.

* Quality Assured Visitor Attraction

Location
Follow A595 to Whitehaven & then
town centre signs to S harbour

Opening
Tue–Sun 10am–5.30pm (4.30pm in
winter)
Please phone for details

Admission
Adult £4.50, Child £2.90, Concs £3.60

Contact
West Strand,
Whitehaven CA28 7LY

t 01946 592302
w thebeacon-whitehaven.co.uk
e thebeacon@copelandbc.gov.uk

---

697 Windermere

Lakeland Pony Trekking

1 hr+   Apr–Sep

Lakeland pony trekking offers horse riding for all ages
and abilities including short, hill, farm and trail rides.
All are undertaken with qualified staff and on suitable
mounts for each rider, ranging from ex-competition
horses to native breeds.

* Treks from ½ hour to 1 day

Location
On A592, 2½ miles from Windermere

Opening
Daily: 10am–4pm, booking essential

Admission
From £15, please phone for details

Contact
Limefitt Park, Trout Beck,
Windermere LA23 1PD

t 015394 31999
w lakelandequestrian.co.uk

698 Accrington

Oswaldtwistle Mills Shopping Village

2½ hrs   All year

A family attraction, set within a working mill and its grounds, Oswaldtwistle Mills offers an interesting range of facilities and shopping. Retail therapy with a twist.

* Sweet factory
* Indoor children's play area

Location
Accessible from M65 junction 7, M62, A58 & M6 junction 29

Opening
Daily: Mon–Sat 9.30am–5.30pm;
(8pm Thu), Sun 11am–5pm;
11 Nov–19 Dec Mon–Thu 9.30–10pm

Admission
Free

Contact
Moscow Mill, Colliers Street,
Oswaldtwistle,
Accrington BB5 3DE

t 01254 871025
w o-mills.co.uk

699 Blackpool

Blackpool Illuminations

2 hrs   Sep–Nov

Britain's biggest and brightest light show shines brilliantly for 66 nights from September to November each year. It stretches for 6 miles and lights up the sky for miles around. Displays include alien space ships, pirates, jelly monsters and Tiffany lamps.

* View the giant clifftop tableaux
* Festival of Light throughout the town

Location
Central Promenade

Opening
Daily: Sep–5 Nov

Admission
Free

Contact
Blackpool Tourism,
1 Clifton Street FY1 1LY

t 01253 478222
w visitblackpool.com
e tourism@blackpool.gov.uk

© Tony Stuchbury www.ajsphotos.co.uk

The Blackpool Piers

4 hrs+   Easter–Nov

Blackpool's Piers are fantastic entertainment for all the family. Great rides for older children are Adrenaline Zone and the Crazy Mouse rollercoaster. Ride the famous big wheel, dodgems, waltzers, carousel, pepita and Noah's Ark.

* Children's entertainer (all piers)
* Fairground rides (South & Central Piers)

Location
North Pier on North Promenade;
South Pier on South Promenade;
Central Pier on Central Promenade

Opening
Daily: Easter–Nov from 10am

Admission
Free, except North Pier (50p toll)
Charges for individual rides

Contact
c/o Leisure Parks Ltd,
97 Church Street, Blackpool FY1 1HU

t 01253 629600
w blackpoollive.com

Blackpool Pleasure Beach

4 hrs+   Mar–Nov

Visit the entertainment adventure capital, with more rollercoasters than any other amusement park, including the Pepsi Max Big One and the new Spin Doctor. There's also the Beaver Creek Theme Park for younger children and award-winning shows.

* Ride Pepsi Max Big One the tallest fastest rollercoaster in Europe at 235ft high & turning at speeds of up to 87mph.

Location
From M6 junction 32 follow brown tourist signs to Blackpool S Shore, then to Pleasure Beach

Opening
Mar–Nov, please phone for details

Admission
A range of tickets are available, please phone for details

Contact
Ocean Boulevard,
Blackpool FY4 1EZ

t 0870 444 5566
w blackpoolpleasurebeach.com

Blackpool

Blackpool Sea Life Centre

2 hrs   All year

The Sea Life Centre houses one of Europe's largest marine collections. It has more than 40 fascinating displays, allowing exciting close-up encounters with marine life, including sharks.

* The only sea snakes on show in Britain

Location
On Blackpool's Golden Mile between Central Pier & the Tower, leave M55 at junction 4

Opening
Daily: 10am–8pm

Admission
Adult £8.95, Child £6.50, Concs £7.50

Contact
The Promenade, Blackpool FY1 5AA

t 01253 622445
w sealife.co.uk
e slcblackpool@leisureparks.com

Blackpool

Blackpool Tower & Circus

5 hrs+   Easter–Nov

Visit Blackpool's answer to the Eiffel Tower to enjoy the aquarium, dinosaur ride, indoor adventure play area and family entertainment at the Hornpipe Gallery, then be delighted by the award-winning circus.

* Please phone for details of evening entertainment
* Take the Walk of Faith 380 ft above the promenade

Location
Take M55 for Blackpool & follow signs

Opening
Daily: Easter–May 10am–6pm; Jun–Nov 10am–11pm

Admission
Tower & Circus Adult £14, Child £12, Concs £10

Contact
Leisure Park Ltd, 97 Church Street, Blackpool FY1 4BJ

t 01253 622242 /01253 292029
w blackpooltower.co.uk
e website@leisure-parcs.co.uk

Blackpool

Sandcastle Tropical Waterworld

4 hrs+   All year

A water-based leisure complex with four pools, it offers a variety of thrills including water-slides, a children's pool, a wave pool, white-knuckle water chutes and a new interactive water play area.

* Quality Assured Visitor Attraction

Location
On South Promenade

Opening
Please phone for details

Admission
Please phone for details

Contact
South Promenade, Blackpool FY4 1BB

t 01253 343602
w sandcastle-waterworld.co.uk

Blackpool

Wyreside Ecology Centre

2 hrs   All year

A visitor centre set in the heart of the Wyre Estuary Country Park, the Wyreside Ecology Centre provides an excellent base for nature trails and riverside walks.

* Riverside path suitable for blind visitors
* Cycles available for hire for disabled visitors

Location
Follow M55, then A585 & B5268

Opening
Daily: Mar–Oct 10.30am–4.30pm Nov–Apr 11am–3pm

Admission
Free

Contact
Wyre Estuary Country Park, River Road, Thornton, Blackpool FY5 5LR

t 01253 857890
w wyrebc.gov.uk
e rreeves@wyrebc.gov.uk

Bolton Aquarium

2 hrs   All year

If you are curious about catfish, partial to piranhas or want to be knowledgeable about knifefish, visit Bolton's unique aquarium. Fish from around the world can be seen in an environment designed to offer an insight into their hidden lives.

* One of the oldest aquariums in the UK
* Predatory blue-head knifefish from Venezuela

Location
In town centre

Opening
Mon–Sat 9am–5pm;
closed Bank Hols

Admission
Free

Contact
Le Mans Crescent, Bolton BL1 1SE

t 01204 332211
w boltonmuseums.org.uk
e museums@bolton.gov.uk

Bolton Museum & Art Gallery

2 hrs   All year

Bolton Museum and Art Gallery has something for the whole family. Visit the Ancient Egypt Gallery, Costume, Local History and the Story of Bolton, Natural History and Wildlife on Your Doorstep, as well as a temporary exhibition gallery with up to six exciting exhibitions.

* Varied programme of events & exhibitions
* Ancient Egyptian sculpture The Priest

Location
In town centre

Opening
Mon–Sat 9am–5pm;
closed Bank Hols

Admission
Free

Contact
Le Mans Crescent, Bolton BL1 1SE

t 01204 332211
w boltonmuseums.org.uk
e museums@bolton.gov.uk

Burrs Activity Centre

1 hr+   All year

Children will have lots of fun at this outdoor activity centre, where they can try canoeing, climbing, orienteering, hiking, kayaking, abseiling and archery.

* Function room – accommodation in a bunk house

Location
Leave M66 at junction 2, follow A58 to
Bolton, then take B6214

Opening
Daily: Please phone for details

Admission
Free. Charges for activities

Contact
Woodhill Road, Bury BL8 1DA

t 0161 764 9649
w activity-centre.freeserve.co.uk
e burrs@activity-centre.freeserve.
co.uk

Bury

East Lancashire Railway

3 hrs+   All year

This mainly steam-hauled service runs between Hayward, Bury, Ramsbottom and Rawtenstall every weekend. Visitors can break their journey at any station to visit the shops in quaint Ramsbottom and the stalls at Bury Market.

Location	Admission
In town centre. Accessible from A56, A58 & M66	Adult £9.50, Child & Concs £6.50
Opening	Contact
Sat–Sun 9am–5pm; May–Sep also Wed–Fri 10am–4.30pm	Bolton Street Station, Bury BL9 0EY
	t 0161 764 7790
	w east-lancs-rly.co.uk
	e admin@east-lancs-rly.co.uk

Carnforth

Docker Park Farm Visitor Centre

4 hrs+   All year

Get up close to the animals at this working livestock farm with horses, pigs, sheep, goats and poultry. Visitors can hold some of the animals, including rabbits and chickens, and enjoy pony rides and lamb bottle feeding.

* Collect eggs & feed poultry
* Tractor rides during holidays

Location	Admission
Exit M6 at junction 35 on to B6254	Adult £4.50, Child £3.50
Opening	Contact
Mar–Oct daily 10.30am–5pm; Nov–Feb weekends 10.30am–4pm	Arkholme, Carnforth LA6 1AR
	t 01524 221331
	w dockerparkfarm.co.uk

Chorley

Camelot Theme Park

4 hrs+   Apr–Oct

There is fun for all the family here, with breathtaking rides and nailbiting medieval jousting tournaments. The Whirlwind, a spinning rollercoaster, will keep even the most courageous thrill-seekers happy.

* Birds of prey show
* Park Hall hotel on site

Location	Admission
Leave M6 at junction 27/28 & M61 at junction 8	Adult £16, Child £16, Concs £12
Opening	Contact
Daily: Apr–Oct 10am–5pm. Please phone for details	Park Hall Road, Charnock Richard, Chorley PR7 5LP
	t 01257 452100
	w camelotthemepark.co.uk
	e kingarthur@camelotthemepark.co.uk

© Tony Stuchbury www.ajsphotos.co.uk

712 Clitheroe

Clitheroe Castle Museum

½ hr   Feb–Dec

Clitheroe Castle Museum brings to life the history and geology of the Ribble Valley. It has an Edwardian kitchen, a cloggers shop and an C18 mine.

* Special events
* Set in 16 acres of grounds

Location
Castle Hill

Opening
Easter–Oct Mon–Sat 11.15am–4.30pm,
Sun 1pm–4.30pm
Mar–Apr Sat–Wed 11.15am–4pm;
Feb & Nov–Dec Sat 11.15am–4pm,
Sun 1pm–4pm

Admission
Adult £2, Child 50p, Concs £1

Contact
Castle Hill, Clitheroe BB7 1BA
t 01200 424635/425566
(tourist information)
w ribblevalley.gov.uk
e museum@ribblevalley.gov.uk

713 Colne

British in India Museum

1 hr   Apr–Sep

An interesting museum full of artefacts relating to the British in India. On display are Indian regimental ties, paintings, photographs of military and civilian subjects, model soldiers, medals, coins, picture postcards, postage stamps, toys and examples of Indian dress.

* Shows British & Indian military artefacts
* Learn about the people behind the Raj

Location
Take A56–A6068 between Burnley & Keighley

Opening
Apr–Sep Wed & Sat 2pm–5pm

Admission
Adult £3, Child 50p

Contact
Hendon Mill, Nelson BB9 8AD
t 01282 613129

714 Fleetwood

Farmer Parr's Animal World

3½ hrs   All year

More than 20 acres of farmland to explore here, with a collection of more than 200 farm animals and rare breeds, including poultry and pets. There are both outdoor and indoor areas.

* Autism Initiatives pottery shop
* Pony & tractor rides

Location
Follow M55 to Fleetwood, then take A585 (Fleetwood Road & Amounderness Way). Opposite Cala Gran Caravan Park

Opening
Daily: 10am–5pm

Admission
Adult £4.25, Child £3, Concs £3.50

Contact
Wyrefield Farm, Rossall Lane, Fleetwood FY7 8JP
t 01253 874389/770484
w farmerparrs.com

Lancaster Castle

1 hr+   All year

One of the best-preserved and hardest-working castles in the country and still used today as a court and prison. Visitors can see where the Lancashire Witches were tried and condemned to die, the Hanging Corner where prisoners were hanged, dungeons and the Drop Room.

* Display of heraldic shields in the Shire Hall
* Beautiful Gillow furniture in jury room

Location
Castle is off St Georges Quay in city, at end of Vicarage Lane

Opening
Daily: 10am–5pm
Admission by guided tour only

Admission
Adult £4, Child & Concs £2.50

Contact
Castle Parade, Lancaster LA1 1YJ
t 01524 64998
w lancastercastle.com
e christine.goodier@mus.lancscc.gov.uk

Leighton Hall

2 hrs   May–Sep

Explore the past of an old, Lancashire family, wander through the grounds and pretty gardens and witness displays by trained birds of prey. This interesting historical building has large grounds with a maze, woodland walk and collection of birds of prey.

* C19 walled garden, landscaped parkland & woodland
* Entertaining guides reveal the family's history

Location
Junction 35A of M6, North Carnforth

Opening
May–Sep Tue–Fri & Sun 2pm–5pm
(12.30pm in Aug)

Admission
Adult £5.50, Child £4, Concs £5

Contact
Carnforth LA5 9ST
t 01524 734474
w leightonhall.co.uk
e info@leightonhall.co.uk

717 Lancaster

Williamson Park & Butterfly House

1½ hrs · All year

Bring the family to Williamson Park to visit the Ashton Memorial, a Victorian folly, a conservation garden and a tropical butterfly house.

* Mini beasts & animal centre
* Small mammal enclosure

Location
Follow Lancaster signs from A6/M6 junction 33 or 34. Follow brown tourist signs from city

Opening
Daily: Apr–Sep 10am–5pm; Oct–Mar 10am–4pm

Admission
Adult £4, Child £2.50, Concs £3.50

Contact
Williamson Park, Quernmore Road, Lancaster LA1 1UX

t 01524 33318
w williamsonpark.com

718 Leigh

Pennington Flash Country Park

4 hrs+ · All year

Roam nearly 500 acres of country park, surrounding a 172-acre lake. World-renowned as a bird-watcher's paradise, this is a popular beauty spot, lake and nature reserve. More than 230 bird species have been recorded.

* 9-hole pay & play golf course
* 7 viewing hides

Location
Take A572 from town centre & A580 from Manchester & Liverpool

Opening
Daily: Ranger on site 8.30am–dusk

Admission
Free. Car park charge

Contact
Helens Road, Leigh WN7 3PA

t 01942 605253
w wlct.org
e pfcp@wlct.org

719 Leyland

Worden Arts & Crafts Centre

2 hrs+ · Apr–Sep

Set in 157 acres of parkland, this arts and crafts centre has a fully-equipped theatre, six craft workshops and an exhibition display room.

* Maze
* Garden for the blind

Location
Leave M6 at junction 28 & follow signs for Worden Arts Centre

Opening
Park Daily: 8.30am–8.30pm
Arts & Crafts Centre Please phone for details

Admission
Free

Contact
Worden Park, Worden Lane, Leyland PR25 1DJ

t 01772 455908
w worden-arts.co.uk

720 Littleborough

Hollingworth Lake Country Park

4 hrs+ · All year

A country park consisting of a lake and surrounding countryside, with boating, a nature reserve, trails, events, guided walks, a visitor centre, play areas and picnic sites.

* Refurbished visitor centre with new exciting exhibits

Location
Leave M62 at junction 21 & take B6225. Follow brown tourist signs

Opening
Daily: Apr–Sep 10.30am–6am; Oct–Apr 11am–4pm

Admission
Free. Car park charge

Contact
Rakewood Road, Littleborough OL15 0AQ

t 01706 373421
w rochdale.gov.uk

721 Nelson

Pendle Heritage Centre

2 hrs+   All year

Situated in the beautiful Pendle landscape, the Heritage Centre is the perfect starting point for a variety of local walks. Stroll through the C18 walled garden or take the woodland walk, stopping at the medieval cruck barn to visit the farmyard animals.

* Cruck-frame barn
* Pendle Witches exhibition

Location
Leave M65 at junction 13 & take A682 on to B6247

Opening
Daily: 10am–5pm

Admission
Please phone for details

Contact
Park Hill, Barrowford, Nelson BB9 6JQ

t 01282 661701
e tic@htnw.co.uk

722 Ormskirk

Cedar Farm Galleries

½ day   All year

There are contemporary crafts, farm animals and a funky playground at these galleries, which include nine working craft retail studios, where makers can be seen at work and commissions are taken.

* New art & yoga workshops
* Pots of Fun pottery painting studio

Location
From M6 junction 27 follow brown tourist signs. At crossroads in Mawdesley village turn into Gorsey Lane & then into Back Lane

Opening
Tue–Sun & Bank Hol Mon 10am–5pm

Admission
Free

Contact
Back Lane, Mawdesley, Ormskirk L40 3SY

t 01704 822038
w cedarfarm.net

723 Preston

National Football Museum

2 hrs   All year

Travel on a journey through football's history. Learn how the game was invented, how it has developed over the last 150 years, and what the future will hold for players and supporters. Discover the individuals and teams who have helped to shape the game we know today.

* Football Hall of Fame exhibit
* Enjoy our new penalty shoot out game

Location
2 miles from junction 31, 31A or 32 on M6, follow signs

Opening
Tue–Sat 10am–5pm, Sun 11am–5pm

Admission
Free

Contact
Sir Tom Finney Way, Deepdale, Preston PR1 6RU

t 01772 908442
w nationalfootballmuseum.com
e enquiries@nationalfootballmuseum.com

724 Preston

Leisure Lakes

4 hrs+   All year

The 30 acres of lakes with sandy beaches provide the perfect base for a wide range of water pursuits, from windsurfing and canoeing to sailing and jet-skiing. A 20-bay driving range offers professional golf tuition for adults and children.

* Mountain bike centre

Location
Off A565, 6 miles from Southport & 10 miles from Preston

Opening
Daily: 9am–7pm

Admission
Adult £2.50, Child £2 or £5 per car. Additional charges for some activities

Contact
Mere Brow, Tarleton, Preston PR4 6JX

t 01772 813446
e gab@leisurelakes.co.uk

725 Rawtenstall

Ski Rossendale

2 hrs+ All year

Ski Rossendale is the North's premier ski centre. Open all year round, it is ideal for beginners and expert skiers alike. Set amid trees and parkland, it commands a superb view over the Rossendale Valley.

* Intermediate slope is 80 yards long
* Novices please phone before visiting

Location
Follow M66 to Rawtenstall.
Centre is on town outskirts

Opening
Daily: Mon–Fri 10am–10pm,
Sat 1pm–6pm, Sun 9am–6pm

Admission
Adult £15, Child £9

Contact
Haslingden Old Road,
Rawtenstall BB4 8RR

t 01706 226457
w ski-rossendale.co.uk
e info@ski-rossendale.co.uk

726 Rochdale

Whitworth Water Ski & Recreation Centre

4 hrs+ Apr–Oct

The aim of the centre, run in conjunction with an able-bodied ski club, is to teach people of all disabilities how to water-ski and to help them integrate with able-bodied members. Full instruction and equipment are provided.

* Banana & Ringo rides
* Bikes for disabled visitors

Location
Take A671 from Rochdale

Opening
Apr–Oct Mon–Fri 9.30am–dusk,
Sat–Sun 8am–dusk

Admission
Free. All activities individually priced,
please phone for details

Contact
Cowm Reservoir, Tong Lane
Whitworth, Rochdale OL12 8BE

t 01706 852534
w whitworth-waterski.co.uk
e andynflo@whitworthwaterski.co.uk

727 Rufford

Rufford Old Hall

2 hrs+ Mar–Oct

Rufford is one of Lancashire's finest C16 buildings, famed for its spectacular Great Hall, where it is believed Shakespeare once performed. There's lots to entertain children here, with quizzes and trails through the house and garden.

* Fine collections of C16–C17 oak furniture
* Arms, armour & tapestries

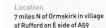

Location
7 miles N of Ormskirk in village
of Rufford on E side of A59

Opening
25 Mar–29 Oct Sat–Wed 1pm–5pm
Please phone to check opening hours
before visiting

Admission
House & Gardens Adult £4.90,
Child £2.50
Gardens £2.80, £1.30

Contact
Rufford, Ormskirk L40 1SG

t 01704 821254
w nationaltrust.org.uk
e ruffordoldhall@ntrust.org.uk

©National Trust Photographic Library

Wigan

Haigh Country Park

5 hrs+   All year

Explore and enjoy this country park that offers
woodland trails and a wide variety of events and
activities including archery, rock climbing and abseiling.

* Free Sunday afternoon entertainment
* 9 & 18-hole golf complex

Location
Near B5238 & B5239

Opening
Park **Daily:** Dawn to dusk
Visitor centre **Daily:** 9am–5pm

Admission
Free

Contact
Haigh, Wigan WN2 1PE

t 01942 832895
w haighhall.net
e hhgen@wict.org

Wigan

Rumble Tumble

1½ hrs   All year

Children can have fun and be challenged in this giant
indoor play zone, which includes a supervised free-fall
slide (for children over five only), ball pools for both
toddlers and older children, a bouncy castle and much
more for all energetic children.

* Birthday party groups accommodated by prior arrangement

Location
Off A49, in Wallgate

Opening
Daily: 10am–7pm

Admission
Before 3pm: Child (under-4) £1.85.
After 3pm: £3. Weekends & hols £3.50
for 1½ hrs

Contact
10 Tower Enterprise Park,
Great George Street,
Wigan WN3 4DP

t 01942 494922

Airport Tour Centre

2 hrs+   All year

Children interested in aeroplanes will love this tour of the airport. Trained guides explain in detail the inner workings of the airport's various busy departments. Prebooking is essential.

Location
Leave M56 at junction 5

Opening
Daily: 9am–9pm

Admission
Adult £5, Child £4, Concs £5

Contact
Terminal 1,
Manchester Airport,
Manchester M90 1QX

t 0161 489 2442
w webmaster.tasmanchester.com
e tourcentre@tasmanchester.com

Castlefield Urban Heritage Park & Visitor Centre

1 hr+   All year

For a great family day out, Castlefield has it all: numerous museums, the remains of the Roman fort of Mamucium, a canal, pleasant walks, boat trips and frequent events in the outdoor arena. Perfect for picnics on a fine day.

* Britain's first urban heritage park

Location
In city centre, follow signs for the Museum of Science & Industry

Opening
Park Daily: please phone for details

Admission
Free

Contact
Castlefield, Manchester

t 0161 234 3157
w visitmanchester.com

Jewish Museum of Manchester

2 hrs   All year

Manchester's Jewish Museum is unique as it is housed in a former Spanish and Portuguese synagogue. The former Ladies Gallery tells the history of Manchester Jewry using pictures, documents, room settings and handsets with testimonies from people of the past.

* Lavish Moorish décor & stained glass

Location
On A665, 1 mile from city centre

Opening
Mon–Thu 10.30am–4pm
Sun 10.30am–5pm;
closed Sat & Jewish hols

Admission
Adult £3.95, Child & Concs £2.95

Contact
190 Cheetham Hill Road,
Manchester M8 8LW

t 0161 834 9879
w manchesterjewishmuseum.com
e info@manchester
jewishmuseum.com

Manchester Art Gallery

4 hrs+   All year

Enjoy some family fun in the Clore Interactive Gallery or take part in a wide range of events. Highlights include outstanding Pre-Raphaelite paintings, craft and design and C20 British art. An exciting exhibitions programme offers the best in visual art and design.

* Collection spans 6 centuries of fine & decorative art
* Exceptional for C19 British paintings

Location
In city centre

Opening
Tue–Sun 10am–5pm;
closed Mon except Bank Hols

Admission
Free

Contact
Mosley Street, Manchester M2 3JL

t 0161 235 8888
w manchestergalleries.org

734 Manchester

Manchester Museum

1 hr   All year

The museum's collections include fossils, minerals, natural history specimens, archaeology, a unique collection from ancient Egypt, living reptiles and amphibians in the award-winning vivarium, and an interactive exhibition on the human body.

* Ethnology collections from South America
* Collections of fossils & minerals

Location
In Oxford Road to S of city centre

Opening
Daily: Tue–Sat 10am–5pm,
Sun–Mon & Bank Hols 11am–4pm

Admission
Free. Special events may charge

Contact
The University of Manchester,
Oxford Road,
Manchester M13 9PL

t 0161 275 2634
w museum.manchester.ac.uk
e michael.rooney@manchester.ac.uk

735 Manchester

Museum of Science & Industry

4 hrs+   All year

The museum comprises five buildings over a 7½-acre site and tells the story of the history, science and industry of Manchester, the world's first industrial city. Stimulate the senses in Xperiment, an interactive science gallery.

* Steam engines & locomotives
* Morphis simulator rides

Location
On Liverpool Road in Castlefield,
signed from city centre

Opening
Daily: 10am–5pm

Admission
Free. Exhibitions may charge

Contact
Liverpool Road, Castlefield,
Manchester M3 4FP

t 0161 832 2244
w msim.org.uk
e marketing@msim.org.uk

736 Manchester

Museum of Transport

2 hrs   All year

Housed in a former bus depot, this wonderfully quirky museum is packed with vintage vehicles, including buses, fire engines and lorries, some 100 years old. There are vehicles from horse-drawn through to the earliest models of the Metrolink trams.

* Biggest collection of vintage buses in the UK

Location
1 mile N of city centre at N end of Boyle Street, next to Queen's Road bus garage

Opening
Mar–Oct Wed, Sat, Sun & Bank Hols 10am–5pm;
Nov–Feb 10am–4pm;
closed Christmas & New Year

Admission
Adult £4, Child & Concs £2

Contact
Boyle Street, Cheetham, Manchester M8 8UW

t 0161 205 2122
w gmts.co.uk
e email@gmts.co.uk

737 Manchester

Old Trafford Museum & Tour

2 hrs   All year

See the Manchester United trophy room, kits through the ages, and memorabilia of the 'greats', from Charlton to Cantona, Best to Beckham. A stadium tour takes you to the players' tunnel, the dressing room, the dugout and more.

* Play your own commentary on United games
* Multi-award winner

Location
From Chester Road (A56), turn into Sir Matt Busby Way, or use Old Trafford Metrolink station

Opening
Daily: 9.30am–5pm
Museum closes 30 mins before kick-off, please phone for details of times & to book tours

Admission
Museum Adult £5.50,
Child & Concs £3.75

Contact
Sir Matt Busby Way, Old Trafford, Manchester M16 0RA

t 0870 442 1994
w manutd.com

738 Manchester

People's History Museum

2 hrs   All year

Discover the extraordinary story of ordinary people, with interactive exhibits looking at their lives at work, home and leisure over the past 200 years.

* From mill workers to the first professional footballers
* Housed in an Edwardian pumping station

Location
Via A6, M602, M62, A56. Follow signs to Castlefield

Opening
Tue–Sun & Bank Hols 11am–4.30pm;
closed Good Fri

Admission
Free

Contact
The Pump House, Bridge Street, Manchester M3 3ER

t 0161 839 6061
w peopleshistorymuseum.org.uk
e info@peopleshistorymuseum.org.uk

739 Manchester

Trafford Ecology Park

2 hrs+   All year

Once an industrial wasteland, Trafford Ecology Park has now been transformed into a thriving activity centre and haven for wildlife. Visitors can see the displays, take part in the events, or simply discover the wealth of wild flowers, trees, birds and animals that flourish there.

* Centred on a reclaimed boating lake
* Based in Europe's largest industrial estate

Location
From M602 take A576. From M60 junction 9 take A5081

Opening
Mon–Fri 9am–5pm;
closed weekends & Bank Hols

Admission
Free

Contact
Lake Road, Trafford Park,
Manchester M17 1TU

t 0161 873 7182
w trafford.gov.uk
e ecology.reception@groundworks.
gov.uk

740 Northenden

Wythenshawe Park

4 hrs+   All year

This C16 hall is set in 275 acres of parkland, offering a range of leisure facilities. Beautifully maintained, it has numerous sporting attractions including several football pitches, tennis courts, bowling greens and children's play areas.

* Museum, gallery & glasshouses
* Farm centre

Location
Just off M56, 4 miles from Manchester
Airport

Opening
Park Daily: Dawn–dusk
Please phone for details of opening
times of other facilities

Admission
Please phone for details

Contact
Wythenshawe Road, Northenden,
Manchester M23 0AB

t 0161 998 2117
e s.west@manchester.gov.uk

741 Salford

Ordsall Hall Museum

2 hrs   All year

Ordsall Hall is a haunted Tudor manor house in the surroundings of inner city Salford. Visitors can admire the impressive Great Hall, Star Chamber and Tudor Kitchen.

* Family events
* Exhibitions programme

Location
Signed from A57 & A5063

Opening
Mon–Fri 10am–4pm, Sun 1pm–4pm;
closed Good Fri, Easter Sun &
Christmas

Admission
Free

Contact
Ordsall Lane, Salford,
Manchester M5 3AN

t 0161 872 0251
w salford.gov.uk/leisure/museums
e ordsall@btopenworld.com

742 Liverpool

The Beatles Story

2 hrs   All year

The award-winning Beatles Story is the ultimate tribute to Liverpool's most famous sons – John, Paul, George and Ringo. The magical history tour takes the visitor on a trip from the Cavern Club, through the years of Beatlemania and Flower Power to the eventual break-up of the group.

* New living history audio tour
* Personal insights from those who really knew the Fab Four

Location
Follow signs to Albert Dock

Opening
Daily: 10am–6pm, (last admission 5pm)

Admission
Adult £8.99, Child £4.99, Concs £5.99

Contact
Albert Dock, Britannia Vaults, Liverpool L3 4AD

t 0151 709 1963
w beatlesstory.com

---

743 Liverpool

Croxteth Hall & Country Park

2 hrs+   Apr–Sep

Enjoy a great day out at Croxteth! Historic Croxteth Hall comes to life with character figures, conversations to eavesdrop on and even smells in the rooms. Everyone will have fun meeting the animals on Home Farm, while the walled garden is a haven of peace and tranquillity.

* Kids can let off steam in the adventure playground
* Explore 500 acres of heritage countryside

Location
Leave M57 at junction 4 & take A580 towards Liverpool

Opening
Daily: Easter–Sep 10.30am–5pm

Admission
Adult £4.20, Child & Concs £2.10

Contact
Croxteth Hall Lane, Liverpool L12 0HB

t 0151 228 5311
w croxteth.co.uk
e croxtethcountrypark@liverpool. gov.uk

744 Liverpool

Everton Football Club

2 hrs   All year

Discover at first hand what goes on behind the scenes at Goodison Park. Walk down the tunnel to the roar of 40,000 fans, visit the dressing room where the players get changed and see where they relax and celebrate or commiserate after a game.

Location
3 miles N of city centre

Opening
Daily: closed on match days

Admission
Adult £8.50, Child & Concs £5
Prebooking essential

Contact
Goodison Park, Liverpool L4 4EL
t 0870 442 1878
w evertonfc.com
e boxoffice@evertonfc.com

745 Liverpool

Knowsley Safari Park

3 hrs+   All year

Enjoy a drive through Knowsley Safari Park: 500 acres of rolling countryside, where some of the world's wildest animals roam free including camels, buffalo, white rhino, emu, wallabies, elephants, giraffes and lions.

* Reptile house is home to snakes, iguanas, lizards, scorpions & stick insects

Location
Leave M62 at junction 6, M57 at junction 2 & follow signs

Opening
Daily: Mar–Oct 10am–4pm;
Nov–Feb 10.30am–3pm

Admission
Adult £9.50, Child & Concs £6.50

Contact
Prescot, Merseyside L34 4AN
t 0151 430 9009
w knowsley.com
e safari.park@knowsley.com

746 Liverpool

Liverpool Football Club Museum & Tour Centre

1 hr   All year

A must for any Liverpool fan, young or old. The museum includes a display of the club's trophies and films on the history of the club. Visit the dressing room, walk down the tunnel to the sound of 45,000 cheering fans, touch the famous 'This is Anfield sign', and sit in the team dugout.

* Film takes visitors through the life of the club
* Hillsborough memorial tribute to 96 fans who died at Hillsborough

Location
3 miles from city centre, 4 miles from M62, 7 miles from end of M57 & M58

Opening
Daily: 10am–5pm
Museum last admissions 4pm
(closes 1 hr before kick-off)

Admission
Adult £9, Child & Concs £5.50

Contact
Anfield Road, Liverpool L4 0TH

t 0151 260 6677
w liverpoolfc.tv
e events@liverpoolfc.tv

747 Liverpool

Liverpool Planetarium

1 hr   All year

Enjoy an exciting visual experience of space in a domed auditorium at this planetarium. The support programme *Nightwatch* takes a look at the night sky.

* 30-minute performance

Location
In city centre. Follow signs from M62

Opening
Daily: Mon–Fri with shows at 2.30pm, 3.15pm & 4.05pm, Sat–Sun at 1.15pm, 2.15pm, 3.15pm & 4.05pm

Admission
Free

Contact
William Brown Street, Liverpool L3 8EN

t 0151 478 4283
w liverpoolmuseums.org.uk
e jennifer.mchale@liverpoolmuseums.org.uk

748 Liverpool

National Wildflower Centre

2 hrs   Apr–Sep

A family-friendly visitor attraction that promotes the creation of new places for wildflowers and their importance to the environment. There are demonstration gardens, a plant nursery and a rooftop walkway.

* Children's play area
* Wall with climbing handles

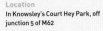

Location
In Knowsley's Court Hey Park, off junction 5 of M62

Opening
Daily: Apr–Sep 10am–5pm

Admission
Adult £3, Child free, Concs £1.50

Contact
Court Hey Park, Knowsley L16 3NA

t 0151 738 1913/722 8292
w nwc.org.uk
e info@nwc.org.uk

749 Liverpool

Speke Hall, Garden & Estate

2 hrs   Mar–Dec

One of the most famous half-timbered houses in the country, dating from 1530. A fully equipped Victorian kitchen and servants' hall enable visitors to see behind the scenes. The nearby Home Farm is a restored model Victorian farm building with orchard.

* Fine Jacobean plasterwork & carved furniture

Location
8 miles SE of central Liverpool, next to Liverpool airport, signed

Opening
Mar–Oct Wed–Sun 1pm–5.30pm;
Nov–Dec Sat–Sun 1pm–4.30pm

Admission
Adult £6.25, Child £3.50

Contact
The Walk, Speke, Liverpool L24 1XD

t 0151 427 7231
w nationaltrust.org.uk
e spekehall@nationaltrust.org.uk

750 Liverpool

Tate Liverpool

2 hrs   All year

Bring the children for a cultural day out at Tate Liverpool, the home of the National Collection of modern art in the North of England. Part of the historic Albert Dock, it has four floors of art to appreciate, free daily talks, a shop and a café.

* Photography, printmaking, painting & sculpture
* Video, performance art & installations

Location
Walking distance from Liverpool Lime Street station, signed from city centre

Opening
Tue–Sun 10am–5.50pm

Admission
Tate Liverpool Free
Exhibition Adult £4, Child free, Concs £3

Contact
The Colonnades, Albert Dock, Liverpool L3 4BB

t 0151 702 7400
w tate.org.uk/liverpool
e liverpoolinfo@tate.org.uk

751 Liverpool

Williamson Tunnels

1 hr   All year

When you enter Williamson Tunnels, you enter a strange underground kingdom that has lain beneath the city of Liverpool since the early C19. Visitors can see and touch the brick and sandstone workings of this key section of the tunnels.

* Entertaining commentary from an expert guide

Location
From city centre head towards Edgehill

Opening
Summer Tue–Sun 10am–5pm;
Winter Thu–Sun 10am–4pm,
Tue & Wed open by arrangement;
Oct & Feb half-terms open daily

Admission
Adult £3.50, Child £2, Concs £3

Contact
The Old Stableyard, Smithdown Lane Liverpool L7 3EE

t 0151 709 6868
w willliamsontunnels.co.uk
e enquiries@willliamsontunnels.co.uk

752 Liverpool

Yellow Duckmarine

1 hr   All year

This unique amphibious city tour takes you through the historic city, docks and waterfront. On dry land, visit the Pier Head, St George's Hall, both cathedrals, Chinatown and the Philharmonic Hall, before you 'splash down' into the Salthouse Dock.

Location
Follow brown tourist signs from M62 or city centre to the Albert Dock

Opening
Daily: 11am–4pm

Admission
Adult £9.95, Child £7.95, Concs £8.95

Contact
32 Anchor Courtyard,
Britannia Pavilion, Albert Dock,
Liverpool L3 4AS

t 0151 708 7799
w theyellowduckmarine.co.uk

753 Skelmersdale

Beacon Country Park

All day   All year

There is space to walk, run, ride horses or bikes, fly kites, or just get away from it all and relax at Beacon Country Park. The park consists of more than 300 acres of rolling countryside with a combination of flowing meadows and woodlands.

* 18-hole golf course & driving range
* Heritage trail & orienteering course

Location
Leave M6 at junction 27, & M58 at junction 5

Opening
Daily: 7am–10pm

Admission
Free

Contact
Beacon Lane, Upholland,
Skelmersdale WN8 7RU

t 01695 622794
w westlancsdc.gov.uk
e beacon.park@westlancsdc.gov.uk

754 Southport

Formby

2 hrs   All year

This nature reserve is home to one of Britain's last thriving colonies of red squirrels. These can be seen in the pine trees, while the shoreline attracts waders such as oystercatchers and sanderlings. As well as the beautiful beach, there are miles of walks across the sand dunes.

Location
15 miles N of Liverpool, 2 miles W of Formby, 2 miles off A565 & 6 miles S of Southport

Opening
All year: Dawn–dusk

Admission
Free. Car park £3.30

Contact
Blundell Avenue, Formby L37 1PH

t 01704 878591
w nationaltrust.org.uk
e formby@nationaltrust.org.uk

755 Southport

Model Railway Village

2 hrs   Mar–Sep

Set within sheltered gardens, this beautiful miniature village has more than 200 1:18 scale models including watermills, churches, shops and houses. There is also a garden gauge railway.

Location
From M6 (junction 26 N or junction 31 S). Opposite Royal Clifton Hotel, next to marine lake footbridge

Opening
Daily: Mar–Sep 10am–5pm
(6pm in Jul–Aug; last admission 1 hr before closing)

Admission
Adult £2.95, Child £2.50, Concs £2

Contact
Lower Promenade, Kings Gardens,
Southport PR8 1RB

t 01704 214266
w southportmodelrailwayvillage.co.uk

World of Glass

2 hrs   All year

Take a journey of discovery into one of the most common substances on earth. Watch live demonstrations of glassblowing by resident artists and wander through a maze of tunnels that are the remains of the oldest glassmaking tank furnace in the world.

* Gift shop & cafeteria
* Fun zone with distorting mirrors & kaleidoscopes

Location
Leave M62 at junction 7 & M6 at junction 24, then head into town centre

Opening
Tue–Sun & Bank Hols 10am–5pm

Admission
Adult £5.30, Child & Concs £3.80

Contact
Chalon Way East,
St Helens WA10 1BX

t 08700 114466
w worldofglass.com
e info@worldofglass.com

Mersey Ferries River Explorer Cruise

1 hr+   All year

This cruise along the River Mersey takes 50 minutes and has a recorded commentary. A stop-off at the Wirral Terminal allows for a visit to an aquarium, children's play area, shop and café.

* Space-themed children's play area at Seacombe
* New space port

Location
Pier Head Liverpool is signed from Albert Dock. Follow signs on M53 for Seacombe & Woodside-on-Wirral

Opening
Daily: Mon–Fri 10am–3pm,
Sat, Sun & Bank Hols 10am–6pm

Admission
Adult £4.80, Child £2.60, Concs £3.50

Contact
Victoria Place, Seacombe,
Wallasey CH44 6QY

t 0151 330 1444
w merseyferries.co.uk
e info@merseyferries.co.uk

Historic Warships at Birkenhead

3 hrs   All year

Visitors to HMS *Plymouth* will experience what life is like on the high seas. On the submarine HMS *Onyx* they can imagine shadowing a target vessel while looking through the periscope. Guided tours are available.

* U534, the last U-boat to leave Germany in WWII
* LCT 7074, last surviving LCT of D-Day landings

Location
Leave M53 at junction 1 & follow signs to All Docks. Signed from there

Opening
Apr–Sep 10am–5pm;
Oct–Mar 10am–4pm

Admission
Adult £6, Child £4, Concs £5

Contact
East Float, Dock Road, Birkenhead
CH41 1DJ

t 0151 650 1573
w warships.freeserve.co.uk

Alnwick Castle, Northumberland

North East

Durham Northumberland Tyne & Wear

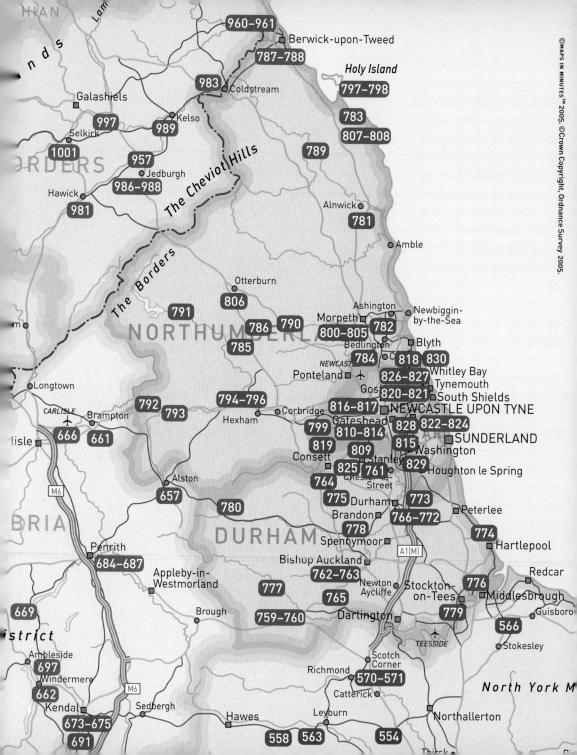

960–961
Berwick-upon-Tweed
787–788

Holy Island

797–798

783

807–808

983
Coldstream

Galashiels

997
Kelso
989

Selkirk

1001

957

Jedburgh

986–988

Hawick

981

789

Alnwick
781

Amble

The Cheviot Hills

Otterburn
806

Ashington
Newbiggin-
by-the-Sea

The Borders

791

786 **790**
Morpeth
800–805
782

785
Bedlington
Blyth

NEWCASTLE
784
C
818 **830**

Ponteland
826–827
Whitley Bay

Gos
820–821
Tynemouth
South Shields

Longtown

792
793

794–796

Corbridge
816–817
NEWCASTLE UPON TYNE

CARLISLE
Brampton
Hexham
799
Gateshead
828 **822–824**

666 **661**
810–814
815
SUNDERLAND

819
809
Washington

lisle
Consett
825 **761**
829
Houghton le Spring

764
Stanley
Chester-le-
Street

Alston
775
Durham
773

657
766–772
Peterlee

780
Brandon
774

M6
778
Spennymoor
Hartlepool

BRIA
DURHAM
A1(M)

Penrith
Bishop Auckland
776
Redcar

684–687
762–763
Stockton-
on-Tees

Appleby-in-
Westmorland
777
Newton
Aycliffe
Middlesbrough

669
Brough
765
Guisboro

759–760
Dartington
779
566

strict
TEESSIDE
Stokesley

Ambleside
697

Windermere
662
Scotch
Corner
North York M

Kendal
Richmond
570–571

673–675
Sedbergh
Catterick
Northallerton

691
Hawes
Leyburn

558 **563**
554

759 Barnard Castle

Barnard Castle

1 hr+   All year

Towering high above the River Tees, this C12 stone castle was once one of the largest castles in northern England, the principal residence of the Baliol family, and a major power base in the many conflicts between England and Scotland.

* Beautiful views of River Tees
* Home to Richard III & Henry VII

Location
In Barnard Castle town, off Galgate on A688

Opening
Daily: Apr–Sep 10am–6pm;
Oct 10am–4pm; Nov–Mar Thu–Mon 10am–4pm

Admission
Adult £3, Child £1.50, Concs £2.30

Contact
Barnard Castle
t 01833 638212
w english-heritage.org.uk

760 Barnard Castle

Bowes Museum

3 hrs   All year

A French-style château housing one of Britain's finest museums. Collections in the museum include paintings, textiles, furniture and ceramics. There are beautiful gardens for children to wander through and fascinating exhibitions throughout the year.

* Set in 23 acres of parkland, with parterre garden
* Outstanding temporary art exhibition programme

Location
Just off A66, 20 mins from Scotch Corner (A1)

Opening
Daily; 11am–5pm

Admission
Adult £7, Child free, Concs £6

Contact
Barnard Castle DL12 8NP
t 01833 690606
w bowesmuseum.org.uk
e info@bowesmuseum.org.uk

761 Beamish

Beamish, The North of England Open-Air Museum

4 hrs+   All year

Beamish is an extraordinary day out for the whole family. Touch, taste and experience the past at this living open-air museum, which vividly illustrates life in the Great North in the early C19 and early C20.

* Costumed guides explain each attraction
* Former European Museum of the Year

Location
Follow signs from junction 63 of A1(M)

Opening
Apr–Oct daily 10am–5pm;
Nov–Apr Tue–Thu & Sat–Sun 10am–4pm

Admission
Adult £15, Child £9, Concs £12
Nov–Mar £6 per person

Contact
Beamish DH9 0RG
t 0191 370 4000
w beamish.org.uk
e museum@beamish.org.uk

762 Bishop Auckland

Hamsterley Forest

   2-4 hrs   All year

Covering some 2,000 hectares, Hamsterley Forest has something for everyone – play and picnic areas, several walks and cycle routes ranging from a 1½ mile easy-access footpath to a 7-mile black cycle route and downhill descent course for the more adventurous.

* Largest forest in County Durham
* New cycle routes

Location
From A68 at Witton-le-Wear follow brown tourist signs

Opening
Forest Daily; 7.30am-sunset
Visitor centre Apr-Oct Mon-Fri 10am-4pm, Sat-Sun 11am-5pm
Please phone for details of Nov-Dec

Admission
Free. Toll for forest drive & car park charge (£2 per car)

Contact
Redford, Bishop Auckland DL13 3NL
t 01388 488312
w forestry.gov.uk

763 Bishop Auckland

Harperley POW Camp

   1 hr   All year

Harperley was one of the few purpose-built POW camps in Britain. It housed low-risk prisoners, first from Italy and then from Germany. At its height it held 1,500 prisoners. In addition to the museum, there is a garden centre and a farm shop.

* Children's outdoor play area
* Featured in the BBC programme *Restoration*

Location
Approximately 250m from junction of A68 & A689 near village of Crook

Opening
Daily; 10am-5pm

Admission
Free

Contact
Firtree, Crook,
County Durham DL15 8DX
t 01388 767098
w powcamp.com
e info@powcamp.com

764 Consett

Mister Twisters, Consett

   1 hr+   All year

This exciting indoor play and party centre includes a multi level soft play climbing frame, inflatable temple and spooky tomb. There is a separate under-5s play village with a baby crawling pit and activity room. There are also centres in Gateshead and Hartlepool.

* Large Visitor Attraction of the Year finalist in 2003

Location
From A1(M) take A691 to Consett. From Gateshead take A692 to Consett

Opening
Daily: Sun-Thu 9am-7pm,
Fri-Sat 9am-8pm

Admission
School hols Mon-Fri Child (1-3) £2.95,
Child (4-12) £3.45

Bank Hols, Sat-Sun Child (1-3) £3.45,
Child (4-12) £3.95 (Additional adult 50p)

Contact
Unit 40, No. 1 Industrial Estate,
Medomsley Road,
Consett DH8 6TW
t 01207 500007
w mistertwisters.co.uk

765 Darlington

Raby Castle

  3 hrs+   Easter-Sep

Raby Castle is a magnificent example of a medieval castle in Teesdale. A wonderful day out for the family, with stunning rooms to wonder at, walled gardens, a deer park and a children's adventure playground.

* Great kitchen little altered in 600 years
* Paintings by Reynolds & other Old Masters

Location
1 mile N of Staindrop on A688

Opening
Easter weekend 11am-5.30pm;
May & Sep Wed & Sun 11am-5.30pm;
Jun-Aug Sun-Fri 11am-5.30pm

Admission
Adult £9, Child £4, Concs £8

Contact
PO Box 50, Staindrop,
Darlington DL2 3AH
t 01833 660 202
w rabycastle.com
e admin@rabycastle.com

766 Durham

Crook Hall Gardens

1 hr+   Easter–Sep

Crook Hall is a Grade I listed medieval manor house. If you are scared of spooks, avoid the haunted Jacobean room, home to the ghost of the White Lady. Outside you can visit the moat pool, wildflower meadow and orchard or find your way out of the maze.

* Fruit trees wreathed in rambling roses
* 'A tapestry of colourful blooms', according to Alan Titchmarsh

Location	Admission
Short walk from Durham's Millburngate shopping centre, opposite Gala Theatre	Adult £4, Concs £3.50
Opening	**Contact**
Easter–Jul & Sep Sun only 1pm–5pm; Aug Sat–Thu & Bank Hols 1pm–5pm	Frankland Lane, Sidegate, Durham DH1 5SZ
	t 0191 384 8028
	w crookhallgardens.co.uk
	e info@crookhallgardens.co.uk

768 Durham

The DLI Museum

2 hrs+   All year

Enter the world of County Durham Light Infantry soldiers and their families. Dramatic and interactive displays and a set walk let you see for yourself what their lives were like. Our art gallery runs a programme of exhibitions related to all aspects of visual art.

* Dress up as a soldier
* Hands-on experience of exhibits

Location	Admission
½ mile NW of Durham city centre, off A691, near railway station	Adult £3, Child £1.25, Concs £2
Opening	**Contact**
Daily: Apr–Oct 10am–5pm; Nov–Mar 10am–4pm	Aykley Heads, Durham DH1 5TU
	t 0191 384 2214
	w durham.gov.uk/dli
	e dli@durham.gov.uk

767 Durham

Diggerland

3 hrs+   Feb–Nov

Based on the world of construction machinery, this is a unique adventure park where children and adults can experience the thrill of riding and driving real JCBs and dumpers in safety.

* Educational day out with a difference
* New Diggerland tractors & Spin Dizzy ride

Location	Admission
Exit A1(M) at junction 62. Head W, signed to Consett. After 6 miles turn left at roundabout, signed to Langley Park, then turn right into Riverside Industrial Estate	Adult/Child £2.50, under–2s Free, Concs £1.25. Additional charge to drive/ride mechanical vehicles
Opening	**Contact**
Feb–Nov weekends, Bank Hols & school hols 10am–5pm	Langley Park DA7 9TT
	t 08700 344437
	w diggerland.com

769 Durham

Durham Castle

1 hr   Mar–Sep

Built by William the Conqueror in 1072 as a fortress, the castle has been in constant use for more than 900 years and is one of the largest Norman castles in England. It was also once a bishop's palace and today provides accommodation for the university.

* World Heritage Site
* Entrance by guided tour only

Location
Durham city centre. Uphill walk or bus No. 40 to Palace Green

Opening
Daily: mid-Mar–mid-Apr, Jul–Sep
10am–12.30pm & 2pm–4.30pm
Other times usually Mon, Wed, Sat–Sun afternoons but please phone to confirm

Admission
Adult £5, Child & Concs £2.50

Contact
Durham DH1 3RW

t 0191 334 3800
w durhamcastle.com
e university-college.www@durham.ac.uk

770 Durham

Kascada Leisure Complex

2 hrs   All year

Situated in the heart of historic Durham, the Kascada Leisure Complex has excellent leisure facilities, with 20 bowling lanes using the latest computerised technology.

* Arcadia – fully interactive video arcade
* Diner Express fast-food bar

Location
From A1(M) take A690 towards Durham, take last right at Gilesgate roundabout, into Claypath, right at traffic lights then left into The Sands (follow signs for coach park)

Opening
Daily: Mon–Fri 11am–11pm, Sat–Sun 10am–11pm

Admission
Adult £3.95, Child & Concs £2.95 (shoe hire 90p)

Contact
Walkergate DH1 1SQ

t 0191 383 0300
w kascadabowl.com

771 Durham

Old Fulling Museum of Archaeology

1 hr   All year

This old mill has become one of the most photographed buildings in the North East. It now houses the Museum of Archaeology among whose striking exhibits is a major collection of Roman inscriptions from the north of England and an outstanding collection of Samianware.

* Artefacts from ancient Greece & Rome
* Medieval finds from Durham city centre

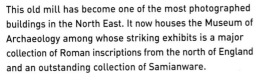

Location
Just below cathedral in city centre

Opening
Apr–Oct 11am–4pm;
Nov–Mar Fri–Mon 11.30am–3.30pm

Admission
Adult £1, Child & Concs 50p

Contact
The Banks, Durham DH1 3EB

t 0191 334 1823
e fulling.mill@dur.ac.uk
w dur.ac.uk/fulling.mill

772 Durham

Prince Bishop River Cruiser

1 hr   All year

The *Prince Bishop* river cruiser sails on the River Wear. It offers the best views of Durham Cathedral, Durham Castle and the bridges. The trip includes a commentary that will suit children of all ages. There is wheelchair access to the upper deck and saloons.

* Sun deck & onboard barbecue
* 1-hour Santa Cruises in Dec

Location
Cruiser is found below Prince Bishop shopping centre in Durham

Opening
Please phone for details

Admission
Adult £4.50, Child £2, Concs £4

Contact
The Boathouse, Elvet Bridge, Durham DH1 3AH

t 0191 386 9525

773 Gilesgate Moor

Top Gear Indoor Karting

2 hrs+   All year

Top Gear is a go-karting leisure centre. It provides indoor go-karting fun for everyone from 8 to 88 (minimum height requirement 1.4 metres) and is a great place for family birthdays.

* New go-karts recently arrived
* Regular race meetings

Location	Admission
From A1(M) take A690 towards Durham & follow brown tourist signs	£20 per person for 30 laps £25 per person for 40 laps
Opening Daily: Mon–Fri 12noon–9pm Sat–Sun 9am–7pm	**Contact** 13 Renny's Lane, Gilesgate Moor DH1 2RS
	t 0191 386 0999 w durhamkarting.co.uk e durhamkarting@lineone.net

774 Hartlepool

Hartlepool's Maritime Experience

4–6 hrs   All year

Built in Bombay in 1816–17 for the princely sum of £23,000, HMS *Trincomalee* is the oldest ship afloat in the UK. Today you can experience what life was like on board. Visit the captain's cabin, the bread room, the sleeping quarters, the quarter deck, even the toilets.

* Excellent disabled access to most decks
* One of several attractions around Historic Quay

Location	Contact
Follow signs for Hartlepool Historic Quay	HMS *Trincomalee* Trust, Jackson Dock, Hartlepool TS24 0XZ
Opening Daily: 10am–5pm	t 01429 860077 w hartlepoolmaritimeexperience. com
Admission Adult £6.25, Child £3.75, Concs £4.75	e info@hartlepoolmaritime experience. com

775 Lanchester

Hall Hill Farm

2 hrs   Mar–Oct

There is a wide range of friendly animals to meet face to face including fluffy chicks, baby lambs, pigs, donkeys, ponies and rabbits. Then there are more unusual animals such as llamas, wallabies and Highland Cattle. Tractor rides take you around this working farm.

* Fantastic views of Durham countryside
* Children's playground

Location	Admission
10 miles W of Durham off B6296, S of Lanchester	Adult £4.20, Child £3.20, Concs £3.80
Opening Mar–Sep daily 10.30am–5pm; Sep–Oct Sat–Sun 10.30am–5pm	**Contact** Lanchester, Durham DH7 0TA
	t 01388 731333 w hallhillfarm.co.uk e info@hallhillfarm.co.uk

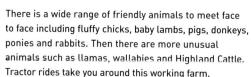

776 Middlesbrough

Dorman Museum

1 hr   All year

The Dorman recently reopened after a major construction programme that has created a diverse range of galleries and exhibitions. The museum, first opened in 1904, now houses hands-on science sections such as H_2O and Earth in Space as well as local history displays.

* Learn the story of Linthorpe Pottery
* Constantly changing art exhibitions

Location
Centre of Middlesbrough, at junction of Ayresome Street & Linthorpe Road

Opening
Apr–Oct Tue–Sun 10am–5.30pm;
Nov–Mar Tue–Sun 9am–4.30pm

Admission
Free

Contact
Linthorpe Road, Middlesbrough
TS5 6LA

t 01642 813781
w dormanmuseum.co.uk
e dormanmuseum@middlesbrough.gov.uk

777 Middleton-in-Teesdale

Bowlees Picnic Area

½ day   All year

This picnic area is in a sheltered side valley of Teesdale. There are four beautiful waterfalls in the site and more falls alongside a footpath that leads to Gibson's Cave.

* Visitor centre nearby
* Undisturbed limestone quarry

Location
On B6277, 2½ miles NW of Middleton-in-Teesdale

Opening
Daily: 24 hrs

Admission
Free

Contact
nr Middleton-in-Teesdale DL12 0XF

t 0191 383 3594
w durham.gov.uk
e rangers@durham.gov.uk

778 Spennymoor

Whitworth Hall Country Park

3 hrs   All year

Feed the red and fallow deer in this 73-acre historic parkland. There is an ornamental lake, a Victorian walled garden, a woodland garden and indoor and outdoor play facilities for children. Special events are arranged throughout the year.

* Feed the ducks
* Charity fun days & car shows

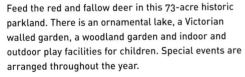

Location
7 miles W of Durham & A1.
At A1 (junction 61) join A688 signed for Spennymoor. Continue following signs for Whitworth Hall Hotel

Opening
Daily: noon–dusk

Admission
Free

Contact
nr Spennymoor DL16 7QX

t 01388 811772
w whitworthhall.co.uk

779 Stockton on Tees

Four Seasons White Water Rafting

2 hrs   Feb–Nov

A nationally recognised centre for canoeing, kayaking and white-water rafting. The tidal River Tees guarantees white water all year with fast-flowing rapids carrying you down the course on an exhilarating and adrenalin-fuelled trip. Equipment can be hired.

* Customizable difficulty for beginners and experts
* Training for all levels

Location
On N bank of River Tees near Tees Barrage Bridge, Stockton on Tees

Opening
All year – booking advised
Please phone for details

Admission
From £15

Contact
Tees Barrage, Stockton on Tees
TS18 2QW

t 01642 678000
w 4seasons.co.uk
e kanu@4seasons.co.uk

780 Upper Weardale

Killhope Lead Mining Museum

4 hrs   Easter–Oct

Wearing hard hat, cap-lamp and wellies, you are guided down the original tunnel of a lead mine to find out about the lives of the miners who toiled here. There is a woodland walk too.

* Warm clothes required even during summer
* Winner of Family Friendly Museum Award 2004

Location
Off A689 between Stanhope & Alston

Opening
Daily: Easter–Oct 10.30am–5pm

Admission
Adult £6, Child £3, Concs £5.50
No under-4s allowed in mine

Contact
The North of England Lead Mining Museum, nr Cowshill, Upper Weardale DL13 1AR
t 01388 537505
w durham.gov.uk/killhope
e killhope@durham.gov.uk

781 Alnwick

Alnwick Castle

2 hrs+   Apr–Oct

This medieval castle has wonderful Renaissance furnishings inside its walls. The Regiment Museum of the Royal Northumberland Fusiliers is housed in the Abbott's Tower along with the museum of local archaeology and the Percy Tenantry volunteers.

* Home to Percy family for 700 years

Location
Alnwick, 35 miles N of Newcastle upon Tyne, 1 mile from A1

Opening
Daily: Apr–Oct 11am–5pm

Admission
Adult £7.95, Child £2.95, Concs £7.50

Contact
Alnwick NE66 1NQ
t 01665 510777
w alnwickcastle.com
e enquiries@alnwickcastle.com

782 Ashington

Wansbeck Riverside Park

2–5 hrs   All year

An award-winning country park with a delightful camping and caravan site, plus a wide range of activities on hand, many of which are on the water. There is a play area, a paddle pool and an island nature reserve.

* Picnic & play areas
* 4-mile riverside walk

Location
Take A1068. Park is located between Ashington & Bedlington

Opening
Daily: 8am–dusk

Admission
Free

Contact
Green Lane,
Ashington NE63 8TX
t 01670 843444

783 Bamburgh

Bamburgh Castle

2 hrs   Mar–Oct

This magnificent coastal castle contains collections of furniture, paintings, arms and armour. The rocky outcrop became a royal centre in AD547. The present fortress has a museum room, grand King's Hall, Cross Hall, armoury and Victorian scullery for children to explore.

* Still home to the Armstrong family
* Exhibits include fine furniture, tapestries & arms

Location
20 miles S of Berwick-upon-Tweed by B1342

Opening
Daily: mid-Mar–Oct 11am–4.30pm

Admission
Adult £6, Child £2.50, Concs £5

Contact
Bamburgh NE69 7DF
t 01668 214515
w bamburghcastle.com
e bamburghcastle@aol.com

784 Bedlington

Plessey Woods Country Park

2–4 hrs   All year

This country park is set in 100 acres of woodland, meadow and riverside, with a good network of paths and bridleways linking the surrounding area.

* Children's play area
* Visitor centre with displays

Location
On A192; just off A1068 & close to A1

Opening
Parkland Daily: All reasonable times
Car park Daily: Dawn–dusk

Admission
Car park £1

Contact
nr Bedlington NE22 6AN
t 01670 824793
w northumberland.gov.uk
e plesseywoods@northumberland.gov.uk

785 Bellingham

Heritage Centre, Bellingham

2 hrs   Apr–Oct

This small folk museum situated in the old railway station yard houses photographs, artefacts and memorabilia recording the life and times of the people of the North Tyne Valley and Redewater Valley.

* The Border Counties Railway
* Special attractions for children

Location
Follow B6320 from Hexham to Bellingham (17 miles). Heritage Centre is in Woodburn Road, in Station Yard opposite Hillside Estate

Opening
Easter–Oct Thu–Mon 10.30am–4.30pm
Please phone for details

Admission
Adult £1, Child (5–16) & Concs 50p

Contact
Station Yard, Woodburn Road, Bellingham, Hexham NE48 2DF
t 01434 220050

786 Belsay

Bolam Lake Country Park

2–4 hrs   All year

Bolam Lake Country Park has everything for a fun family day out. There is a lake surrounded by beautiful woodland and meadows with paths and picnic areas. It is ideal for bird-watching.

* Lakeside walk made by local architect John Dobson

Location
Signed from A696 at Belsay & B6524 at Whalton

Opening
Park Daily: All reasonable times
Car park Daily: Dawn–dusk
Café Weekends, Bank Hols & school hols
Please phone for details

Admission
Free. Car park up to 1 hr £1, over 1 hr £2

Contact
nr Belsay NE20 0HE
t 01661 881234

787 Berwick-upon-Tweed

Berwick Barracks Museum & Art Gallery

All year

The barracks are home to a number of attractions, including 'By Beat of Drum', showing what life was like for British infantry soldiers until Queen Victoria's reign. The regimental museum tells the history of the King's Own Scottish Borderers.

* One of the first purpose-built barracks
* Walk on ramparts affords great views of River Tweed

Location	Contact
Off Church Street in town centre	The Parade, Berwick-upon-Tweed PD15 1DF
Opening	
Daily: Easter–Sep 10am–6pm (5pm in Oct); Nov–Mar Wed–Sun 10am–4pm	t 01289 304493
	w english-heritage.org.uk
Admission	
Adult £3.30, Child £1.70, Concs £2.50	

788 Berwick-upon-Tweed

Pot-a-Doodle-Do

2 hrs   Feb–Dec

An oasis of creativity for all – there is a wide range of art and craft activities to try, as well as a large children's play area, quad-bike trekking, fishing and country walks. Friendly staff are on hand to help make sure your day is the best it can be.

* Wooden wigwam village accommodation new for 2006
* Mosaicmaking – part of national curriculum in history

Location	Contact
On A1, S of Berwick-upon-Tweed	Borewell Farm, Scremerston, Berwick-upon-Tweed TD15 2RJ
Opening	
Daily: Easter–Oct 10am–5pm; 31 Oct–Easter Wed–Sun 10am–4pm; closed Jan	t 01289 307107
	w potadoodledo.com
	e info@potadoodledo.com
Admission	
Free. Pay-as-you-go activities	

789 Chillingham

Chillingham Castle

1 hr+   May–Sep

This medieval fortress has Tudor additions, a torture chamber and dungeon, and a woodland walk. It also glories in beautifully furnished rooms and an Italian topiary garden with herbaceous borders.

* Beautiful grounds with commanding views
* Formal gardens & woodland walks open to public

Location	Contact
Signed from A1 & A697	Chillingham NE66 5NJ
Opening	
May–Sep Sun–Fri 12noon–5pm; Oct–Apr by appointment	t 01668 215359
	w chillingham-castle.com
	e enquiries@chillingham-castle.com
Admission	
Adult £6, Child £3 (under-5s £1), Concs £5.50	

790 Cambo

Wallington Estate

2–4 hrs   All year

The impressive grounds surrounding the historic house of Wallington have plenty of walks, covering formal gardens, woodland and high moorland, plus an adventure playground.

* Redecorated & refurbished in 2004
* Fine collection of doll's houses

Location	Admission
12 miles W of Morpeth & 6 miles NW of Belsay	House & Grounds Adult £7.30, Child £3.65
	Grounds only Adult £5.20, Child £2.60
Opening	**Contact**
House 1 Apr–5 Sep Wed–Mon 1pm–5.30pm (4.30pm in Oct)	Cambo, Morpeth NE61 4AR
Grounds Daily: Apr–Oct 10am–7pm (6pm in Oct); Nov–Mar 10am–4pm	t 01670 773600
	w wallington@nationaltrust.org.uk

791   Falstone

Kielder Water Leaplish Waterside Park

6 hrs+   All year

Situated in the North Tyne Valley, this waterside park is surrounded by breathtaking scenery and has a 27-mile shoreline. There are facilities and activities to suit all ages.

* Luxury Scandinavian-style holiday lodges
* Adventure playground

Location
8 miles from Scottish border, 12 miles N of Bellingham at top of Kielder Reservoir; 45 mins N of Hexham

Opening
Daily: some facilities are seasonal
Please phone for details

Admission
Activities priced individually

Contact
Leaplish Waterside Park, Falstone, Hexham

t 0870 2403549
w nwl.co.uk/kielder
e kielder.holidays@nwl

792   Greenhead

Roman Army Museum

2 hrs   Feb–Nov

Ever wanted to be a Roman soldier? Here you can watch the recruiting film, fill in the join-up sheet and join the Roman army for a day. Learn about weapons, uniforms, pay, training and what soldiers did in their free time.

* Superb eagle's eye film & virtual tour of Hadrian's Wall
* Fascinating display of Roman military objects

Location
Off B6318, nr Greenhead, 3 miles from Haltwhistle. Follow heritage signs for Hadrian's Wall & Roman Museum

Opening
Daily: Feb–Mar 10am–5pm; Apr–Sep 10am–6pm; Oct–Nov 10am–5pm

Admission
Adult £3.50, Child £2.20, Concs £3

Contact
Greenhead CA6 7JB

t 016977 47485
w vindolanda.com
e info@vindolanda.com

793   Haltwhistle

South Tyne Trail

3 hrs+   All year

This former railway line is open to walkers of all ages, and for much of its length to cyclists and horse-riders. The trail has excellent views of the South Tyne Valley and it includes the spectacular Lambley Viaduct.

* Interpretation displays near Coanwood
* Self-guided trail

Location
Runs for 13 miles between Haltwhistle & Alston parallel to A689. Best access from Haltwhistle, Alston & car parks at Featherstone Park & Coanwood (for Lambley Viaduct)

Opening
Daily: All reasonable times

Admission
Free

Contact
The Railway Station, Station Road, Haltwhistle NE49 0AH

t 01434 322002

794 Hexham

Cherryburn

1 hr   Mar–Oct

This delightful cottage, with farmyard, garden and play lawn, was once home to the artist, engraver and naturalist Thomas Bewick. Visitors can enjoy an exhibition of his work and see demonstrations of wood engraving and handprinting from woodblocks.

* Occasional demonstration of printing
* Stunning views of valley of the River Tyne from garden

Location	Contact
Take A695 to Mickley Square & follow signs, 11 miles from Hexham	Station Bank, Mickley, nr Stocksfield NE43 7DD
Opening	t 01661 843276
18 Mar–29 Oct Thu–Tue 11am–5pm (last admission 4.30pm)	w nationaltrust.org.uk
	e cherryburn@nationaltrust.org.uk
Admission	
Adult £3.50, Child £1.75	

796 Hexham

Vindolanda

2½ hrs   Feb–Nov

A fascinating Roman fort and settlement lying just to the south of Hadrian's Wall. On the site itself stands a full-size replica of a section of Hadrian's Wall in both stone and timber, giving the visitor a true idea of the impressive might of the monument.

* Full-sized reconstructions of Roman temple and shop
* Rare & fascinating personal documents to read

Location	Contact
Take A69 & B6318 near village of Bardon Mill, then follow signs	Chesterholm Museum, Bardon Mill, Hexham, Northumberland NE47 7JN
Opening	t 01434 344277
Apr–Sep 10am–6pm; Feb–Mar & Oct–Nov 10am–5pm	w vindolanda.com
	e info@vindolanda.com
Admission	
Adult £4.95, Child £3, Concs £4.10	

795 Hexham

Housesteads Roman Fort, Hadrian's Wall

1 hr+   All year

Children will be fascinated to encounter life as it was on Rome's northernmost frontier at Housesteads – a jewel in the crown of Hadrian's Wall and the most complete Roman fort still standing in Britain. There is also an indoor museum to explore.

* The best-preserved of 16 forts along the Wall
* Dramatic countryside

Location	Contact
Take B6318, 2¾ miles NE of Bardon Mill	Hexham NE47 6NN
Opening	t 01434 344363
Daily: Apr–Sep 10am–6pm; Oct–Mar 10am–4pm	w nationaltrust.org.uk
	english-heritage.org.uk
Admission	e housesteads@english-heritage.org.uk
Adult £3.60, Child (5–16) £1.80, Concs £2.70	

797 Holy Island–Lindisfarne
Lindisfarne Castle

½ hr   Feb–Dec

Perched atop a rocky crag, accessible only across a causeway at low tide, the castle offers a real adventure. Originally a Tudor fort, it was converted into a private house in 1903 by the young Edwin Lutyens.

* Charming walled garden planned by Gertrude Jekyll
* Check crossing times before making a long journey

Location
Holy Island, 6 miles E of A1, across causeway

Opening
2 Feb–20 Feb daily; 12 Mar–30 Oct Tue–Sun;
Times vary depending upon tides, usually 10.30am–3pm or 12noon–4pm

Admission
Adult £5, Child £2.50

Contact
Holy Island,
Berwick-upon-Tweed TD15 2SH
t 01289 389244
w nationaltrust.org.uk

798 Holy Island–Lindisfarne
Lindisfarne Priory

1 hr+   All year

Lindisfarne was founded in the C7 by St Aidan, razed by the Vikings in 793, rebuilt in C12 and destroyed again in the C16, by Henry VIII who used the stones to build Lindisfarne Castle. The priory is reached by a causeway accessible only at low tide so check tide times.

* Anglo–Saxon carvings in museum
* Refurbished museum

Location
Holy Island, 6 miles E of A1, across causeway

Opening
Daily: Apr–Sep 10am–6pm; Mar &Oct 10am–4pm; Nov–Mar Sat–Mon 10am–2pm Times vary depending on tides

Admission
Adult £3.60, Child £1.80, Concs £2.70

Contact
Holy Island,
Berwick-upon-Tweed TD15 2RX
t 01289 389200
w english-heritage.org.uk

799 Low Prudhoe
Tyne Riverside Country Park

2–4 hrs   All year

This delightful country park includes a riverside walk that links through to Newcastle upon Tyne. It can also offer canoeing access to the river, and there are orienteering courses and several prime picnic locations.

* Off-road cycle route
* Children's play area

Location
On A695, just off A69

Opening
Daily: All reasonable times (car park dawn–dusk)

Admission
Free. Car park charge

Contact
Station Road,
Low Prudhoe NE42 6NP
t 01661 834135
w northumberland.gov.uk
e tyneriverside@northumberland.gov.uk

800 Morpeth
Belsay Hall, Castle & Gardens

3 hrs   All year

This wonderful estate has a C14 castle, C17 manor house and C19 neoclassical hall set in 30 acres of landscaped gardens and grounds, including quarry gardens with a microclimate where rhododendrons are found in bloom even in the middle of winter.

* 2 acres of rhododendrons at their best May–Jun
* Formal terraces & winter garden, original planting

Location
In Belsay, 14 miles NW of Newcastle upon Tyne on A696

Opening
Apr–Sep daily 10am–6pm;
Oct daily 10am–4pm;
Nov–Mar Thu–Mon 10am–4pm

Admission
Adult £5.30, Child £2.70, Concs £4

Contact
Belsay NE20 0DX
t 01661 881636
w english-heritage.org.uk

801 Morpeth

Carlisle Park

1–3 hrs   All year

Situated on the riverside in Morpeth, Carlisle Park's attractions include woodland and riverside walks, a castle, the William Turner Herb Garden, an aviary, tennis courts, bowling greens, a play area, an ancient woodland walk, a C12 castle and an C11 motte.

* Green Flag award & Quality Assured Visitor Attraction
* Tennis, paddling pool, picnic areas & beautiful gardens

Location	Admission
Follow signs to Morpeth town centre, then Carlisle Park is within walking distance of many car parks, as well as bus station & train station	Free
	Contact
	Castle Morpeth Borough Council, Kylins Centre, Morpeth NE61 2EQ
Opening	
Park Daily: All reasonable times	t 01670 500777
Turner Garden Daily: 7.30am–dusk	w castlemorpeth.gov.uk
Sporting Facilities Apr–Oct 10am–9pm	e firstcall@castlemorpeth.gov.uk

802 Morpeth

Cragside House, Gardens & Estate

3 hrs+   Apr–Dec

Described as the palace of a modern magician, Cragside was at the cutting edge of technology when built in the 1880s. It had hot and cold running water, central heating, telephones, a passenger lift and a Turkish bath suite and was lit by hydro-electricity.

* Used to impress important armaments customers
* 3-acre rock garden, fruit house & Italian garden

Location	Contact
1 mile N of Rothbury on B6341	Rothbury, Morpeth NE65 7PX
Opening	t 01669 620333
Estate Apr–Oct 10.30am–7pm	w nationaltrust.org.uk
1 Nov–17 Dec 11am–4pm	e cragside@nationaltrust.org.uk
Admission	
Adult £5.70, Child £2.60	

803 Morpeth

Cresswell Dunes

1 hr+   All year

This site is in the southern section of Druridge Bay, a 5-mile sandy beach with nationally important wildlife and beautiful dunes. Close by are the amenities of Cresswell village and the bird-watching hide at Cresswell Pond.

* Go rockpooling
* Expert guides available

Location	Admission
Follow signs to Cresswell from A1068 Ashington–Amble road, then take unnamed road leading N out of Cresswell	Free
	Contact
	Castle Morpeth Borough Council, Coopies Lane, Morpeth NE61 6JT
Opening	
Daily: All reasonable times	t 01670 535000
	e sam.talbot@castlemorpeth.gov.uk

804 Morpeth

Druridge Bay Country Park

2-4 hrs   All year

At Druridge Bay you can enjoy lakeside walks and 5 miles of beautiful beach. Visitors can also windsurf and use nonmotorised boats (by permit, available from the information centre or ticket machine).

* Different events throughout the year
* Annual kite festival

Location
Off A1068

Opening
Park Daily: All reasonable times (car park dawn-dusk)
Café Weekends, Bank Hols & local school hols
Please phone for details

Admission
Free . Car park up to 2 hrs £1, all day £2

Contact
Hadston, Morpeth NE61 5BQ

t 01670 760968
w northumberland.gov.uk

805 Morpeth

Scotch Gill Woods Local Nature Reserve

1-3 hrs   All year

Otters and dippers can be seen in the River Wansbeck, which runs along Scotch Gill Woods. Red squirrels are present here, as well as at the adjacent nature reserves of Bracken Bank and Davies Wood (accessible from the same car park).

* Always wear appropriate clothing & footwear

Location
Follow B6343 from Morpeth for ½ mile, turn right into car park at 1st bridge over river

Opening
Daily: All reasonable times

Admission
Free

Contact
Castle Morpeth Borough Council, Coopies Lane, Morpeth NE61 6JT

t 01670 535000
w castlemorpeth.gov.uk
e sam.talbot@castlemorpeth.gov.uk

806 Rochester

Brigantium

1 hr   Easter-Oct

This archaeological reconstruction centre has plenty to stimulate the young explorer. Wander round the Roman British farm, round house, willow maze, mesolithic hunting camp, Roman defences and road, and marvel at the Bronze Age burial and stone circle.

* Display & video room
* Dowsing courses

Location
On A68 from Jedburgh or Corbridge or A696 from Newcastle

Opening
Daily: Easter-Oct 10.30am-4.30pm
Special visits & guided tours can be booked in advance

Admission
Adult £2.50, Child & Concs £1.50

Contact
Rochester Café,
Rochester NE19 1RH

t 01830 520801

807 Seahouses

Farne Islands

2-3 hrs   Varies

Take the whole family on a boat trip to the Farne Islands. They house a bird reserve hosting around 70,000 pairs of breeding birds, from 21 species. Puffins can be seen in season, and the islands are also home to a large colony of grey seals throughout the year.

* Most famous seabird sanctuary in Britain
* Views of Bamburgh Castle

Location
Islands are 2-3 miles off N Northumberland coast. Take B1340, then a boat from Seahouses harbour

Opening
Please phone for details

Admission
May-Jul Adult £5, Child £2.50
All other times £4, £2

Contact
Seahouses

t 01665 721099
w nationaltrust.org.uk

808 Seahouses

Marine Life Centre & Haunted Kingdom

2–3 hrs   Feb–Oct

The museum and aquarium include a touch pool for crabs and other sea life and an exhibition with audio-visual conversations between fishing families. Visitors can also enjoy virtual-reality displays in our cinema.

* 50,000-litre trout pond
* Reconstructed fisherman's house

Location	Contact
Off B1340 on the coast	8–10 Main Street, Seahouses NE68 5RG
Opening	
Daily: 28 Feb–31 Oct 10.30am–5pm	t 01665 721257
	w marinelifecentre.co.uk
Admission	
Adult £2.50, Child & Concs £2	

809 Dunston

Whickham Thorns Outdoor Activity Centre

1 hr+   All year

This activity centre offers plenty of excitement, including an assault course, a climbing wall, cycle hire, a ski slope, archery and orienteering. There is also a snowboarding club.

* High-ropes aerial assault course new in 2005
* First boulder park in the North East

Location	Admission
Off A1 on opposite side of motorway from MetroCentre	Free. Please phone for activity prices
Opening	Contact
Daily: Mon–Fri 11am–10pm, Sat 11am–6.30pm, Sun 12noon–3pm; closed Bank Hols	Market Lane, Dunston, Gateshead NE11 9NX
Please phone for details	t 0191 433 5767
	w gateshead.gov.uk

810 Gateshead

BALTIC

1 hr+   All year

Housed in a 1950s grain warehouse, this contemporary art centre has five galleries, artists' studios, a cinema/ lecture space, a media lab, a library, an archive for the study of contemporary art and a retail outlet.

* Constantly changing programme of exhibitions
* Displays of work by artists in residence

Location
Gateshead Quayside, 10 min walk from town centre

Opening
Times vary, please phone for details or visit the website

Admission
Free

Contact
South Shore Road,
Gateshead NE8 3BA

t 0191 478 1810
w balticmill.com
e info@balticmill.com

811 Gateshead

Bill Quay Farm

2 hrs   All year

Bring your children to this lovely urban farm to enjoy spectacular views of the River Tyne and to meet farmyard breeds, both traditional and unusual. The farm includes a green retreat for wildlife.

* Family picnic area

Location
Take A185 from Heworth interchange, turn left down Station Road (1¼ miles from Heworth) & take 1st left at crossroads

Opening
Daily: 12noon–5pm
Some buildings have restricted access, please phone for details

Admission
Free

Contact
Hainingwood Terrace,
Bill Quay,
Gateshead NE10 0UE

t 0191 433 5780

812 Gateshead

The New Metroland

3 hrs+   All year

Among the many children's attractions here are a
rollercoaster, a pirate ship, swinging chairs, dodgem
cars, a children's railway, a ferris wheel, aeroplanes,
helicopters, slides and climbing nets.

* Europe's largest indoor fun-fair
* Mr B's Amusement Arcade

Location	Admission
Take A1(M) to Gateshead MetroCentre	Please phone for details
Opening	**Contact**
Term time Mon–Fri from	39 Garden Walk, MetroCentre,
12noon; in school hols Mon–Sat	Gateshead NE11 9XY
10am–8pm, Sun 11am–6pm	t 0191 493 2048
	w metroland.uk.com

813 Gateshead

Saltwell Park

1-3 hrs   All year

At Saltwell Park you can enjoy bedding displays,
a rose garden, a wooded den, a children's play
area and a boating lake. There are brass bands
at the bandstand and bowls during the summer.

* Original and genuine Victorian public garden
* Saltwell Tower – a Gothic mansion

Location	Contact
Off A184 or A692 S of Newcastle upon	East Park Road,
Tyne	Gateshead NE8 5AX
Opening	t 0191 433 5900
Daily: 7.30am–dusk	w gateshead.gov.uk/saltwellpark
Admission	e saltwellpark@gateshead.gov.uk
Free	

814 Gateshead

Shipley Art Gallery

2 hrs   All year

Shipley Art Gallery is home to a collection of more than
700 pieces by the country's leading craftmakers. It
includes studio ceramics, glass, metalwork, jewellery,
textiles and furniture. The exhibition Made in Gateshead
tells the fascinating history of the town.

* Art Kart with materials, puzzles, jigsaws and activities
  sheets for all ages

Location	Admission
Off A167. Nearest Metro station is	Free
Gateshead. Limited free street park-	**Contact**
ing outside gallery	Prince Consort Road,
Opening	Gateshead NE8 4JB
Daily: Mon–Sat 10am–5pm, Sun	t 0191 477 1495
2pm–5pm;	w twmuseums.org.uk/shipley
closed Good Fri, 25, 26 Dec & 1 Jan	

815 Jarrow

Bede's World & St Paul's Church

3 hrs   All year

Discover what life was like for St Bede, who established a monastery and church here in the C7. During the summer enjoy a range of children's activities, including tours of an Anglo-Saxon demonstration farm, story telling, tilemaking, archery and breadmaking.

* Herb garden based on Anglo-Saxon & medieval plants
* Anglo-Saxon demo farm, complete with animals

Location	Admission
Near S end of Tyne Tunnel, off A185	Adult £4.50, Child & Concs £3
Opening	**Contact**
Apr–Oct Mon–Sat 10am–5.30pm, Sun 12noon–5.30pm (4.30pm in Nov–Mar) Church closed during services	Church Bank NE32 3DY
	t 0191 489 2106
	w bedesworld.co.uk
	e visitorinfo@bedesworld.co.uk

816 Newcastle upon Tyne

Discovery Museum

3 hrs   All year

Explore Newcastle's past, from Roman times to the present day. See Tyneside inventions that changed the world and take a walk through changing fashions. The Discovery Museum offers a fun approach to science and a great day out for all the family.

* See Roman, Norman & medieval Newcastle upon Tyne
* Find out about life along the River Tyne

Location	Contact
Short walk from Newcastle Central station	Blandford Square, Newcastle upon Tyne NE1 4JA
Opening	t 0191 232 6789
Daily: Mon–Sat 10am–5pm, Sun 2pm–5pm	w twmuseums.org.uk/discovery
	e discovery@twmuseums.org.uk
Admission	
Free	

817 Newcastle upon Tyne

Life Science Centre

3 hrs+   All year

There's always something new at the Life Science Centre. Meet your 4-billion-year-old family, explore what makes us all different, test your brainpower and enjoy the thrill of the Crazy Motion ride.

* Mars Quest space exhibition
* Open-air ice rink in Times Square during Christmas period

Location	Admission
From S take A19, A184, A69 or A1 into Newcastle upon Tyne. From N take A69 into Newcastle upon Tyne. 1 min from Central station	Adult £6.95, Child £4.50, Concs £5.50
	Contact
	Times Square, Newcastle upon Tyne NE1 4EP
Opening	t 0191 243 8210
Daily: Mon–Sat 10am–6pm, Sun 11am–6pm (last admission 4pm)	w lifesciencecentre.org.uk
	e info@life.org.uk

818 North Shields

Stephenson Railway Museum

1 hr   May–Sep

Relive the glorious days of the steam railway at the Stephenson Railway Museum. Take a ride on a steam train and discover the impact of coal and electricity on the lives of ordinary people. There are activities and events to suit all ages.

* Many activities throughtout the year
* Please phone for details of days & times of steam train rides

Location	Contact
Well signed from junction of A19/A1058	Middle Engine Lane, North Shields NE29 8DX
Opening	t 01912 007146
May–Sep Tue–Thu 11am–3pm	w twmuseums.org.uk/stephenson
Sat, Sun & Bank Hols 11am–4pm	e stephenson@twmuseums.org.uk
Admission	
Free	

819 Rowlands Gill

Gibside

3 hrs   All year

Gibside is one of the North's finest landscapes, embracing many miles of riverside and forest walks. The park is very child-friendly with woods to explore, streams to paddle in and wildlife to look out for, including deer, kingfishers, herons and even badgers.

* Former home of Queen Mother's family
* Newly restored green house & stables

Location	Admission
6 miles SW of Gateshead on B6314	Adult £3.50, Child £2
Opening	Contact
Grounds Mar–Oct Tue–Sun & Bank Hols 10am–6pm; Nov–Feb 10am–4pm	nr Rowlands Gill, Burnopfield NE16 6BG
Chapel Apr–Oct Tue–Sun 11am–4.30pm	t 01207 541820
	w nationaltrust.org.uk
	e gibside@nationaltrust.org.uk

820 South Shields

Arbeia Roman Fort

2 hrs   All year

Arbeia was an essential part of a mighty frontier system. Built in approximately AD160, it guarded the entrance to the River Tyne. See excavated remains, plus stunning reconstructions of original buildings and displays of finds discovered at the site.

* 3 reconstructed buildings on their original sites
* Time Quest archaeological dig

Location
10 min walk from South Shields Metro & bus station, signed from Ocean Road

Opening
Easter–Sep Mon–Sat 10am–5.30pm, Sun 1pm–5pm; Oct–Easter Mon–Sat 10am–3.30pm

Admission
Free

Contact
Baring Street,
South Shields NE33 2BB

t 0191 456 1369
w twmuseums.org.uk

821 South Shields

Pier Amusements Centre

2 hrs   All year

At the Pier Amusements Centre you can play Quasar, a futuristic game in which each player is armed with a laser gun and shoots the opposition to win points.

Location
On pier front at South Shields.
Reached via A183, A1018 or A185

Opening
Daily: 10am–10pm

Admission
Please phone for details

Contact
Pier Parade, South Shields NE33 2JS

t 0191 455 3885

822 Sunderland

National Glass Centre

2 hrs   All year

Discover how glass has been used since it was invented in 5,000BC. See it magnify a bee's knee and a fly's tongue 100 times, listen to a glass orchestra, have fun with crazy mirrors, and hear how glass is used to protect astronauts when they re-enter the earth's atmosphere.

* Home of International Institute for research in glass

Location
Signed from all major roads

Opening
Daily: 10am–5pm

Admission
Adult £5, Child & Concs £3

Contact
Liberty Way,
Sunderland SR6 0GL

t 0191 515 5555
w nationalglasscentre.com
e info@nationalglasscentre.com

823 Sunderland

Souter Lighthouse

1 hr+   Feb–Nov

Built in 1871, Souter boasted the most advanced lighthouse technology of its day. The lighthouse is full of interest for children. They can see the engine and rooms, the Victorian keeper's cottage and the light tower itself.

* When operational, light could be seen from 26 miles
* See the engine room & cramped living quarters

Location	Contact
2½ miles S of South Shields on A183	Coast Road, Whitburn, Sunderland SR6 7NH
Opening	
Daily: Feb–local half-term 11am–5pm;	t 0191 529 3161
Easter–6 Nov Sat–Thu 11am–5pm	w nationaltrust.org.uk
(last admission 4.30pm)	e souter@nationaltrust.org.uk
Admission	
Adult £3.80, Child £2.20	

824 Sunderland

Sunderland Museum & Winter Gardens

4 hrs   All year

This museum tells the story of Sunderland. It includes paintings by L S Lowry and exciting hands-on exhibits and interactive displays. The stunning Winter Gardens will stimulate the senses with more than 1,500 flowers and plants – a showcase of the world's natural beauty.

* Good facilities for disabled visitors
* Many educational exhibits

Location	Contact
In city centre on Burdon Road	Burdon Road, Sunderland SR1 1PP
Opening	
Daily: Mon–Sat 10am–5pm,	t 0191 553 2323
Sun 2pm–5pm	w twmuseums.org.uk/sunderland
	e sunderland@twmuseums.org.uk
Admission	
Free	

825 Sunniside

Tanfield Railway

2 hrs+   All year

Tanfield is a 3-mile steam railway and the oldest existing railway in the world. Travel into the scenic Causey Woods where the 1727 Causey Arch bridge is the centrepiece in a deep valley with walks and display boards giving the C18 railway history of the area.

* Large collection of locally built locomotives
* Oldest working engine shed in Britain

Location	Contact
On A6076 Stanley–Gatehead road	Old Marley Hill, Sunniside, Gateshead NE16 5ET
Opening	
Daily: Viewing only	t 0191 388 7545
Please phone or visit the website	w tanfield-railway.co.uk
for details	e tanfield@ingsoc.demon.co.uk
Admission	
Train ride Adult £5, Child (5–14) £2.50,	
Concs £3.50	

826 Tynemouth

Blue Reef Aquarium

1 hr+   All year

The ultimate undersea safari, Blue Reef brings the magic of the undersea world alive. Explore the drama of the North Sea and the dazzling beauty of a spectacular coral reef. This giant tropical ocean tank has its own underwater tunnel and more than 30 living displays.

* Quality Assured Visitor Attraction
* See Asian short-clawed otters

Location
From A19, take A1058 to town centre & follow brown tourist signs

Opening
Daily: Mar–Oct 10am–5pm; Nov–Feb 10am–4pm

Admission
Adult £5.50, Child £3.75, Concs £4.95

Contact
Grand Parade, Tynemouth NE30 4JF
t 0191 258 1031
w bluereefaquarium.co.uk
e tynemouth@bluereefaquarium.co.uk

827 Tynemouth

Tynemouth Priory & Castle

1 hr   All year

A burial place of saints and kings, this commanding castle has provided defence against the Vikings, medieval Scotland, Napoleon and C20 Germany. The Benedictine priory was founded in 1090 on the site of an ancient Anglian monastery.

* Restored magazines of a coastal defence gun battery on view at weekends

Location
In Tynemouth, near North Pier

Opening
Daily: Apr–Sep 10am–6pm;
Oct 10am–4pm; Nov–Mar Thu–Mon 10am–4pm

Admission
Adult £3.30, Child £1.70, Concs £2.50

Contact
Tynemouth
t 0191 257 1090
w english-heritage.org.uk

828 Wallsend

Segedunum Roman Fort, Baths & Museum

2 hrs+   All year

The last outpost of Hadrian's Wall, Segedunum has stood on the banks of the River Tyne since AD122. It was built to protect the coast from barbarians in the North, and was once home to 600 Roman soldiers. There are hands-on displays of life in Roman Britain.

* The most extensively excavated site in Britain
* 100ft high viewing tower plus audio guide

Location
1 min walk from Wallsend Metro & bus station

Opening
Apr–Aug 9.30am–5.30pm;
Sep–Oct 10am–5pm;
Nov–Mar 10am–3.30pm

Admission
Adult £3.50, Child & Concs £1.95

Contact
Buddle Street, Wallsend NE28 6HR
t 0191 236 9347
w twmuseums.org.uk

829 Washington

Wildfowl & Wetlands Trust Washington

3 hrs **All year**

The trust is home to more than 500 ducks, geese, swans and flamingos. Many birds will take food from your hand. The annual highlight is the downy duckling days (May to July) when visitors can see young birds take their first wobbly steps in the nursery.

* Nuthatch sighted in 2003 for first time in 10 years
* See waders, kingfishers, snipe, shovelers & flamingos

Location
E of Washington, 4 miles from A1(M)

Opening
Daily: *summer* 9.30am–5.30pm; *winter* 9.30am–4pm

Admission
Adult £5.95, Child £3.75, Concs £4.75

Contact
Pattinson,
Washington NE38 8LE
t 0191 416 5454
w wwt.org.uk
e info.washington@wwt.org.uk

830 Whitley Bay

Whitley Bay Ice Rink

½ day **All year**

Whitley Bay Ice Rink offers something for everyone. Come and enjoy a morning of tenpin bowling. The ice rink is also a concert venue. Family skate and disco sessions are available as well.

* Fantastic fun on the ice
* Snacks & drinks available

Location
From S take A1 through Tyne Tunnel, then A1058. From Newcastle upon Tyne take A1058

Opening
Daily: Please phone for details

Admission
Adult £4, Child £3.50 (£1.50 skate hire)

Contact
Hillheads Road,
Whitley Bay NE25 8HP
t 0191 291 1000
e icerink@ukonline.co.uk

Crail, Fife

Scotland

Central Scotland Grampian
Highlands & Islands Southern Scotland

831 Aberfeldy

Aberfeldy Watermill

1 hr   All year

The mill built in 1825 and renovated in the early 1980s, has had further renovations to open it in this present form. The original machinery has been retained and the huge 5m waterwheel can usually be seen in operation generating electricity to power its lighting.

* Book shop and gallery
* Literary events throughout the year

Location
Aberfeldy is on A827 between Loch Tay–Pitlochry

Opening
Daily: Mon–Sat 9.30am–5.30pm, Sun 12noon–5pm

Admission
Free

Contact
Mill Street, Aberfeldy PH15 2BG

t 01887 822896
w aberfeldymill.com
e info@aberfeldymill.com

832 Aberfeldy

Highland Adventure Safaris

2 hrs   All year

An exciting way to experience the exhilaration and freedom of this beautiful part of the Highlands. Visitors can bring the great outdoors a little closer by trying out Land Rovers on Ecotours, wildlife-watching trips or an exciting off-road driving experience.

* Families, groups or individuals catered for
* Skills courses available

Location
From A827 at Aberfeldy, follow B846 for 2 miles past Castle Menzies until you see the signs

Opening
Daily: 9am–5pm
Please phone for details

Admission
Prices vary, please phone for details

Contact
Drumdewan, Aberfeldy, Perthshire PH15 2JQ

t 01887 820071
w highlandadventuresafaris.co.uk
e info@highlandadventuresafaris.co.uk

833 Aberfoyle

Forest Hills Watersports

½–1 day   All year

The centre offers a range of 'wet' and 'dry' activities that can be combined or enjoyed individually. Watersports of all descriptions are available in addition to quad biking, mountain biking and 4×4 drives.

* Equipment available for hire
* Courses taught by qualified instructors

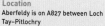

Location
Off junction 10 of M9 & junction 16 of M8. Follow signs for Aberfoyle, then to Forest Hills Watersports, 4 miles along B829

Opening
Daily: *summer* 9.30am–7pm
winter 10.30am–5pm

Admission
Activities priced individually

Contact
Kinlochard, Aberfoyle, Stirlingshire FK8 3TL

t 01877 387775
w goforth.co.uk
e info@goforth.co.uk

834 Angus

Barrie's Birthplace

½ hr   Apr–Sep

J M Barrie, the creator of Peter Pan, was born here in 1860, one of a handloom weaver's ten children. See the imaginative exhibition and discover how the outside wash house served as Barrie's first theatre.

* Audio programme
* Near Kirriemuir Camera Obscura

Location
Take A901/A926 in Kirriemuir, 6 miles NW of Forfar

Opening
Jul–Aug daily 11am–5pm;
Sun all year 1pm–5pm;
Apr–Jun & Sep Sat–Wed 12noon–5pm

Admission
Adult £5, Child £4, Concs £4

Contact
9 Brechin Road, Kirriemuir, Angus DD8 4BX

t 01575 572646
w nts.org.uk/barrie.html
e barriesbirthplace@nts.org.uk

835 Brechin

Brechin Castle Centre

2 hrs+   All year

Brechin Castle is a country park with a working model farm covering 65 acres and a children's activity area with a new adventure castle. Take a ride on the miniature railway or enjoy a stroll along the nature trail.

* Scottish Tourist Board 4-Star Visitor Attraction
* Santa at Christmas

Location
Between Aberdeen & Dundee, off A90; on A935 to Brechin turn off, well signed from there

Opening
Daily: Mon-Sat 9am-6pm, Sun 10am-6pm

Admission
Adult £2, Child £1

Contact
Haughmui, by Brechin, Angus DD9 6RL

t 01356 626813
w brechincastlecentre.co.uk
e enquiries@brechincastlecentre.co.uk

836 Comrie

Auchingarrich Wildlife Centre

2 hrs+   All year

Set in 100 acres of Perthshire countryside, the centre has animals and birds from all over the world. Attractions include falconry displays, indoor and outdoor play areas, animal and chick handling, a unique bird hatchery and the Highland Castle Centre.

* More than 150 species of animals & birds
* Hatchings every day Easter-October

Location
On B827, 2 miles N of Comrie

Opening
Daily: 10am-5pm

Admission
Adult £5.50, Child & Concs £4

Contact
Glascorrie Road, Crieff, Perthshire PH6 2JS

t 01764 679469
e auchingarrich@wilton.sol.co.uk

837 Crieff

The Famous Grouse Experience at Glenturret Distillery

1 hr+   All year

The stunning audio-visual tour takes you on an airborne journey with The Famous Grouse. Visitors swoop over numerous famous Scottish landmarks – from Loch Ness to Edinburgh Castle. Afterwards stroll along a nature trail or enjoy a picnic in the grounds.

* Audio-visual presentation
* Award-winning famous restaurant

Location
Off A85, 1 mile from Crieff

Opening
Daily: 10am-6pm (last tours at 4.30pm)

Admission
Tours Adult £3.95-£6.95 depending on tour, Child £2.50

Contact
Glenturret Distillery, The Hosh, Crieff, Perthshire PH7 4HA

t 01764 656565
w famousgrouse.com
e enquiries@famousgrouse.com

838 Dundee

Discovery Point

1 hr+   All year

Discovery Point is home to Captain Scott's ship, *Discovery*, which was built in Dundee for his expedition to the Antarctic, and the Verdant Works, winner of the European Industrial Museum of the Year Award. It has original working machinery, and computer and hands-on displays.

* State-of-the-art multimedia exhibitions
* Scottish Family Attraction of the Year 2004

Location
In city centre, opposite train station

Opening
Daily: Apr–Oct Mon–Sat 10am–6pm,
Sun 11am–6pm;
Nov–Mar Mon–Sat 10am–5pm,
Sun 11am–5pm

Admission
Adult £6.45, Child £3.85, Concs £4.90

Contact
Discovery Quay, Dundee DD1 4XA

t 01382 201245
w rrsdiscovery.com
e info@dundeeheritage.co.uk

839 Dundee

Sensation: Dundee

2 hrs+   All year

If you thought science was boring, this centre may help you rethink. The hands-on experiments, live workshops and investigations bring science to life. Discover how we use our five senses to interact with the world around us in 12 specially designed exhibits.

* Scottish Family Attraction of the Year 2003
* New 1.4million Roborealm

Location
In city centre, 5 min walk from
Dundee station. Follow brown tourist
signs

Opening
Daily: 10am–6pm (5pm in winter)

Admission
Adult £6.50, Child & Concs £4.50

Contact
Greenmarket, Dundee DD1 4QB

t 01382 228800
w sensation.org.uk
e staff@sensation.org.uk

840 Dunfermline

Dunfermline Abbey & Palace

1 hr   All year

The elegant ruins of Dunfermline Abbey are what is left of a great Benedictine abbey founded by Queen Margaret in the C11. Robert the Bruce was buried in the choir and the royal palace next door, also partially ruined, was the birthplace of Charles I.

* Substantial parts of the abbey nave remain
* Next to the ruin of the royal palace

Location
Off M90, in town centre

Opening
Apr–Sep daily 9.30am–6.30pm;
Oct–Mar Mon–Wed & Sat
9.30am–4.30pm, Sun 2pm–4.30pm

Admission
Adult £2.50, Child £1, Concs £1.90

Contact
St Margaret Street, Dunfermline,
Fife KY12 7PE

t 01383 739026
w historic-scotland.gov.uk

841 Dunfermline

Knockhill Racing Circuit

3 hrs   All year

Get behind the wheel of a Formula First single-seater racing car or rally car, go off-road in a 4×4 or be driven round the racing circuit by a professional. Alternatively, sit back and enjoy the races. Choose from British touring cars, superbikes, stock cars and Formula Woman.

* Hands-on driving experiences
* Relaxing hospitality at race events

Location
Signed from M90 junction 4

Opening
Daily: 9am–6pm

Admission
Prices vary depending on event, please phone for details

Contact
Dunfermline, Fife KY12 9TF

t 01383 723337
w knockhill.co.uk
e enquiries@knockhill.co.uk

842 East Lothian

Museum of Flight

2 hrs+   All year

Man's fascination with flight is celebrated at this protected WWI and WWII airfield. See the R34 airship which took off from East Fortune on a record-breaking transatlantic flight in 1919.

* See a Britten-Norman Islander, an aircraft described as the most versatile in the world

Location
Off A1, 20m E of Edinburgh

Opening
16 Mar–Oct daily 10am–5pm;
Nov–Mar Sat–Sun 10am–4pm

Admission
Adult £5, Child free, Concs £4

Contact
East Fortune Airfield,
East Lothian EH39 5LF

t 01620 880308
w nms.ac.uk/flight/

843 Edinburgh

Almond Valley Heritage Centre

3 hrs   All year

This is an innovative museum exploring the history and environment of West Lothian with award-winning children's activities and interactive displays. The centuries-old farm buildings are home to a variety of friendly animals that the children can see and pet.

* Demonstrations & seasonal activities
* Gift shop

Location
Signed from M8 junction 3,
2 miles from motorway

Opening
Daily: 10am–5pm

Admission
Adult £3, Child £2

Contact
Millfield, Livingston
West Lothian EH54 7AR

t 01506 414957
w almondvalley.co.uk
e info@almondvalley.co.uk

844 Edinburgh

Bedlam Paintball, Edinburgh

3 hrs+   All year

Get the ultimate adrenaline rush at Bedlam Paintball. Be prepared to utilise tactics, teamwork and quick thinking as you experience all the multiple game scenarios available here.

* Other venues at Glasgow & Edzell
* For children aged 12 yrs+

Location
If travelling from Edinburgh, Fife, Falkirk, Stirling, Livingston & surrounding areas, Bedlam is off A8000

Opening
Daily: from 10am

Admission
From £20 per person, please phone for details

Contact
Milton Wood, Dundas Estate,
South Queensferry, Edinburgh

t 07000 233526
w bedlam.co.uk
e info@bedlam.co.uk

845 Edinburgh

The Cadies & Witchery Tours

1–2 hrs   All year

Witchery Tours take a light-hearted look at tales of witchcraft, plague and torture. Explore the eerie alleyways and creepy courtyards of the Old Town with your ghostly guide, who will blend history with humour and fact with fable.

* 'Jump-ooters' make ghastly appearances
* Re-enactments & live performances

Location
In city centre, off the Royal Mile

Opening
Daily: tours operate 7pm–10pm, please phone to check times & availability

Admission
Adult £7.50, Child (over 5) £5, Child (under 5) free

Contact
84 West Bow (Victoria Street), Edinburgh EH1 2HH

t 0131 225 6745
w witcherytours.com
e lyal@witcherytours.demon.co.uk

846 Edinburgh

Edinburgh Butterfly & Insect World

3 hrs+   All year

Walk through an indoor tropical rainforest inhabited by thousands of the world's most beautiful butterflies. Also Don't forget to visit the unique Scottish honey-bee zone.

* Bugs & Beasties section
* Meet the Beasties handling sessions

Location
3 miles S of city centre on A702. Just off the bypass, A720 at Gilmerton exit

Opening
Daily: summer 9.30am–5.30pm; winter 10am–5pm

Admission
Adults £5, Child & Concs £3.85

Contact
Dobbies Garden World, Lasswade, Edinburgh EH18 1AZ

t 0131 663 4932
e edinburgh-butterfly-world.co.uk
e info@edinburgh-butterfly-world.co.uk

847 Edinburgh

Edinburgh Crystal Visitor Centre

2 hrs   All year

Edinburgh Crystal Visitor Centre displays the entire Edinburgh Crystal range as well as unique pieces created by our cutters and engravers. See the craftsmen at work engraving and cutting glass, and watch all the processes involved in glass making on TV.

* VIP hands-on Tour

Location
30 mins S of city centre. From the city bypass, take A701 S for 4 miles, following signs for Penicuik

Opening
Mon–Sat 10am–5pm

Admission
Free

Contact
Penicuik, Midlothian EH26 8HB

t 01968 675128
w edinburgh-crystal.com
e visitorcentre@edinburgh-crystal.co.uk

848 Edinburgh

Edinburgh Castle

1 hr+   All year

A majestic landmark that dominates the city's skyline, Edinburgh Castle is the most visited of Scotland's historic buildings. Perched on an extinct volcano and offering stunning views, this fortress is a powerful national symbol, and part of Edinburgh's World Heritage Site.

* Guided & audio tours
* The Scottish Crown Jewels & the Stone of Destiny

Location
In city centre, at top of Royal Mile

Opening
Daily: Apr–Sep 9am–6pm; Oct–Mar 9am–5pm

Admission
Adult £9.80, Child £3.50, Concs £7.50

Contact
Castle Hill, Edinburgh EH1 2NG

t 0131 225 9846
w historic-scotland.gov.uk

867 Fife

Scottish Fisheries Museum

1 hr+   All year

The Scottish Fisheries Museum tells the story of Scottish fishing and its people from the earliest times to the present. There are many fine paintings and photographs on display as well as a variety of real and model boats, fishing gear and other accoutrements.

* Overlooks a beautiful harbour
* Regular calendar of events and exhibitions

Location	Admission
Leave M90 at junction 3, then follow A92 to Anstruther	Adult £4.50, Child free, Concs £3.50
Opening	**Contact**
Daily: Apr–Sep Mon–Sat 10am–5.30pm, Sun 11am–5pm; Oct–Mar Mon–Sat 10am–4.30pm, Sun 12noon–4.30pm	St Ayles, Harbourhead, Anstruther, Fife KY10 3AB t 01333 310628 w scotfishmuseum.org e info@scotfishmuseum.org

868 Fife

Scottish Vintage Bus Museum

2 hrs   Apr–Oct

Possibly Britain's largest collection of historic buses dating from the 1920s to the 1980s. There are beautifully restored buses to see in the main exhibition hall, as well as buses under restoration in the large workshops.

* Regular bus rallies
* Fire engines

Location	Contact
On B915, near Dunfermline. Follow signs to museum from M90 junction 4.	Commerce Park, Lathalmond, nr Dunfermline, Fife KY12 0SJ
Opening	t 01383 623380
Easter–early Oct Sun only 12.30pm–5pm	w busweb.co.uk/svbm
Admission	
Adult £3, Concs £1.50	

869 Fife

St Andrews Aquarium

1 hr+   Apr–Oct

Enjoy a sense of discovery and enjoyment at St Andrews Aquarium, which welcomes you to the wonderful world of the sea and its inhabitants – from shrimps to sharks, octopuses to eels, rays to seals.

* More than 30 exhibition tanks
* Touch some of the fish

Location	Contact
At Bruce Embankment near Royal & Ancient Golf Club	The Scores, St Andrews, Fife KY16 9AS
Opening	t 01334 474786
Daily: Easter–end Oct Mon–Fri 10am–5pm Sat–Sun 10am–6pm	w standrewsaquarium.co.uk e info@standrewsaquarium.co.uk
Admission	
Adult £5.95, Child £3.95, Concs £4.95	

870 Glamis by Forfar

Glamis Castle

2 hrs+   Mar–Dec

This is a place of legends and fairy tales. It has been a royal residence since 1372 and was the childhood home of HM Queen Elizabeth The Queen Mother, birthplace of HRH The Princess Margaret and legendary setting for Shakespeare's famous play *Macbeth*.

* Rich variety of furnishings, tapestries & art
* Extensive estate & formal gardens

Location	Contact
On A94, between Aberdeen & Perth	The Castle Administrator, Estates Office, Glamis by Forfar, Angus DD8 1RJ
Opening	t 01307 840393
Daily: Mar–Oct 10am–6pm; Nov–23 Dec 11am–3pm	w glamis-castle.co.uk e enquiries@glamis-castle.co.uk
Admission	
Adult £7, Child £3.80, Concs £5.70	

871 Glasgow

Calderglen Country Park

2 hrs   All year

This is a large country park with a myriad of activities. The visitor centre has a good range of displays and a Hidden Worlds wildlife experience. There is also a children's zoo, conservatory, adventure playground and miles of fascinating trails to follow.

* Scottish Tourist Board 4-star award

Location
In Calderglen Country Park in East Kilbride on Strathaven Road, just out of town

Opening
Park: Daily: All reasonable times
Visitor centre: Daily: summer 10.30am–5pm; winter 11.30am–4pm

Admission
Free

Contact
East Kilbride G75 0QZ

t 01355 236644
w southlanarkshire.gov.uk

872 Glasgow

Clydebuilt Scottish Maritime Museum

2 hrs   All year

Clydebuilt charts the development of Glasgow and the River Clyde from 1700 to the present day. It tells the story of Glasgow's rivers, its ships and its people, through award-winning audio-visuals, computer interpretation, hands-on displays and video.

* 5-star museum attraction
* Take control of a real steam engine

Location
At junctions 25 & 26 on Glasgow's M8

Opening
Mon–Sat 10am–5.30pm,
Sun 11am–5.30pm

Admission
Adult £4.25, Child £2.50, Concs £3

Contact
Braehead Shopping Centre,
Kings Inch Road,
Glasgow G51 4BN

t 0141 886 1013
w scottishmaritimemuseum.org
e clydebuilt@tinyworld.co.uk

873 Glasgow

Falls of Clyde Visitor Centre & Wildlife Reserve

2 hrs+   All year

The Falls of Clyde Wildlife Reserve includes ancient gorge woodland along both sides of the River Clyde, with its famous and spectacular waterfalls. The visitor centre has an exhibition and offers a programme of educational events and guided walks in the reserve.

* Watch nesting peregrine falcolns (Mar–Jun)
* Badger watching

Location
Visitor centre is in New Lanark, which is signed from all major routes and lies 1 mile S of Lanark

Opening
Reserve: Daily: summer 8am–8pm; winter during daylight hours

Admission
Reserve Free

Visitor centre Adult £3, Child free, Concs £2

Contact
Falls of Clyde Reserve, New Lanark, Lanarkshire ML11 9DB

t 01555 665262
w swt.org.uk
e fallsofclyde@swt.org.uk

©G Burns

874 Glasgow

Glasgow Police Museum

1 hr+   All year

Visit the museum of Britain's first police force to gain historical insight into the people and the events that contributed to the founding, development and progress of the force. See how this pioneering force helped shape law enforcement throughout the world.

* International police exhibition
* Over 5,000 exhibits

Location
From London Road, via James Morrison Street, or Saltmarket via St Andrew's Street, or Greendyke Street via Turnball Street

Opening
Daily: Apr–Oct 10am–4.30pm (12noon opening on Sun); Nov–end Mar Tue 10am–4.30pm, Sun 12noon–4.30pm

Admission
Free

Contact
68 St. Andrew's Square, Glasgow G1 5MR

t 0141 552 1818
w policemuseum.org.uk
e curator@policemuseum.org.uk

875 Glasgow

Glasgow Science Centre

2 hrs+   All year

The Glasgow Science Centre has hundreds of hands-on exhibits over three floors, where visitors can interact with real experiments and phenomena. The centre also includes a planetarium that offers the chance to see the thousands of stars that fill our night sky.

* Imax cinema
* Several new exhibitions for 2006

Location
Opposite the Scottish Exhibition Centre & Moat House Hotel on River Clyde

Opening
Daily: 10am–6pm

Admission
Adult £6.95 Child & Concs £4.95

Contact
50 Pacific Quay, Glasgow G51 1EA

t 0141 420 5000
w glasgowsciencecentre.org
e admin@gsc.org.uk

876 Glasgow

Glasgow Ski & Snowboarding Centre

1 hr+   All year

An artificial ski and snowboarding centre with three slopes that caters for children of all levels and offers lessons in group or private sessions. Floodlit slopes allow visitors to enjoy the facilities well into the evening.

* Race training & freeride clubs
* Kids' toboggan (5 yrs+) & tubing (10yrs+) parties

Location
In Bellahouston Park off Junction 23 of M8

Opening
Daily: summer Mon–Fri 9.30am–9pm, Sat–Sun 9.30am–6pm; winter Mon–Thur 9.30am–11pm, Fri–Sun 9.30am–9pm

Admission
Activities individually priced Please phone for details

Contact
16 Dumbreck Road, Glasgow G41 5BW

t 0141 4274991
w ski-glasgow.co.uk
e info@ski-glasgow.co.uk

877 Glasgow

Lamont City Farm

2 hrs   All year

Come and meet all sorts of animals, including sheep, goats, horses, ponies, pigs, rabbits, chinchillas, chipmunks, guinea pigs, hens, ducks, geese and Highland cows.

* Under-5s play area
* Snack bar

Location
On M8 travel to St James roundabout & take Erskine cut-off. At 3rd round-about turn left then 1st right into Barhill Road

Opening
Daily: 10.30am–4.30pm (3.30pm in winter)

Admission
Families free, (donations welcomed) Groups please phone for details

Contact
Barhill Road, Erskine, Renfrewshire PA8 6BX

t 0141 812 5335
w farmgarden.org.uk

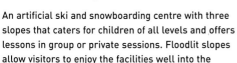

878 Glasgow

Motoring Heritage Centre

1 hr   All year

The centre's display tells the story of Scotland's motoring history with fine cars and unique archive film. Guided tours are available. The Motoring Heritage Centre is housed in the building that was once occupied by Europe's largest car manufacturer.

* 2-star visitor attraction

Location
In Alexandria within walking distance of Balloch by Loch Lomond. Follow A82 to Balloch

Opening
Mon, Fri & Sat 10am–5.30pm, Sun 11am–5pm
closed Tue–Thu

Admission
Adult £1.50, Child 75p, Concs £1

Contact
Loch Lomond Outlets,
Main Street, Alexandria,
West Dunbartonshire G83 0UG
t 01389 607862
w motoringheritage.co.uk

879 Glasgow

Museum of Scottish Country Life

3 hrs   All year

Set in 170 acres of farmland, with a Georgian farmhouse and steadings, this museum gives an insight into the working lives of the people of Scotland.

* Exhibition building
* Historic farm & demonstrations

Location
Just off A749 or A726 S of Glasgow & W of East Kilbride

Opening
Daily: 10am–5pm

Admission
Adult £4, Child (4–13) free, Concs £3

Contact
West Kittochside,
East Kilbride G76 9HR
t 01355 224181
w nms.ac.uk
w info@nms.ac.uk

880 Glasgow

Museum of Transport

2 hrs   All year

The museum uses its collections of vehicles and models to tell the story of transport by land and sea, with a unique Glasgow flavour. Here you will find the oldest surviving pedal cycle and the finest collection in the world of Scottish-built cars.

* World-famous makes such as Argyll & Albion

Location
In city's West End, opposite Kelvingrove Art Gallery & Museum

Opening
Daily: Mon–Thu & Sat 10am–5pm,
Fri & Sun 11am–5pm

Admission
Free

Contact
Kelvin Hall, 1 Bunhouse Road,
Glasgow G3 8DP
t 0141 287 2720
w glasgowmuseums.com

881 Glasgow

People's Palace

2 hrs+   All year

The People's Palace is Glasgow's social history museum and a chance to learn the story of the people and city of Glasgow from 1760 to the present. You can see paintings, prints and photographs displayed alongside a wealth of historic artefacts, film and computer interactives.

* Discover how a family lived in a typical single-end Glasgow tenement

Location
Short walk from city centre

Opening
Daily: Mon–Thu & Sat 10am–5pm,
Fri & Sun 11am–5pm

Admission
Free

Contact
Glasgow Green, Glasgow G40 1AT
t 0141 271 2951
w glasgowmuseums.com

882 Glasgow

The Piping Centre

2 hrs   All year

The Piping Centre houses the National Museum of Scotland's fine collection of bagpipes, making it the most authoritative display of its kind. The priceless collection is presented in a lively audio-visual format that is as entertaining as it is enlightening.

* 4-star Museum Attraction

Location	Contact
In Glasgow, off junction 16 of M8 & along A804 towards the E	30–34 McPhater Street, Glasgow G4 0HW
Opening	t 0141 353 0220
Daily: 9am-9pm; closed Sun in winter	w thepipingcentre.co.uk
	e reception@thepipingcentre.co.uk
Admission	
Adult £3, Child & Concs £2	

883 Glasgow

Scotkart

1 hr+   All year

Experience the thrill, the speed and the buzz of Scotland's largest and fastest indoor go-karting centre. This indoor circuit features 200cc race go-karts. All the equipment, instruction and computer timings are included in the price.

* 200cc race karts
* Track includes a flyover and tunnel

Location	Child £10 per session (12 mins)
Follow Clydebank signs along expressway then Dunbarton road. At Yoker look for brown tourist signs, Scotkart is 200 yrds from Yoker station	£1 for insurance
	Contact
	John Knox Street, Clydebank, Glasgow G81 1NA
Opening	t 0141 951 8900
Daily: 12noon–10pm	w scotkart.co.uk
	e race@scotkart.co.uk
Admission	
Adult £12 per session (12 mins),	

884 Glasgow

Tall Ship in Glasgow Harbour

1 hr+   All year

Built in 1896, the tall ship *Glenlee* circumnavigated the globe four times. Discover her rich history, depicted on board, and gain a real sense of what it was like to live and work on board in her seafaring days. Special events include pirate crafts and seafaring superstitions.

* Exhibition tells the *Glenlee* story
* Visitor centre

Location	Contact
Off M8 junction 19, follow brown thistle signs	100 Stobe Cross Road, Glasgow G3 8QQ
Opening	t 0141 222 2513
Daily: Mar–Nov 10am–5pm; Dec–Feb 11am–4pm	w thetallship.com
	e info@thetallship.com
Admission	
Adult £4.95, Child £2.50, Concs £3.75 (one child free with paying adult)	

885 Kenmore

Scottish Crannog Centre

1 hr   Mar–Nov

Visit Scotland's only authentic recreation of an Iron Age loch-dwelling. Discover why these ancient people built their homes out over the water, and how they lived. Guided tours, exhibits, video and ancient crafts bring the past to life.

* Shore-based exhibition with audio-visual presentation
* Tour the real thing

Location	Contact
Croft-na-Caber just S of Kenmore	Kenmore, Loch Tay, Perthshire PH15 2HY
Opening	t 01887 830583
Mar–Oct daily 10am–5.30pm; Nov Sat–Sun 10am–4pm (last tours 4.30pm)	w crannog.co.uk
	e info@crannog.co.uk
Admission	
Adult £4.75, Child £3, Concs £4	

886 Kinloch Rannoch

Loch Rannoch Watersports & Quads

4 hrs+   All year

Try your hand at a variety of water-based activities, from canoeing and windsurfing to sailing, motor boating and kayaking. A comprehensive range of courses is available, run by fully qualified staff. The centre also boasts a 4 star hotel.

* Reindeer safaris at Christmas
* Quad bike & field sports centre (for ages 14+)

Location	Admission
Signed for Kinloch Rannoch off A9 N of Pitlochry	Activities priced individually
Opening	**Contact**
Daily: *summer* 9.30am–9pm; *winter* 10.30am–5pm	Kinloch Rannoch, Perthshire PH16 5PS
	t 01882 632242
	w goforth.co.uk

887 Kircaldy

Craigencalt Ecology Centre

1 hr   All year

The Ecology Centre provides environmental education and information across a wide range of subjects. It is the home of the UK's first 'Earthship', a building created from waste and natural materials to be self-sufficient in energy and water.

* Community woodland & organic garden
* Workshops and events

Location	Admission
Take B923 off A921 between Burntisland & Kirkcaldy. Located beside Kinghorn Loch	Free
Opening	**Contact**
Daily: 10am–5pm Earthship by arrangement	Craigencalt Farm, Kinghorn Fife KY3 9YG
	t 01592 891567
	w cfec.org.uk
	e cfec@freeuk.com

888 Kirriemuir

Peel Farm

1 hr+   Feb–Dec

There are many animals and birds to see at Peel Farm, as well as a walk along a varied and interesting farm trail that includes a gorge and waterfall and even a red deer park.

* Farm shop
* Antiques

Location
20 miles N of Dundee, off B951 from Kirriemuir or B594 from Alyth

Opening
Apr–Dec daily 10am–5pm;
Feb–Mar Sat–Sun 10am–4pm

Admission
Free

Contact
Lintrathen, by Kirriemuir, Angus DD8 5JJ

t 01575 560205
w peelfarm.com
e Frances@peelfarm.com

889 Linlithgow

Linlithgow Palace

1 hr   All year

Set in its own park and beside Linlithgow Loch, this is a magnificent ruin of a great royal palace. A favoured residence of Stuart royalty, it was the birthplace of both James V and Mary, Queen of Scots.

* North range has a fine Renaissance facade
* Oldest working fountain in Britain

Location
On A803/M9, in town centre

Opening
Apr–Sep daily 9.30am–6.30pm;
Oct–Mar Mon–Sat 9.30am–4.30pm,
Sun 2pm–4.30pm

Admission
Adult £4, Child £1.60, Concs £3

Contact
Kirkgate, Linlithgow, West Lothian EH49 7AL

t 01506 842896
w historic-scotland.gov.uk

890 New Lanark

New Lanark World Heritage Site

2 hrs+   All year

This beautifully restored conservation village was once Britain's largest cotton-manufacturing centre and is the birthplace of Robert Owen's reforms. Now a World Heritage Site, New Lanark's award-winning visitor centre features the amazing Millennium Experience.

* Award-winning visitor centre
* Accommodation available at New Lanark Mill Hotel

Location	Contact
Off M74 junction 13, signed off all routes	New Lanark Mills, South Lanarkshire ML11 9DB
Opening	t 01555 661345
Daily: Jun–Aug 10.30am–5pm; Sep–May 11am–5pm	w newlanark.org
	e trust@newlanark.org
Admission	
Adult £5.95, Child & Concs £3.95	

891 Perth

Dewar's Centre

3 hrs+   All year

Come and brush up on your curling skills, or take a deep breath and learn to skate for the first time. Everyone is catered for, including the little ones, with Tiny Tots on Ice.

* 8–rink indoor bowling arena
* Superb catering facilities

Location	Contact
Situated in centre of Perth	Glover Street, Perth PH2 0TH
Opening	t 01738 624188
Daily: but please check before visiting as times vary	w conferencescotland.com
	e info@curlingscotland.com
Admission	
£4.90 (under 5s free)	

892 Perth

Noah's Ark

2 hrs   All year

Noah's Ark is a specially equipped children's soft play barn for under-12s. There are three separate areas to ensure the safety of all the children. Indoor go-karting is available seasonally. Also enjoy a game of tenpin bowling with family and friends.

* 4–star Visitor Attraction
* Ceramic studio & trampolines

Location	
On W edge of Perth, ½ mile from A9	Karting £3.50 for 5 mins, £4 for 5 mins in twin karts
Opening	**Contact**
Soft play Daily	Old Gallows Road, Perth PH1 1QE
Please phone to confirm times	t 01738 445568
Admission	w noahs-ark.co.uk
Adult Free, Child (over-5) £4.25, Child (under-5) £3.75	

893 Pitlochry

Atholl Country Life Museum

1 hr   May–Sep

This lively museum explores the reality of country life and the social history of the Atholl people. It uses detailed facts, 100 historical photographs, and stories set in a wide range of imaginative displays.

* Gamekeeper's corner
* Display of stuffed wild animals

Location
Turn off A9 for Blair Atholl, 7 miles N of Pitlochry

Opening
Daily: Easter & May–Sep
1.30pm–5pm;
Jul–Aug from 10am on weekdays

Admission
Adult £3, Child £1, Concs £2.50

Contact
Blair Atholl, Pitlochry,
Perthshire PH18 5SP

t 01796 481232
w blairatholl.org.uk
e janet.cam@virgin.net

894 Pittenweem

Kellie Castle & Garden

2 hrs   All year

This beautiful castle was started in 1360, though much of the present building was built in the C16 and early C17. Don't miss the Victorian nursery with its fascinating collection of dolls and toys. Outdoor attractions include Victorian stables and a charming walled garden.

* Fine example of domestic architecture
* Delightful dovecote

Location
On B9171, 3 miles from Pittenweem

Opening
Castle Daily: Easter & May–Sep
1pm–5pm
Gardens Daily: 9.30am–5.30pm

Admission
Castle Adult £8, Child & Concs £5
Gardens £3, £2

Contact
Pittenweem, Fife KY10 2RF

t 01333 720271
w nts.org.uk
e information@nts.org.uk

895 Plean

Plean Country Park

3 hrs+   All year

This beautiful Victorian estate provides extensive woodland walks, parkland, a picnic area and great orienteering courses. There is also a fine walled garden and beautiful wild flower meadows.

* Varied events throughout the year
* Horse trails

Location	Contact
Off M9, M80 & M876, S of Stirling	Viewforth, Stirling FK8 2ET
Opening	t 01786 442541
Daily: dawn–dusk	w stirling.gov.uk/countryside
Admission	
Free	

896 St Andrews

British Golf Museum

½ hr+   All year

Ever wondered where the word golf comes from? Why there are 18 holes on a golf course? Why golfers shout 'fore'? Here you'll learn the answers and many more interesting facts besides. The museum tells the story of British golf from its origins to the present day.

* Regular calendar of events
* Guided walks on the Old Course (summer only)

Location	Contact
Signed from town centre	Bruce Embankment, St Andrews, Fife KY16 9AB
Opening	t 01334 460046
Apr–Oct Mon–Sat 9.30am–5.30pm, Sun 10am–5pm; Nov–Mar daily 10am–4pm	w britishgolfmuseum.co.uk
	e alisonwood@randagc.org
Admission	
Adult £5, Child £2.75, Concs £4	

897 St Andrews

Scotland's Secret Bunker

1 hr+   Apr–Oct

Hidden beneath a farmhouse is a 24,000 sq ft secret nuclear bunker. Walk down the 150m entrance tunnel and through the 3 ton blast-proof doors to discover 24,000 sq ft of secret accommodation. Up to 300 staff would have lived here for up to 3 months at a time.

* Built in complete secrecy in the 1950s
* Discover how they would have survived & you wouldn't

Location	Contact
On B940, between St Andrews & Anstruther	Crown Buildings, Troywood, nr St Andrews, Fife KY16 8QH
Opening	t 01333 310301
Daily: Apr–Oct 10am–6pm (last admission 5pm)	w secretbunker.co.uk
	e mod@secretbunker.co.uk
Admission	
Adult £7.20, Child £4.50, Concs £5.95	

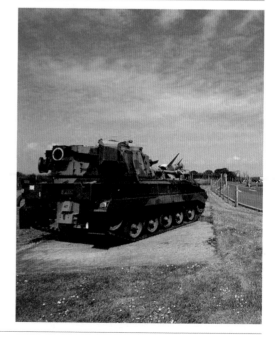

898 Stirling

Bannockburn Heritage Centre

½ hr+   Feb–Dec

Situated at the site of the famous battlefield where
Robert the Bruce routed the forces of Edward II to win
freedom for the Scots from English domination,
the centre contains an exhibition on the period of the
battle and an audio-visual presentation of the battle.

* Wars of independence exhibition

Location
Off M80/M9 junction 9, 2 miles S
of Stirling

Opening
Daily: Feb–Mar Nov–Dec
10.30am–4pm
Apr–Oct 10am–5.30pm

Admission
Adult £5, Child £4, Concs £4

Contact
Glasgow Road, Whins of Milton,
Stirling, Stirlingshire FK7 0LJ

t 01786 812664
w nts.org.uk

899 Stirling

Blair Drummond Safari & Adventure Park

4 hrs+   Mar–Oct

See a fascinating collection of animals from all over the
world, including elephants, giraffes, lions, tigers, and
rhino. You can take a safari to Chimpanzee Island, watch
the performing sea lion show or visit the Pet Farm.

* Three African rhino
* Adventure playground & giant Astraglide

Location
In Blair Drummond by junction 10 of
M9, 4 miles along A84 towards
Callander

Opening
Daily: 25 Mar–23 Oct 10am–5.30pm
(last admission 4.30pm)

Admission
Adult £9.50, Child & Concs £5.50

Contact
Blair Drummond, Stirling,
Stirlingshire FK9 4UR

t 01786 841456
w blairdrummond.com
e enquiries@blairdrummond.com

900 Stirling

The MacRobert Centre

  2 hrs+ All year

The MacRobert Centre is a premier children's art venue and Scotland's first dedicated children's theatre. It includes projection facilities for animation and other film work produced by children, and there is a fully supervised crèche involving children in art activities.

* Ideal for children with special needs
* Evening shows for adults

Location
Off A9, follow signs to University of Stirling

Opening
Daily: 10am–late
Please phone for details

Admission
Varies, please phone for details

Contact
University of Stirling,
Stirling FK9 4LA

t 01786 466666
w macrobert.org
e macrobert-arts@stir.ac.uk

901 Stirling

Stirling Castle

  1 hr+ All year

Stirling Castle is considered by many to be the grandest of Scotland's castles perching on a rocky outcrop. There is a medieval kitchens display and an exhibition on what life was like in the Royal Palace.

* Audio guides in six languages
* Regimental Museum of the Highlanders

Location
Off M9, in old town

Opening
Daily: Apr–Sep 9.30am–6pm;
Oct–Mar 9.30am–5pm
(last admission 45 mins before closing)

Admission
Adult £8, Child £3, Concs £6

Contact
Esplanade, Stirling,
Stirlingshire FK8 1EJ

t 01786 450000
w historic-scotland.gov.uk

902 Aberdeen

Aberdeen Maritime Museum

1 hr+   All year

Discover what it is like to live and work on a massive oil platform in the middle of the North Sea. Using models, real equipment and computer displays, the exhibitions bring the maritime experience to life. There are models of fast clipper ships and fishing displays.

* Incorporates Provost Ross's House, built in 1593
* Offers a spectacular viewpoint over the busy harbour

Location	Contact
On the harbour	Shiprow, Aberdeen AB11 5BY
Opening	t 01224 337700
Daily: Mon–Sat 10am–5pm,	w aagm.co.uk
Sun 12noon–3pm	e info@aagm.co.uk
Admission	
Free	

903 Aberdeen

Beach Leisure Centre

4 hrs+   All year

Relax at this amazingly equipped leisure centre specifically geared for families. The pool has four flumes, a fountain and rapids. There's also a fitness studio, health suite with sauna and steam room, a climbing wall and sports hall.

* Free crèche
* Refurbished café

Location	Contact
Next to beach at Aberdeen	Beach Promenade
	Aberdeen AB24 5NR
Opening	t 01224 647647
Please phone for details	w aberdeencity.gov.uk
Admission	e info@aberdeencity.gov.uk
Facilities individually priced	

904 Aberdeen

Codona's Pleasure Fair

3 hrs+   All year

Codona's amusement park is packed with more than 30 sensational rides and attractions for all the family. There are fun children's rides and, for the white knuckle fans, there's the giant Log Flume and 360° Looping Star rollercoaster.

* New 100ft ferris wheel
* Dodgems, haunted house, waltzers & crazy train

Location	Admission
Travelling from the S take A90.	Rides priced individually
Coming from Inverness take A96	
Inverness–Aberdeen route. Once	**Contact**
in Aberdeen follow signs to Aberdeen	Beach Boulevard,
Fun Beach	Aberdeen AB24 5NS
Opening	t 01224 595910
Daily: 10am–midnight	w codonas.com
Please phone for details	

905 Aberdeen

Gordon Highlanders Museum

2 hrs   Apr–Oct

Relive the compelling and dramatic story of one of the British Army's most famous regiments through the lives of its outstanding personalities and of the kilted soldiers of north-east Scotland.

* Tartan Day, National Garden Day
* Interactive displays

Location	Admission
Off Queens Road, known as Highland	Adult £2.50, Child £1, Concs £1.50
Tourist Route in & out of Aberdeen	
Opening	**Contact**
Apr–Oct Tue–Sun 10.30am–4.30pm,	St Luke's, Viewfield Road,
Sun 1.30pm–4.30pm (closed Mon),	Aberdeen AB15 7XH
Nov–Mar open by appointment only	t 01224 311200
	w gordonhighlanders.com
	e museum@gordonhighlanders.com

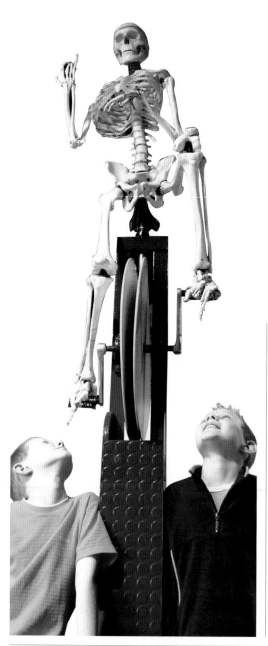

906 Aberdeen

Satrosphere

2 hrs   All year

Satrosphere offers fun for families and for grown-ups who love to explore, experiment and find out how the world works. Look into infinity, light up a plasma dome, step inside a bubble or make a skeleton ride a bike – it's all possible at Satrosphere.

* Interactive shows
* Workshops

Location	Contact
Off Beach Boulevard & Links Road near Patio Hotel	The Tramsheds, 179 Constitution Street, Aberdeen AB24 5TU
Opening Daily: 10am–5pm	t 01224 640340 w satrosphere.net
Admission Adult £5.50, Child & Concs £4	e satrosphere@satrosphere.net

907 Ballater

Balmoral Castle & Estate

1 hr+   Apr–Jul

See inside one of the Queen's residences, visit the ballroom and the formal and vegetable gardens, or enjoy an audio-visual display. Other activities on the estate include pony-trekking, a Land Rover safari, guided walks, fishing and trailer rides.

* Access to grounds, gardens, exhibitions, shops, tea room & ballroom

Location	Contact
Off A93, between Ballater & Braemar	Estates Office, Balmoral Estates, Ballater, Aberdeenshire AB35 5TB
Opening Daily: Apr–Jul 10am–5pm (ast admission 4pm)	t 01339 742534 w balmoralcastle.com
Admission Adult £6, Child £1, Concs £5	e info@balmoralcastle.com

908 Ballater

The Old Royal Station, Ballater

½ hr   All year

This renovated railway station features royalty and railway exhibitions with commentary and audio-visual presentations about Royal Deeside. A Victorian carriage will be arriving in April for display in an exhibition.

* 4–Star Speciality Attraction
* Restaurant

Location
In the centre of the picturesque Deeside village of Ballater, on A93 Aberdeen–Braemar road

Opening
Please phone for details

Admission
Free

Contact
Station Square, Ballater AB35 5AB

t 01339 755306
w visitscotland.com
e ballater@visitscotland.com

909 Drumoak

Drum Castle, Garden & Estate

2–4 hrs   Apr–Sep

The late C13 keep, fine adjoining Jacobean mansion and the additions of Victorian lairds make Drum Castle unique. The building is set in spectacular grounds, which contains a garden of historic roses, woodland trails and a children's playground.

* Old Wood of Drum is a Site of Special Scientific Interest

Location
Off A93, 3 miles W of Peterculter, 8 miles E of Banchory & 10 miles W of Aberdeen

Opening
Daily: Apr–May & Sep 12.30pm–5.30pm; Jun–Aug 10am–5.30pm

Admission
Please phone for details

Contact
Drumoak, Banchory, Aberdeen & Grampian AB31 5EY

t 01330 811204
w drum-castle.org.uk
e drum@nts.org.uk

910 Forres

Findhorn Heritage Icehouse

1 hr   May–Sep

Explore underground arched chambers built 150 years ago to store ice for packing salmon on the way to London. The chambers are now used to display all aspects of the salmon net fishing industry. Visit the Heritage Centre where the history and ecology are graphically displayed.

* Junior quiz to complete
* See the unique Findhorn Class yacht

Location
From Forres take the B9089 to Kinloss, then B9011 to Findhorn and follow signs.

Opening
Jun–Aug daily 2–5pm;
May & Sep Sat–Sun 2–5pm

Admission
donations welcomed

Contact
North Shore, Findhorn,
Forres, Moray IV36 3YL
t 01309 690659
w findhornbay.net
e s.eibbor@tesco.net

911 Fraserburgh

The Museum of Scottish Lighthouses

2 hrs+   All year

Located in Scotland's oldest lighthouse, the museum tells the history of Scotland's lighthouses. There are multi screen audio-visual presentations and a guided tour to the top of the fully restored lighthouse where visitors can enjoy panoramic views of the Buchan coast.

* Largest collection of lighthouse equipment in the UK
* The first lighthouse built on top of a fortified castle

Location
In town centre

Opening
Daily: Apr–Jun & Sep–Oct Mon–Sat
11am–5pm, Sun 12noon–5pm;
Jul–Aug Mon–Sat 10am–6pm, Sun
11am–6pm; Nov–Mar Mon–Sat
11am–4pm, Sun 12noon–4pm

Admission
Adult £5, Child £2, Concs £4

Contact
Kinnaird Head, Stevenson Road,
Fraserburgh AB43 9DU
t 01346 511022
w lighthousemuseum.co.uk

912 Huntly

Leith Hall

3 hrs+   Apr–Sep

The home of the Leith family since 1650, the mansion house contains interesting personal possessions and a military exhibition. The estate has a garden with two ponds, a bird hide, an ice house and stables.

* Halloween events
* Easter egg hunt

Location
On B9002, 1 mile W of Kennethmont
& 34 miles NW of Aberdeen. Signed
off A96

Opening
Easter weekend & May–Sep
Fri–Tue 12noon–5pm
(last admission 4.15pm)

Admission
Varies according to ticket type
Please phone for details

Contact
Kennethmont, Huntly,
Aberdeenshire AB54 4NQ
t 01464 831216
w nts.org.uk
e l.padgett@nts.org.uk

913 Macduff

Macduff Marine Aquarium

1 hr+   All year

This most northerly of Scotland's aquariums has several unique features, including the main tank, which is open to the air. There are touch tanks, a ray pool, rock pool and in shore displays with a wealth of aquatic life to admire and sometimes even touch.

* Estuary & deep-reef exhibits
* Feeding times & dive sessions

Location
A short walk from Macduff town
centre, just E of harbour. Reached via
A98, A947 or A96

Opening
Daily: 10am–5pm

Admission
Adult £4.75, Child £2.25, Concs £2.75

Contact
11 High Shore, Macduff
Banffshire AB44 1SL
t 01261 833369
w marine-aquarium.com
e macduff.aquarium@aberdeenshire.
   gov.uk

914 Mintlaw

Aberdeenshire Farming Museum

2 hrs   Apr–Oct

Discover 200 years of farming and family life at this museum, set within a delightful country park. The C19 farm buildings house displays on Scotland's rich agricultural history. There is also a working 1950s-style farm.

* Collection of farming artefacts
* Sensory garden

Location	Admission
1 mile W of Mintlaw on A950	Free
Opening	**Contact**
Daily: May–Sep 11am–4.30pm; Apr & Oct weekends only 12noon–4.30pm	Aden Country Park, nr Mintlaw, Aberdeenshire AB42 5FQ
Park All year	t 01771 622807
Please phone for details	w aberdeenshire.gov.uk/heritage

915 New Pitsligo

Northfield Farm Museum

1–2 hrs   May–Sep

This unique collection depicts working and family life on North East farms over the last 100 years. Admire a wealth of exhibits such as tractors, motorbikes, farm implements, household items and an engineer's workshop.

* Unique private collection of farm machinery
* 1920s tractors

Location	Contact
10 miles SW of Fraserburgh, just off A98	New Pitsligo, nr Fraserburgh, Aberdeenshire AB43 6PX
Opening	t 01771 653504
Daily: May–Sep 11am–5.30pm	
Admission	
Adult £1.50, Child & Concs 75p	

916 Peterhead

Peterhead Maritime Heritage

1 hr+   Jun–Aug

This heritage centre offers a historic look back at the Peterhead experience of fishing and whaling, and gives a brief insight into the oil industry. An observation box with telescopes provides breathtaking views out across the bay.

* 3-star speciality attraction

Location	Admission
Overlooking Peterhead Bay & beside beach and marina. Reached via A90 or A950	Free
	Contact
Opening	South Road, Peterhead, Aberdeenshire AB42 2YP
Daily: Jun–Aug 10.30am–5pm, Sun 11.30am–5pm	t 01779 473000
	w aberdeenshire.gov.uk

917 Ardrishaig

Lochfyne Miniature Railway

1 hr   Apr–Sep

Enjoy a ride on this miniature 10¼in-gauge steam railway that winds a picturesque route along the length of Ardrishaig Front Green from Greenend station to the John Smith Memorial Garden.

* Fun for all the family
* Regular timetable

Location
2 miles S of Lochgilphead on A83 Campbeltown road, 40 miles S of Oban

Opening
Apr–Sep Sat–Sun from 12.30pm (weather permitting)

Admission
Rail fare £1

Contact
19 Macintyre Terrace, Lochgilphead, Argyll PA31 8TF
t 01546 602918
e bryanpassey@talk21.com

918 Aviemore

Cairngorm Reindeer Centre

½ hr   Feb–Dec

Travel in a cavalcade to see 150 reindeer ranging free in the Cairngorms. Under the supervision of a guide, visitors can feed, stroke and photograph the reindeer. All ages, even babies in back carriers can come. Book well in advance for Christmas sleigh-pulling events.

* Guided tours on the hills (weather permitting)
* Learn more about these fascinating creatures

Location
6 miles E of Aviemore

Opening
Daily: Feb half-term, Apr & Oct–Dec 11am; May–Sep 11am & 2.30pm

Admission
Adult £8, Child & Concs £4

Contact
Glenmore, Aviemore, Invernessshire PH22 1QU
t 01479 861228
w reindeer-company.demon.co.uk
e info@reindeer-company.demon.co.uk

919 Aviemore

The Fun House

2 hrs   All year

The Fun House is a first choice for family entertainment. A wealth of activities include mini golf, a tree house, tenpin bowling, air hockey and soft play areas. There is also a crèche for toddlers and an American Diner.

* 3 Star Visitor Attraction

Location
Off B970, on a wooded riverside estate of 65 acres (on the ski road)

Opening
Daily: 10am-6pm

Admission
Please phone for details

Contact
Hilton Coylumbridge Hotel, Aviemore, Invernessshire PH22 1QN
t 01479 813081
w aviemorefunhouse.co.uk

920 Aviemore

Strathspey Steam Railway

2 hrs   May–Sep & Dec

This steam railway runs between Aviemore and Boat of Garten and on to Broomhill, near Nethy Bridge. The railway beautifully evokes the steam era of the 1950's and 1960's and runs through unspoilt countryside with fabulous mountain views.

* 3-Star Visitor Attraction

Location
Boat of Garten is off A95 between Aviemore & Grantown-on-Spey, or off B970 between Nethy Bridge & Inverdruie

Opening
Daily: end May–end Sep & selected days in Dec, please phone for details

Admission
Adult £9.50, Child £4.75, Concs £7

Contact
Aviemore Station,
Dalfaber Road, Aviemore,
Invernessshire PH22 1PY

t 01479 810725
w strathspeyrailway.co.uk

Strathspey Steam Railway©

---

921 Ballindalloch

Ballindalloch Castle

2 hrs+   Easter–Sep

This magnificent C16 castle, known as 'the Pearl of the North', has been the family home of the MacPherson-Grants since 1546. Through its romantic gardens flow the Rivers Spey and Avon. The 'Biggles' author Captain W E Johns lived at nearby Pitchroy Lodge.

* Ballindalloch herd of Aberdeen Angus cattle
* Golf facilities available, subject to prior arrangement

Location
14 miles NE of Grantown-on-Spey on A95

Opening
Easter–Sep Sun–Fri 10.30am–5pm

Admission
Please phone for details

Contact
Ballindalloch, Banffshire
AB37 9AX

t 01807 500206
w ballindallochcastle.co.uk
e enquiries@ballindallochcastle.co.uk

---

922 Balmaha

Loch Lomond National Nature Reserve

3 hrs   All year

This beautiful reserve includes five of the loch's islands, each supporting oak woodland, and the mouth of the River Endrick has fen, grassland and swamp woodland. Visit Inchailloch Island in May–June for woodland wildlife and winter–early spring for wildfowl.

* Wonderful camp & picnic site
* Remains of a C13 parish church

Location
Inchailloch is reached by ferry from Balmaha boatyard

Opening
Daily: wardens present Apr–Sep

Admission
Free

Contact
Loch Lomond & Trossochs National Park, Balmaha Visitor Centre

t 01389 722600
w lochlomond-trossachs.org
e info@lochlomond-trossachs.org

923 Barcaldine

Scottish Sealife & Marine Sanctuary

2½ hrs   All year

Nestling on the shore of Loch Creran, Scotland's leading marine animal rescue centre cares for abandoned seal pups and also has resident common seals and otters. The centre combines a spectacular aquarium with a busy rescue and rehabilitation facility.

* 3-star Marine Attraction
* New displays added regularly

Location
10 miles N of Oban on A828

Opening
Mar–Oct daily 10am–5pm (last admission 4pm); winter time vary please phone for details

Admission
Adults £9.50, Child (3-14) £6.95, Concs £7.50

Contact
Sanctuary, Barcaldine
By Oban, Argyll PA37 1SE

t 01631 720386
w sealsanctuary.co.uk
e oban@sealife.fsbusiness.co.uk

924 Birsay

Kirbuster Museum

1 hr+   Mar–Oct

The custodian at this folk museum describes the farming life of the past. The museum boasts the last traditional peat-burning central hearth and stone neuk bed in Northern Europe. There are also displays of farming equipment and a traditional Victorian garden.

* Putting green
* Livestock in grounds

Location
In Kirbuster, Birsay

Opening
Daily: Mar–Oct 10am–1pm, 2pm–5pm

Admission
Free

Contact
Kirbuster, Birsay
Orkney KW17 2LR

t 01856 771268
m orkney.gov.uk/heritage
e museum@orkney.gov.uk

925 Carrbridge

Landmark Forest Theme Park

5–6 hrs   All year

Scotland's favourite heritage park, Landmark has a wide range of fun, discovery and adventure activities for all ages in all weather, including a wild-water coaster, a red squirrel nature trail, a steam-powered sawmill and a wildforest maze.

* 4-Star Speciality Attraction
* Treetop trail

Location	Admission
7 miles N of Aviemore, 23 miles S of Inverness just off A9 at Carrbridge	Adult £8.95, Child (over 4) £6.90, Child (under 4) free
Opening	Contact
Daily: April–mid-July 10am–6pm; mid-Jul–mid-Aug 10am–7pm; Sep–Mar 10am–5pm	Main Street, Carrbridge, Invernessshire PH23 3AJ
	t 01479 841613
	w landmark-centre.co.uk
	e landmarkcentre@btconnect.com

926 Corrigal

Corrigall Farm Museum

2 hrs   Mar–Oct

This museum is a fully renovated Orkney farm cottage, complete with its peat fire and box beds. A kiln, parish weaver's loom and other traditional crafts help you to catch a flavour of the farming and domestic life of the Orkney people from the C18 to the C20.

* Various livestock
* Horse-drawn farm machinery

Location	Contact
Signed from main Kirkwall–Stromness road	Midhouse, Corrigall, Harray KW17
Opening	t 01856 771411
Mar–Oct Mon–Sat 10.30am–1pm & 2pm–5pm, Sun 2pm–7pm	w orkney.gov.uk/heritage
	e museum@orkney.gov.uk
Admission	
Free	

927 Culloden

Culloden Battlefield

1 hr+   Feb–Dec

This was the site of one of the most infamous battles in Scottish history, when more than 1,500 Jacobites were killed. Today it is a poignant and haunting location. The visitor centre has a fascinating exhibition, including an audio-visual programme.

* Permanent exhibition of weapons used in the battle
* Audio-visual programme

Location	Contact
On B9006, 5 miles E of Inverness	The National Trust for Scotland, Culloden Moor, Inverness IV2 5EU
Opening	t 01463 790607
Daily: Apr–Oct 9am–6pm Nov–Dec & Feb–Mar 11am–4pm	w nts.org.uk/culloden
	w information@nts.org.uk
Admission	
Adult £5, Child & Concs £4	

928 Dornoch

Historylinks Museum

1 hr+   All year

This small museum is packed with 700 years of history – the treachery and violence of the Picts and Vikings, feuding clans, and the shameful burning of Scotland's last condemned witch.

* Activities & quizzes
* Dressing up for children

Location	Admission
In Dornoch town centre, 2 miles from A9	Adult £2, Child Free
Opening	Contact
Easter week & Jun–Sep daily 10am–4pm; May Mon–Fri 10am–4pm; Oct–Mar Wed–Thu 10am–4pm	The Meadows, Dornoch, Sutherland IV25 3SF
	t 01862 811275
	w historylinks.org.uk
	e historylinks@connectfree.co.uk

929 Drumnadrochit

Loch Ness Monster Exhibition Centre

1 hr+   All year

Through photographs, descriptions and film footage, this exhibition presents the evidence about the existence of the Loch Ness Monster. It also highlights the efforts of various search expeditions, by both individuals and respected institutions, such as Operation Deepscan.

* Travel round the loch, view places & meet locals
* Exhibition cinema in eight different languages

Location
On A82, W of Inverness

Opening
Daily: Apr–Oct 9am–9pm;
Nov–Mar 9am–5pm

Admission
Adult £5, Child £3.50, Concs £3.95

Contact
Drumnadrochit, Invernessshire
IV63 6TU

t 01456 450342
w lochness-centre.com
e donald@lochness-centre.com

---

930 Elgin

Elgin Cathedral

2 hrs   All year

The superb remains of a majestic and beautiful C13 cathedral that was almost destroyed in 1390 by Alexander Stewart, the infamous Wolf of Badenoch. You can also visit the bishop's home at Spynie Palace, 2 miles north of the town.

* Joint ticket available with Spynie Palace
* 4–star Historic Site Attraction

Location
Elgin Cathedral can be found just N of the centre of Elgin by following brown tourist signs.

Opening
Apr–Sep daily 9.30am–6.30pm
Oct–Mar Sat–Wed 9.30am–4.30pm

Admission
Adult £3.30, Child £1.30, Concs £2.50

Contact
Historic Scotland, Longmore House,
Salisbury Place, Edinburgh EH9 1SH

t 01343 547171
w historic-scotland.gov.uk
e hs.explorer@scotland.gov.uk

---

931 Fochabers

Moray Firth Wildlife Centre

2 hrs+   Feb–Dec

A wildlife centre with exhibitions about dolphins, ospreys, otters and wildfowl. It is run by the Whale and Dolphin Conservation Society, with children's activities available throughout the summer.

* Nature reserve adjacent
* Wildlife activity holidays

Location
On A96 at mouth of River Spey,
5 miles N of Fochabers

Opening
Feb–Mar Sat–Sun 10.30am–5pm;
Apr–Oct daily 10.30am–5pm;
Oct–Dec Sat–Sun 10.30am–5pm

Admission
Free

Contact
Fochabers, Moray IV32 7PJ

t 01343 820339
w mfwc.co.uk
e wildlifecentre@wdcs.org

932 Fort William

Treasures of the Earth

1hr   Feb–Dec

One of Europe's finest collections of gemstones, crystals and fossils are set in simulated caves, caverns and mining scenes. There are casts of T-Rex and a sabre-toothed tiger, together with fossil fish and dinosaur bones.

* Dinosaur Diorama
* Shop with a range of gemstones, crystals and jewellery

Location
In Corpach by Fort William

Opening
Daily: *summer* 9.30am–7pm; *winter* 10am–5pm; Closed Jan

Admission
Adult £3.50, Child £2, Senior £3

Contact
Corpach, Fort William, Invernessshire PH33 7JL

t 01397 772283

933 Fort William

Vertical Descents

3 hrs+   All year

This adventure centre offers canyoning, white-water rafting, paintballing, fun yakking, adventure holidays, adrenaline sports, adventure travel, mountain biking, abseiling, and a bridge swing (like a bungee with a swing). No previous experience is required.

* All necessary clothing & equipment provided

Location
Off A82, 7 miles S of Fort William

Opening
All year; closed Christmas hols

Admission
£35 per person (half-day canyoning)
Activities individually priced

Contact
Inchree Falls, Inchree, Onich, nr Fort William PH33 6SE

t 01855 821593
w activities-scotland.com
e verticaldescents@yahoo.com

934 Glencoe

Glencoe Visitor Centre

1 hr   All year

Built in 2002, this state-of-the-art eco-friendly centre is built from timber, insulated with sheep's wool and heated by burning local wood chips. The exhibition covers the ecology and geology of Glencoe, mountaineering and the history of Glencoe.

* Summer events programme
* Display on the history of mountaineering in the glen

Location
On A82, between Glasgow & Fort William

Opening
Daily: Mar 10am–4pm;
Apr–Aug 9.30am–5.30pm;
Sep–Oct 10am–5pm;
Nov–Feb Thu–Sun 10am–4pm

Admission
Adult £5, Child & Concs £4

Contact
Ballachulish, Argyll PH49 4LA

t 01855 811307
w nts.org.uk
e sborland@nts.org.uk

935 Inverary

Inverary Jail

1 hr+   All year

Sit and listen to trials in the 1820 courtroom. Talk to guides dressed as warders, prisoners and the matron. Visit the two prisons and experience the sounds and smells as they would have been.

* View a Black maria prison transport vehicle
* Try the crank machine, whipping table & hammocks

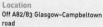

Location	Admission
Off A82/83 Glasgow–Campbeltown road	Adult £5.95, Child (4–16) £3, Concs £3.95
Opening	Contact
Daily: Apr–Oct 9.30am–6pm; Nov–Mar 10am–5pm (last admission 1 hr before closing)	Church Square, Inveraray, Argyll PA32 8TX
	t 01499 302381
	w inverarayjail.co.uk
	e info@inverarayjail.co.uk

936 Inverness

Inverness Dolphin Cruises

1 hr+   Mar–Oct

Enjoy a 1½–hour cruise on the *Daniel Quilp* out on the Moray Firth, where you will see the most northerly resident colony of dolphins in the world, common and grey seals, porpoise, Minke whales, red kites and ospreys.

* Room for 50 passengers
* Commentary from professional guide

Location	Admission
Boat leaves from Inverness harbour	Adult £12.50, Child £9, Concs £10
Opening	Contact
Daily: Mar–end Oct; cruises leave at 10.30am, 12noon, 1.30pm, 3pm & 4.30pm (& 6pm in Jul–Aug)	Shore Street Quay, Shore Street Inverness IV1 1NF
	t 01463 717900
	w inverness-dolphin-cruises.co.uk
	e info@inverness-dolphin cruises.co.uk

937 Inverness

Inverness Terror Tour

1 hr+   All year

Led by Davy the Ghost, this walking tour of horror and laughter takes you through the streets of Inverness. Hear gruesome stories along the way of witches, ghosts, and other ghastly happenings before ending at the haunted tavern, where a free drink is provided.

* Witches, ghosts, torture & murders

Location	Contact
Outside Tourist Information Centre on Bridge Street	Tourist Information Centre, Bridge Street, Inverness IV2 3BJ
Opening	t 07730 831069
Daily: 7pm	e davytheghost@btinternet.com
Admission	
Adult £7, Child £5, Concs £6.50	

938 Isle of Barra

Kisimul Castle

1 hr+   Mar–Sep

The historic restored seat of the MacNeils of Barra, chiefs of the Clan MacNeil. Located on an island, it is reached by a small boat from the village of Castlebay.

* Real & lived-in castle
* Fabulous views of Castlebay

Location	Admission
In Castlebay, Isle of Barra, reached by a small boat from Castlebay (5 min trip, weather permitting).	Adult £3.30, Child £1.30, Concs £2.50
Opening	Contact
Daily: Mar–Sep, 9.30am–6.30pm (last admission 6pm)	Castlebay, Isle of Barra, Western Isles HS9 5XD
	t 01871 810313
	w historic-scotland.gov.uk
	e hs.explorer@scotland.gsi.gov.uk

939   Isle of Lewis

The Black House Museum

1 hr   All year

Visit a traditional Isle of Lewis thatched crofter's cottage, or black house. Now a museum it is fully furnished, complete with attached barn, byre, stackyard and peat fire. The visitor centre has fascinating information about Hebridean life.

* Interactive displays
* 5-star Scottish Tourism Award

Location
In Arnol village, Isle of Lewis

Opening
Apr–Sep Mon–Sat 9.30am–6.30pm;
Oct–Mar Mon–Sat 9.30am–4.30pm

Admission
Adult £4, Child £1.60, Concs £3

Contact
Arnol, Isle of Lewis,
Western Isles HS2 9DB

t 01851 710395
w historic-scotland.gov.uk
e hs.explorer@scotland.gsi.gov.uk

940   Isle of Raasay

Raasay Outdoor Centre

4 hrs+   Apr–Oct

Raasay Outdoor Centre is situated in the historic mansion of Raasay House. Try your hand at sailing around the seas of Skye, kayaking around Raasay's sheltered bays or rock climbing and abseiling in some of the island's most beautiful locations.

* Whole range of outdoor activities
* Café & fine restaurant

Location
Isle of Raasay is a 15-min ferry journey from Isle of Skye. There is a direct bus route from Inverness & Glasgow

Opening
Daily: Apr–Oct 8am–11pm or fully residential
Please phone for details

Admission
Free (activities range from £15)

Contact
Rassay House, Isle of Raasay,
by Kyle IV40 8PB

t 01478 660266
w raasay-house.co.uk

Arnol Blackhouse©

941 Isle of Skye

Bella Jane Boat Trips

3 hrs+   Mar–Oct

Bella Jane Boat Trips take you to the world-famous Loch Coruisk and the seal colony at the heart of the Cuillin on the Isle of Skye. During the journey you will see a wealth of sea life and enjoy breathtaking scenery.

* 4-star Visitor Attraction
* Aquaxplore excursions to Canna & Rum

Location	Contact
Take B8083 from Broadford to Elgol for 15 miles (45 mins by car)	Elgol, Isle of Skye IV49 9BJ
	t 0800 731 3089 (from 7.30am)
Opening	w bellajane.co.uk
Daily: Mar–Oct. Trip times vary, please phone for details	e david@bellajane.co.uk
Admission	
£10–£20 Please book in advance	

942 Isle of Skye

The Bright Water Visitor Centre

1 hr   Apr–Oct

The centre offers a unique child-friendly, interactive experience that unfolds the area's dramatic history and celebrates the wealth of local wildlife. It also commemorates Gavin Maxwell, author of *Ring of Bright Water*.

* 3-star Speciality Attraction
* Visit the Stevenson Lighthouse

Location	Contact
Take Kyleakin exit at Skye round-about (at the end of the Skye Bridge)	The Pier, Kyleakin, Isle of Skye IV41 8PL
Opening	t 01599 530040
Apr–Oct Mon–Fri 10am–4pm	w eileanban.org
Admission	e enquiries@eileanban.org
Free, donations requested	

943 Isle of Skye

Family's Pride II Glass-bottom Boat Trips

1 hr   Mar–Oct

Cruise in the spectacular Bay of Islands in a glass-bottomed boat. See seals, birds and porpoises above deck, then step below and see the amazing sights of the underwater world.

* Frequent daily sailings

Location	Admission
In Broadford, Isle of Skye, 8 miles from Skye Bridge	Adult £9.50, Child (Under-12) £4.75
	Contact
Opening	5 Scullamus, Breakish
Daily: Mar–Oct 10.30am–4.45pm	Isle of Skye IV42 8QB
	t 0800 783 2175
	w glassbottomboat.co.uk

944 Kincraig

Working Sheepdogs

1 hr   All year

Participate in the working day of a Highland shepherd and his dogs. Help to shear a sheep and bottle feed orphan lambs. Meet the friendly pups and feed the Highland cows.

* 2-star Wildlife and Nature Attraction
* Live performances

Location
On a working farm, 5 miles S of Aviemore & 5 miles N of Kingussie on B9152

Opening
Daily: demonstrations at 12noon & 4pm;
Private bookings available

Admission
Please phone for details

Contact
Leault Farm, Kincraig,
Invernessshire PH21 1LZ

t 01540 651310

945 Kingussie

Highland Folk Museum, Newtonmore

3 hrs   All year

Get a fascinating glimpse into 300 years of Highland life at this re-creation of a thriving C18 farming township with clockmaker's workshop and working croft. See how Highland people adapted to the harsh environment, and enjoy demonstrations of traditional skills and crafts.

* 4-star Visitor Attraction
* Vintage buses on site

Location
On A86, ¼ mile N of Newtonmore

Opening
Please phone for details

Admission
Please phone for details

Contact
Duke Street, Kingussie,
Invernessshire PH21 1JG

t 01540 661307
w highlandfolk.com
e highlandfolk@highland.gov.uk

946 Kingussie

Highland Wildlife Park

3 hrs+   All year

Enjoy a wild day out in the Cairngorm National Park. Drive through the scenic main reserve then explore the rest of the park on foot. There are wolves, otters, reindeer, lynx, pine martens, capercaillie and more.

* 4-star Visitor Attraction
* Educational tours & talks

Location
Off A9, 7 miles S of Aviemore, 2½ hrs from Edinburgh

Opening
Daily: Apr–May & Sep–Oct 10am–6pm; Jun–Aug 10am–7pm; Nov–Mar 10am–4pm; last entry 2 hrs before closing (if heavy ice or snow please phone before visiting)

Admission
Please phone for details

Contact
Kincraig, Kingussie,
Invernessshire PH21 1NL

t 01540 651270
w highlandwildlifepark.org
e info@highlandwildlifepark.org

© Haken Halilhan www.halilhan.dynu.com

947 Kirkwall

The Orkney Museum

3 hrs   All year

Visit this C16 town-house museum to discover the history of Orkney. From prehistory to the C20, the story of Orkney is told through archaeological and social history exhibits, ranging from a Scar Viking boat burial through to a 300-year-old calculator.

* C16 Scottish vernacular architecture
* Beautiful gardens

Location
Kirkwall, Orkney, opposite St Magnus Cathedral

Opening
May–Sep Mon–Sat 10.30am–5pm, Sun 2–5pm; Oct–Apr Mon–Sat 10.30am–12.30pm & 1.30pm–5pm

Admission
Free

Contact
Tankerness House, Broad Street, Kirkwall, Orkney KW15 1DH
t 01856 873191
w orkneyheritage.com
e museum@orkney.gov.uk

948 Kirkwall

Scapa Flow Visitor Centre & Museum

2 hrs+   All year

A British Navy base during WWI and WWII, Scapa Flow is now a museum with many interesting relics from the war days. Advance booking is required for the ferry from Houton to Lyness.

* Artefacts from HMS *Hampshire*
* Display on HMS *Royal Oak*

Location
Near Lyness Pier, on island of Hoy

Opening
Daily: May–Sep Mon–Sat 9am–4.30pm, Sun please phone for details; Oct–Apr Mon–Fri 9am–4.30pm

Admission
Free

Contact
Lyness, Hoy, Kirkwell, Orkney KW16 3NT
t 01856 791300
w orkney.gov.uk/heritage
e museum@orkney.gov.uk

949 Kyle of Lochalsh

Seaprobe *Atlantis*

1 hr+   Apr–Oct

In this fabulous semi submersible, glass-bottomed boat, you can enjoy views of a WWII shipwreck, kelp forests, fish, jellyfish, sea urchins, starfish and occasional dolphins and whales. Visit seal and bird colonies, and look out for otters.

* 4-star Visitor Attraction
* Comprehensive commentary during the voyage

Location
Off A87 at Kyle of Lochalsh; boat departs from below Lochalsh Hotel (follow the brown tourist signs)

Opening
Daily: Easter–Oct 10am–evening

Admission
For 1 hr trip Adult £12, Child (3–12) £6

Contact
Kyle Tourist Information Centre Old Ferry Pier, Kyle of Lochalsh, IV40 8AQ
t 0800 980 4846
w seaprobeatlantis.com
e seaprobe@msn.com

950 Lairg

Ferrycroft Countryside Centre

2 hrs   Apr–Oct

A hands-on family-oriented visitor centre displaying the natural and archaeological history of an area rich in beauty and wildlife. The centre guides the visitor through the changes in land use in the area from the ice age to the present day.

* Indoor & outdoor play areas
* Countryside ranger

Location
Central Sutherland, on the shore of Loch Shin

Opening
Daily: Apr–May & Sep & Oct 10am–4pm; Jun–Aug 10am–5pm

Admission
Free

Contact
Lairg, Sutherland IV27 4AZ
t 01549 402160
w lairghighlands.org.uk
e ferrycroft@croftersrestaurant.fsnet.co.uk

951 Lewis

Lewis Karting Centre

Varies   All year

Arrive and drive at this outdoor go-karting centre. There are go-karts for hire for children aged eight and upwards and a Kiddie Kart section for the younger driver on a safe inflatable circuit.

* Sessions include briefing, kit & 12 minutes on the track
* Maclaren-style 2-seater coming soon

Location
4 miles S of Stornoway on A859

Opening
Please phone for details

Admission
Please phone for details

Contact
Creed Enterprise Park, Lochs Road, Stornoway, Isle of Lewis HS2 9JN
t 01851 700222
w lewiscarclub.co.uk
e enquiries@lewiscarclub.co.uk

952 Liddle

Tomb of the Eagles

1 hr+   All year

A visit to the Tomb of the Eagles gives a valuable insight into the life of our Neolithic ancestors. Visitors are given the opportunity to handle some of the original artefacts.

* Guided tour of Bronze Age house
* Children's indoor play area

Location
South Ronaldsay, Orkney. Overlooking the Pentland Firth, on Orkney mainland

Opening
Daily: Mar–Oct 9.30am–6pm; Nov–Feb by arrangement

Admission
Please phone for details

Contact
Liddle, South Ronaldsay, Orkney KW17 2RW
t 01856 831339
w tomboftheeagles.co.uk
e info@tomboftheeagles.co.uk

TombEagles©

961 Berwick-upon-Tweed

Paxton House & Country Park

2 hrs   Apr–Oct

This beautiful C18 Palladian country house has lots of activities for young people. Younger children can follow the Paxton Ted house trail and for older children there is an activity guide. Outside there is a Nature Detective trail and an adventure playground.

* 5-star historic house
* Children's summer activities

Location
On B6461, 3 miles from A1 Berwick-upon-Tweed bypass

Opening
House Daily: Apr–Oct 11am–5pm (last tour 4pm)
Garden Daily: Apr–Oct 10am–sunset

Admission
House & Garden Adult £6, Child £3
Garden only £3, £1.50

Contact
Berwick-upon-Tweed TD15 1SZ

t 01289 386291
w paxtonhouse.com
e info@paxtonhouse.com

962 Caerlaverock

WWT Caerlaverock Wetlands Centre

½ day   All year

Caerlaverock has a 1,400-acre wild nature reserve with modern hides and observation towers linked by a network of screened approaches. In winter see thousands of barnacle geese and watch twice-daily feeds of wild swans.

* Self-catering accommodation available
* Badger-watching & summer nature trail

Location
9 miles SE of Dumfries along Solway Coast Heritage Trail

Opening
Daily: 10am–5pm

Admission
Adult £4.40, Child (over 4) £2.70, Child (under 4) free, Concs £3.60

Contact
Eastpark Farm, Caerlaverock, Dumfriesshire DG1 4RS

t 01387 770200
w wwt.org.uk
e info.caerlaverock@wwt.org.uk

963 Castle Douglas

Cream O'Galloway

3 hrs   All year

A natural experience for the whole family, in which you can enjoy the adventure playground, nature trails, dog walk and beautiful scenery.

* 4-Star Visitor Attraction
* Ice-cream factory with viewing gallery

Location
In SW of Scotland. From A75 near Gatehouse-of-Fleet, take road to Sandgreen. Turn left after 1½ miles

Opening
Please phone for details

Admission
Adult £1.50, Child £3

Contact
Rainton, Gatehouse-of-Fleet, Castle Douglas DG7 2DR

t 01557 814040
w creamogalloway.co.uk
e info@creamogalloway.co.uk

964 Castle Douglas

Threave Garden, House & Estate

3 hrs   All year

A garden for all seasons, best known for its springtime display of daffodils. Herbaceous beds are colourful in summer and the trees and heather striking in autumn.

* Visitor centre with exhibitions
* Baronial house

Location
Off A75 near Castle Douglas

Opening
House Apr–Oct Wed–Fri & Sun
11am–3.30pm (guided tours)
Garden Daily: 9.30am–sunset

Admission
Please phone for details

Contact
Castle Douglas,
Dumfries & Galloway DG7 1RX

t 01556 502575
w nts.org.uk
e tjones@nts.org.uk

965 Coldingham

St Abb's Head Nature Reserve

2–4 hrs   All year

This national nature reserve is an important site for cliff-nesting seabirds in summer. Visitors can watch them wheeling and diving below the high cliffs and take guided walks with a ranger.

* Formed by extinct volcano

Location
Off A1107, 2 miles N of Coldingham

Opening
Daily: All reasonable times

Admission
Free

Contact
Ranger's Cottage,
Northfield, St Abb's,
Eyemouth, Borders TD14 5QF

t 018907 71443
w nts.org.uk
e krideout@nts.org.uk

966 Creetown

Creetown Heritage Museum

1 hr   Apr–Oct

An exhibition of Creetown past and present, shown through a large collection of historical photographs, artefacts, audio and video presentations and hands-on activities including exploring the beautiful Wigtown Bay nature reserve.

* 3-star Speciality Museum
* Location for the film *The Wicker Man*

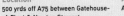

Location
500 yrds off A75 between Gatehouse-
of-Fleet & Newton Stewart

Opening
Apr–Oct Sun–Tue & Thu–Fri
11am–4pm; Easter Week daily;
Jun–Aug also open Wed

Admission
Adult £1.50, Child & Concs 75p

Contact
91 St John Street, Creetown,
Newton Stewart DG8 7JE

t 01671 820471
w creetown-heritage-museum.com

967 Dalbeattie

Dalbeattie Museum

1 hr   Apr–Sep

This museum gives an insight into things we used in the past. Visitors can view and handle household utensils and children's games, as well as agricultural, quarrying and bobbin making tools. There is also a model of the *Titanic* and an exhibition on the disaster.

* True story of First Officer Murdoch of *Titanic* fame

Location
On corner of Southwick Road
& high street in town centre

Opening
Daily: Apr–Sep Mon–Sat 10am–4pm,
Sun 2pm–4pm

Admission
Adult £1, Child free, Concs 50p

Contact
1 Southwick Road,
Dalbeattie DG5 4BS

t 01556 610437
e tommy.ullvele@wanadoo.co.uk

968 Dumfries

Caerlaverock Castle

1 hr+   All year

With its moat, twin-towered gatehouse and imposing battlements, Caerlaverock Castle is the epitome of the medieval stronghold. The castle's turbulent history owes much to its proximity to England, which brought it into border conflicts.

* Children's adventure park & nature trail
* Video presentation available

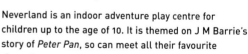

Location	Contact
8 miles SE of Dumfries on B725	Caerlaverock, Dumfries, Dumfriesshire DG1 4RU
Opening	t 01387 770244
Daily: Apr–Sep 9.30am–6.30pm; Oct–Mar 9.30am–4.30pm	w historic-scotland.gov.uk
Admission	
Adult £4, Child £1.60, Concs £3	

©Tony Stuchbury www.ajsphotos.co.uk

969 Dumfries

Dumfries Museum & Camera Obscura

1 hr   Mar–Oct

Set in its own gardens, Dumfries Museum & Camera Obscura is situated in a converted windmill. From the camera you can see a panoramic view of Dumfries. The museum is a treasure house of the history of Dumfries & Galloway.

* Prehistoric reptile footprints
* Tools & weapons from the area's oldest people

Location	Admission
In town centre	Museum Free
Opening	Camera Obscura Adult £1.80, Child 90p, Concs 90p
Daily: Apr–Sep Mon–Sat 10am–5pm, Sun 2pm–5pm; Mar & Oct Tue–Sat 10am–1pm 2pm–5pm	Contact
	Rotchell Road, Dumfries DG2 7SW
	t 01387 253374
	w dumfal.gov.uk/museums
	e dumfriesmuseum2dumfal.gov.uk

970 Dumfries

Neverland Adventure Play Centre

1 hr   All year

Neverland is an indoor adventure play centre for children up to the age of 10. It is themed on J M Barrie's story of *Peter Pan*, so can meet all their favourite characters.

* Suitable for children 1–10 years old
* Set in original site of the book

Location	Contact
In town centre, reached via A75, A76 or A701	Park Lane, Dumfries, Dumfriesshire DG1 2AX
Opening	t 01387 249100
Daily: 10am–5pm	w mabiefarmpark.co.uk
Admission	
Adult free, Child £2	

RobertBurnsCenter©

971 Dumfries

Old Bridge House Museum

1 hr+   Apr–Sep

Visit Dumfries's oldest house, now a museum of everyday life. You can see the family kitchen, nursery and bedroom of a Victorian home and pay a visit to an early dentist's surgery.

* 3-star Visitor Award
* Worksheets for children

Location
At end of Old Bridge on Maxwelltown bank of River Nith

Opening
Daily: Apr–Sep Mon–Sat 10am–5pm, Sun 2pm–5pm

Admission
Free

Contact
Mill Road, Dumfries DG2 7BE

t 01387 256904
w dumgal.gov.uk/museum
e dumfriesmuseum@dumgal.gov.uk

972 Dumfries

Robert Burns Centre

1 hr   All year

Situated in an old mill building, this museum is dedicated to the history and literature of the legendary Scottish poet Robert Burns.

* 4-star Visitor Award
* Film theatre

Location
On Mill Road by River Nith at Old Wear on Maxwelltown Bank

Opening
Daily: Apr–Sep Mon–Sat 10am–8pm, Sun 2pm–5pm; Oct–Mar Tue–Sat 10am–1pm, 2pm–5pm

Admission
Free

Contact
Mill Road, Dumfries DG2 7BE

t 01387 264808
w dumgal.gov.uk/museum
e dumfriesmuseum@dumgal.gov.uk

973 Dumfries

Robert Burns House

1 hr   All year

This is the house in which the famous poet Robert Burns died. It has been preserved in its original condition and contains many original artefacts and manuscripts.

* Children's worksheets available
* Original desk and chair where he wrote his best known poems

Location	Admission
Burns Street, off Shakespeare Street, next to Brooms Road car park	Free
Opening	**Contact**
Daily: *summer* Mon–Sat 10am–5pm, Sun 2pm–5pm; *winter* Tue–Sat 10am–1pm, 2pm–5pm	Burns Street, Dumfries DG1 2PS t 01387 255297 w dumgal.gov.uk/museum e dumfriesmuseum@dumgal.gov.uk

974 Dumfries

Shambellie House Museum of Costume

2 hrs+   Apr–Oct

Step back in time and experience Victorian and Edwardian elegance in this museum showing original costumes in appropriate room settings. Take a fascinating look at fashion and social etiquette of the era, before enjoying a pleasant stroll in the wooded gardens.

* Tea rooms
* Regular events for families

Location	Contact
7 miles S of Dumfries on A710, Solway coast road	New Abbey, Dumfries Dumfriesshire DG2 8HQ
Opening	t 01387 850375
Daily: Apr–Oct 10am–5pm	w nms.ac.uk
Admission	e info@nms.ac.uk
Adult £3, Child (under 12) free, Concs £2	

975 Dundonald

Dundonald Castle

1 hr   Apr–Oct

The castle's association with the Stuarts gives Dundonald its special importance. It was built by Robert Stuart in 1371 to mark his succession to the throne of Scotland.

* 4-star Historic Attraction
* Available for wedding ceremonies

Location	Contact
In village of Dundonald on A759, 6 miles from Ayr & 3 miles from Kilmarnock	Winehouse Yett, Dundonald, Ayrshire KA2 9HD
Opening	t 01563 851489
Daily: Apr–Oct 10am–5pm	w dundonald.org.uk
Admission	e info@dundonald.org.uk
Adult £2.50, Child &Concs £1.25	

© Tony Stuchbury www.ajsphotos.co.uk

976 Eyemouth

Eyemouth Museum

1 hr   Apr–Oct

This museum has exhibitions on fishing, farming, milling, wheelwrighting and blacksmithing. One of the highlights is a large tapestry that commemorates the great east coast fishing disaster of 1881 in which 189 local fishermen were drowned.

* 3 star visitor attraction
* Temporary exhibitions on the first floor gallery

Location
In town centre

Opening
Daily: Apr–Jun & Sep Mon–Sat 10am–5pm, Sun 12noon–3pm; Jul–Aug Mon–Sat 10am–5pm, Sun 12noon–4pm; Oct Mon–Sat 10am–4pm

Admission
Adult £2.50, Child free, Concs £2

Contact
Auld Kirk, Manse Road, Eyemouth

t 018907 50678

977 Fairlie

Kelburn Castle & Country Centre

4 hrs+   All year

Kelburn is a historic country park with a castle that dates back to the C13. There are exotic gardens, and a beautiful glen with waterfalls and deep gorges to explore. Take a tour of the castle or visit the new falconry centre.

* Adventure course and pet corner
* Horse riding available

Location
On A78 between Ayr & Greenock

Opening
Daily: Easter–Oct fully 10am–6pm; Nov–Easter (grounds & riding centre only) daily 11am–5pm

Admission
Adult £6.50, Child & Concs £4.50

Contact
South Offices, Fairlie, Ayrshire KA29 0BE

t 01475 568685
w kelburncountrycentre.com
e admin@kelburncountrycentre.com

978 Fenwick

Rowallan Activity Centre

2–4 hrs   All year

Whether you want to play football, learn to ride or discover the thrill of paintballing, this multi functional indoor and outdoor centre has something for everyone. Test your head-for-heights on the climbing wall or simply unwind in the new health club with swimming pool.

* Crèche & beauty shop
* Amusement arcade

Location
From A77 Glasgow–Kilmarnock road (near Fenwick) turn (at the Fenwick Hotel) on to B751 towards Kilmaurs. Centre is 1 mile on the left

Opening
Daily: 8am–late

Admission
Free

Contact
Melklemosside, Fenwick, Ayrshire KA3 6AY

t 01560 600769
w rowallanac.com

979 Galston

Loudoun Castle Family Theme Park

4 hrs+   Apr–Sep

A great day out for all the family is certain here, with rides and entertainment to suit all ages, in a historic setting. New live shows featuring Rory & The Gang! run throughout the day.

* Twist & Shout rollercoaster
* New Dougall McDougal's farm

Location
On A719 on edge of Galston

Opening
Daily: Mid-May–Aug 10am–5pm
Open some days in Apr & Sep, please phone for details

Admission
Please phone for details

Contact
Galston, Ayrshire KA4 8PE

t 01563 822296
w loudouncastle.co.uk
e loudouncastle@btinternet.com

980 Gretna Green

Gretna Green World Famous Blacksmith's Shop

1 hr+   All year

Visit the blacksmith's shop where many 16-year-olds married after eloping from England. The centre also has an exhibition about the history of Gretna Green, a coach museum with horse-drawn carriages, a native breeds' park with Highland cattle, and a play park.

* One of Scotland's earliest visitor attractions
* Site of thousands of weddings since the C18

Location
Just off the M74, just N of border

Opening
Daily: Apr–Sep 9am–early evening;
Oct–Mar 9am–5pm

Admission
Exhibition Adult £3, Child & Concs £2.50

Contact
Gretna Green Group Ltd,
Headless Cross, Gretna Green,
Dumfries & Galloway DG16 5EA

t 01461 338441
w gretnagreen.com
e info@gretnagreen.com

981 Hawick

Drumlanrig's Tower

1 hr   Mar–Oct

Drumlanrig's Tower interprets Hawick's turbulent history from medieval times, using the latest audio-visual technology. The exhibition is housed in a beautifully restored period building.

* Exhibition tells the story of the house
* Display of watercolours by the artist Tom Scott

Location
In Hawick high street

Opening
Daily:
Apr–Jun & Sep–Oct Mon–Sat
10am–5pm, Sun 1pm–5pm;
Jul–Aug Mon–Sat 10am–6pm,
Sun 1pm–5pm; winter times vary,
please phone for details

Admission
Adult £2.50, Child free, Concs £1.50

Contact
1 Towerknowe, Hawick TD9 9EN

t 01450 373457

982 Heathhall

Dumfries & Galloway Aviation Museum

3 hrs   Easter–Oct

Founded in 1977 by a group of aviation enthusiasts and based on a former WWII airfield, the museum is located in and around the original 3-storey-high control tower. It is now home to engines, memorabilia and records of personal histories.

* 3 star Visitor Attraction
* Huge collection of artefacts

Location
On Heathhall Industrial Estate, easily accessed from A75 Dumfries bypass. From town centre follow A701 Edinburgh road

Opening
Easter–Oct Sat–Sun 10am–5pm; Jul–Aug Wed–Fri 11am–4pm

Admission
Adult £2.50, Child & Concs £1.50

Contact
Heathhall Industrial Estate, Heathhall, Dumfries DG13PH

t 01387 251623
w www.dumfriesaviationmuseum.com
e alammin@hotmail.com

983 Hirsel

Coldstream

4 hrs+   All year

The seat of the Home family, Coldstream has interesting grounds with a museum and craft centre. There are extensive nature trails through the woodland and grounds where you may catch a glimpse of the well-known Douglas pedigree Highland Cattle.

* Birthplace of the Coldsteam Guards
* Once a rival to Gretna Green

Location
15 miles from Berwick-upon-Tweed on A698

Opening
Museum Daily: 10am–5pm
Garden & Grounds Daily: dawn–dusk

Admission
Free. Car park £2

Contact
Douglas & Angus Estates, Hirsel Country Park, Hirsel TD12 4LP

t 01573 224144
w hirselcountrypark.co.uk
e rogerdodd@btconnect.com

984 Innerleithen

Robert Smail's Printing Works

1–2 hrs   Jun–Sep

At this restored printing works, visitors will discover how the industry worked at the beginning of the C20. See the printing presses in action and try your hand at old-fashioned typesetting.

* Secrets of the printing works
* Shop

Location
6 miles E of Pebbles

Opening
Jun–Sep Thu–Mon 12noon–5pm, Sun 1–5pm; also open Good Fri–Easter Mon

Admission
Adult £5, Child & Concs £4

Contact
7–9 High Street, Innerleithen, Borders EH44 6HA

t 01896 830206
w nts.org.uk
e smail@nts.org.uk

RobertSmailPrintingWorks©

985 Isle of Arran

Brodick Castle, Garden & Country Park

3 hrs+   Apr–Oct

With a history dating back to the Vikings, Brodick Castle offers a wonderful day out of heritage, nature and relaxation. The castle boasts an impressive collection of sporting pictures and trophies, while the gardens and park offer delightful trails.

* Waymarked trails & wildlife garden
* Various events held throughout the year

Location
Take ferry from Ardrossan to Brodick for the connecting bus to castle

Opening
Castle Daily: Apr–Oct 11am–4pm (3pm closing in Oct)
Country Park Daily: 9.30am–sunset

Admission
Please phone for details

Contact
Isle of Arran

t 01770 302202
w nts.org.uk
e brodickcastle@nts.org.uk

986 Jedburgh

Jedburgh Castle Jail & Museum

1 hr+   Mar–Oct

A C19 reform prison with displays interpreting the history of Jedburgh. This is one of the most haunted buildings in Scotland and has an ever-changing programme of exhibitions.

* 3-Star Museum Attraction
* Outdoor play area

Location
Off A68 Jedburgh road

Opening
Daily: Mar–Oct Mon–Sat
10am–4.30pm, Sun 1pm–4pm

Admission
Adult £2,Child (under-16, accompanied) & Scottish Border residents free, Concs £1.50

Contact
Castlegate, Jedburgh TD8 6QD

t 01835 864750

987 Jedburgh

Jedforest Deer & Farm Park

3 hrs+   Easter–Oct

At this modern working farm you can see deer herds and rare breeds as well as your favourite farm animals. There is a conservation area pond, wildfowl, picnic and barbecue area. Colour coded nature trails wind through the woodlands.

* Birds of prey displays & tuition
* Feeding the animals

Location
5 miles S of Jedburgh on A68

Opening
Daily: Easter–Aug 10am–5.30pm;
Sep–Oct 11am–4.30pm

Admission
Adult £4, Child & Concs £2.50

Contact
Mervinslaw Estate,
Jedburgh, Roxburghshire TD8 6PL

t 01835 840364
w aboutscotland.com/jedforest/
e mervinslaw@ecosse.net

988 Jedburgh

Mary Queen of Scots Visitor Centre

1 hr   Mar–Nov

A fine C16 fortified house with period rooms set in a formal garden of pear trees. The visitor centre tells the story of the life of the tragic queen, who visited Jedburgh in 1566. Artefacts include a lock of Mary's hair and weapons from Carberry Hill battlefield.

* One of Scotland's top visitor attractions
* See some of Mary's possessions

Location
On A68 in centre of Jedburgh, SE of Selkirk

Opening
Daily: early Mar–Nov Mon–Sat
10am–4.30pm, Sun 11am–4.30pm

Admission
Adult £3,Child (under-16, accompanied) & Scottish Border residents free, Concs £2

Contact
Queen Street, Jedburgh TD8 6EN

t 01835 863331

989 Kelso

Floors Castle

2 hrs   Apr–Oct

This fairy tale castle is set in parkland that abounds with fauna and wildlife. Look out for oystercatchers, herons, tawny owls and red squirrels or have fun in the adventure playground, which has a flying fox, swings, a slippery dip and other fun games.

* Various sporting activities (golf, shooting) on offer
* Works by well-known artists, including Matisse

Location
On edge of Kelso

Opening
Daily: Apr–Oct 10am–4.30pm

Admission
Adult £6, Child £3.25, Concs £5

Contact
Kelso, Roxburghshire TD5 7SF

t 01573 223333
w floorscastle.com
e marketing@floorscastle.com

990 Kilmarnock

Galleon Centre

2 hrs+   All year

This leisure facility has a swimming pool and ice rink, as well as a games hall that is suitable for badminton, football, basketball and table tennis. There is also a bowling hall, a comprehensive fitness suite and two bars serving a range of healthy refreshments.

* Trampolining clubs
* Swimming & skating lessons

Location	Contact
In Kilmarnock town centre, follow the signs	99 Titchfield Street, Kilmarnock KA1 1QY
Opening	t 01563 524014
Daily: Mon–Fri 7am–11pm,	w galleoncentre.com
Sat 8am–6pm, Sun 9am–11pm	e adminoffice@galleoncentre.com
Admission	
Adult £1.05, Child 85p, Concs 80p	
Various activities priced individually	

991 Kilmarnock

The Garage

2 hrs+   All year

The Garage offers entertainment and fun for all the family. There is indoor go-karting and 12 lanes of bowling, plus a soft play area with ball pools, swings, slides and chutes.

* Helmets & safety suits provided
* Viewing gallery

Location	Contact
Off A77	36–40 Grange Street, Kilmarnock
Opening	t 01563 573355
Daily: 10am–midnight	w garageleisure.co.uk
Admission	e thegarage@kilmarnock10.freestyle.
Free, activities priced individually	co.uk

992 Kilmarnock

Scottish Maritime Museum

1 hr+   All year

Irvine Harbour was once one of Glasgow's main trading ports. There are many facilities, from the Magnum Leisure Centre to bird-watching on the river estuary. There are fine walks and rides with magnificent views of the Firth of Clyde on the beach.

* Guided tours throughout the day
* Explore a large collection of vessels moored at pontoons

Location	Contact
W of Kilmarnock on the A71. 10 min walk from Irvine train station	Harbourside, Irvine, Ayrshire KA12 8QE
Opening	t 01294 278283
Daily: 10am–5pm	w scottishmaritimemuseum.org/irvine
Admission	
Adult £3, Child & Concs £2	

993 Kilwinning

Dalgarven Mill Museum

1 hr+   All year

A country life museum in a C16 restored grain mill converted to house an extensive collection of Ayrshire memorabilia and costume – farming and domestic. The museum tells the story of the self-sufficient, pre-industrial rural community of Dalgarven.

* 3-star Visitor Attraction
* River beach & wildflower meadows

Location	Admission
On A737 between Kilwinning & Dalry	Please phone for details
Opening	Contact
Easter–Oct Tue–Sun 10am–5pm;	Dalgarven Mill, Dalry Road,
Nov–Easter Tue–Fri 10am–4pm,	Kilwinning, Ayrshire KA13 6PL
Sat–Sun 10am–5pm	t 01294 552448
	w dalgarvenmill.org.uk
	e admin@dalgarvenmill.org.uk

994 Kirkcudbright

Galloway Wildlife Conservation Park

2–3 hrs   All year

This wildlife park has plenty to entertain all the family, including new South America exhibits, a play area, apets corner and free snake encounters (depending on the weather).

* 27-acre site
* More than 200 animals

Location
1 mile from Kirkcudbright on B727, turn up the hill at Royal Hotel. Signed from A75

Opening
Daily: Mar–Oct 10am–5pm; Nov–Feb Sat–Sun 10am–4pm

Admission
Adult £4.50, Child £2.50, Concs £3.50

Contact
Lochfergus Plantation, Kirkcudbright, Dumfries & Galloway DG6 4XX
t 01557 331645
w gallowaywildlife.co.uk
e info@gallowaywildlife.co.uk

995 Kirkpatrick Fleming

Robert the Bruce's Cave

1 hr+   Mar–Nov

This world-famous ancient monument marks the site where Robert the Bruce hid in a cave during the wars of independence. See the abundance of wildlife around, including red squirrels and deer.

* Camping available
* Cycling & fishing

Location
Follow brown tourist signs from Gretna

Opening
Daily: Mar–Sep 9.30am–9pm; Oct–Nov 9.30am–5pm (closing times may vary)

Admission
Please phone for details

Contact
Cove Farm, Cove Estate Kirkpatrick Fleming, Dumfries & Galloway DG11 3AT
t 01461 800285
w brucescave.co.uk
e enquiries@brucescave.com

996 Largs

The Viking Experience

1 hr   Feb–Nov

Travel back in time to AD825 and experience the sounds and smells of a homestead beside a Norwegian fjord. Meet resident Vikings who will tell sagas associated with Viking life and culture. Visit the longhouse with views over the fjord and see longships moored outside.

* Shows begin regularly
* Leisure facilities, soft play centre & theatre

Location
On the Largs seafront

Opening
Daily: Apr–Sep 10.30am–5.30pm; Mar & Oct 10.30am–3.30pm; Feb & Nov Sat 12.30pm–3.30pm, Sun 10.30am–3.30pm

Admission
Adult £4, Child & Concs £3

Contact
Vikingar, Greenock Road, Largs, Ayrshire KA30 8QL
t 01475 689777
w vikingar.co.uk
e info@vikingar.co.uk

997 Melrose

Three Hills Roman Centre & Fort

4 hrs+   All year

The most important Roman military complex between Hadrian's Wall and the Antonine Wall guarded and secured the crossing of the River Tweed at Newstead in the C1 and C2 AD. Excavations have revealed much of what went on there. See finds from 1905 to 1910.

* See millennium milestone & timber tower
* Viewing platforms & information boards

Location
Market Square in Melrose

Opening
Daily: Apr–Oct 10.30am–4.30pm Nov–Mar by appointment please phone for details

Admission
Walks Adult £3, Child free, Concs £2.50
Exhibition £1.50, £1, £1

Contact
Ormistram, Melrose TD6 9PN
t 01896 822651
w trimontium.net

998 Newton Stewart

Galloway Red Deer Range

2 hrs   Jun–Sep

This attraction has a viewpoint near the road from which beautiful red deer can be observed in their natural habitat. Visitors to the range can also walk among the deer, photograph them and even touch them, under supervision – a memorable experience.

* Guided tours in summer
* See & hear roaring stags during the rutting season

Location
On A712, 3 miles SW of Clatteringshaws Loch

Opening
End of Jun–mid-Sep Tue & Thu 11am–2pm, Sun 11am–2.30pm
Tours Tue & Thu 11am & 2.30pm, Sun 2.30pm

Admission
Adult £3.50, Child £1.25, Concs £2.50

Contact
Red Deer Range Car Park, nr Clatteringshaws, Newton Stewart, Dumfries & Galloway DG7 3SQ
t 01671 402420
w forestry.gov.uk/gallowayforestpark
e galloway@forestry.gsi.gov.uk

999 Saltcoats

North Ayrshire Museum

1 hr   All year

Visit the newly refurbished North Ayrshire Museum and discover the history of this region from prehistoric times to the present day. Exhibits include a reconstructed Victorian cottage, maritime models and archaeology displays.

* Rich variety of artefacts
* Industrial history

Location
Just off A78 & A738

Opening
Mon–Tue & Thu–Sat 10am–1pm & 2pm–5pm

Admission
Free

Contact
Manse Street, Saltcoats, Ayrshire KA21 5AA
t 01294 464174
w north-ayrshire.gov.uk/museums
e namuseum@north-ayrshire.gov.uk

Halliwell'sHouse©

1000 Sanquhar

Sanquhar Tolbooth Museum

1 hr   Apr–Sep

Housed in a fine C18 tolbooth, this museum charts the life of ordinary Upper Nithsdale people. Exhibits recreate life in a local jail and tell the story of the mines and the local knitting tradition.

* Housed in a fine C18 tolbooth
* Community life in times past

Location
In town centre

Opening
Apr–Sep Tue–Sat 10am–1pm &
2pm–5pm, Sun 2pm–5pm

Admission
Free

Contact
High Street, Sanquhar, Dumfries
& Galloway DG46BN

t 01659 50186
w dumfriesmuseum.demon.co.uk
e dumfriesmuseum@dumgal.gov.uk

1001 Selkirk

Halliwell's House Museum

1 hr   Apr–Oct

Step back in time in Halliwell's House and discover the building's former use as a home and ironmonger's shop. It also tells the story of the historic burgh of Selkirk. The Robson Gallery has regular contemporary craft exhibitions.

* Guided tours (by arrangement)
* Children's play area

Location
Just off Market Place in heart of
Selkirk. Selkirk can be reached by A7
from Galashiels

Opening
Daily: Apr–Sep Mon–Sat 10am–5pm
(5.30pm in Jul–Aug), Sun
10am–12noon; Oct Mon–Sat
10am–4pm

Admission
Free

Contact
Halliwell's Close, Market Place,
Selkirk TD7 4BL

t 01750 720096
e museums@scotborders.gov.uk

Index

Acknowledgements
& Picture Credits

The Publishers would like to acknowledge the important contribution the British Tourist Authority made to this publication through the use of images from its website, *www.britainonview.com*.

The publishers would like to thank The National Trust, The National Trust for Scotland and English Heritage who kindly supplied photographs for use with their entries.

The publishers would also like to thank all contributors who provided information, and particularly all those who kindly supplied photographs. Particular thanks go to Tony Stuchbury (www.ajsphotos.co.uk).

Compiled, edited and designed by Butler and Tanner. Edited by Libby Willis. Design and layout by Lyn Davies and Carole McDonald. Project Manager Nick Heal. Special thanks to Carl Luke and Jennie Golding.